IRISH SOCIAL POLICY IN CONTEXT

BY THE SAME EDITORS

CONTEMPORARY IRISH SOCIAL POLICY

edited by
Suzanne Quin, Patricia Kennedy,
Anne O'Donnell and Gabriel Kiely

Contemporary Irish Social Policy provides a comprehensive review of the range of social policy provision in Ireland – education, income maintenance, employment, housing and health – together with chapters relating to different categories of consumers of services including children, people with disabilities, older people, Travellers and the growing population of refugees and asylum seekers in Ireland. Key areas of policy development concerning youth, drugs and the criminal justice system are also examined.

Each chapter is complete in itself, providing description and analysis of current policy, an overview of its historical development and discussion of current and future issues in the field. A table of the main policy developments, a bibliography, and a list of recommended reading are given at the end of each chapter. The contributors include academics, researchers and managers of services in the public and voluntary sectors.

Intended especially as a textbook for students of social policy, it is also a basic reference book for anyone wishing to gain an understanding of current social policy provision in Ireland. *Contemporary Irish Social Policy* is a companion volume to *Irish Social Policy in Context* by the same editors.

ISBN 1 900621 24 X   Published July 1999

Irish Social Policy
in Context

edited by

Gabriel Kiely
Anne O'Donnell
Patricia Kennedy
Suzanne Quin

University College Dublin Press
Preas Choláiste Ollscoile Bhaile Átha Cliath

First published 1999 by University College Dublin Press,
Newman House, 86 St Stephen's Green, Dublin 2, Ireland

Cataloguing in Publication data available from the British Library

Index by John Loftus
Typset in Bantry, Ireland, in 11/12½ Bembo and Gill Sans by Elaine Shiels
Printed in Ireland by Colour Books, Dublin

Contents

This book is dedicated to the memory of Linda Marie Kiely

Preface

This book is designed as a textbook on Irish Social Policy. It is a companion book to *Contemporary Irish Social Policy* by the same editors. This volume addresses the context of Irish Social Policy by bringing together chapters on aspects of Irish Social Policy that have relevance to specific policy measures. The book traces the historical development of Irish Social Policy and addresses some of the major influences, such as the impact of the European Union, on policy formation. It locates Ireland in a comparative context and discusses Ireland as an example of the mixed economy of welfare. The book also analyses the policy-making process, the financing of policy measures and policy evaluation. Some specific aspects of particular relevance to the development and understanding of social policy in Ireland, including the treatment of women, the concept of citizenship, the rise in the significance of partnerships, the place of the family, the understanding and measurement of poverty, and the role of consumer participation are treated in separate chapters. The book also includes a chapter on new initiatives in policy formation in the public sector.

In preparing this book, the editors carefully designed its contents to meet the needs of students of Social Policy. As lecturers and researchers in social policy, they were motivated by the need to provide up-to-date and comprehensive material on Irish Social Policy which would be easily accessible to anyone with an interest in the subject. This volume, in conjunction with the companion volume *Contemporary Irish Social Policy*, meets this need. The editors were also motivated to produce these books by the rise in interest in Irish Social Policy as reflected in the recent development of an active Irish Social Policy Association.

The authors were invited to contribute a chapter on a specified topic and were selected according to their expertise in the specific area. Care was taken to include a cross-section of people in the field of social policy to include academics, researchers and practitioners in the public and voluntary sectors.

While this book was designed primarily as a text on Irish Social Policy, it should be of interest to a much wider readership. Although a companion volume to *Contemporary Irish Social Policy*, it is also a stand-alone volume providing the reader with a descriptive analysis and discussion of issues of concern to the development of social policy in Ireland. Therefore, in addition to being a textbook, it is also a basic reference book for anyone wishing to gain an understanding of the context in which current Irish Social Policy is located.

Gabriel Kiely
Anne O'Donnell
Patricia Kennedy
Suzanne Quin
Dublin, February 1999

1
Introduction:
From Colonial Paternalism to National Partnership: An Overview of Irish Social Policy

Gabriel Kiely

Ireland's social welfare system had its origins in the Poor Relief Act of 1847. This Act, as Burke describes in her chapter, was a meagre form of outdoor relief which the British government was compelled to introduce because of the inability of the Poor Relief (Ireland) Act (1838) to deal not only with poverty in Ireland, but also the ravages of the Great Famine in 1845-47. Outdoor relief, while available in Britain, was not included as part of the Poor Law in Ireland. At the time, Ireland was under direct British rule from London and a part of the United Kingdom since the Act of Union in 1800. However, it was treated differently and less favourably than any other part of the Kingdom, being more like a colony than an integral part of the Union. This different treatment goes back even to the Elizabethan Poor Laws of 1601, the provisions of which did not apply to Ireland. Thus the Irish Poor Law, which was the first nationwide provision for the poor, came to represent in many people's minds, as Burke points out, the injustice of British rule in Ireland. Outdoor relief, with its origins in paternalistic colonialism, continued, although greatly modified since its introduction in 1847, as the basis of Irish income support until it was finally replaced by the Social Welfare (Supplementary Welfare Allowance) Act in 1975.

The foundations of the health service also have their origins in the Great Famine, with the passage of the Medical Charities Act in 1851. The dispensary system established by this Act continued as the basis of the health service until radically reformed following the Health Act 1970 and the establishment of regional health boards. Unlike social welfare and the health services, the provision of a state primary school education system had its origins less in a desire by the British government to respond to a social need, than an attempt to meet the needs of political and cultural assimilation as Burke in her chapter points out. From the late eighteenth and early nineteenth centuries, Ireland already had the beginnings of a separate school system, with strong Catholic and nationalist roots. Thus in 1831, prior to the introduction of a state-run primary school system in Britain, the National Board of Education was established in Ireland to provide such a system. Although there were difficulties initially concerning the non-denominational aspects of these schools, the issue was ultimately resolved with the churches effectively gaining control of this state system. This control has persisted up to the present and it was only with the introduction of free second-level education in 1967 that the state began to gain some measure of control.

It was not until the beginning of the twentieth century that a more broad range of social policies were introduced. These were known as the Liberal Reforms and included the Children's Act (1908), which up to the 1990s continued to be the primary legislation governing the protection of children, the Old Age Pension Act 1908, and the National Insurance Act 1911. The National Insurance Act (1911) was highly significant as the first social protection in Britain and Ireland to give an insured worker and subsequently his family a right to relief. However, the medical benefit of the Act was not included in its application to Ireland. In this case, the restrictions were due not to a reluctance on the part of the British government, but because of opposition from interests within Ireland (Burke). Nonetheless, as Burke points out, this important social policy (i.e. a scheme of National Insurance) was implemented in Ireland while the country was still under British rule.

The advent of Irish independence in 1922 did not see an upsurge in social legislation or provisions. In fact, one of the first acts of the new Irish state in the field of social policy was to reduce by ten per cent the old age pension in 1924. The conservatism of the new state, coupled with a poor economy and the influence of the Catholic Church, were major factors affecting the dearth of social legislation and provisions right up to the time Ireland joined the European Union in 1973.

The influence of the Catholic Church on the development of Irish social policy was at its greatest in the first few decades of the new Irish state. It culminated with the Constitution of 1937, which reflected Catholic moral and social teaching on all matters relating to the economic and social life of the citizens of the nation. The influence was particularly strong in relation to sexual morality, the family and the

position of women in Irish society. The ideology concerning the
of women, as Kennedy states in her chapter, when combine
concern about male unemployment, became institutionalized in the tax
and social welfare systems. This is illustrated, for example, by an employment bar in certain areas, including the civil service, on married women
which was only removed in 1973, and the discrimination in certain
social welfare provisions against female employees, some of which
continued up to as late as 1986.

Concerns with sexual morality were tied in to the Catholic Church's
teaching on the family which espoused the precepts of subsidiarity and
non-intervention. It was here, as Kiely in his chapter points out, that the
seeds of family policy for the first half of the twentieth century were
sown. However, the principle of non-intervention was not applied with
the same rigour when it came to regulating people's sexual behaviour, as
reflected in the Censorship of Films Act (1923), the Censorship of
Publications Act (1929), and the Criminal Law Amendment Act (1935)
which banned the sale and importation of contraceptives. This concern
with sexual morality has continued up to the present, as reflected in the
two abortion referenda, opposition to the introduction of the legalized sale
of contraceptives, and opposition to changes in the Constitution allowing
the introduction of divorce. Articles 41 and 42 of the Constitution are in
effect a statement of the Catholic Church's teaching on the family.
While these articles reflected the culture and values of Ireland at the
time, they did, however, as Burke observes, store up problems for future
policy makers trying to draft adequate child protection laws. As Conroy
puts it, in her chapter, these were not issues of cost, but rather of the
dominant values of the time.

In the early decades of the Irish state, the economic resources were
just not there to support any radical social policy measures. Economic
survival was the priority. In addition, dependency ratios were very high
due to high birth rates and emigration. Poverty, unemployment and
emigration were the scourges of Irish society with an economy based on
agriculture and protectionism. It was not until 1958, with the introduction
of the first programme for economic development, that any changes
started to come about. The principle of subsidiarity espoused by the
Catholic Church conveniently matched the state's inactivity in the field
of social policy, thus leaving the churches, the voluntary sector and the
family as the main, and in some cases the only, suppliers of social services.
While the Beveridge Report in Britain of 1942 sent shock waves around
the world (as Burke describes it), its only tangible effect in Ireland was
the introduction by the Irish government of a children's allowance
scheme in 1944, one year ahead of its introduction in Britain.

Overall, social policies developed on a piecemeal basis with no comprehensive or integrated plan. The state responded to specific needs often only in response to political pressure to do so, and reluctantly. Even in the 1960s, despite economic expansion, social progress was very limited. Conroy argues that the difficulty was not a refusal to change or lack of knowledge, but different perspectives on social policy. During this period, she cites as an example of these different perspectives the dominance of the medical model in policy developments in cases of child abuse, with the eventual development of an investigative model of child abuse in the 1990s and the institutionalization of social services in general with the establishment of the regional health boards.

To some extent, Ireland's entry to the European Union in 1973 marked a watershed in Irish social policy, particularly with regard to the position of women, with the introduction of a wide range of women's benefits which were, as Conroy puts it, grafted onto the welfare system. These benefits, she says, were part of a broad restructuring of gender and motherhood which granted new individual entitlements to women. Many of these changes were prompted by the recommendations of the Commission on the Status of Women (1972), but as Doyle points out in her chapter, the implementation of many of these recommendations had as much to do with Ireland's accession to the EU as with the importance with which the recommendations were viewed.

The 1970s also saw a change in direction in policies affecting the family, as Kiely shows, with the removal of the marriage ban on employment (1973), the introduction of a range of new measures which benefited families, including the Health (Family Planning) Act (1979), which finally legalized family planning services. The old non-interventionist approach to the affairs of the family were at last showing signs of erosion with the state now taking a more active, if still somewhat reluctant, approach to family policy.

Ireland, as Kennedy shows in her analysis of the treatment of women in Irish social policy, typified a strong male breadwinner-type state in which disincentives such as the lack of childcare continued to make it difficult for women, and in particular mothers, to access well-paid full-time employment. However, while Ireland has lagged behind most of Europe in terms of equality legislation and has still some distance to go before achieving equal treatment of men and women, in its efforts to catch up it has moved ahead of other member states of the EU in some areas. Doyle shows in her chapter that this is especially so for sexual harassment and employment equality legislation, as for example with the Employment Equality Bill 1997. Many of the remaining obstacles, particularly to equal treatment of women in the labour force, are attitudinal and structural and cannot be solved by legislation alone. Women, as Kennedy says, are earners and carers. Integrating both of these roles and sharing them equally with men are a challenge faced by all member states of the European Union. However, progress is slow, with Ireland, as Kennedy and Doyle show, still having high pay differentials between men and women, a low level of labour-force participation by mothers, and a high concentration of women in low-paid part-time jobs. This slow progress is reflected in the fact that it was not until 1999 that a National Childcare Strategy was published which addressed the need for affordable quality childcare for children of working parents. The lack of childcare provision continues to be one of the main obstacles to equal opportunities for women and especially for mothers and their participation in the labour force.

Conroy, in her analysis of the lack of progress in social policy in the 1960s and 1970s, identifies the European Community, social reformers and workers' representatives as the social actors who were instrumental in addressing social policy on a mass scale. Largely as a result of the influence of these major social actors, coupled with the recession of the 1980s giving rise to the acceptance of the notion that the state could not respond to meet the needs of massive poverty, emigration and employment, Irish social policy adopted a new model of centralized collective bargaining at the end of the 1980s. The first national agreement between the social partners (i.e. the government, the trade unions and the employers) was a watershed in Irish social policy, as it marked the beginning of partnership as a basis of a new approach. As a result of the subsequent national agreements which included a much wider range of community interests, Ireland leap-frogged (as Conroy describes it) from a state which did not have a comprehensive set of social policies, into the mainstream of national policy making. *The Programme for Economic and Social Progress* (PESP) (1990–93) contained proposals for a fundamental structural reform including an assault on long-term unemployment and a restructuring of the social services, in particular social welfare, the health services, education and housing.

These national agreements were also a significant factor in bringing about a steady growth in the economy in the 1990s, with low inflation, reduced unemployment, a dramatic drop in emigration and a substantial rise in Gross National Product. Ireland, as Fitzgerald in her chapter shows, saw a sharp fall in dependency ratios, with an expanding young work force, an older generation depleted by emigration, and a relatively high birth rate. The so-called 'Celtic Tiger' was born, and with it came not only the resources to support social development, but the political will to do so. While most of Europe was cutting back on its social programmes, Ireland was expanding. However, rather than adopting the welfare state model of many European countries, Ireland developed or drifted into, as Conroy says, a mixed economy of welfare based on partnership. Such a development was almost inevitable, given Ireland's strong tradition of voluntarism and its well-established and vibrant private sector, especially in the areas of health-care provision and education.

In his chapter, Fanning describes this mixed economy of welfare as consisting of a balance of welfare provision within society between the public and private, voluntary and informal sectors. He distinguishes the use of the term 'mixed economy' of welfare in Ireland from the use of that term which describes the recent tendency in welfare states to shift the balance of welfare provision away from the state. In Ireland, the balance between the various providers of welfare he calls welfare pluralism with the state continuing to provide or purchase services on behalf of its citizens, whether through direct provision or grant aid, subsidies or tax relief to other sectors which provide welfare services.

In Ireland, as Fitzgerald in discussing the financing of social services shows, health, education and social welfare account for about two-thirds of current government spending. This is in the form of directly funded services and tax relief on specific spending items such as mortgage interest relief, pension contributions and private health insurance. Most of this spending is funded from general taxation. Income from other sources such as hospital charges, she points out, comes to only a small fraction of the total. EU Structural Funds, although providing much-needed financial support to assist Ireland's industrialization, amounted to only about three per cent of GNP for the period 1994–99. Because the market is a poor mechanism for allocating social services for several reasons, as Fitzgerald argues, there is also a market fringe providing them in addition to the mainstream collective provision. It is this mix of direct state provision, coupled with services provided by the private, voluntary and informal sectors often with substantial financial support from the state either in the form of direct financial aid or tax reliefs, that constitute the Irish mixed economy of welfare.

Where Irish social policy fits in a comparative context is difficult to say. Perhaps this is why it is not included in many comparative studies or where it seems an awkward fit in whatever category it is placed. Many of the studies fail to take account, as O'Donnell in her chapter argues, of specific features of the Irish situation such as its colonial past and its recent transition from a rural society which had an economy based on agricultural production or indeed its recent economic boom. Depending on the variables used in the typology, it has been variously classified as a Latin Rim, Anglo-Saxon, and even Scandinavian. Perhaps the difficulty is not so much with the idiosyncratic features of the Irish welfare state

but with, as O'Donnell points out, the deficiencies of existing classification approaches. Ireland's welfare regime is in a process of change
and after decades of minimum intervention, it is only now engaging in
comprehensive social development. Where that development will lead is
unclear, but two things seem certain: it is breaking with its highly
conservative past and it is not heading in the direction of the classic
model of the European welfare state.

One of the driving forces behind the development of Irish social
policy in recent decades has been a national concern about the high
number of people, and in particular families, living in poverty. Despite
Ireland's increased economic well-being, the number of people living in
poverty, as measured by income lines alone, has increased. However, as
Johnston in her chapter on poverty in Ireland shows, the numbers of
people experiencing poverty, when combined with deprivation as measured by deprivation indicators, have fallen slightly, as has the depth of
poverty, i.e. how far people are below the poverty lines. Johnston also
shows that if the poverty lines of 50 per cent of average incomes are held
constant, but uprated for inflation, that the percentage below the relative
poverty lines decreased, from 20 per cent in 1987 to eight per cent in 1994.

This concern with poverty, as discussed by Langford in her chapter,
received great impetus from the various EU Anti-Poverty Programmes
and the Structural Funds which provided not only resources to tackle
poverty and the related problem of unemployment, but a social policy
approach to the wider concerns embraced by the concept of social
exclusion, based on the principles of participation, partnership and multidimensionality. Poverty was now accepted as being a structural problem.
This resulted in what Langford calls the democratization of structures, with
the representation of groups addressing social exclusion on the National
Economic and Social Forum and the National Economic and Social
Council. Arising out of these changes, the current national programme
(*Partnership 2000*) agreed between the government and the social partners
has, as Langford puts it, at its heart, the need for an ongoing targeted
strategy across a range of government departments and agencies to
combat social exclusion. In addition, the government published in 1997
a *National Anti-Poverty Strategy* (NAPS) which mainstreams anti-poverty
policy in Ireland and sets out a strategy for a ten-year period.

The NAPS is one example of how recent governments in Ireland
have opened up citizen participation in policy formation. Carroll, in her
chapter, discusses a number of these initiatives and other strategic planning
approaches used both to cut across different government departments
and to include a wide range of inputs from others in the planning process,
whether as experts, consumers or citizens. This approach recognizes the

complexity and interrelatedness of social policies and the responsibility, as Carroll describes it, of government to act as custodian of the common future balancing present demands with those of future generations. Iredale describes the various forms of consultation in policy formation as encouraging active citizenship which promotes participative democracy. These various participants are what Earley calls gatekeepers who function to regulate the level and flow of demand directed towards the political system. Decisions about social policy are, however, as Earley says, the end-product of a complex and rather untidy process in which a disparate series of people and institutions are involved.

Thus there needs to be a balance between partisan politics and political control (Iredale). In the past, pressure groups, for example, representing the interests of particular consumer groups, were instrumental in seeing much needed policy changes for those they represented. This ad hoc approach did not, however, lend itself to the development of an overall national coordinated social policy. It would appear from Carroll's analysis of current trends in policy formation that there now seems to be the emergence, if not of an overall coordinated social policy, at least of the acceptance of the need for such planning and the political will to move in that direction.

Arising out of these changes in approach to the formation and implementation of social policy has been an increased reliance on partnership between the government and the social partners. Thus we find that the organization of welfare in Ireland, as Rush in his chapter shows, is being increasingly influenced by the concept and adopted strategy of social partnership which emerged in 1987 with the first national agreement between the social partners (employers, trade unions and farming community). This tripartite corporatism, as Rush points out, replaced the post-colonial elite of earlier years. Since then the role of social partnership has developed with national agreements now being credited with much of the current success of the Irish economy. From a somewhat narrow base initially, representation within the national partnership mechanism has broadened and is now inclusive of a wide cross-section of interests. The so-called four pillars of national social partnership now consist of representatives of farming organisations, trade unions, community and voluntary organizations, and employer and business organisations. This social partnership, as Rush shows, is not just at national level. It is also a vibrant part of local community development. Ireland has moved since the beginnings of industrialization in the late 1950s, through a modernization process in the administration and type of its welfare regime, from what Rush calls residual state centralism, to participative local and national social partnership.

This new model of social policy based on partnership has fundamental implications for citizenship, as D'Arcy explains, in so far as citizenship is about the involvement of people in the community in which they live. However, a balance has to be found between social rights on the one hand, and duty and obligation on the other. This balance, D'Arcy goes on to argue, is emerging in Irish social policy as reflected, for example, in a recent Department of Social Welfare (1997) Green Paper. The Green Paper included in its definition of citizenship the active role of people, communities and voluntary organizations in decision making and thus extending the concept of formal citizenship from the basic civil, political, social and economic rights to one of direct democratic participation and responsibility. While such a concept of citizenship may appear to be largely aspirational, the development of the partnership model provides a mechanism for its realization. If, however, this is achieved remains to be seen; many, including D'Arcy, argue that not all citizens have gained this citizenship, as illustrated for example by the treatment of women in Irish social security.

The need for research to evaluate policy outcomes is essential if these aspirations are to be fulfilled. In addition, as Winston shows in her chapter, evaluation is highly significant both for those implementing the policy and those at its receiving end. However, while there has been a growth, as Winston describes it, in the 'evaluation industry' in Ireland, much of this research is carried out for accountability purposes or to investigate the efficiency of cost-effectiveness of programmes. In the field of social policy there is less funding available for programme evaluation, although this has increased in recent years. In addition, in recognition of the importance of research, government departments, commissions and expert working groups now almost routinely build in some sort of evaluation research when engaging in policy formation. This research provides information which, together with personnel and structures, are what Earley identifies as the required resources that the policy-making system must itself have in order to process the demands of policy change. Carroll, in her chapter, offers several examples of this process.

Redistribution of resources is a function of all modern nation states. How this is achieved constitutes in one sense the state's social policy. In the early nineteenth century this was expressed in the form of paternalistic colonialism in which the British government reluctantly intervened to offset the devastation of rampant poverty in Ireland and later the ravages of the Great Famine. The early years of independence continued this paternalistic approach as policy was formulated by a post–colonial elite which in the 1950s and 1960s consisted of some dynamic, imaginative and innovative civil servants. It was not until the 1970s that this approach to social policy, which was non–interventionist in nature, began to change. The change both coincided with and was prompted by Ireland's accession to the European Economic Community. The late 1980s and early 1990s saw the emergence of a new approach to social policy based on the ideology of national social partnership.

Partnership is now one of the main driving forces behind Ireland's developing social policy. While the notion of partnership is not new; its application in Ireland is somewhat unique. Perhaps this is why various comparative social policy studies have difficulty fitting Ireland into their typologies. National partnership between the government and the social partners is an evolving model of welfare states. Its primary difference from other models is the process by which policy is developed. Traditionally, partnerships have been based on bargaining between the social partners in situations where the state intervenes in the economy. In Ireland, social solidarity and deliberation are also key elements in the partnership process. Comparative studies tend to focus more on outcomes than process and thus they can neglect to address this important dimension of welfare regimes. The social partnership model evolving in Ireland has a number of distinctive features which include: the inclusion of social policy concerns at a national level as part of the negotiations between the social partners in arriving at national agreements; the inclusion of a wide range of interests – including the socially excluded – in these negotiations; the extension of partnerships beyond the national level to local communities; the emphasis on social solidarity and deliberation; and the setting in place of mechanisms for policy implementation and policy monitoring.

Of its nature, social policy is value-based and therefore constantly struggling to find a balance between what are often conflicting demands. How these demands are reconciled can be as important as the policies themselves. National social partnership is one way of achieving this reconciliation and ultimately the attainment of the social policy objective of an inclusive society. Partnership has facilitated the achievement of Ireland's current prosperity. Whether it equally achieves a socially inclusive society remains to be seen.

2

Foundation Stones of Irish Social Policy, 1831–1951

Helen Burke

INTRODUCTION

This chapter introduces the reader to the foundation stones from which many of modern Ireland's social policies were built. While it focuses primarily on the foundations laid down by government, both British and Irish, by tracing the evolution of social legislation and how it affected Irish people in the nineteenth and in the first half of the twentieth century, the contribution of other major influences on the shaping of social policy, such as the economy, the churches and voluntary organizations, is also acknowledged.

Social policy between 1831 and 1951 is broken down into three periods in this chapter:

(a) *The nineteenth century* in which a rigid poor law system came to Ireland – a system that was broken open by the great famine; in which health services began to develop and education became a major policy issue at both primary and university level.

(b) *1900–21*, when Ireland's social policy benefited from the Liberal reforms in Britain which brought the old age pension and national insurance to Ireland; when the Government of Ireland Act 1920 partitioned the country leaving the six north-eastern counties under British rule, and the struggle for independence led, after the Treaty with Britain, to the establishment of Saorstat Éireann/The Free State in the south in 1922.

(c) *1922–51*, when survival, not social policy, was the main preoccupation of the new Irish state in the politically and economically difficult years of the 1920s and 1930s as much of Europe fell to fascism. This section examines the conservative nature of the new Irish state and its usually cautious approach to social policy; how the challenge posed by the establishment of a welfare state in Britain and Northern Ireland after the Second World War was handled; and the effects of the failure of the Mother and Child Scheme not only on Irish social policy, but on the politics of this island.

THE POOR LAW AND MEDICAL CHARITIES, 1831–1900

Poverty was rampant in Ireland during the first half of the nineteenth century. The country's problems were those of a misgoverned society, deeply rooted in its political, economic and social systems. After the passage of the Act of Union in August 1800, the British administration, operating from Dublin Castle, had adopted a more interventionist policy in Ireland than heretofore and in 'areas like education, public health and emergency public works, where intervention became both more decisive and more extensive in Ireland than in contemporary Britain. The idea of a centralized and impartial administrative ethos was applied early on, reflecting the inefficiency of Irish local government, the inadequacy of the gentry and the poverty of the parishes' (Foster, 1988: 290). Thus was established a centralist approach to tackling social problems and to the delivery of social policies in this country, an approach that has persisted to this day.

By the 1830s, Irish poverty was spilling over into the English cities where thousands of destitute Irish emigrants, most of them illiterate and unskilled, went in search of work. For example, 10,000 adult Irishmen 'who subsisted on mendicancy' were found in Liverpool in 1834 (Jackson, 1963: 83) and that is just one of the cities to which the Irish went. The new English Poor Law was passed in 1834. The British establishment had grown tired of their old Elizabethan poor law, claiming that its lax administration and relatively generous approach to the able-bodied poor had made large sections of the population dependent on poor relief. The members of the English Royal Commission on the Poor Law were determined that under the new poor law the able-bodied poor would be forced to find work and 'persuaded themselves that, by and large, those who sought employment could find it' (Checkland and Checkland, 1974: 42). These beliefs were enshrined in the 1834 Poor Law Report and in the new English poor law which was firmly based on a deterrent workhouse system. Thus with the fervour of poor law reform raging in England and aggravation mounting against both the destitute Irish immigrants and the absentee Irish landlords dancing their way around the London season, it is not surprising that determination grew in Westminster to try and tackle Ireland's terrible poverty and to do so in such a way that in the future Irish property would be made to pay for Irish poverty.

So for the third time that century a new commission was set up to advise the government on what to do about Irish poverty. Richard Whately, Church of Ireland Archbishop of Dublin, who was appointed by the King as chairman of the *Royal Commission of Inquiry into the Conditions of the Poorer Classes in Ireland*[1] in September 1833, was a very exceptional man. Professor of Political Economy at Oxford when he was invited to take up the See of Dublin in 1831, he found it hard to leave his pleasant academic life in Oxford, for what he knew would be a difficult assignment in Dublin (Whately, 1866: 101). Soon after his arrival in Ireland, Whately was appointed chairman of the new and controversial Board of National Education (see pp. 17–18).

In 1833, Whately led the ten-man Irish Royal Commission with great courage. He took a totally different approach to the poor from that of the English Commissioners. Like any development worker in the late twentieth century, Whately knew that his Commission had two choices: either they could just suggest measures to deal with the destitute (as the English Commission had done by developing their workhouse system), or they could try and understand the causes of Ireland's daunting poverty and prevent it escalating in the future, as well as suggest measures to deal with it in the present. The British government were very annoyed when they realized the line he was taking – why didn't he hurry up and just recommend a workhouse system for Ireland? Whately and his fellow commissioners ignored these hints and carried on with their own agenda (Burke, 1987: 24–7). They painted a graphic picture of the extent and depth of Ireland's dreadful poverty. They calculated that if the workhouse system was adopted in Ireland, accommodation would be required for 2,385,000 people, such was the extent of destitution. But they completely rejected the extension of the workhouse system to Ireland, stating eloquently:

> the difficulty in Ireland is not to make the able-bodied look for employment, but to find it profitably for the many who seek it . . . we see the labouring class are eager for work, that work there is not for them and they are therefore, and not from any fault of their own, in permanent want. (Third Report Irish Commissioners, 1836: 5).

Instead, they recommended a bold plan for economic and social development as well as help for organisations and institutions dealing with the disabled and the poorest people. Their reports had two major problems. First of all the Commissioners failed to agree on how their plan could be financed and secondly their recommendations demanded much more state intervention by Britain in Ireland than that Whig government, influenced as it was by the philosophy of *laissez-faire*, was prepared to countenance.

But the British government could not just ignore the Irish Royal Commission's reports so they sent over to Ireland an emissary who they knew would recommend precisely what they wanted to hear. He was George Nicholls, once a seafarer and canal designer, now a poor law reformer in England, who even before he had set foot in Ireland had told the British government that Ireland needed a workhouse system. After a hasty tour of the country he recommended the extension of the new poor law to Ireland (Burke, 1987: 38–44). His report was readily accepted by the cabinet and so the Act for the More Effectual Relief of the Destitute Poor in Ireland, 1838, was passed – a peculiar name for a workhouse system, all the more so given that it was the first statutory provision for the poor in Ireland. It came to be known as The Poor Relief (Ireland) Act, 1838. George Nicholls was rewarded with the job of setting up the workhouse system in Ireland. He estimated that 100 workhouses, each holding 800 people, would be sufficient, but subsequently revised this upwards to provide 100,000 places.

The Workhouse System

The country was divided into unions and in each union a workhouse was built. A board of guardians was elected in each union and they had to levy a compulsory rate to finance the workhouse. There was no provision in the 1838 Act for outdoor relief; the only relief was that provided in the workhouse, indoor relief, as it was called. The granting of relief was at the discretion of the guardians and no poor person, however destitute, could be held to have a statutory right to relief under the Irish poor law. The Poor Law Commission in London was the central authority for the Irish poor law. It issued detailed instructions on the strict rules for running the workhouse, the segregation of families inside the house, the work of the inmates, the discipline, the diet, the clothing, everything was strictly laid down from London under the poor law principle of less eligibility, i.e. that conditions inside the workhouse must be worse than those of the poorest labourers existing beyond the workhouse walls. From the outset the people feared and detested the workhouse; it came to represent in many people's minds the injustice of British rule in Ireland. Thus Ireland's first nationwide provision for the poor was hated, not only by those who dreaded the thought of ending up in the workhouse, but by property owners who resented having to pay rates to maintain it.

The Great Famine

The Irish poor law was soon set an impossible task – that of trying to cope with the ravages of the great famine. The potato crop failed in 1845, in 1846 and again in 1848. The failure of the potato was a disaster of mammoth proportions because two-thirds of the population of over eight million people were dependent on agriculture for their livelihood. The majority of the people lived on very small holdings, with potatoes as their staple diet. Sir Robert Peel, who was the British Prime Minister during the first year of the great famine, had served in Ireland for six years as Chief Secretary. Going on experience garnered during the many minor famines earlier that century, he reacted swiftly by importing Indian meal for distribution in the most stricken areas, mobilizing the Board of Works to provide employment and encouraging the intervention of local relief committees. Peel's initiative did much to mitigate the worst effects of the first year of the famine. But Peel was replaced as Prime Minister by Lord John Russell in June 1946. Peel was a great loss; he had always sought to be fair to Ireland (Kerr,1982:350). Russell's administration, strongly influenced by Sir Charles Trevelyan at the Treasury, was much more rigidly *laissez-faire*, i.e. the opposite to interventionist. Although conditions were even worse in the autumn and winter of 1846–7, no more Indian meal was imported, the philosophy of the new government being to let the local unions, the local market and relief committee deal with the situation. The different reactions of these two governments to the great famine is a classic example of how ideology influences social policy.

As the famine deepened and spread, thousands and thousands of desperate people stormed the workhouses for assistance. The workhouses were full to overflowing; the guardians tried desperately to provide extra accommodation. Stables, mills, out-buildings, were taken over as auxiliary workhouses. Conditions in these overcrowded premises were appalling and death and disease spread rapidly through them. Workhouse staff, doctors and clergy who ministered to the sick died too. The catastrophe overwhelmed the workhouses and broke open the poor law's rigid system.

Outdoor Relief

When the dead and dying were being found along the roadside after the terrible winter of 1847, Russell's government was forced to move. First they copied the Quakers' soup kitchen scheme but, when this proved inadequate as the situation further deteriorated, they passed the Poor Relief Extension Act, 1847, which allowed the guardians to grant a meagre

·elief to special categories of destitute people, for example
having two or more legitimate children (Burke, 1987:
ludicrous restriction which the guardians ignored, but
ow far removed the Russell administration was from
what was happening in Ireland. It was the intention of
…·aaury that outdoor relief would be just a temporary measure until
the famine was over. However, a desperate people fought determinedly
to hang on to this limited form of relief and it thus became the ancestor
of Ireland's social welfare system, albeit a mean and restrictive ancestor.

Nobody knows exactly how many people died during the great famine,
but it is generally accepted that around a million people died and another
one and a half million emigrated. The west and southwest of the country
suffered most, with many parishes losing over half their population. The
parish of Goleen in west Cork, for example, had 12,627 people in 1841,
but by 1851 there were only 6611 (O'Donovan, 1997: 56).

Medical Charities

Then, as now, starving people were subject to all sorts of diseases and
infections. Although Ireland had a scattered array of voluntary dispensaries
and quite an impressive number of hospitals by nineteenth-century
standards, the embryonic health services then existing were totally
incapable of coping with the ravages wrought by the great famine. The
need for an organized system of 'medical relief' had featured in most of
the early-nineteenth century reports and debates about an Irish poor law.
The Irish medical profession were so concerned that they would lose
control to lay administrators in any new system of medical relief, that
between 1836 and 1838 they sent observers to Westminster to monitor
debates on medical charities and the poor law (Woods, 1988: 145).
Resistance to the cost of a nationwide system of medical charities, plus
effective lobbying by the medical profession, stalled any progress on this
front prior to the famine. But the horrors of the great famine swept all
these worries aside, and in 1851 the Medical Charities Act was passed.
Under that act every union in the country was divided into dispensary
districts and a dispensary doctor was appointed to each district. His brief
was to deliver medical care and medicines to the poor. The service was
paid for by the poor rate and was a very welcome addition to the poor
law. Woods ends her definitive study of the evolution of dispensary
policy in Ireland thus:

> The dispensary system provided a nation-wide community based medical
> service for persons unable to pay for private medical care. It brought a
> doctor who also served as a Registrar for births and deaths (after 1863),

within reach of the whole population. It provided rudimentary health education, a vaccination service, a midwifery service to some areas, and care for all who needed it in periods of epidemic disease. The dispensary system instituted measures for the improvement of public health and a forum for the conduct of research into disease. It lasted for 121 years before it was radically reformed. (Woods, 1988: 149)

On 21 June 1851, there were 265,170 inmates in the Irish workhouses, the highest number ever recorded (Burke, 1987:128). After that the numbers declined as social conditions slowly improved. This left some free capacity in the workhouses which was very often taken up by patients referred by the dispensary doctors who needed hospital beds for their patients. The cities, particularly Dublin, had several good voluntary hospitals but rural areas had very few. The workhouses gradually came to fill this lacuna by providing a very basic hospital service throughout the country that was to grow eventually into the state hospital system.

EDUCATION 1831–1900

Primary Education

While several continental countries, such as Switzerland, France, Holland and the Scandinavian countries, had become involved in state-run systems of primary education in the early years of the nineteenth century, not so with Britain, because of the influence of *laissez-faire* on that country's social policy formation. However, for Ireland things were different. Perhaps, as Coolahan suggests, a state-run system of national education 'could serve politicising and socialising goals, cultivating attitudes of political loyalty and cultural assimilation. The danger of separate school systems operating without official supervision needed to be countered'(1981: 4). Such a separate school system with strong Catholic and nationalist roots had been growing apace thanks to the work of pioneers like Nano Nagle and her Presentation nuns in Cork in the 1770s, and subsequently in Dublin and other large towns, and Edmund Rice, who started teaching street children in Waterford in 1802 and later founded the Irish Christian Brothers. Both of these orders were committed to bringing free education to poor Irish children.

In 1831 the National Board of Education was set up to run a state-supported primary school system. Archbishop Richard Whately was made its first chairman and this turned out to be an even more difficult job than chairing the Irish Royal Commission on Poor Relief. The goal of this initiative was to provide a free, non-denominational, primary education system where children of all religions would be educated together in secular subjects, but they would be taught religion by members of their own faith (Coolahan, 1981: 4). To attempt to develop an integrated school system in a country that was deeply divided along religious lines, with very strong animosities and suspicions across that divide, was brave indeed, but it was deeply resented by all the churches, even by members of Whately's own Church of Ireland. Notwithstanding the opposition of the churches to the National Board of Education and their schools, these schools proved highly popular with the people. In 1849 around 500,000 children were attending the 4,321 national schools (Foster, 1988: 341). What the churches wanted was state support for their own church-run schools. They lobbied government for that relentlessly and from the 1870s onwards this was gradually introduced. At the turn of the century, the Catholic hierarchy was able to declare that the national system of education, despite its name, was *de facto* denominational in practice. So ended this experiment in integrated education in Ireland. If Whately's dream for a non-denominational system of education in Ireland had succeeded, would Northern Ireland have avoided the thirty years of civil strife it experienced at the end of the twentieth century?

Secondary Education

In the nineteenth century the majority of children in Ireland left school after they had completed primary school. Secondary schools were very much the preserve of the middle and upper classes and these classes were expected to pay for that schooling themselves. The secondary schools were private institutions and as there were no required qualifications for secondary teachers at that time, the quality of the education varied considerably. The Intermediate Education Act, 1878, provided some funding on the basis of results achieved in the public examinations to the denominational secondary schools, but the churches firmly resisted any encroachment by the state into the management of secondary schools. Some schools accepted children from poor homes for a nominal fee or charged nothing at all. It was only after the establishment of the Irish Free State in 1922 that the Department of Education devised a system of providing capitation grants for pupils in recognized schools and incremental salaries for recognized secondary teachers (Coolahan, 1981: 53), thereby laying down basic standards for second level education. It was only in 1967 that free second-level education came to this part of Ireland (see p. 38).

University Education

The only university in Ireland in 1831 was Trinity College, Dublin University, which was founded in 1591, and remained a Protestant university until well into the twentieth century. Until 1873 there was a religious test for entry; after that date some Catholics went to Trinity, but it still retained its close ties with the Church of Ireland and the ascendancy class. By mid-nineteenth century, pressure had built up for a state-endowed Catholic university in Ireland. This was resisted by the British who, aware of the sectarian animosities on this island, always tried to ensure that the institutions they established in the nineteenth century were non-denominational in character, be they workhouses, national schools or universities. Instead they agreed to support non-denominational Queen's Colleges, with one in Belfast, Cork and Galway, founded in 1845. The Queen's Colleges were condemned by Rome. The Catholic bishops set about founding their own Catholic University in Dublin. In 1851 they invited John Henry Newman, the great Oxford scholar and convert to Catholicism, to come and be its first Rector. It opened in 1854 at 86 St Stephen's Green. However Newman, finding he could not get on with Paul Cullen, the powerful and domineering Catholic Archbishop of Dublin, resigned in 1859. The Catholic University struggled on, without proper funding or a charter. The Jesuits took it over in 1883; for them too it proved an impossible task. The Catholic bishops continued to warn their flock against attending Trinity or the Queen's Colleges and kept up the pressure for funding for a university acceptable to Catholics. Finally the British government compromised and in 1908 established the National University of Ireland with an non-denominational charter and colleges in Dublin, Cork and Galway, but with a sufficiently broadly based senate and governing bodies to allow scope for influence from the Catholic hierarchy (Whyte, 1980: 18), if that was so desired. These colleges, UCD, UCC and UCG replaced the Catholic University and two of the Queen's Colleges, while the remaining college in Belfast, became a separate university, Queen's University, Belfast – a precursor of partition to follow twelve years later?

THE LIBERAL REFORMS 1900–21

The Liberal led government in Britain that enacted the Irish Universities Act, 1908, had come to power in 1905 on a turn of the century wave of social reform. Many factors coalesced to make this an era of radical change. Although universal suffrage still lay in the future, the franchise had extended during the second half of the nineteenth century. Politicians

ʰat they would have to do more now to win and hold the
ɟorking-class man. Furthermore there was the rise of
..., which had forced Bismarck into establishing new forms of
..ɟial insurance to bind the German workers into his new Germany.
Government now had a clearer picture of what needed to be done thanks
to the mould-breaking social surveys of Charles Booth (1889–1903) and
Seebohm Rowntree (1901) which revealed, at the dawn of the new
century when the British Empire was at its zenith, that thirty per cent
of the population at home were living below the poverty line. These
surveys helped to destroy the Victorian myth that poverty was a person's
own fault by clearly identifying for the first time the causes of poverty as
old age, sickness, under-employment and unemployment caused by the
economic conditions.

The social policies put in place between 1908 and 1911 set out to try
and tackle these problems and more. They are known as 'the Liberal
Reforms'. This is something of a misnomer, for while the Liberal Party
members were the major players in this government, they were supported
by the Irish Party and by the members of the new Labour Party in
Westminster, so it was in reality what we would describe today as a
coalition government. For reasons of space only three of these reforms –
three with a lasting effect on Irish social policy – are discussed here.

Children Act 1908

The new century brought with it a new approach to children, less harsh
and more protective than heretofore. This act epitomized those changes
and came to be called the Children's Charter. It repealed 39 earlier
measures dealing with children. Imprisonment of children was now
forbidden and remand homes were set up to deal with children awaiting
trial in the new juvenile courts established by this act. Although it
predated the insights of modern psychology, the focus of this act was on
treatment rather than punishment, more on trying to prevent cruelty to
children by their parents, and on the protection of children at risk. The
idea was to try and make parents more responsible for their children. It
became an offence to allow one's child to beg or smoke. The act was
strong on aspiration but weak in implementation, particularly in Ireland
where it long outlived its relevance for children at risk in the rapidly
changing world of the second half of the twentieth century.

Old Age Pension Act 1908

When this Act was finally passed by Parliament, it marked the end of a long campaign for pensions for the elderly, since prior to this legislation the only sources of financial assistance for badly off older people were outdoor relief from the poor law or private charity. Literally thousands of older people opted to go hungry rather than to seek help from these sources. This 1908 Act was certainly not over-generous. It provided a pension of five shillings (25p) per week for people over seventy years of age who passed a strict means test. It was paid for out of general taxation. In order to qualify for a full pension one's income had to be less than £21 per annum. This original act also had a respectability clause which tried to bar the work-shy and the recent prisoner from eligibility but, as this clause proved inoperable in practice, it was repealed in 1919 (Bruce, 1965: 155–6). The fact that it was included at all in the original act illustrates that the Victorian concept of 'the deserving poor' was still around in 1908, indeed it is a phrase that can still be heard even in 1998! But even if this pension seems very grudging by today's standards, it was enormously popular when enacted, with far more people applying for it than the government expected.

National Insurance Act 1911

Winston Churchill and David Lloyd George were the two politicians that steered this legislation around the vested interests opposed to it, such as the insurance companies and the medical profession, and through parliament. They could not have been two more contrasting men. Churchill, the aristocrat would one day lead Britain successfully through the Second World War and lead the Conservative Party. Lloyd George, the Welsh radical, hated the landowning classes and all that they stood for. His People's Budget in 1909 had set the trap that forever curbed the power of the House of Lords (Bruce, 1965: 181–3). Both men shared a passion for politics and for improving the lot of ordinary people.

The National Insurance Act was based on a three-cornered system of contributory insurance, with a weekly, flat rate contribution from the employee, the employer and the state. In return for these contributions insured workers built up rights to certain benefits when sick or unemployed. This was the most important thing that the 1911 Act did; it broke away completely from the poor law by giving the insured worker and, subsequently his or her family, a right to relief.

Part I of the Act (for which Lloyd George was responsible) provided health insurance. All employees earning less than £160 per year had to be insured, except that certain groups like teachers and civil servants, who had occupational pensions already, were allowed to stay outside the net. In return for his contributions, the insured worker was entitled to medical benefit (i.e. free treatment and medicines when sick) from the doctor of his choice on the local panel; sickness benefit of 10 shillings a week (50p) while out of work due to illness, certified by one's doctor, for up to 26 weeks. If after that a worker was still certified as unfit to go back to work, he could apply for disablement benefit (5 shillings a week) for a further 26 weeks. An insured worker also received free treatment in a sanatorium for himself or his family if suffering from tuberculosis, the major killer disease of the time that was highly infectious. That was why the family was included in this provision, to encourage as many TB patients as possible to come forward for treatment. Finally a maternity benefit, 30 shillings' worth of maternity services, was provided for an insured worker's wife on confinement.

Part II, Unemployment Insurance, was Churchill's responsibility. Britain was the first country in the world to have state provision of unemployment insurance, so the government proceeded very cautiously into these unknown waters. At first it applied to certain industries only, those especially vulnerable to fluctuations in employment. Under this section the insured worker got unemployment benefit of seven shillings (35p) per week from the second to the fifteenth week of unemployment in return for his contributions, as long as he had not turned down an offer of another job in his field.

These benefits were described at the time as just life-belt measures, intended to tide the worker over a bad patch. Although meagre enough by present day standards they were regarded by very many people as very progressive innovations in Britain in 1911 and were, of course, greatly enhanced as time went on. However the reception given to the 1911 Act in Ireland was far from positive.

Irish Reaction to the 1911 National Insurance Act

The *Irish Independent*, never a radical newspaper, led Irish opposition to the bill, harping on the cost of the contributions for both employees and employers, rather than on its benefits. It was, to the *Independent,* another example of Britain's penal taxation on Ireland and the paper called for Ireland's exclusion from the act. The Irish Catholic hierarchy entered the fray in June 1911; they too opposed the application of the bill to Ireland (Barrington, 1987: 49–50). Their statement said they could understand the value of a scheme like this for an industrial nation like England, but considered it inappropriate in Ireland where only a fraction of the population were wage earners. Taking a very similar line to the *Irish Independent,* they argued that the cost would be too heavy a burden for small Irish firms and shopkeepers and would therefore increase unemployment. Barrington's analysis is very interesting:

> the bishops viewed the issues raised by the bill through predominantly rural and capitalist eyes and from the standpoint of the farmer and small trader. No reference was made to the needs of the increasingly desperate working class in the cities. It seems the bishops did not fully understand the bill and the range of benefits offered (1987: 50).

Barrington goes on to wonder if the bishops had been lobbied to oppose the bill by disgruntled members of the Irish Party, or by the medical profession or the business community. Ireland is a small place where lobbying is easy. But at least on this occasion the bishops made their views public, unlike their intervention in the Noel Browne affair some forty years later (see pp. 28–30 below).

The Irish Party and the medical profession were divided on the bill. Contract practice was as unpopular with the Irish medical profession as it was with their colleagues in Britain. Furthermore, grafting an insurance scheme onto the dispensary system would have been both complicated and costly and Whitehall had no clear ideas on how exactly that could be done. While most dispensary doctors were in favour of the scheme, others feared a loss of income through a reduction in the number of private patients. Those in favour of the scheme demanded very high payments for their participation. Seeing what a tangled web of reactions his bill was getting in Ireland, that wily politician Lloyd George said he would let a committee of the Irish Party, on whose support he was dependent in Westminster, advise him on the implementation of the bill in Ireland. With Home Rule just around the corner, the Irish Party had to be more cautious than usual about expenditure on health services in Ireland, as they believed they would be running the show themselves in the near future. The compromise that was eventually arrived at meant that the National Insurance Act was applied to Ireland, except for medical benefit. So this important social policy – a scheme of National Insurance – was implemented in Ireland while the country was still under British rule. The scheme was cheaper in Ireland than in Britain, because Irish contributors did not have to pay for medical benefit. But sadly, the opportunity of radically reforming the Irish health services was sacrificed when the medical benefit section was thrown out.

Nor did Home Rule come as easily as the Irish Party had hoped in 1911. The Ulster unionists had rallied against the first two Home Rule Bills in 1886 and 1893. They were even more frightened now that the

Parliament Act of 1911 had broken the power of their protectors in the House of Lords. Under the leadership of Sir Edward Carson and Captain James Craig, they were even more determined to rebel against any Home Rule Bill for Ireland. After the Liberals introduced the third Home Rule Bill in April 1912, the vast majority of Ulster Protestants pledged themselves in the Solemn League and Covenant to repudiate the authority of any parliament forced on them (Lee, 1992: 1–6). There was, according to Lee, a 'sense of inalienable superiority' among Ulster unionists that led them to dismiss their Catholic neighbours as a lower species (1992: 4). They threw down the gauntlet; Ulster would fight rather than accept Home Rule.

As it happened, events overtook both the Ulster unionists and that reforming Liberal government with the outbreak of the First World War in 1914. Home Rule was no longer a priority for the British government; it was postponed until after the war. Ulstermen fought bravely in Flanders, as did thousands of men from all over Ireland. Then, after what Lloyd George described as their blood-stained stagger to victory, the war ended in November 1918. But all had changed utterly. Even though they had won the war, Britain no longer ruled the world and bit by bit the British Empire began to break up. The first sign of this was the short and bloody Easter Rising in Dublin that shook the city for five days of confusion and bloodshed in April 1916. The country did not rise in support of Pádraig Pearse and his fellow rebels. It seems that it was only after the British started executing the leaders of the Easter Rising in May 1916 that support for their cause widened. This is not an essay on political history, so suffice it to say that the Easter Rising of 1916 plus the Unionist rebellion against Home Rule put in process a sequence of events that led to the setting up of Dáil Éireann in Dublin in January 1919, the Government of Ireland Act and partition in 1920, the War of Independence in the south and the Treaty of 1921. Out of these events emerged two separate states on this small and troubled island. The six north-eastern counties became Northern Ireland which remained a part of the United Kingdom. The other twenty-six counties became the Free State in 1922 and later the Republic of Ireland in 1949. The Irish Constitution of 1922 granted universal suffrage, so women in the Free State were able to vote six years before women in Northern Ireland or in Britain. It also provided a proportional representation system of voting as part of the agreement with Britain that the Protestant minority would be protected (Lee, 1992: 82).

SURVIVAL 1922–51

The Treaty had ended the war with Britain, but that Treaty very soon led to a bitter civil war at home. The pro-treaty side won the vote in the Dáil to accept the Treaty, but that debate crystallized the real differences between the two sides and the enormous rivalry between Michael Collins and Eamon de Valera. A bitter civil war ensued. Collins was killed in an ambush in August 1922 yet still the war persisted until the following year. That awful civil war split the new state down the middle, even dividing families and friends. It also spawned two new political parties, Cumann na nGaedhael (later to change its name to Fine Gael) and Fianna Fáil, led by de Valera who decided to bring his party back into the Dáil and constitutional politics in 1927.

Not only had the new Irish state to deal with the aftermath of civil war, but it had come into being at the worst possible time, when the western economies were slipping into a recession so deep that it culminated in the Wall Street Crash on 24 October 1929 and the great depression – an economic depression that did not really end until the build up to the Second World War. So the real achievement of the leaders of the new Irish state in the inter-war years was that, unlike Germany, Spain or Italy, they did not let the country fall into fascism and dictatorship. In spite of all this economic and political trauma, Irish people held onto their hard-won, new democracy. This was a great achievement indeed.

There was no money to spend on social services. Some attempt was made to honour the pledge made in the Democratic Programme of the First Dáil (January 1919) to abolish 'the present odious, degrading and foreign Poor Law System' by continuing the amalgamation of unions, the replacement of some workhouses by county homes and the abolition of boards of guardians, a process of reforming local government that had started in 1920. That Cumann na nGaedhael government, led by W.T. Cosgrave, was both very short of money and very conservative in outlook. While there were genuine suspicions that some people drawing the old age pension were under seventy years of age (age was impossible to prove because of the late arrival of compulsory registration of births in Ireland), it is still hard to understand how the government could have cut ten per cent off the old age pension in 1924. Cumann na nGaedhael was never allowed by their political opponents to forget this insensitive act.

A Conservative State

The ideology of the new state was deeply conservative. In his autobiography, Seán Ó'Faoláin described the 1920s in Ireland as a 'time when the Catholic Church was felt, feared and courted on all sides as the dominant power' (1965: 264). Writing of this period in his great book, *Church and State in Modern Ireland,* John Whyte explains:

> if the government proved on the whole willing to listen to the Church, there is no need to explain this as simply due to political necessity. Ministers were products of the same culture as the bishops and shared the same values. There was only one Protestant in the government, Ernest Blythe, and his austere Ulster outlook seems to have fitted in well enough with the Catholic puritanism of his colleagues (1980: 36).

Whyte documents thoroughly how this puritanism was exercised: the Censorship of Films Act, 1923; the Intoxicating Liquor Acts, 1924 and 1927; rejection of Divorce Bills 1925; Censorship of Publications Act, 1929.

When Fianna Fáil came to power in 1932 they continued down the same path by banning the sale and importation of contraceptives in the 1935 Criminal Law Amendment Act. More restrictions followed in the 1936 Conditions of Employment Act, as Pauline Conroy's important research on industrial women workers shows. That act gave the Minister power, after due consultation, to prohibit the employment of female workers in industrial work or to fix the number of female workers employed (Conroy, 1987: 82–6). Conroy shows how congruent this law was with de Valera's 1937 Constitution. The 1937 Constitution put the family centre stage and afforded to the family 'inalienable and imprescriptible rights, antecedent and superior to all positive law' (article 41.1.1), thereby storing up problems for future policy makers trying to draft adequate child protection laws. It was equally clear that the woman's place was in the home; her roles were those of mother and homemaker (article 41.2.1 and 2). Divorce was outlawed (article 41.3.2). The Constitution was firmly rooted both in the Catholic social teaching of that era and in the culture and values of Ireland at that time.

Improvements in Social Welfare

Unemployment was a major problem in western countries during the 1930s. Fianna Fáil introduced two measures to help the unemployed. The first was the 1933 Unemployment Assistance Act. It was a means-tested, weekly allowance for anyone seeking work and unable to find it who was outside the insurance net or who had run out of benefit. It also included small farmers. The second was the Public Assistance Act, 1939, which was really a tidying up of poor law outdoor relief and medical relief. Outdoor relief was renamed Home Assistance. This was a discretionary means-tested allowance and any adult could apply for it, regardless of age, nationality or place of residence. Need was the only test applied. Someone dependent on another benefit (e.g. social insurance or the old age pension) could apply for home assistance to top up that benefit, if necessary. It was also there for people with no benefits such as a prisoner's family. Medical Assistance was also means-tested and discretionary. It provided the lower income group with the dispensary service and free hospital and specialist care but with no choice of doctor.

Widows and orphans were included in the social welfare system in 1935. Where a family was already covered by national insurance, that cover was now extended to include widows and orphans and, for those outside the insurance net, a means-tested allowance for widows and orphans was made available.

The Second World War and the Beveridge Report

Much to the annoyance of the British Prime Minister, Winston Churchill, de Valera managed to keep Ireland out of the Second World War. Once again thousands of Irish people emigrated to Britain to join the forces or to work in British industry or agriculture. Emigration had continued as one of Ireland's major problems – it had not ceased after the famine or with independence. When things were going particularly badly in Britain's war against Germany, Churchill asked one of his Labour Ministers, Greenwood, to find someone to write a plan for reconstruction after the war. Churchill saw this as a morale-boosting exercise for the war weary British people, as much as anything else. The man chosen was William Beveridge, a distinguished academic with a long track record in public service. His report, *Social Insurance and Allied Services*, was published in November 1942. The plan was, in effect, to build a more equitable society after the war. It set out to rid the country of want – what we would call poverty today. To do that, it proposed a universal, comprehensive system of social insurance to cover all the hazards of life from cradle to the grave. It argued that such a comprehensive system would be effective only if three underlying assumptions were also met: full employment to generate income, fuel the economy and pay for universal benefits; a national health service to get rid of Britain's two-tiered health service and instead try to make the best possible health service available to all; and a children's allowance to help with the cost of rearing large families. It was an instant success, hugely popular at home. The Beveridge Report was not only a blueprint for the future; it caught and built on the social solidarity of wartime Britain. The British Labour party adopted the Beveridge report as its political manifesto and in the post war election won a landslide victory.

The advent of the welfare state in Britain, the first in the world, made shock waves around the world, no more so than in Ireland. The idea of a children's allowance scheme, particularly one to assist low-income families with several children, had been around since before the war but had been opposed by the Department of Finance. Then in 1944 when Fianna Fáil was looking for something to increase its popularity at the polls, a universally available children's allowance that would give half a crown (12.5p) per week for the third and subsequent children was given to all families in the land. So Ireland introduced children's allowances a year before the British. The influence of Beveridge can be seen, too, in other areas.

Ruth Barrington's book reveals that the Irish Department of Local Government and Public Health[2] 'had a coherent and radical blueprint for the reform of the health services by the end of 1945. This included a long term strategy to provide a free health service and short term priorities to improve the treatment of tuberculosis and other specialist conditions and to protect the health of mothers and children' (1987: 167). However this daring plan, like Whately's more than a century before, ran into huge obstacles because it was too radical and therefore out of tune with the ideology of the day. The first Fianna Fáil Bill, 1945, which sought to introduce compulsory measures to treat and prevent TB – the major killer of the day – and to provide free services for mothers and children, was regarded as too oppressive. Their second Bill in 1947 likewise ran into trouble with both the doctors and the hierarchy, but this was not made public at the time. Then Fianna Fáil went out of office before the 1947 Act was implemented and a new inter-party government, led by John A. Costello of Fine Gael, came to power. He appointed the young and energetic Dr Noel Browne, from the new Clann na Poblachta Party, Minister for Health on his first day in the Dáil. Browne threw himself wholeheartedly into reforming the Irish health services. Greatly aided by all the preparatory work that had been done in the Department of Health,[3] in no time at all a free and comprehensive health system to tackle the scourge of TB was established and was most successful in getting the TB death rate down.

The Mother and Child Scheme[4]

In 1950, Browne moved on to try and implement his evolving plan for a comprehensive health service for mothers and children. Browne received the cabinet's approval on two important points of principle:

to remove the remaining compulsory elements, that might h
infringed on parental rights from the 1947 Act, and to keep it as a f
scheme, i.e. it would not be means-tested (Whyte, 1980: 200–1). Then
Browne pressed on to implement his scheme. He was very much a
loner and did not consult his cabinet colleagues about the problems
he encountered.

Powerful vested interests were determined to block the Mother and
Child Scheme. The details of Browne's conflict with the Irish Medical
Association and the Catholic hierarchy are not covered in this chapter,
but they have been thoroughly analysed elsewhere (Barrington, 1987;
Browne, 1986; Deeny, 1989; Lee, 1992; Whyte, 1980). Suffice to say
that in 1950 the medical profession and the Catholic hierarchy were
totally opposed to a free, state-run, health service for mothers and
children. To many members of the medical profession, the scheme
looked far too much like the beginning of a national health service that
would limit their income and autonomy. The bishops did not want the
state intruding, as they saw it, into the domain of the family and were
nervous about the health education aspects of the scheme, afraid it might
advocate contraception. Browne thought he had reassured them but he
had not. Behind closed doors, both the bishops and the medical
profession put pressure on the Taoiseach and members of the cabinet to
drop or drastically change the scheme. The government found itself in
an impossible position fighting both the bishops and the doctors. Noel
Browne was asked to compromise, to make it a means-tested scheme.
He refused and resigned in April 1951, releasing the correspondence
between the hierarchy, the Taoiseach and himself to the press. He
wanted the people to know what had happened his scheme.

With Browne's departure from office, the dream of establishing a
universally available health service in Ireland collapsed. The controversy
over the Mother and Child Scheme had profound effects on the
development of social policy in this country. It identified the forces
ranged against a universally available health service in this part of Ireland.
The supporters of means-tested services had won the day. This inevitably
led to the creation of a tortuously complicated system for the provision
and funding of health services in the Republic. But perhaps of even
greater consequence to the people of this island, the controversy exposed
for all to see the readiness of the Catholic hierarchy to interfere with
government in an effort to shape the laws of the land to their beliefs,
thus reinforcing that old, divisive Orange shibboleth, that 'Home Rule
means Rome Rule'. This crisis then, plus the coming of the welfare state
to Northern Ireland, deepened the border between North and South.
The year 1951 was a bad one for social policy in Ireland, for Ireland itself

and particularly for women and children in the Republic who lost the chance of getting a comprehensive health service.

So, what can we conclude from this overview of the foundation stones of Irish social policy? First of all that the economy of a country is an important factor in shaping its social policy, for a very poor country cannot afford generous social services. However, the economy is by no means the only factor, for a country's unique history and cultural values are equally important in influencing policy, for example the failure of the attempt to establish an integrated system of primary education in Ireland in the nineteenth century. The chapter shows that the social policies that Ireland inherited from Britain were indeed a mixed bag: some were punitive, like the workhouse system; others were very positive, like the old age pension and national insurance scheme. The poor law, Ireland's first nationwide provision for the poor, was a tightly controlled centralized system, thus setting a precedent for a centralist approach to policy making in Ireland. The power of the Roman Catholic church as an ideological force and as a key player in shaping Irish social policy emerges strongly from this chapter, for example the omission of medical benefit from the 1911 National Insurance Act in Ireland and in the defeat of the Mother and Child Scheme in 1951. The medical profession emerged here too as careful guardians of their own professional interests and incomes. Thus governments come up with policies, then legislation to tackle certain issues, but these policies have to be mediated through the competing forces of pressure groups working for change and those competing pressure groups seeking to kill off the new initiative. One of our tasks as social scientists is, through sound research, to feed ideas for policy initiatives into government that help to build a better world, as we saw William Beveridge, Charles Booth and Seebohm Rowntree do in this chapter.

NOTES

1 The full name of the Irish royal commission was: *The Commission of Inquiry into the Conditions of the Poorer Classes in Ireland, and into the various Institutions at present established by Law for their Relief and also whether any, and what, further Remedial Measures appear to be requisite to Ameliorate the Condition of the Irish Poor or any portion of them.*

2 The Department of Local Government and Public Health was divided into two new departments in 1947, the Department of Health and the Department of Social Welfare.

3 See note 2 above.

4 Much of this section has already appeared in Helen Burke, *The Royal Hospital, Donnybrook, 1743–1993,* Dublin, 1993.

RECOMMENDED READING

Barrington, R. (1987) *Health, Medicine and Politics*. Dublin: Institute of Public Administration.
Burke, H. (1987) *The People and the Poor Law in 19th Century Ireland*. Dublin: WEB.
Whyte, J. (1980) *Church and State in Modern Ireland 1923–1979*. Dublin: Gill & Macmillan (first published 1971).

REFERENCES

Barrington, R. (1987) *Health, Medicine and Politics*. Dublin: Institute of Public Administration.
Beveridge, W. (1942) *Social Insurance and Allied Services*. London: HMSO.
Bruce, M. (1965) *The Coming of the Welfare State*. London: Batsford.
Browne, N. (1986) *Against the Tide*. Dublin: Gill & Macmillan.
Bunreacht na hÉireann/Constitution of Ireland (1937) Dublin: Stationery Office.
Burke, H. (1987) *The People and the Poor Law in 19th Century Ireland*. Dublin: WEB.
Carney, C (1985) 'A Case Study in Social Policy: The Non-Contributory Old Age Pension', *Administration*, 33: 483.
Checkland, S.G. and E.O.A. Checkland (eds) (1974) *The Poor Law Report of 1834*. Harmondsworth: Penguin.
Conroy, P. (1987) 'The Position of Women Workers in Overseas Manufacturing Plants in Ireland: A Social Study', PhD thesis, University College Dublin.
Coolahan, J. (1981) *Irish Education: History and Structure*. Dublin: Institute of Public Administration.
Cousins, M. (1995) *The Irish Social Welfare System, Law and Social Policy*. Dublin: Round Hall Press.
Deeny, J. (1989) *To Cure and to Care: Memoirs of a Chief Medical Officer*. Dún Laoghaire: Glendale Press.
Edwards, R.D. and T.D. Williams (eds) (1994) *The Great Famine*. Dublin: Lilliput Press (first published 1957).
Foster, R.F. (1988) *Modern Ireland 1600–1972*. London: Allen Lane.
Garvin, T. (1996) *1922: The Birth of Irish Democracy*. Dublin: Gill & Macmillan.
Jackson, J.A. (1963) *The Irish in Britain*. London: Routledge & Kegan Paul.
Kerr, D.A. (1982) *Peel, Priests and Politics*. Oxford: Clarendon Press.
Lee, J.J. (1992) *Ireland 1912–1985: Politics and Society*. Cambridge University Press (first published 1989).
Ó Cinnéide, S. (1969) *A Law for the Poor*. Dublin: Institute of Public Administration.
O'Donovan, M.R. (1997) 'Goleen (Kilmoe) Parish in Famine Times', *Mizen Journal*, 6.
Ó Faoláin, S. (1965) *Vive Moi! An Autobiography*. London.
Ó Gráda, C. (1997) *A Rocky Road: The Irish Economy since the 1920s*. Manchester: University Press.
Powell, F. (1991) *The Politics of Irish Social Policy 1660–1990*. New York: Edwin Mellen Press.
Reports of the Commissions for Inquiring into the condition of the Poorer Classes in Ireland. (1835, 1936) London: Government Publications.
Whately, E.J. (1868) *Life and Correspondence of Richard Whately, DD*. London.

Whyte, J. (1980) *Church and State in Modern Ireland 1923–1979*. Dublin: Gill &
    Macmillan (first published 1971).
Woodham-Smith, Cecil (1962) *The Great Hunger, Ireland 1845–9*. London: Hamish
    Hamilton.
Woods, A.A. (1988) 'The Evolution of Dispensary Policy in Ireland, 1766–1872',
    MSocSc thesis, University College Dublin.

3
From the Fifties to the Nineties: Social Policy Comes Out of the Shadows

Pauline Conroy

INTRODUCTION

Social policy has been described by David Donnison (1975) as those actions which deliberately or accidentally effect the distribution of resources, status, opportunities and life chances among social groups and categories of people within a country, and thus help shape the general character and equity of its social relations. Social policy may also be viewed as the institutionalized control of services and organizations to maintain or change social structures and values (Townsend, 1981). Social policies articulate themselves through an interconnected provision or non-provision of a range of programmes, services, fiscal systems, laws, regulations, rights and entitlements. All these arrangements go to make up welfare states or welfare regimes.

The relative importance of the state, the market, the family or voluntary sector provision in a welfare regime is one of the core differences between countries (Lewis, 1993: 2). In this chapter, the changing focus of Irish social policy during the post-war decades is analysed. The shifting balance between state or public provision on the one hand, and provision by family or the voluntary sector on the other, will be identified. This balance has been described as the mixed economy of welfare (Mayo, 1994: 22) (see Chapter 4, pp. 51–69). In this mixed economy, the most significant sources of front-line care in personal social services are the family, friends and neighbours caring for children, the elderly, those with physical disabilities, learning difficulties or mental illness. Irish people in general give a high support to welfare, compared with other countries. Peillon (1995) attributes the reasons for this support not so much to people's social circumstances, as to the values they hold.

THE FIFTIES – A RATIONALE FOR WELFARE

The ending of the Second World War was not a moment of great upheaval for Ireland. The Irish and British economies were closely interlocked. Yet the challenge of providing homes, health and jobs for tens of thousands of returning soldiers did not arise as it had in France or Germany or the UK. The underlying thinking and policies which had developed in the 1930s and 1940s, as described by Burke in Chapter 2 (pp. 11–32), continued on into the fifties and sixties. The 1950s were a period of economic stagnation, high unemployment and mass emigration. However, it was also the decade that witnessed one of the most defining social debates of the second half of the century: the debate over the Mother and Child Scheme proposed by Minister of Health, Noel Browne, in 1951. The defeat of his attempt to introduce a form of universal national health service for pregnant and nursing mothers and children up to sixteen years was to carry echoes across the subsequent decades. This manifested itself in timidity in relation to introducing radical social changes, however well researched or required, and the absence of a social policy in the first attempts at economic planning.

The 1950s saw the emergence of new ideas and vibrant debates about a modern social science. The absence of universal, or even widespread, public health, education and social services did not pass in silence. Lectures in social science and economics had begun in University College, Dublin in the 1930s. The concepts of social science which were in wide circulation were strongly related to the teachings of the Catholic Church on social policy. In his *Primer of the Principles of Social Science*, written for schools, Canon Cronin wrote:

> The Church . . . is the divinely appointed guardian of the moral law and therefore it is her business to expound our rights and our duties in justice and charity even in temporal matters. (Cronin, 1934: 35)

The circulation of alternative, more secular ideas concerning economy and society gained currency with the founding of the People's College Adult Education Association by trade unionists in 1948.[1] The College obtained a grant from the George Bernard Shaw Trust in 1952 and developed lecture courses and summer schools (Dardis Clarke, 1986). The College suffered accusations of 'secularism' and was deprived of public funding in its early years. By 1954, a rival centre had appeared. A Catholic Workers College was opened with Church approval in Ranelagh in 1954 and immediately obtained a Corporation grant. The College was later to become the National College of Industrial Relations.

These were not the only new centres of social ideas. A Social Study Conference had been launched in 1952 as an independent voluntary organization with the aim of creating an enlightened public opinion based on Christian principles. This movement attracted two hundred or more participants, workers, employees, and others to formal lectures and discussions. Their subject matter was of high social significance: the dilemma of the citizen (1953); private enterprise and social responsibility (1954); can Ireland afford a living wage? (1955). The Social Study Conference was founded on an all-Ireland basis and met North and South, but not in the Diocese of Dublin. Its discussions of Irish social problems which might eventually be addressed by social policy quickly attracted a rival.

In 1954, the Dublin Institute of Catholic Sociology was established under the auspices of the Archbishop of Dublin, John Charles McQuaid. The following year a new edition of *A Manual of Social Ethics* was published by the Rev James Kavanagh for students of the Institute which was later to become the Dublin Institute of Adult Education (Kavanagh, 1956). The Manual stated:

> The State does not exist to do for individuals and families what they can do reasonably well themselves: the State should not supplant them when they can partly do things but should supplement their efforts (Kavanagh, 1956: 54).

To this intersecting and overlapping array of opposing voices may be added the Catholic Social Studies Conference, which addressed social issues on a mass scale, but this time inside the Diocese of Dublin in the unlikely venue of the National Stadium, more frequently used for boxing matches. The mobilization of opinion on social policy and social topics was widespread in the fifties but ignored in public policy. The several competing centres of discussion can be interpreted as a precursor to the Second Vatican Council of the sixties.

The Irish Housewives Association (IHA), founded in 1942, was particularly active during the 1950s in attempting to better the appalling social conditions of the majority of the population. They were among the first to advance the rights of citizen as 'consumer' and member of a family, a hitherto relatively unknown idea. As such, they campaigned to lower the price of bus fares and campaigned for controls over the price of coal, coke (a form of cheap coal used by workers' families), bread and jam (Tweedy, 1992: 105). Their actions carried a logic. In the absence of extensive public social welfare and social provision, individuals were at the mercy of market forces to meet their needs. The view of the IHA was that market forces needed to be regulated by the State.

In the 1950s the family – a national and cultural preoccupation – was treated as the basic unit of social welfare. Not everyone was able to form a family, nor did every couple unit have children. Despite considerable resistance from the Minister of Justice of 1950, General MacEoin opposed the legalization of adoption on the grounds that it would be against charity and against the common law of justice (Shatter, 1977: 163). Many of the fears expressed at the time were reflected in the Adoption Act which was passed in 1952. The rights of parents of abandoned children were strongly supported and the shared religion of the child and the adoptive parents were given extensive consideration. The child as a person was not at the centre of the legislation. These were not issues of costs but rather of the dominant values of the time.

An entire generation of people left Ireland during the 1950s. Tens of thousands of young boys and girls, men and women took the boat to Holyhead or the plane to America. The school leaving age was fourteen years, so emigration started young. These young emigrants did not return and their children became the London Irish or Irish Americans of today. The work of an entire Commission was devoted to emigration and population problems.

A mention of the fifties frequently attracts immediate reference to the document which was to herald a change in development of the economy (Brown, 1985). That document was the *White Paper on Economic Development* of 1958 (White Paper, 1958). It proposed a new interventionist approach to investment and productivity in agriculture and the opening up of the economy to foreign investment in industry. There was no social plan for health, for education, for housing. Social provision was to be postponed until prosperity had increased.

THE SIXTIES – THE DILEMMA OF SOCIAL REFORM

The 1960s saw an explosion of new social ideas. There was broadcasting from a national television station and the Second Vatican Council was held. Vatican II was interpreted as conveying a new social message, namely that the 'common good embraces the sum total of all those conditions of social life which enable individuals, families and organizations to achieve complete and efficacious fulfilment' (Healy and Reynolds, 1992: 23). There was a start to the American war in Vietnam, the commemorations of the fiftieth anniversary of the 1916 uprising, the rise of the civil rights movement in the United States and then in Northern Ireland. These global events had an impact on Ireland. They provided a backdrop to the first and second programmes for economic expansion which were supposed to modernize the economy. But the process proved more complex.

The new industrial workers, who were to produce the national wealth in factories rather than farms, lived in poor and underdeveloped conditions. There was no national health service. Secondary education was fee-paying and formal industrial training was unknown. Slum clearance had yet to be completed. The socially insured part of the working population was small.

Deeny (1971), in his detailed study of the Irish labour force, paints a bleak picture of the 1960s. Between 1961 and 1966, some 608,939 people emigrated from the country amounting to 33 per cent of young men aged 20 to 24 years, and 30 per cent of young women. About one in five of the population depended in whole or in part on a weekly social welfare payment. The working conditions of 90,000 urban and rural labourers were very poor, with 80 per cent having left school at 14 years old or younger (Deeny, 1971: 80). There was an urgent need for change.

This was immediately manifest in the reform programme published by the Fine Gael party in 1965, known as *Planning the Just Society*. The document broke with the tradition of viewing all state social intervention as an outsider's intrusion into the family and the voluntary sector. Arguing specifically against a narrow interpretation of the principle of subsidiarity, the 175-page text proposed development of education, health, welfare and children's services to reach the vast majority of the people.

The sixties saw the emergence of proposals to abolish the nineteenth-century Poor Law health system of dispensary doctors. These were to be replaced by a choice of doctor and right for the poor to obtain prescriptions from a chemist (White Paper, 1966). Equivalent reforms in social welfare did not see the light of day with the contributory pension (1961) being the most significant landmark of the decade (Cousins, 1995: 30).

Street protests against slums and tenements and Court challenges by the homeless were the marks of one of the first social protest movements: the Dublin Housing Action Group. In 1966, the fiftieth anniversary of the 1916 uprising, a new Housing Act was passed to permit public investment in housing grants and to organize the letting of public housing (Housing Act, 1966). The problems were acute. Forty-four per cent of Dublin Corporation's then 50,000 houses were shared by more than one family (Care, 1972: 39). The collapse of slum housing was a factor in the passage of the 1969 Housing Act which allowed the demolition of houses unfit for human habitation.

It was in the field of education that the biggest change occurred. In 1966, a government report, part-funded by the OECD, entitled *Investment in Education*, produced a first statistical study of the educational system. The results were depressing. Secondary education was inaccessible for the mass of pupils and primary education was failing those pupils who left the education system with no certificate at all. In 1967, the Minister for Education, Donough O'Malley, introduced a system of free secondary education and a school transport system, for those secondary schools that wished to participate (Brown, 1985: 251). Within a year, an extra 15,000 pupils had enrolled at school, revealing a suppressed demand for education in the population at large.

Despite a decade of economic expansion, of inward foreign investment and growth in manufacturing employment, the sixties were limited in their social achievements. The Second Programme for Economic Expansion did not deliver social change.

> . . . the Second Programme was mainly concerned with economic matters, regarded as a means to social progress, but was not associated with a complementary social programme. Neither the social implications of economic growth, nor the dependence of social progress on the rate of economic expansion, was got across sufficiently clearly to the public at large. (ICTU, 1968: 8).

Attitudes were gradually changing in the general population as to the need for widespread social and welfare interventions and reforms, but the results were in many instances too limited to have an impact on the general living and working conditions. In May 1968 a student revolt sparked off uprisings in universities across Europe. In the same period, Soviet tanks suppressed the democratic reform movement in Czechoslovakia, behind the then 'Iron Curtain' between Eastern and Western Europe. These global events impinged on a social thinking relatively untouched since before the Second World War. They injected a concept of rights and justice into a field of social policy hitherto dominated by welfarism and charity. For the first time, ideas and concepts of social policy could be garnered from outside the UK.

The breaking-down of barriers happened in Ireland too. In 1968, a civil rights movement appeared in Northern Ireland in which thousands of students and young people took part seeking an end to discrimination in employment, voting and housing. Between 1969 and 1974, nearly a quarter of all households in Belfast moved house from fear or intimidation. Some left Northern Ireland; some fled south. The Troubles had begun (O'Dowd et al., 1980: 133).

Gender barriers were challenged. The first fertility guidance clinic opened in Dublin in 1969, as women openly defied Catholic teaching and the law in a search for a means to control their fertility. With the enactment of the 1967 Abortion Act in England, Irish women quietly left at once for England to terminate pregnancies. Attitudes towards the situation of these women exiles was to cause a crisis in Ireland sixteen years later.

SOCIAL MOVEMENTS AND SOCIAL STAGNATION

The 1970s was a decade of social movements influencing or trying to impact on social policy. The more philosophical dissent of the fifties had by now crystallized into a range of movements whose vibrancy contrasted with the paucity and drabness of social development. According to NESC (1996: 6):

> The major economic events of the 1970s for Ireland were the two oil crises, 1973 and 1979, and membership of the EEC. Joining the EMS [European Monetary System] on its establishment in 1979 was also of great significance.

From a social policy perspective, an alternative agenda to macroeconomic trends can be constructed. The emergence of competing views as to the direction of social policy introduced a pluralism into social policy discussion. An example of such competing views was the debate between a welfare approach to juvenile justice and a justice approach – 'a return to the classic criminological principles of Victorian society' (Powell, 1995: 39). This was a hallmark of the 1970s.

The failure to address social policy on a mass scale was publicly reversed by no less than three social actors in the early 1970s: the European Community, social reformers and workers' representatives. With such strong institutional forces in favour, one might have expected substantial change. In a discussion document of 1972 the Irish Congress of Trade Unions stated:

> From time to time the Trade Union Movement puts forward proposals of various kinds for the extension and improvement of social services but it has not yet formulated a coherent, comprehensive programme for social development and the elimination of poverty. This omission should be remedied and the social priorities of the Trade Union Movement clearly set out. (ICTU, 1972a)

Among the trade union priorities were reductions in school class size from 40 pupils, an increase in social welfare payments and especially children's allowances, a target of 20,000 public houses to be built and an increase in public expenditure on health. The discussion paper of the ICTU was prepared in the context of a national wage agreement

(Employer–Labour Conference, 1976) and thus may be viewed as the precursor to the *Programme for Economic and Social Progress* (PESP, 1991), which combined social and economic policy in a single policy framework some 25 years later (Craig, 1994).

The ICTU proposals on social policy can also be viewed in the framework of the visible rediscovery of poverty in Ireland (Daly, 1989: 13), arising from research and discussion at the Kilkenny Conference of the Council of Social Welfare in 1971 (Brown, 1988). At that conference, research on the extent of poverty in Ireland was reviewed. Using a system of threshold measurements, as described by Room (1995), it was estimated that one million people were living at or below levels of transfer payments which were assessed as below the minimum necessary for subsistence.

The influence of Ireland's membership of the European Community in 1973 on social policy is difficult to estimate and quantify, but, according to Mangan (1993: 81), has been arguably more important than legislation. The Irish Labour Party and, later, the Irish Commissioner for Social Affairs, Patrick Hillery, had been extremely influential in drafting the first social action programme of the European Community. This programme, keeping well within the limits of subsidiarity, proposed the progressive establishment of social standards in living and working conditions across Europe. It allowed for action in relation to elderly people, people with disabilities, school leavers and women. It provided the basis for the first European programme to combat poverty (1975–80) (Commission, 1973) (see Chapter 6, pp. 90–113).

The ink was hardly dry on Ireland's membership of what was then popularly referred to as the Common Market, than a process of opting-out of social provisions commenced, which was to continue to the present day. In 1974, the government of Ireland requested and was refused permission from the European Commission to derogate from the introduction of equal pay between women and men for equal work under Article 119 of the Treaty of Rome. At the time, women workers' hourly earnings in Ireland were only 56 per cent of those earned by men (ICTU, 1972a). In 1978, Ireland made no moves to introduce equal treatment between women and men in social security schemes. This second opt-out was contested through the European and Irish courts for 18 years, when the last compensatory back-payments were finally made to Irish claimants. A pattern of stripping-out social clauses and provisions from international agreements started in the 1970s to prevent global thinking on integrated socio-economic development from tainting the economism which overshadowed Irish social policy (see Chapter 7, pp. 114–38).

By the early seventies, some major policy issues had been identified. The representatives of charitable endeavour and workers were ready to move forward and act; a favourable European climate was available. However, the response to the newly convergent focus on social policy and the extent of poverty in particular did not articulate itself in a major realignment of policy and reform. The meaning of social policy in public policy was too narrowly defined. The views of Townsend (1981: 25) on the UK could also apply to Ireland:

> Administrative and professional, including academic, élites have fostered a narrow, and relatively weak, version of the scope and meaning of the term 'social policy'. Social objectives have been transmuted by the state into economic objectives, but also minimised or fragmented.

Townsend's comments go some way to explaining why a broad-based concept of social policy was not accepted for over a decade from its enunciation in the seventies by Donnison (1975) and later reconfirmed by the National Economic and Social Council (NESC, 1981). On the latter occasion, NESC argued that:

> the concept of a modern welfare state embraces not only the extensive provision of social services to those in need but also the acceptance by Government, on behalf of the whole community, of a responsibility, at least in part, for the general well-being of the people (NESC, 1981: 11).

This included fiscal and monetary policy, a framework of legal rights and obligations and public programmes in health, education, housing and welfare.

In the absence of a comprehensive concept and practice of welfare, it was in fragmented sectoral fields that the differences of views on social policy were fought out during the 1970s. It was not, as is commonly thought, that there was a refusal to change or lack of knowledge on the need for new social policies, rather, there were different perspectives on social policy.

Social expenditure on both cash and non-cash benefits did increase during the 1970s. Expenditure on housing increased for example. About 40 per cent of the housing stock in 1989 had been built since 1971 (Blackwell, 1988: 10). But overall, the expected redistribution of resources between those in need and those with less need did not take place (NESC, 1988). A part of the answer may be found in the fact that as a proportion of government public expenditure or expressed as a proportion of the public capital programme, expenditure on social services fell during the 1970s (NESC, 1981, Table 2).

Ferguson (1996: 5–36) illustrates the point well for the case of children. He shows that it was during the 1970s that the medical model of policy development in cases of child abuse took hold with state ownership of the issue. This was despite intense struggles by voluntary groups to advance an alternative child centred and welfare approach. The significance of these 1970s debates was to find its trajectory in an investigative model of child abuse in the 1990s. The medical model was also institutionalized for social services in general under the Health Act of 1970, when the eight regional health boards were given responsibility for welfare – a field which in other countries is directed by social service departments.

In the field of poverty reduction, a national committee on pilot schemes to combat poverty was set up in the seventies to organize a new national anti-poverty strategy between 1975 and 1980. The scheme closed in considerable controversy concerning the extent to which the state should stimulate and subsidize local action for social change. The Employment Equality Agency was established in 1977. Its first priorities were directed towards creating a climate in which women and men could work together on an equal footing in relation to pay and working conditions (Hayes, 1995). In terms of legislation the Anti-Discrimination (Pay) Act, 1974, the Employment Equality Act, 1977 and the Unfair Dismissals Act, 1977 were the first instruments of protective legislation against non-discrimination, introduced in quick succession in the 1970s. Elsewhere, voluntary groups, concerned not just with charity but with justice, such as the student-based Free Legal Advice Centres (CASE, 1979) and the Prisons Study Group (1973), began to introduce not just alternative views and opinions but detailed alternative policies ready for implementation.

The 1970s were important for women. The formation of the First Commission on the Status of Women was a landmark in institutional change. A range of special women's benefits were introduced and grafted onto the welfare system: prescribed relatives allowance (1968); deserted wives allowance (1970); deserted wives benefit (1973); unmarried mothers benefit (1973); prisoners wives benefit (1974); single women's allowance (1974). These category-based benefits were part of a broader restructuring of gender and motherhood which granted new individual entitlements to women but simultaneously reasserted their status as wives, mothers, daughters and unpaid carers (Yeates, 1995; Conroy Jackson, 1993).

The competing perspectives on social policy circulating in the UK at that time (Williams, 1989: 17), such as welfare collectivism and welfare reformism were weakly implanted in Irish social science thinking and rarely if ever expressed in text. Yet, by the end of the seventies, the pressures for change were intense and new public institutions had emerged, albeit at the margins of the main government departments. A number of important legislative enactments had been successful and the way was open for the next phase of policy development: a departure from the fifties.

THE EIGHTIES: RECESSION AND REAPPRAISAL

The opening paragraphs of the *Report of the Commission on Social Welfare* (1986) typifies the policy atmosphere of the 1980s when 37 per cent of the population were in receipt of a weekly social welfare payment under a system that had been evolving since 1908 and had not been examined since 1947.

> Despite the dramatic growth in the social welfare system in terms of the numbers affected and the amount of resources involved, the development of the system has progressed without any fundamental review. (1986: xiii)

Faced with a gargantuan task, the Commission produced a 430-page report of research and costed proposals favouring a gradual reform of social welfare. Core priority was given to improving the basic payments, focusing on child support, extra payments for long-term beneficiaries and the extension of free fuel and electricity allowances. The Report did not recommend a different system but it did recommend some deep changes. Most, but not all, of its core priorities were accepted but have only gradually been implemented over a ten-year period. The focus on child support is interesting in that average completed family size did not alter significantly between 1946 and 1981 (Nic Ghiolla Phádraig and Clancy, 1995: 90).

The proposals to reform social welfare came at a bad time. The early eighties were deeply recessionary in Europe. The numbers unemployed had crossed a psychological threshold of over 200,000. Between 1979 and 1986, some 95,000 people had emigrated (NESC, 1989: 109). These were some of the issues that were discussed by the National Planning Board (1984).

It was by now widely recognized by decision makers that improvements were needed in housing, health, education and social welfare. How these were to be achieved without increasing public expenditure through the employment of more teachers, social workers and nurses was the dilemma. The OECD (1982) warned the government of Ireland against any moves towards increasing government expenditure, towards allowing real wage increases or increasing borrowing. Social developments, as a consequence, would have to be postponed or rely on an increase in taxation of those already at work.

Public opinion and public awareness of these complex dilemmas were not acute. The early years of the eighties were seized by a different social convulsion: the campaign to amend the Constitution by inserting a new amendment granting equal right to life to the mother and the unborn foetus – an anti-abortion amendment (Jackson, 1987, Barry, 1992).

Abortion had been illegal in Ireland since the nineteenth century and no political party planned to introduce any law on the subject. Not since the Mother and Child Scheme of the 1950s had a subject so divided the country and engendered such an atmosphere of crisis and it was the same subject, namely pregnancy and maternity. The eighth Amendment to the Constitution was passed in 1983. A referendum on a constitutional amendment to introduce divorce was rejected in 1986.

Local social action, local community work, local area-based responses, especially in the voluntary sector, grew during the 1980s. The voices of those in extreme poverty, or their advocates, were more frequently heard speaking of the homeless, the poverty of those with disabilities, the plight of Travellers without halting sites (Crickley and Devlin, 1990). A number of interpretations can be advanced for this phenomenon. The focus on local dimensions may have contained an implied retreat or distance from the polarization of national social debate into opposed moral camps. The emphasis on local action may have been an expression of the rise of civil society as a force in social policy and a response to the effects of spiralling unemployment on badly hit districts. Research evidence suggests that the nature of poverty changed over the eighties, with a large share of poor households experiencing unemployment compared with the seventies when poor households were more likely to contain persons outside the labour market (Nolan and Callan, 1994).

The capacity of the State to offer solutions to problems of such magnitude as poverty, emigration and unemployment was questioned during the eighties. The minor piecemeal reforms of the style of the 1970s were not sufficient to have substantial and rapid impact. The calling into question of the Keynsian welfare state was not unique to Ireland but was commonplace throughout the western world of that period. The trend is well described by Taylor (1995: 41):

> The central thrust of many developments in the welfare state during the 1980s was to tighten the grip on entitlement policing. Social rights, as an attribute of citizenship, have been gradually eroded as governments sought to reduce public expenditure, privatise public industry and reassert the primacy of individual self help.

By the end of the eighties, social policies in the spheres of health, education, housing and social welfare had developed their own dualism or apartheid. A tri-layered system of social welfare was still in position of social insurance, social assistance and the old nineteenth century Poor Law Outdoor Relief, renamed as supplementary welfare. While low-income households derived benefits based on social contributions, the same contributions produced little for middle-class households.

For the latter, tax allowances on mortgage interest, private health and pension contributions functioned as a form of residual welfare provision. Public social housing stock was reduced by sales and low rates of public housing building.

This loosening of beliefs in an ever-expanding welfare state, with ever enlarged capacity to produce houses, benefits, and hospital beds, was dealt a blow in the 1980s. In Ireland, as in the UK, the state and its departments have been extensively criticized for being over-centralized and over-interventionist. The principle of a universal right to minimum income payments, and accessible health education and justice systems has been undermined. This critical ethos has been sustained by frequently demeaning conditions prevailing for those seeking to obtain social and welfare payments and resources. Faced with the failing claims of a would-be welfare state to treat its citizens fairly and equally, the concept of a universal set of social rights, entitlements and resources is itself an issue of debate, particularly in the UK (Walker and Walker, 1996: 253).

In this context, the devolution and decentralization of services and provisions have an empowering appearance and carry greater resonance of a welfare society. A welfare society is one where people recognize responsibilities towards each other in the first instance. The role of the state is to provide an enabling environment for groups and individuals to provide services for and between themselves, to facilitate local employment, local services and local participation. The welfare society has both positive and negative aspects. A positive aspect is the revitalizing of the individual as a participant in society and in decision making. A negative aspect is a drift towards particularism or an undermining of universal rights and entitlements (Spicker, 1996: 229). These general concepts have special utility in understanding how Irish public social policy at the end of the eighties took a turn in a new direction towards centralized collective bargaining, and later developed a strong local development dimension. The first agreement between governments, unions and employers was called the *Programme for National Recovery* and ran from 1988 to 1990. It was its successor in the nineties that marked a shift in social policy.

THE NINETIES – PARTNERSHIP AS THE WELFARE SOCIETY

By the end of the eighties and the early nineties, social policy in Ireland had skipped a so-called phase. That missing phase was the development of a comprehensive set of social policies, of resources, rights, entitlements and systems of redistribution. In a leapfrog effect, social policy passed directly into the mainstream of national policy making by incorporation into negotiated centralized collective bargaining. *The Programme for*

Economic and Social Progress (PESP) 1990–93 did just that. The PESP was one of a series of national agreements between employers, farmers, milk suppliers, cooperatives, construction industry, the ICTU and the Government to adopt a long-term development strategy over a decade. The PESP contained proposals for the nineties such as:

> a programme of fundamental structural reforms, especially a continuation of the radical tax reform begun under the *Programme for National Recovery*, a major assault on long-term unemployment and a restructuring of our social services, in particular social welfare, the health services, education and housing (PESP, 1991: 8).

A chapter of PESP was devoted to area based strategies to combat long-term unemployment through the establishment of local partnership companies throughout the country. Reviewing the PESP, the National Economic and Social Forum, established in 1993 to include voluntary organizations, was critical (NESF, 1993) noting that the programme's benefits were not shared equally and did not take account sufficiently of problems of unemployment, poverty and social exclusion. Further negotiations led to a *Programme for Competitiveness and Work* (1991) and a Programme entitled *Partnership 2000 for Inclusion Employment and Competitiveness* (1996).

Preparations for the Partnership 2000 programme included submissions from eight voluntary organizations or networks on social development. This provided a part of the voluntary sector with a status akin to those of trade unions, or employers' and farmers' organizations. The Programme included chapters on social inclusion and a new focus on equality with proposals for improving family income supplement as an in-work benefit to top up wages and combat poverty as well as proposals to make the education system more equal. It contained no proposals on social insurance or housing stock or structure.

The 1990s has been the decade of the non-governmental organization, as a new agent of service provision, of change and of representativeness. The role of the voluntary sector has changed, at times driven by forces faster than its own development. Community groups, voluntary organizations, projects and local associations are now repeatedly canvassed to supply views, opinions and submissions on every subject from the development of docklands to the future of services for people with disabilities. Severely underfunded for such a scale of participation in the policy-making process, many organizations have experienced difficulties in providing volunteers and staff for the process.

In 1992 the *Protocols to the Maastricht Treaty of European Union* inserted opt-outs on abortion in Ireland and restrictions on compensatory back payments for equal treatment in pensions. In 1998 Ireland obtained a six-month derogation on the introduction of a parental leave Directive which had been drafted with the aim of enabling women and men to reconcile their working and family lives better. The principle of advancing the economic without the social was still alive at the dawn of the twenty-first century. When it comes to gender, unpaid work and the provision of care, Ireland has 1950s policies sitting on twenty-first century aspirations.

Yet, while dynamic changes have occurred in the area of local services, area-based developments and community development, some new and intractable social issues have surfaced in Irish society. The arrival of the first waves of asylum-seekers in the nineties has severely tested the capacity of the society and its services to tolerate or integrate outsider groups, as the treatment of Irish Travellers has posed over recent decades. The rapid and fatal spread of heroin among the youth in very disadvantaged areas has created great pain and social turmoil. The overcrowding of some prisons with addicted, ill, young prisoners as well as the plight of the homeless have not yet revealed cracks and fissures in the partnership ethos.

The social legacies of the fifties and sixties returned to haunt Irish society in the 1990s on several fronts. The disclosure of mass child sexual abuse both in families and in religious-run orphanages revealed an unpleasant underside. The evidence of physical abuse of children in orphanages and the trafficking and export of babies of unmarried mothers to the United States during the fifties and sixties was provided by survivors and the adopted children themselves. The existence of incest and the cruel and inhumane treatment of victims were a matter of public concern. Abortion, although by now constitutionally permissible in certain cases, remained without legal expression with the consequence that child pregnancy continued to provoke socio-moral crisis.

Contrary to European trends and without an oil crisis, the Irish economy grew during the nineties in terms of output and exports. Tax revenues were buoyant. Inflation was low and stable. The traditional excuse for evading social reform was gone. A surplus was available for social development. At this very point of time, the convergence criteria for economic and monetary union prescribed restraint in public expenditure, to maintain low inflation and low public borrowing.

From the fifties to the nineties, social resources, status and opportunities have changed among social groups and categories in Irish society. Instead of moving towards a welfare state, Ireland has developed, or rather drifted, towards a mixed economy of welfare. The state, the voluntary sector and the family each play a distinct part in social provision. The distributional arrangements between these are underpinned by strong meritocratic and gender biased thinking. Thinking is meritocratic in that those with less measured or medicalized abilities, those in pregnancy and maternity, those with disabilities, or less measured learning achievements are deemed more suited to have their needs met by the voluntary and family sector. While a number of important advances in social resources and capacities (NESC, 1996: 51) have been achieved, they have been accompanied by social and economic restructuring which has increased or frozen inequalities in certain spheres. These disparities are partly caused by poverty and social exclusion and are partly attributable to structural inequality and discrimination.

NOTE

1 The author is grateful to Máire O'Leary for access to her personal archive on these subjects.

RECOMMENDED READING

Brown, T. (1985) *Ireland, A Social and Cultural History 1922–1985*. Dublin: Fontana Press.
Conroy Jackson, P. (1993) 'Managing the Mothers, The Case of Ireland', pp. 72–91 in J. Lewis (ed.), *Women and Social Policies in Europe*. London: Edward Elgar.
Donnison, D. (1975) *An Approach to Social Policy*. Report No 8. Dublin: NESC.
Mangan, I. (1993) 'The Influence of EEC Membership on Irish Social Policy and Social Services', pp. 60–81 in S. Ó Cinnéide (ed.), *Social Europe: EC Social Policy and Ireland*. Dublin: Institute of European Affairs.

REFERENCES

Barry, U. (1992) 'Movement Change and Reaction, The Struggle over Reproductive Rights in Ireland', pp. 107–18 in A. Smyth (ed.), *The Abortion Papers*. Dublin: Attic Press.
Blackwell, J. (ed.) (1988) 'Towards an Efficient and Equitable Housing Policy', *Administration*, special issue, 36 (4), Dublin: Institute of Public Administration.
Brown, T. (1985) *Ireland, A Social and Cultural History 1922–1985*. Dublin: Fontana Press.
Brown, T. (1988) 'Poverty in the Republic of Ireland', pp. 15–26 in E. Hanna (ed.), *Poverty in Ireland*, Social Study Conference, Lurgan: Ronan Press.
Care Memorandum on Deprived Children and Children's Services in Ireland (1972) Dublin: Care.
CASE (1979) *Journal of Civil Rights, Social and Welfare Law*. Dublin: Coolock Community Law Centre.

Commission of the European Communities (1973) *Guidelines for a Social Action Programme*. Brussels: Commission of the European Communities.

Conroy Jackson, P. (1993) 'Managing the Mothers, The Case of Ireland', pp. 72–91 in J. Lewis (ed.), *Women and Social Policies in Europe*. London: Edward Elgar.

Council of the European Communities (1992) *Treaty on European Union*. Luxembourg: Office for Official Publications of the European Communities (reproduction of the text as signed in Maastricht on 7 February 1992).

Cousins, M. (1995) *The Irish Social Welfare System, Law and Social Policy*. Dublin: Round Hall Press.

Craig, S. (1994) *Progress Through Partnership*. Dublin: Combat Poverty Agency.

Crickley, S. and M. Devlin (1990) 'Community Work in the Eighties – an Overview', pp. 53–80 in Community Workers Co-op, *Community Work in Ireland*. Dublin: Combat Poverty Agency.

Cronin, M. (1934) *Primer of the Principles of Social Science*. Dublin: M. H. Gill.

Daly, M. (1989) *Women and Poverty*. Dublin: Attic Press.

Dardis Clarke, R. (ed.) (1986) *The Story of the People's College*. Dublin: O'Brien Press.

Deeny, J. (1971) *The Irish Worker: A Demographic Study of the Labour Force in Ireland*. Dublin: Institute of Public Administration.

Donnison, D. (1975) *An Approach to Social Policy*. Report No 8. Dublin: NESC.

Employer-Labour Conference (1976) *Report to the Employer Labour Conference on the National Agreements of 1970, 1972, 1974 and 1975*. Dublin, 29 January.

Ferguson, H (ed.) (1996) *Administration*, 44 (2): 5–36.

Hayes, K. (1995) *Employment Equality Agency, 1995 Annual Report*. Dublin: EEA.

Healy, S.J. and S.M. Reynolds (1992) *Power Participation and Exclusion*. Dublin: Conference of Major Religious Superiors, (Ireland), Justice Commission.

Investment in Education (1966). Dublin: Stationery Office.

Ireland Housing Act 1966.

Ireland Housing Act, 1969.

ICTU (1968) *Trade Union Information*. Dublin: ICTU

ICTU (1972a) *Discussion Document on Economic and Social Development*, Annual Delegate Conference. Dublin: ICTU

ICTU (1972b) *Trade Union Information*, No. 173/6 August. Dublin: ICTU.

Jackson, P. (1987) 'Outside the Jurisdiction, Irish Women Seeking Abortion', pp. 203–23 in C. Curtin, P. Jackson and B. O'Connor (eds), *Gender in Irish Society*. Galway: Galway University Press.

Kavanagh, J. (1956) *Manual of Social Ethics*. Dublin: Gill.

Lewis, J. (ed.) (1993) *Women and Social Policies in Europe: Work, Family and the State*. Aldershot: Edward Elgar.

Mangan, I. (1993) 'The Influence of EEC Membership on Irish Social Policy and Social Services', pp. 60–81 in S. Ó Cinnéide (ed.), *Social Europe: EC Social Policy and Ireland*. Dublin: Institute of European Affairs.

Mayo, M. (1994) *Community and Caring – The Mixed Economy of Welfare*. London: Macmillan.

National Planning Board (1984) *Proposals for Plan 1984–87*. Dublin: Stationery Office.

NESC (1981) *Irish Social Policies Priorities for Future Development*, No. 61. Dublin: NESC.

NESC (1988) Redistribution through state social expenditure in the Republic of Ireland 1973–1980, No. 85. Dublin: NESC.

NESC (1989) *The Economic and Social Implications of Emigration*, No. 90. Dublin: NESC.

NESC (1996) *Strategy into the 21st Century*, No 99. Dublin: NESC.

NESF (1993) *Negotiations on a Successor Agreement to the PESP*, Forum Report No. 1, November. Dublin: NESF.

Nic Ghiolla Phádraig, M. and P. Clancy (1995) 'Marital Fertility and Family Planning in Dublin', pp. 87–112 in I. Colgan McCarthy (ed.), *Irish Family Studies: Selected Papers*. Dublin: UCD Family Studies Centre.

Nolan, B. and T. Callan (eds) (1994) *Poverty and Policy in Ireland*. Dublin: Gill & Macmillan.

O'Dowd, L., B. Rolston and M. Tomlinson (eds) (1980) *Northern Ireland, Between Civil Rights and Civil War*. London: CSE Books.

OECD (1982) *Ireland Economic Surveys 1981–82*. Paris: OECD.

Partnership 2000 for Inclusion, Employment and Competitiveness (1996) Dublin: Stationery Office.

Peillon, M. (1995) 'Support for Welfare in Ireland, Legitimacy and Interest', *Administration*, 43 (3): 3–21.

Powell, F. (1995) 'Deconstructing Juvenile Justice: A Postmodern Policy Dilemma,' *Administration*, 43 (1): 36–56.

Programme for Competitiveness and Work (1994) Dublin: Stationery Office.

Programme for Economic and Social Progress (1991) Dublin: Stationery Office.

Programme for National Recovery (1987) Dublin: Stationery Office.

Prison Study Group (1973) *An Examination of the Irish Penal System*. Dublin: Prison Study Group.

Report of the Commission on Social Welfare (1986) Dublin: Stationery Office.

Reports of the Commission on Emigration and Other Population Problems, 1948–1954 (1956) Dublin: Stationery Office.

Room, G (ed.) (1995) *Beyond the Threshold: The Measurement and Analysis of Social Exclusion*. Bristol: The Policy Press.

Shatter, A. (1977) *Family Law in the Republic of Ireland*. Dublin: Wolfhound Press.

Spicker, P. (1996) 'Understanding Particularism', pp. 220–33 in D. Taylor (ed.), *Critical Social Policy – A Reader*. London: Sage.

Taylor, G. (1995) 'Voluntary Workfare and the Right to Useful Employment', *Administration*, 43 (3): 36–56.

Townsend, P. (1981) 'Guerrillas, Subordinates and Passers-By', *Critical Social Policy*, 1 (2): 22–34.

Tweedy, H. (1992) *A Link in the Chain: The Story of the Irish Housewives Association 1942–1992*. Dublin: Attic Press.

Walker, A. and C. Walker (eds) (1996) *Britain Divided: The Growth of Social Exclusion in the 1980s and 1990s*. London: Child Poverty Action Group.

White Paper (1958) *Economic Development*. Dublin: Stationery Office.

White Paper (1966) *The Health Services and their Further Development*. Dublin: Stationery Office.

Williams, F. (1989) *Social Policy – A Critical Introduction*. London: Polity Press.

Yeates, N. (1995) *Unequal Status, Unequal Treatment: The Gender Restructuring of Welfare: Ireland*. Dublin: WERRC, UCD.

4
The Mixed Economy of Welfare

Bryan Fanning

INTRODUCTION

The role of the state in Ireland, as elsewhere, in securing the welfare of its citizens is one that has developed over time but it is not the case that all welfare is provided through the actions of the state. A mixed economy of welfare has persisted within contemporary society even though it has shifted towards a formal role for the state whose role and responsibilities in the provision of welfare are determined by law. As well as directly providing welfare services funded through taxation, the state has come to regulate the provision of welfare which is purchased by individuals and families or provided by charitable groups and organizations within society. The family remains a key site for informal social care. Beyond the family some redistribution of resources has historically occurred in communities on a charitable or voluntary basis. For example, many hospitals which were developed prior to the twentieth century, by the voluntary endeavours of religious orders and philanthropists, form the basis of much current Irish healthcare provision (Robins, 1960).

As such, the 'mixed economy of welfare' is a term which can be used to describe the balance of welfare provision within a society between the public, private, voluntary and informal sectors. It will be used in this sense throughout this chapter. However, with the emergence of a dominant role for the state in the provision of welfare (the welfare state) in some countries during the twentieth century, the concept of a mixed economy of welfare has been associated with recent tendencies to shift the balance of welfare provision away from the state – by means of privatization or by reduction in state provision – towards a greater reliance on other sectors (Gould, 1993: 67; Macarov, 1995: 250). The term is therefore used to describe a shift from a state-dominated welfare economy to a more mixed economy of welfare (Cochrane, 1993: 274). This second sense of what is meant by 'the mixed economy of welfare' will be revisited later in the chapter (p. 67).

WELFARE PLURALISM

The emergence of the state as a provider and regulator of welfare has given it a central role in shaping the mixed economy of welfare. The provision of welfare through a balance of public, private, voluntary and informal sector activity is referred to as welfare pluralism. This pluralism in the provision of welfare occurs within a mixed economy where the state may directly provide or purchase services on behalf of its citizens or provide grant aid, subsidy or tax relief to other sectors which provide welfare services. It also includes the private purchase of services whether from public, private or voluntary sectors. There are four sectors engaged in the provision of welfare:

• *A Public Sector* which includes welfare provision that is financed and managed by the state.

• *A Private Sector* which provides welfare goods and services for profit to those who can pay. The largest single purchaser of these is often the state. It may, for example, purchase places for public patients in private nursing homes. Individuals might also purchase welfare goods and services from the private sector.

• *A Voluntary Sector* which includes welfare provision on a charitable basis and self-help and mutual-aid groups. The voluntary sector in Ireland complements and supplements state provision. For example, the Society of St Vincent de Paul, a lay religious organization, has been described as operating a 'shadow welfare state' through its provision of welfare services (Department of Social Welfare, 1997: 31). The Irish voluntary sector is the dominant or sole provider in some social service areas such as in the provision for the elderly and those with disabilities.

• *An Informal Sector* consisting of the informal provision of welfare through families and within communities. Examples include the care of children, the aged and people with disabilities by members of their household.

The precise role of the state as provider and regulator is one that has changed over time so that an ongoing restructuring of the welfare economy can be identified with particular shifts when societies agree to extend or change the balance of provision. These shifts emerge through the political process (through legislation and the actions of governments) and through the market which will itself be influenced by state direction through taxation and regulation of its activities.

A pluralism in the provision of welfare suggests that welfare will be paid for in a number of different ways. Voluntary providers may depend on grants from the state, and therefore upon taxation, to some extent as well as upon charitable donations and fees. The Irish voluntary sector receives £487 million annually from the state and the European Union, not including an additional £120 million paid to those working with people with special needs and not including funding for voluntary hospitals (Department of Social Welfare, 1997: 84).

Even the informal sector is influenced by the state in a number of ways. Informal provision may be the expression of personal choice within society but it may also be necessitated by the absence of alternative provision. The state may encourage informal care through the tax or benefit systems. For example, the state encourages informal care by providing tax allowances towards the employment of private nurses (Cousins, 1994: 28). In 1973 benefits for the domiciliary care of 'severely handicapped children' were introduced under Section 61 of the Health Act (1970). The Social Welfare Act (1990) introduced a means-tested Carer's Allowance payable to carers providing full-time care to persons over retirement age or who are disabled (Cousins, 1994: 31). Much informal care, however, consists of unpaid work in the home which is not funded by the state.

THE POLITICAL ECONOMY OF WELFARE

The balance of public sector, private sector, voluntary sector and informal sector provision within a society will be shaped by its values, circumstances and politics. Different countries will have different mixed economies of welfare which reflect a particular combination of ideological, economic and political factors (Mayo, 1994: 24). The Irish mixed economy of welfare might be explained to some extent in terms of a number of such factors.

Catholic Conservatism

One approach to the comparative study of welfare systems which distinguishes between conservative, liberal and social democratic welfare regimes depicts the Irish welfare system as having characteristics of the first category (Esping-Anderson, 1990: 26–30). Conservative welfare regimes are seen as characteristic of countries where Catholic political parties and church influences are strong, the political left is weak and where there has been a history of absolutism and authoritarianism (Cochrane, 1993: 8). Welfare economies are influenced by church advocacy of traditional family forms, with state intervention only as a last resort in accordance with the principle of subsidiarity. Advocacy of corporatist or vocationalist structures, where there would be no direct state control of voluntary provision, aims to consolidate church authority and influence in society. In areas such as education and health, where a role for voluntary providers (historically dominated by religious bodies) developed, resistance to state encroachment would be anticipated. However in areas of welfare provision where there were no traditional voluntary providers, for example in the provision of unemployment and retirement age benefits, a role for the state as provider might not be contested.

Underdevelopment

A second approach to the analysis of mixed economies of welfare examines how the welfare regimes of countries are influenced by levels of capitalist industrialization. Within such an approach, distinctions are perceived between developed or core European countries and those, including Ireland, Greece, Spain, and Portugal, which have been labelled as semi-peripheral (Peillon, 1994: 184). Semi-peripheral countries are variously characterized by underdeveloped economies and a particularly directive role for the state coupled with low levels of welfare provision. A desire to develop the role of the state in the provision of welfare may not be accompanied by the ability to afford extensive provision.

Post-colonialism

Unlike other semi-peripheral European countries, Ireland experienced colonization and came to share the institutional features of an advanced capitalist British economy rather than those of the other semi-peripheral countries (Peillon, 1994: 193). The administrative legacy of colonialism included shared patterns of public administration with Britain which persisted after 1922. However, as part of the British Empire, Ireland also had a separate colonial administration characterized by paternalism and emphasis on military security which resulted in the centralized administration of policing and education (Chubb, 1993: 213). This administration was undertaken by a centralized civil service which, like the Indian civil service, persisted beyond independence. As such, the civil service was marked by an enormous degree of continuity.

THE DEVELOPMENT OF THE IRISH WELFARE STATE

The welfare economy of the Irish Republic was to some extent shaped by aspirations for a Gaelic-Catholic Ireland adopted by those influential in shaping the ideology of the new Irish state. An initial emphasis on isolationism over economic modernization resulted in low standards of living when such standards in the capitalist world were beginning to rise sharply (Fennell, 1993: 57). Subsequently Ireland came to pursue, from the 1950s, a conformist process of modernization while retaining some opposition, through church censure and legal barriers, to social liberalism. Catholic ethos influenced the nature of welfare provision and the strength of the Church as a voluntary provider of welfare, particularly in the areas of education and health, influenced how it continued to be organized (Peillon, 1994: 95). The new status of the Irish language was reflected particularly in education. Irish welfare approaches also reflected the relative dependence on agriculture in comparison to countries such as the UK. These included low taxation, indirect transfers (price support mechanisms) as well direct transfers (benefits) in this area (Cousins, 1997: 229).

The role of the state in Ireland as a provider and regulator of welfare developed in a piecemeal manner after 1922 with a tendency to introduce schemes as an ad hoc response to social problems rather than through coherent and systematic planning (Carney, 1991: 6). The role of the state as provider within the Irish mixed economy of welfare became less developed than in Britain due to resistance to collectivization within Irish society and for reasons of affordability. Nevertheless the Irish state emerged as a significant provider of welfare.

The development of the Irish mixed economy of welfare can be illustrated by posing the following questions:

• Who has the power to provide welfare in society?
• Who pays for welfare in society?

Furthermore, specific mixed economies can be identified in respect of different areas of welfare. This will be illustrated by considering the examples of the mixed economy of health care and the mixed economy of social security in Ireland. Irish health and social security welfare economies will also be examined through comparison with those in Britain by examining how they have diverged from each other.

The Mixed Economy of Health Care

The Irish mixed economy of health care is characterized by a role for the state in direct provision and state regulation and funding of provision by other sectors. The state funds hospital care and visits to doctors 'free at point of access' on a means–tested basis and it subsidizes private health insurance through the tax system, grants to the voluntary sector and some benefits to informal carers. The voluntary sector in Ireland has a long-standing role in the provision and funding of health care which complements statutory provision. In some areas, such as in the provision of personal social services to the elderly and people with disabilities, it is the dominant or sole provider (Department of Social Welfare, 1997: 31).

Voluntary providers may be dependent upon Health Board funding. This was addressed in Section 65 of the 1953 Health Act which stated that a health authority may, with the approval of the minister, give assistance to any body which provides 'a similar service or ancillary to a service which the health authority may provide'. The voluntary sector itself is characterized by a diversity in the goals and organizational forms of voluntary agencies so that there are different relationships for funding and interdependence between voluntary agencies and the health authority. Voluntary providers tend to be more vulnerable and less stable but may also be more flexible than statutory agencies:

Stability is not a function of most voluntary agencies. They often experience a high turnover of staff and members and this, coupled with uncertainties about funding, tend to destabilize them and force them to review and refine their mission constantly (O'Sullivan, 1994: 6).

Voluntary agencies may possess a capacity for flexibility within the mixed economy of welfare because their functions are not limited by statute. They may identify needs not met elsewhere, innovate provision and lobby for its extension to address the needs of marginal or previously ignored groups. Examples of this pioneering role in Ireland can be seen in relation to the development of provision for themselves by people with disabilities and Travellers (for example through the work of St Michael's House and Pavee Point, respectively).

Control of Health Care

Various proposals by the Fianna Fáil government in 1947, the Inter-Party government in 1951 and the Fianna Fáil government in 1953 to introduce what became known as the 'Mother and Child' scheme, demonstrated conflicts around the provision of health services. In particular conflict was engendered by the opposition of Dr Noel Browne, the Inter-Party government's Minister for Health, to the near-monopoly of the religious orders in hospital care and the Church's opposition to socialized, or state controlled, medicine (Foster, 1988: 572).

However, the conflicts which emerged at the time of the reorganization of health provision in Ireland extended beyond those of church and state. Conflicts between general practitioners, as private sector providers of health care, and the state emerged. The Inter-Party government's proposals for free (voluntary) ante and post-natal care for mothers, as well as free medical care for all children under 16 were opposed by general practitioners who feared financial loss and loss of independence should the private practice of medicine be gradually superseded by a salaried state service. Likewise in Britain, the post-war Labour government, seeking to establish the National Health Service, found itself in conflict with the British Medical Association (BMA) over proposals to establish a health-centre programme which would pay general practitioners, in part, through a salary. The BMA campaign on the issue sought to play on doctors' fears that the proposal was the thin edge of a wedge which would turn general practitioners into full-time salaried civil servants. As such, opposition by interest groups to changes in the mixed economies of health care was similar in both cases (Lee, 1989: 316). While general practitioners remained within the private sector in both Britain and the Republic of Ireland, British hospital care was collectivized within the National Health Service, as were the previously voluntary personal social services. In Ireland, however, the role of voluntary providers remained unchallenged.

The development of the role of the state in the provision of health care was influenced by the principle of subsidiarity in Catholic social teaching in that there was active resistance to extending the role of the state in the provision of health and personal social services. However an ideological shift occurred from the 1960s within the Catholic Church, whereby the state was more likely to be criticized for doing too little rather than for encroaching upon existing voluntary provision (Whyte, 1980). The withdrawal of religious personnel from the provision of health and personal social services, as a result of the decline in religious vocations, has created gaps which are increasingly filled by the statutory sector and other voluntary agencies. A recent example of this is the agreement to transfer ownership of Our Lady of Lourdes Hospital in Drogheda to the North Eastern Health Board (Department of Social Welfare, 1997: 31).

An increased preoccupation with the coordination of voluntary and statutory provision within a statutory framework which identifies roles and responsibilities of the different providers is evident in recent legislation and policy proposals. For example, the Child Care Act 1991 placed emphasis on coordination between the health boards and the voluntary sector. Policy proposals contained in *Shaping a Healthier Future: A Strategy For Effective Health in the 1990s* (Department of Health, 1994) considered service agreements between the larger voluntary agencies and the health boards. The *Supporting Voluntary Activity* (Department of Social Welfare, 1997: 22) Green Paper, on the community and voluntary sector and its relationship with the state, advocated an enabling role for the state in the development of the voluntary sector (1997: 22). The mixed economy of health care in Ireland can therefore be seen to have changed over time. The role of the state has increased. The nature of the voluntary sector has changed. Interrelationships between the state and voluntary sectors have developed. These have been shaped by the legacy of subsidiarity, new approaches to partnership in the provision of welfare and the financial dependence of the voluntary sector upon the state.

Payment for Health Care

While the United Kingdom introduced a comprehensive free medical service in 1948 which related treatment to need rather than income, with no charge to patients at points of access (doctors' surgeries, hospitals), in Ireland such comprehensive free provision never emerged. For example, the *White Paper on the Health Services and their Development* (1960) stated:

> The government did not accept that the State had a duty to provide access to medical, dental and other health services free of cost for everyone without regard to individual need and circumstances (quoted by Murie and Birrell, 1972: 11).

Those not entitled to free health care under a means-tested benefit scheme had to pay for health care at points of access. Statutory universal entitlement to some services free of charge was supplemented by charges and by private health insurance. Private insurance schemes were primarily designed to insure against the costs of hospital care and as such did not provide comprehensive health insurance for those not entitled to medical cards, such as the cost of visiting a general practitioner or the full cost of visiting a medical consultant (Nolan, 1991: 131). As such a two-tiered healthcare system developed, which distinguished between a level of publicly available healthcare which was available free at point of access for those with medical cards (though with some charges for others), and additional public and private services where entitlement was based upon ability to pay.

The extent in Ireland of state funding for voluntary organizations in the area of health exceeds that in other areas (O'Sullivan, 1994: 16). Voluntary sector provision of health and personal social services is to a considerable extent dependent upon funding from Health Authorities under Section 65 of the 1953 Health Act. Such funding has tended to be allocated to established groups so as to ensure the continuation of existing services (Duffy, 1993: 334). In 1996 the Department of Health and the Health Boards provided £80 million to the voluntary and community sector. This included £20 million towards childcare services and £13 million towards services provided for people with physical difficulties (Department of Social Welfare, 1997: 84–5). Much of this funding is directed at relatively large agencies which are referred to as 'non-statutory' or 'quasi-statutory' because they have come to share a number of characteristics with statutory providers in terms of organization and administration (O' Sullivan 1994: 16; Duffy, 1993: 333).

In areas where there is no state provision or financial support for provision elsewhere, individuals, families and communities are dependent upon their own resources or support from their families and communities within the informal and voluntary sectors. Much voluntary activity remained dependent upon private fund-raising such as through charitable donations and sponsorship (Powell and Guerin, 1997: 148). Much informal care is provided without assistance from the state. For example, the National Council of the Elderly estimated in 1988 that 50,800 of the 66,300 elderly persons in the community who required care were cared for by other members of the same household (O' Connor et al., 1988). Only a small proportion of these carers (1850 in 1989) were entitled to financial assistance from the state under the criteria of the Prescribed Relative's Allowance (PRA). The PRA was replaced by a means-tested carers' allowance under the Social Welfare Act 1990 under which the number of recipients caring for elderly dependants in the home had risen to 4400 by 1993 (Cousins, 1994: 39–42).

THE MIXED ECONOMY OF SOCIAL WELFARE

The differences between the social welfare systems of Ireland and Britain after 1922 can perhaps be explained as the result of scantier resources within Ireland for a long period after the formation of the state and as a result of the wartime consensus in Britain which resulted in the introduction of comprehensive welfare legislation in 1948 rather than the piecemeal welfare legislation which emerged over a longer period in Ireland. However, in both countries social welfare provision evolved similarly. In both cases, similar taxation-funded systems of state unemployment and retirement age benefits developed. In Ireland, the state developed an uncontested role as provider of social welfare in the absence of such provision having emerged through corporatist institutions (Korpi, 1992: 18). In both Ireland and Britain, the state emerged as the dominant provider of unemployment insurance (although some pluralism can be seen with the existence of some private insurance against unemployment through mortgage insurance and informal insurance where individuals have savings) and developed a significant role in the provision of retirement age welfare.

After Independence, differences quickly emerged between levels of unemployment insurance in Ireland and in Northern Ireland and the latter maintained parity with the rest of Britain through ongoing subsidy from 1925. Subsequently, the introduction of the post-war welfare state within Northern Ireland required levels of expenditure which could not be afforded. Estimates in 1969–70 put the cost of applying Northern Ireland eligibility provisions and benefit rates to Ireland at double Ireland's expenditure on health and social welfare services (Fitzgerald, 1972: 181–7). Since then, however, the gap has narrowed as a result of an Irish economic growth rate of twice that of the United Kingdom since the 1960s, with a resultant doubling of social expenditure as a proportion of the GNP between 1963 and 1980 (Joyce and Ham, 1990: 220). As a result, Ireland's mixed economy of social welfare bears considerable similarities to the United Kingdom in terms of who pays for social welfare. This can be seen in relation to pension systems in both countries.

Pensions

An example of welfare pluralism in the provision of welfare can be seen in how Irish citizens can obtain an income upon reaching retirement age in a number of ways. Firstly, the state provides two forms of pension: the means-tested non-contributory old age pension and the contributory Pay Related Social Insurance (PRSI) pension. These state pensions are referred to as the First Pillar of the Irish pension system (Pensions Board, 1997: 5). The First Pillar provides some degree of income for those at retirement age. The state has a direct role as a provider of pensions.

The Second Pillar consists of occupational pensions which are not provided by the state but through employers or where the self-employed pay contributions to a private pension scheme provided by private sector insurance companies. As there is no statutory requirement upon workers to contribute to a private pension scheme, involvement occurs on a voluntary basis. Their ability to contribute to a private pension scheme depends to some extent on their occupation, earnings and employment conditions. Some companies do not have occupational pension schemes. Those that do may distinguish between permanent and casual employees. Some workers may feel they cannot afford contributions within a private scheme. Occupational pensions are obviously not available to the unemployed. About half of those within the Irish workforce contribute to private occupational schemes of one sort or another (Pensions Board, 1997: 6). The state participates in the Second Pillar in a number of ways. Firstly it provides occupational pensions for its own employees. Secondly it provides tax incentives to those who take out personal pensions within the private sector. The actions by the state in regulating and subsidizing occupational pension schemes influence the extent of participation in them.

A Third Pillar of retirement age income can be realized from accumulated personal wealth not tied up in pension funds such as the proceeds of businesses, investments and assets that are sold or cashed in on retirement. People who have purchased their homes through a mortgage may own them outright by the time they reach retirement age. They may realize some of the capital tied up in their homes either by selling-up and moving to cheaper accommodation, or by securing loans against their homes which are not payable until the property is sold after their deaths, or they may leave their property as an inheritance. Such personal wealth exceeds the amount of wealth tied up in pension funds (Pensions Board, 1997: 20). However such wealth is inequitably distributed in Irish society so that private resources available to people on retirement is also unevenly distributed.

A Fourth Pillar can be identified which consists of the post retirement-age earnings of those who continue working whether full-time, part-time or in new occupations and therefore can top up their earnings from state and private pensions or from other sources of wealth. Its growth can be attributed to some extent to improvements in health and longevity so that retirement now represents a part of the lifecycle of Irish people (Whelan and Whelan, 1988: 1) but can also be attributed to need, where the amounts of coverage provided under the First, Second and Third Pillars combine to provide an inadequate retirement age income. For example, in 1994, 18.6 per cent of households receiving non-contributory old-age pensions and 33.6 per cent of households receiving non-contributory widows' pensions had earnings below the poverty line (Pensions Board, 1997: 12).

Both Ireland and Britain have similar mixed economies of retirement age welfare. In Ireland, of the 415,000 people over 65 years of age, about 325,000 are recipients of non-contributory and contributory (First Pillar) pensions (Pensions Board, 1997: 11). A voluntary system of funded occupational schemes set up by employers, public service schemes run on a 'pay-as you-go' basis and personal pensions arranged by individuals (Second Pillar) provide for employees and the self-employed who did not contribute to the contributory First Pillar scheme. However, coverage among these sectors is lower. In 1995 only 52 per cent of employees, only 27 per cent self-employed and only 12 per cent of farmers had Second Pillar pension coverage (Pensions Board, 1997: 15). Coverage had been low up to the late 1960s and then expanded significantly over the following twenty years but with little expansion since then. In the last ten years the numbers covered have remained static. However, since then the labour force has expanded rapidly and the percentage of coverage has fallen somewhat. Coverage is especially low amongst temporary and part-time employees who have expanded during this period as a percentage of the work force. Only 12 per cent of such employees in service industries have coverage, compared to 48 per cent of full-time permanent employees (Pensions Board, 1997: 15). Nevertheless, there is a high rate of voluntary Second Pillar system coverage in Ireland compared to many other countries: 48 per cent in the UK, 48 per cent in Germany, 31 per cent in Belgium, 15 per cent in Spain and Portugal, 5 per cent in Italy and Greece (Pensions Board, 1997: 77).

While the percentages covered by First and Second Pillar schemes are comparatively high in Ireland, the extent of coverage of First Pillar pensions is below that of all other EU countries as a percentage of after-tax national average income (Pensions Board, 1997: 65). As such while most people will receive First Pillar pensions they are unlikely in themselves to provide adequate levels of income. However, for those who have them, Second Pillar occupational pensions in Ireland are of good quality so that the combined extent of coverage as a percentage of after-tax national average income is higher than some European countries including Britain.

RESTRUCTURING THE MIXED ECONOMIES OF WELFARE

The balance of mixed economies of welfare changed as the role of states in the provision of welfare became extended throughout the twentieth century. From the 1970s, however, the state's role in the provision of welfare in western society has become the subject of economic and ideological challenges (Heclo, 1991: 339–400). For example, in various western countries pressures to reduce state expenditure found ideological justification to reform the role of the state in the provision of welfare with the rise of neo-liberalism. Neo-liberalism challenged the role of the state in the provision of welfare and placed a new emphasis on indi-vidualism, the market and voluntarism. Effectively neo-liberalism was an ideological commitment to the free market within economies where the state had a considerable role in the provision of goods and services (health, social welfare, the utilities and nationalized industries) and in the consumption of goods and services. Neo-liberalism, as such, sought a move towards a 'more' mixed economy of welfare through diminishing the role of the state (Gould, 1993: 7). This restructuring was to be achieved in part through:

- privatization in the provision of services
- deregulation
- privatization of responsibility for risk in the provision of welfare
- a new emphasis on voluntarism

Privatization of Provision

Privatization is generally understood to refer to the replacement of the state by private provision in the sense that the state ceases to be an owner of the relevant assets and employer of the relevant staff. Such privatization occurred during the 1980s in Britain when state monopolies such as gas and telecommunications were sold to the private sector. Similar privatizations of public enterprise occurred in Ireland (Bord Báinne, Irish Life Assurance Company, Nitrigin Éireann Teo. (NET), Irish Continental Lines) but there has been little privatization in the provision of welfare.

One exception occurred in 1989 when the Hospitals Joint Services Board was privatized. The Board supplied linen to the hospitals and had a turnover of £3.8 million in 1988 but had accumulated losses of £3.5 million. The government wrote off these accumulated debts to make the sale of the Board more attractive to the private sector and sold it for £2 million (Sweeney, 1990: 191). This amounted to a very small proportion of state provision in the area of health. Further privatization in the provision of welfare occurred both in Britain and Ireland in relation to public housing where the state, in transferring ownership to tenants, divested itself of responsibility for ongoing repairs and maintenance. While little privatization of state welfare provision occurred in Ireland, there already was, as previously discussed, considerable private provision in areas such as health care and retirement age insurance.

Deregulation

This form of privatization occurs when regulation by the state of some area of activity is eliminated or reduced such as eliminating restrictions upon service providers to provide services at a certain cost or in a certain manner. During the 1980s the British (First Pillar) State Earnings Related Pensions Scheme (SERPS) was deregulated allowing competition from the private sector (Glennester, 1996: 271). In Ireland the Health Insurance Act (1995) deregulated health insurance. The Voluntary Health Insurance Board had provided private health insurance as a virtual state monopoly from 1957, when it was established, until 1997 when BUPA, a British health insurance company, entered into the Irish market.

Privatization of Risk

Social welfare benefits, pensions and access to free at point of use of health provision are all various forms of collective insurance against the risk of poverty due to unemployment or old age or illness. The removal or reduction of such collective insurance results in some privatization of risk. When entitlements to state benefits are cut, people are exposed to private risk whether or not there is some alternative source of insurance available to them. One consequence of the privatization of state health care insurance or pensions is that an individual may decide either to under-invest in health care or pensions or not invest at all.

Emphasis on Voluntarism

Privatization of risk may place new demands on the informal and voluntary sectors. In Britain neo-liberalism produced a new discourse based on the ideas of self-reliance and voluntarism which found expression in the Citizens Charter introduced by John Major's government in 1991. The Citizens Charter emphasized self-reliance, as distinct from reliance upon the state, and customer choice within a mixed economy of state, private and voluntary provision (Lewis, 1998: 322).

The Restructuring of Health Welfare

Following a post-war expansion in public-funded health services in the Republic, in the United Kingdom and in other European countries a new emphasis on efficiency emerged in various health care reform programmes. This was due, in part, to the rising cost of health care resulting from the costs of medical advances and more expensive treatment – in surgery, drug therapy, screening, and diagnosis – and the success of health care in prolonging the lives of people.

A resulting emphasis on promoting efficiency through competition among providers of health care emerged in a number of countries (Joyce and Ham, 1990: 218). In Britain, for example, the National Health Service and Community Care Act (1990) radically changed economic and managerial structures of state health provision by instigating competitive purchasing arrangements within the National Health Service. At one level these reforms resulted in no profound change to a mixed economy of health welfare dominated by a taxation-funded, state-controlled, free at point-of-entry National Health Service. Nevertheless there was increased emphasis on the role of private and voluntary provision and a shift in the role of the state from provider to purchaser of provision, to some extent, which has been characterized as a shift towards welfare pluralism (Lewis, 1998: 75).

In Ireland, some changes occurred within the mixed economy of health care during the same period. These resulted from significant reductions in state expenditure during the 1980s, the introduction of charges for hospital care, some privatization and, most recently, deregulation in the area of private health insurance. Between 1980 and 1988 the numbers employed by Health Boards and Public Voluntary Hospitals fell from 55,647 to 50,671, the number of hospital beds fell from 19,183 in 1980 to 15,225 in 1987 and the number of hospitals fell from 157 to 121 (Joyce and Ham, 1990: 221). These cutbacks occurred within the broader context of public sector reductions during this period. They were not accompanied by changes to the existing mixture of public and private finance of health care. Nevertheless reforms to the Irish health system crystallized existing distinctions between public and private purchase of health care from public, private and voluntary providers.

As noted earlier, interrelationships between the voluntary and statutory sectors have developed in recent years. They have been formalized to some extent through partnership arrangements, the use of contracts as mechanisms of funding of the voluntary sector by the state and the emergence of performance evaluation in relation to contracts (O' Sullivan, 1994: 22; Powell and Guerin, 1997: 161). The National Health Service and Community Care Act (1990) produced similar interrelationships between voluntary providers and the state in Britain.

The Restructuring of Retirement Age Welfare

The issue of the adequacy of and extensiveness of pension cover has been under consideration in Ireland since the 1970s when this was addressed in a Green Paper on a National Income Related Pension Scheme (1976). However proposals to introduce a comprehensive income related pension scheme were not pursued because of economic difficulties and the growing rate of unemployment. Instead priority was given to increasing the level of social welfare payments, including state pensions, and to extending social insurance within the workforce (Pensions Board, 1997: i).

In 1997 the Irish government began considering reforms to the Irish pension system within the context of similar reviews in many other countries for three main reasons:

- Demographic pressures resulting from declining birth rates producing an ageing population profile with a decrease in the ratio of dependants (including pensioners) to non-dependants (taxpayers)

- Difficulties experienced in honouring commitments to previously agreed pension levels as a result of the level of resources now available
- Concern about inadequate income levels amongst those completely reliant upon First Pillar pensions.

Concerns about the first two points are more long term in Ireland than in many other countries owing to a younger population profile. Nevertheless the cost of First Pillar pension provision is estimated to rise from 13.9 per cent of the taxable income of employees in 1990 to 25.1 per cent in 2035. The ratio of pensioners to the employed workforce is expected to rise, particularly from 2010 onwards. A total of 185,000 state employees are entitled to First Pillar contributory pensions. The cost of these public sector pensions is set to rise to 160 per cent of the 1995 cost by 2025 (Pensions Board, 1997: 35). In Britain, current debates about the adequacy and extensiveness of pension cover are located within a wider debate on reforming the welfare state. Concern about future dependency ratios, resulting from a declining workforce, an ageing population of dependants, and about poverty amongst the aged has created an impetus for a reformation of pension policy (Glennester, 1996: 281). In 1997 New Labour floated the concept of 'Do it Yourself' (DIY) or 'stakeholder' welfare under which people would build their 'own personal welfare state'. Suggestions have been made that compulsory Second Pillar pensions, on top of the basic non-contributory pension, could be introduced to ensure that people receive an adequate income on retirement (*The Sunday Times*, 16 January 1998).

The Irish Pension Board's (1997) review fell short of recommending that Second Pillar coverage becomes compulsory. Instead it focused on ways of extending voluntary coverage including tax incentives, the inclusion of part time employees in occupational schemes and reforms to the regulatory framework to facilitate portability of voluntary pensions between jobs. In both Britain and Ireland the need to supplement First Pillar coverage is likely to be addressed through extending Second Pillar coverage with the possibility of a privatization of risk should mandatory Second Pillar coverage replace First Pillar coverage or social unemployment and sickness insurance be replaced by private insurance.

CONCLUSIONS

A mixed economy of welfare has emerged in Irish society with a pluralism in the production of welfare between public, private, voluntary and informal sectors and in the payment for welfare through public and private purchase within these sectors. Different balances of public, private, voluntary and informal welfare have emerged in various areas of provision as have different balances of public and private payment for welfare. The Irish mixed economy is the product of historical, ideological and political factors which have shaped how welfare is paid for and provided. For example, the institutional legacy of British colonialism influenced some welfare provision after 1922 and economic underdevelopment limited levels of welfare provision. Some areas of Irish welfare provision were influenced by Catholic hostility to collectivism so that ideological conflicts emerged in the context of opposition by existing providers to state encroachment on voluntary provision in areas such as health and education. In such cases corporatist or vocationalist welfare arrangements prevailed. In other areas where there were no existing voluntary providers, an extensive role for the state as provider was characterized less by ideological conflict than issues about the availability and allocation of resources. The resultant mixed economy is characterized by a significant role for the state in the provision, funding and regulation of welfare. At the same time, there is also a significant role for an uncollectivized voluntary sector in areas such as health and education. There is also a role for an informal sector which provides care in areas (such as within the home), where the state has not developed a role as provider (the care of young children for example). However, the state provides some funding for informal care in some areas (the care of people with disabilities, for example).

More recently, challenges to the role of the state in the provision and funding of welfare have resulted in some restructuring of welfare economies. They have emphasized a greater role for private purchase of welfare within society (a privatization of risk) and a reduction of the cost of welfare through privatization of state provision or the introduction of competition between public and private providers. In societies with a preponderance of state welfare provision, for example the United Kingdom, such a restructuring can be characterized by a shift towards a 'more' mixed economy of welfare (Cochrane, 1993: 274).

Although the balance within mixed economies of welfare change over time – with implications for the members of societies – ultimately, access to welfare and the extent of welfare are important to people rather than how welfare is provided. For example, the greater extent of and general access to health care in Ireland in comparison to one or two hundred years ago has undoubtedly improved the health and longevity of Irish people. This might be seen in terms of a growth in the mixed economy of health care. On the other hand the quality of health care within a society may improve over time but there may be significant imbalances on its availability within mixed economies of welfare, which do not address issues of equity. Such issues will be pertinent whatever the nature of the mixed economy of welfare.

RECOMMENDED READING

Department of Social Welfare (1997) *Supporting Voluntary Activity: A Green Paper on the Community and Voluntary Sector and its Relationship with the State*. Dublin: Stationery Office.

Faughnan, Pauline (1990) *Voluntary Organisations in the Social Services Field*. Dublin: Social Science Research Centre.

Mayo, M. (1994) *Communities and Caring: The Mixed Economy of Welfare*. Basingstoke: Macmillan.

REFERENCES

Carney, C. (1991) *Selectivity Issues in Irish Social Services*. Dublin: Family Studies Centre.

Chubb, B. (1993) *The Government and Politics of Ireland*. London: Longman.

Cochrane, A. (1993) 'Comparative Approaches to Social Policy', pp. 1–18 in A. Cochrane and A. Clarke (eds), *Comparing Welfare States*. London: Sage.

Coughlan, A. (1984) 'Public Affairs 1916–1966: The Social Scene', *Administration*, 14 (3): 204–14.

Cousins, M. (1994) 'Social Security and Informal Caring: An Irish Perspective', *Administration*, 42 (1): 25–46.

Cousins, M. (1997) 'Ireland's Place in the World of Welfare Capitalism', *Journal of European Social Policy*, 7 (3): 223–35.

Department of Health (1993) *Health Statistics*. Dublin: Stationery Office.

Department of Health (1994) *Shaping a Healthier Future: A Strategy For Effective Health in the 1990s*. Dublin: Stationery Office.

Department of Social Welfare (1997) *Supporting Voluntary Activity: A Green Paper on the Community and Voluntary Sector and its Relationship with the State*. Dublin: Stationery Office.

Dooney, S. and S. O' Toole (1992) *Irish Government Today*. Dublin: Gill & Macmillan.

Duffy, M.J. (1993) 'The Voluntary Sector and the Personal Social Service', *Administration*, 34 (3): 323–44.

Esping-Andersen, G. (1990) *The Three Worlds of Welfare Capitalism*. Cambridge: Polity Press.

Fennell, D. (1993) *Heresy: The Battle of Ideas in Modern Ireland*. Belfast: Blackstaff.

Fitzgerald, G. (1972) *Towards a New Ireland*. London: C. Knight.

Foster, R.F. (1988) *Modern Ireland 1600–1972* . London: Penguin.

Ginsburg, N. (1992) *Divisions of Welfare: A Critical Introduction to Comparative Social Policy*. London: Sage.

Glennester, H. (1996) *Paying for Welfare*. London: Harvester Wheatsheaf.

Gould, A. (1993) *Capitalist Welfare Systems: A Comparison of Japan, Britain and Sweden*. New York: Longman.

Heclo, H. (1991) 'Towards a New Welfare State', in P. Flora and A.J. Heidenheimer (eds), *The Development of Welfare States in Europe and America*. London: Croom Helm.

Hensey, B. (1988) *The Health Services of Ireland*. Dublin: Institute of Public Administration.

Joyce, L. and C. Ham (1990) 'Enabling Managers to Manage: Healthcare Reform in Ireland', *Administration*, 38 (3): 215–37.

Kavanagh, J. (1978) 'Social Policy in Modern Ireland', *Administration*, 26 (3): 318–30.

Korpi, W. (1992) *Welfare State Development in Europe since 1930: Ireland in a Comparative Perspective*. Dublin: Economic and Social Research Institute.

Lee, J.J. (1989) *Ireland 1912–1995: Politics and Society*. Cambridge: Cambridge University Press.

Lewis, G. (1998) 'Coming Apart at the Seams: The Crisis of the Welfare State', in G. Hughes and G. Lewis (eds), *Unsettling Welfare: The Reconstruction of Social Policy*. London: Routledge.

Macarov, D. (1995) *Social Welfare: Structure and Practice*. London: Sage.

Mayo, M. (1994) *Communities and Caring: The Mixed Economy of Welfare*. Basingstoke: Macmillan.

McCashin, T. (1982) 'Social Policy 1957–82', *Administration*, 30 (2): 203–23.

Murie, A. and D. Birrell (1972) 'Social Services in Northern Ireland', *Administration*, 20 (4): 107–32.

Nolan, B. (1991) *The Utilisation and Financing of Health Services in Ireland*. Dublin: Economic and Social Research Institute.

O'Connor, J., E. Smyth and B. Whelan (1988) *Caring for the Elderly: Part 2: A Study of Carers in the Home*. Dublin: National Council for the Aged.

O' Sullivan, T. (1994) 'The Voluntary-Statutory Relationship in the Health Services', *Administration*, 42 (1): 3–24.

Peillon, M. (1994) 'Placing Ireland in a Comparative Perspective', *Economic and Social Review*, 25 (2): 179–95.

Pensions Board (1997) *National Pensions Policy Initiative: Consultation Document*. Dublin: Stationery Office.

Powell, F. and D. Guerin (1997) *Civil Society and Social Policy*. Dublin: A & A Farmer.

Robins, J.A. (1960) 'The Irish Hospital', *Administration*, 8 (2): 145–65.

Sweeney, P. (1990) *The Politics of Public Enterprise and Privatisation*. Dublin: Tomar.

Whelan, C.T. and B.J. Whelan (1988) *The Transition To Retirement*. Dublin: Economic and Social Research Institute.

Whyte, J.H. (1980) *Church and State in Modern Ireland, 1923–70*. Dublin: Gill & Macmillan.

5
Comparing Welfare States: Considering the Case of Ireland

Anne O'Donnell

Comparative social policy can be hard work, as will
become evident. Why inflict it on everyone?
(Jones, 1985: 3)

INTRODUCTION

This chapter introduces the field of comparative social policy analysis
and discusses the case of Ireland in this context. It begins with a discussion of definitional issues, before answering questions as to why and how
comparative social policy analysis takes place. This includes a discussion
of the role of models and typologies within this approach. It briefly
reviews the work of the leading contributors to the debate, referring to
the case of Ireland within these contributions. The work of other writers
who have sought to consider Irish social policy from a comparative
perspective is reviewed. Following this, the methods used in comparative
social policy analysis are evaluated. In conclusion, some of the current
and future issues for comparative social policy analysis are explored.

COMPARATIVE SOCIAL POLICY ANALYSIS

Higgins (1981: 5) usefully reminds us that comparative social policy is
not a field of study but a method of study, and that the phrase itself is
something of a misnomer since it is not the social policies themselves
that are comparative but the study of them. Even the 'comparative
approach' is deemed a misleading term by Jones (1985: 9), as there are
many variants within this approach. As Spicker (1995: 14) states, the
phrase 'comparative social policy' usually refers to cross-national studies,
although this may not necessarily be so, since the term 'comparative'
may relate to comparisons between regions or groups, or to changes over

time within one country. While all of these comparisons are valuable, this chapter is most concerned with cross-national comparisons.

Borrowing from Heidenheimer et al.'s (1975: i) definition of comparative public policy we can say that

> comparative social policy analysis is the study of why, how and to what effect different governments pursue courses of policy action or inaction in relation to the welfare of its citizens.

The Goals of Comparative Social Policy Analysis

Ragin (1994: 108) succinctly describes the goals of comparative social research as exploring diversity, interpreting cultural or historical significance and advancing theory. Higgins (1981: 167) proposes that a comparative analysis of social policy encourages a distinction between the general and the particular, 'whereby without some degree of comparison we are unable to say whether problems of policy are peculiar to certain types of political and economic system or whether problems are inherent in the policies themselves'.

Kennelly and O'Shea (1998: 193) suggest some reasons as to why it is important to analyse the Irish welfare state in a comparative European context. These reasons include the fact that social policy analysis is becoming more comparative in its outlook, as researchers discover that the challenges facing one particular country may be similar to challenges facing other countries, and that the practicality of a European social policy can be explored through comparative social policy analysis.

These justifications sound convincing, although, as Cochrane (1993) states, it may no longer be necessary to make the case for a comparative approach to the study of social policy since it appears to be very much in vogue. He usefully reminds us that

> there is a danger that the new orthodoxy may make it rather too easy to espouse a comparative approach without ever being clear why, or what questions can be most helpfully illuminated through comparison. (Cochrane, 1993: 1)

The danger of this complacency is one of the underlying concerns of this chapter.

Comparative Social Policy Methods

> 'Comparative understanding in the realm of social policy may be desired but it is not easily acquired.' Jones (1985: 5)

To admit that comparison is a desirable pursuit for social policy analysts tells us nothing about how we could most usefully go about such an endeavour, or that this might be easily achieved. The key problem in comparative studies is that of finding the correct balance between description and analysis, according to Higgins (1981: 1). Jones suggests that the first logical step in any comparative exercise is to define what is to be compared and the criteria by which it is to be compared. Ragin (1987: 67) points out that one of the key questions is whether the theory to be tested is properly operationalized. This is a crucial criterion for evaluating comparative social policy efforts. Ideal comparative social policy analysis will state its aims and scope clearly, ask questions to reflect these objectives and acknowledge that the conclusions reached reflect the questions asked.

Models and Types

The process of classification is described by Spicker (1995: 12) and is relevant to this discussion, since the output of much comparative social policy analysis is the formulation of models or typologies, into which welfare states are classified. Spicker suggests that classifications depend on the identification of common elements between cases. Theory is basic to the selection of the criteria for classification, though equally classification is basic to the construction of theoretical explanations. The purpose of models according to Titmuss (1974: 30) is 'not to admire the architecture of the building, but to help us see some order in all the disorder and confusion of facts, systems and choices concerning certain areas of our economic and social life'. Models usually involve the distinction of ideal-types. An ideal-type is defined by Weber (1949: 90) as 'a conceptual purity, a mental construct not to be found empirically anywhere in reality', a utopia. He warns that the construction of abstract ideal-types recommends itself not as an end but a means, a useful reminder to social policy comparativists, who may be tempted to see the models or types of welfare for more than they are.

Spicker (1995: 13) says that 'family resemblance' which tries to identify interrelated clusters of characteristics has an advantage over the use of ideal-types as

> one is not wholly constrained by the theory; if there are other resemblances apart from those which were first looked for, it should be possible to identify them and reassess the material from a range of data that is available.

This concept can be seen in the 'families of nations' work of Castles and Mitchell (1993), which is discussed below (p. 77).

Kennelly and O'Shea (1998: 199) state that the most useful way of understanding the long-term background to the welfare state in Ireland is by reference to the well-established analysis of welfare state regimes, though they acknowledge Cousins's (1997) criticism of the limitations of typologies, especially for post-colonial countries such as Ireland. This work of Cousins is further discussed later in this chapter (p. 81).

COMPARATIVE SOCIAL POLICY APPROACHES: CONSIDERING THE CASE OF IRELAND

A historical review of comparative social policy analysis is useful to enable the consideration of Ireland's position within various frameworks that have been offered. The typologies which are dealt with are those of Jones (1985), Esping-Andersen (1990), Castles and Mitchell (1993), Leibfried (1993) and Lewis (1992). Esping-Andersen's study has been widely acknowledged and has provoked much reaction. It has 'broken the mould of comparative social policy', according to Kemeny (1995: 95) and it is therefore analysed in some detail.

Jones (1985): Patterns of Welfare

As Jones (1985: 79) points out, the most obvious and popular stratagem in comparative analysis of the degrees of welfare in welfare capitalism had been to compare the levels of social spending between the western states as a proportion of GDP and/or as a proportion of total public expenditure. These early comparative studies (for example, Wilensky, 1975) espoused the evolutionary/convergence theory of welfare state development, which held that social expenditure increased with industrialization and increasing national prosperity. The league-table approach which this involved, Jones argued, was 'taking the art of comparison too far, or rather not far enough, whereby qualitative statements have followed from quantitative leads'. Jones (1985: 81) made one of the first attempts to move away from this approach and treated the level of social spending and the 'nature of social policy orientation' as two separate characteristics, which resulted in a two-dimensional picture where low and high spenders can be either '*welfare* capitalists' or 'welfare *capitalists*'.

Although Ireland was not included in Jones's analysis, Irish data from her source (OECD, 1984: 5) will be considered. From this and according to Jones's judgements on spending, Ireland seemed to be a relatively high social spender (27.1% of GNP for 1981) but this clearly tells us a limited amount about what this spending means. When investigating the nature of welfare, Ireland grouped closely to UK and the so-called Scandinavian tradition in relation to the use of income tax to pay for social welfare and in having higher spending on civic public consumption than social transfers.

Ireland was not included in Kraus's data on inequality and so this variable cannot be considered. Ireland would presumably therefore lie with the UK as a 'low spending, welfare capitalist regime'. This is imprecise and obscures the great differences between the two countries' approaches to social policy, particularly in accounting for influencing factors.

This approach could be seen as a useful development of the league-table approach, broadening the scope of comparison. However, although critical of it, Jones did use a league-table approach for the spending variable, albeit with another variable. This consideration of social spending is questionable though the practice continues to date, with Bonoli (1997) most recently following this trend. Bonoli, in his two-dimensional classification, finds Ireland and Britain alone in a quadrant called 'Beveridgean low spenders' characterized by low social expenditure and low contribution-financed social expenditure. Although there is more to the analysis than represented here, a similarity with the work of Jones (1985), as described above, must be admitted.

Esping-Andersen (1990): Three Worlds of Welfare Capitalism

'Ireland is obviously a moveable feast but not one which Esping-Andersen attempted to digest.' Cousins (1997: 226)

Esping-Andersen (1990: 2) carried out his comparative work based on the belief that existing theoretical models of the welfare state were inadequate and that 'the existence of a social programme and the amount of money spent on it may be less important than what it does'. Only 'comparative empirical research' will adequately disclose the fundamental properties that unite or divide modern welfare states, he stated. The comparative approach, Esping-Andersen (1990: 3) claims, is meant to, and will, show that welfare states are not all of one type. He also acknowledged that the Titmussian (1974) approach, proposing residual, institutional and industrial achievement-performance models of welfare, forces researchers to move away from 'the black box of expenditures' and this shift to welfare-state typologies makes simple linear welfare-state rankings difficult to sustain. Admittedly the work of Jones (1985), as described above, and others like Therborn and Roebroek (1986), in their work on full employment commitment, had already addressed this.

Esping-Andersen (1990: 3) chose de-commodification, which he defined as the degree to which people are permitted to make their living standards independent of pure market forces, and social stratification, whereby one's status as a citizen will compete with, or even replace, one's class position, as his central concepts in considering welfare regimes.

He firstly formulated de-commodification indices for pensions, sickness and unemployment using an array of variables, weighted by the population covered by these benefits. Eighteen OECD countries were analysed and the de-commodification scores for the above indices were combined. Esping-Andersen (1990: 51) claims that 'the idea that welfare states cluster into distinct groups becomes more evident when the total combined de-commodification score for the three programs are examined.' He distinguished three groups of countries: the Anglo-Saxon nations which are concentrated at the bottom of the index; the Scandinavian countries which are clustered at the top and the continental countries which are found between these two extremes. He concluded that 'even if this table shows a number of borderline cases, the clustering remains strong.' (Esping-Andersen, 1990: 51)

To investigate social stratification, Esping-Andersen created scored indices for conservative, liberal and socialist regime attributes. The results of this scoring are the appearance of clusters of welfare states, similar to the de-commodification clusters, with countries scoring strong, medium or low according to conservative, liberal and socialist regime attributes. Esping-Andersen thereby formulates a typology of three worlds of welfare capitalism: liberal, conservative and socialist based on the de-commodification and stratification indices. He concluded that, conceptually, we are comparing 'categorically different types of states' (Esping-Andersen, 1990: 20–1).

In the combined de-commodification score ranking, Ireland scored a low degree of de-commodification, being placed fifth lowest of the eighteen OECD countries analysed, below the mean. Within the social stratification indices Ireland scored medium on conservative attributes and low on liberal and socialist attributes. The UK and New Zealand are the only other two countries that do not score strongly on any set of attributes. Ireland, with the UK and New Zealand, scores low on liberalism, although it is found with 'liberal' countries (Canada, Australia and USA) in the de-commodification index. Ireland does not appear to illustrate the conclusions of Esping-Andersen's typology, not obligingly clustering with other countries, nor finding a home easily.

If we conclude from the above that Esping-Andersen's elaborate statistical analysis experiences difficulty in placing Ireland, this is perhaps appropriate, as far as Ireland is concerned, because of the complexity of the elements of its 'welfare stateness', which McLaughlin (1993), O'Connell and Rottman (1992) and Cousins (1997) describe more fully. It does, however, highlight some limitations of Esping-Andersen's analysis. This may be partly because of the focus of Esping-Andersen (1990: 29), who concludes that, in accounting for regime-types, three factors should be of particular importance: 'the nature of class mobilization (especially of the working class); class-political coalition structures; and the historical legacy of regime institutionalization'. These factors do not provide the most insight into the case of Ireland. The failure of the labour movement in Ireland, especially after partition in 1922, and the asocial basis of politics attributable to the nationalist focus and the civil war legacy, which arguably still haunt the Irish political scene, are described by Cochrane (1993: 208) and, in greater depth by Whyte (1974). Room (1995: 106) acknowledges that analysis like Esping-Andersen's is weakened in relation to countries, including Ireland, where 'class interests have not been so uniquely important for patterns of stratification and political order'.

Within Esping-Andersen's framework, however, McLaughlin (1993: 205) did examine the extent to which the Republic embodies the characteristics of a Catholic corporatist welfare regime, which he describes as 'a variant of Esping-Andersen's conservative corporatist regime, applicable to Latin Rim countries and Ireland, which has been largely ignored by social policy theorists'. Room (1991: 180) agrees that a deficiency of welfare classifications is the tendency to treat the various 'conservative' variants under a catch-all label. Some effort is made by Leibfried (1993) (see p. 78) to address this somewhat, by identifying the Latin Rim as a distinct type of welfare regime, he acknowledges. Cochrane (1993: 15) succinctly summarizes Ireland as:

> an example of more conservative, corporatist arrangements, maintaining status differentials with extensive involvement from the Church and clearly conservative attitudes to the position of women. Ireland displays a mix of different elements cutting across regime types . . . showing an uneasy mixture of corporatism and liberalism.

In this context, Cochrane (1993: 12) provides a justification for the case study approach. He discusses the limitations of typologies in comparative research – principally that there are no pure forms, with elements of many models found in each country. It becomes necessary, he concludes, to return to more detailed studies of individual countries or groups of countries, considering 'regime type' as a starting-point. These issues will be discussed further later in this chapter, when evaluating comparative social policy methods (pp. 82–3).

Whether or not Ireland 'fits' well into Esping-Andersen's typology, that is, whether it had explanatory power for Ireland, may seem irrelevant in the light of more fundamental criticisms of his approach, which themselves may explain why Ireland is not easily accommodated in its outcome. There have been many criticisms of Esping-Andersen's approach. It has been challenged on the count of gender-blindness, with the main attacks coming from Taylor-Gooby (1991), Langan and Ostner (1991) and Lewis (1992). Esping-Andersen's variable selection and indices construction are challenged by Castles and Mitchell (1990). The limitations of his static cross-sectional model is addressed by Kangas (1994), who concludes that the 'clustering' of welfare states is contingent on a particular point in time. Kemeny (1995: 90) argues that Esping-Andersen's 'threefold classification does not make a complete break with the traditional 'quantification' approach of earlier perspectives on welfare'. For liberal and socialist read Wilensky's 'laggards' and 'leaders', respectively, he advises.

Contributions to the comparative social policy debate subsequent to the work of Esping-Andersen have often explored the relationship of particular countries to his typology. His model's lack of predictive value for the case of Netherlands is addressed by Kloosterman (1994). Deacon (1992) considers the applicability of existing models, including Esping-Andersen's, to Eastern Europe. Kwon (1997) examined Japan and South Korea in relation to Esping-Andersen's conservative model. Esping-Andersen (1997), while enquiring whether the Japanese welfare state is a hybrid or unique case, uses the opportunity to concede that the criticism of the classification of welfare states can be fertile. This is because it forces the author to re-examine underlying criteria and consider more carefully the countries that do not fit in the overall scheme. Likening this generalization to emphasizing the forest instead of the individual, unique trees, he admits that the forest may in fact bear little resemblance to the reality of the trees.

Castles and Mitchell (1993): Families of Nations

Castles and Mitchell (1993) present 'four worlds of welfare', ostensibly adding a 'Radical' world to Esping-Andersen's typology. This is achieved by tabulating the following three sets of paired variables: household transfers as a percentage of GDP with average benefit; income profit taxes as a percentage of GDP with household transfers as a percentage of GDP; trade union density with non-Right incumbency. The results reveal the existence of a fourth quadrant of countries. (Castles and Mitchell, 1993: 106) As this contains the countries which fit least easily into Esping-Andersen's typology, the authors propose that this grouping may capture a reality undiscovered by his study.

Castles and Mitchell (1993: 124) conclude that Ireland has characteristics which cross-cut the Radical and Liberal worlds. Their analysis captures elements of relevance to Ireland more fully than Esping-Andersen's and is therefore more useful in locating it within a comparative context. As Castles and Mitchell (1993: 125) observe, Ireland has had predominantly rightist government, because the party system was mobilized around 'revolutionary' issues irrelevant to class concerns. Ireland has shared in the English-speaking nations' expenditure laggardliness, but not because it was part of a common family of nations. However, this analysis seems to miss out on Ireland's 'conservative' features, which might place it more readily with Italy in the Conservative quadrant. To have concluded that Ireland had characteristics which cross-cut three worlds, while probably true, may not be very useful to those who wish to classify it.

Leibfried (1993): Four Worlds of Welfare Capitalism

Leibried (1993) confines his analysis to European countries, to examine whether a 'Social Europe' might come about via convergence from the 'bottom up'. His attention centres on the 'interfaces between poverty, social insurance and poverty policy' and he outlines the different consequences that the introduction of a Basic Income scheme might have for each regime (Leibfried, 1993: 139). Rather than focus on 'those policy areas that quantitatively dominate the welfare state, the social insurance systems', Leibfried (1993: 139) claims to concentrate on the 'margins' of the welfare state, 'to test the limits and contents of social citizenship'. He qualitatively assesses four regimes, under the headings of the characteristics of welfare state approach (welfare state as compensator/employer, labour market, economy), the guarantee of the right to work/welfare and Basic Income prospects. He thereby distinguishes four different social policy regimes: the Scandinavian welfare states, the 'Bismarck' countries, the Anglo-Saxon and the Latin Rim countries.

Leibfried does not explicitly place Ireland anywhere but Room (1991: 180) noted that Leibfried fails to resolve how far Ireland should be included in the Latin Rim category and Olsson Hort (1993: 227) places it with the UK as an Anglo-Saxon country. Cook and McCashin (1992: 27) suggest that Ireland can be characterized as in a 'transition' from the Latin Rim model to the Anglo-Saxon one.

The Latin Rim characterization highlights the role of the church, women and the agricultural economy. According to Room (1991: 180), the Latin Rim countries have two related characteristic elements, namely the influence in welfare organization through poverty relief and service provision, and in the non-emergence onto the political agenda of certain key issues elsewhere central to the social policy debate. Siaroff (1994: 90) claims that Ireland is 'often treated as a quasi-Southern European nation anyway', when accounting for his findings of the lack of 'female work desirability in Central and Southern Europe, *plus* Ireland'.

However, there are clear differences between the Latin Rim and Ireland, reflecting cultural and historical differences. Cousins (1997: 231) considers whether or nor Ireland could be usefully compared to a Southern model of welfare and concludes that it cannot be subsumed into a Southern European or peripheral model. Peillon (1994), seeking to consider Ireland comparatively, endeavours to locate it within a category of countries which share similar features, either capitalist/ industrial/advanced or peripheral/semi-peripheral countries. He concludes that Ireland cannot be defined as an advanced capitalist economy although it displays many institutional features associated with such economies. If there is a semi-peripheral type of society, rather than economy, Peillon (1994: 193) suggests that Ireland is not part of this, sharing few of the institutional features of other semi-peripheral countries.

An overall criticism of Leibfried's approach is his ambiguous, and arguably unachieved, claim of concentration on the margins of social policy. It is not clear why he should do so when there are fundamental, and it could be said obvious, differences between regimes. Nor is it clear that he achieved this exploration of the margins. He failed to explain what this would mean and in any event, apart from Basic Income prospects, he looks at entitlement, albeit approached in a qualitative rather than quantitative way. Leibfried's analysis, as well as that of Esping-Andersen, has been criticized on the grounds that it omits gender as a central issue. Langan and Ostner (1991: 132) acknowledge that Leibfried recognizes that women's welfare is an issue and attempts to introduce a gender perspective into his models. They reinterpret Leibfried's models from this perspective and devise a feminist framework in the light of empirical evidence about women's economic and political position under these different regimes. Langan and Ostner (1991: 141) consider the Latin Rim model and characterize it as a 'mixed women's family support economy'. They mainly discuss Italy, with which Ireland can be compared. This reveals similarities in relation to gendered labour market segregation, although many of the factors they consider prove difficult to quantify or qualify.

Lewis (1992): Male Breadwinner Models

The approach of Lewis (1992) builds on the idea that any further development of the concept of 'welfare regime' must incorporate the relationship between unpaid work (done mainly by women in providing welfare) as well as paid work (see Chapter 13, pp. 231–53). Lewis (1992: 159) suggests that the idea of a male-breadwinner family model has served historically to cut across established typologies of welfare regimes.

She suggests that Ireland and Britain are examples of historically 'strong' male-breadwinner states and that this accounts for 'the level and, more importantly, the nature of women's (part-time) labour market partici-pation; the lack of childcare services and maternity rights; and the long-lived inequality between husbands and wives in regard to social security', with a firm dividing line drawn between public and private responsibility (Lewis, 1992: 159). Since Lewis's study, several other gender-sensitive typologies have been proposed, including those of Siaroff (1994) and Shaver and Bradshaw (1995). These studies also explore women's work and welfare and are valuable developments of Lewis's work in this regard. Siaroff (1994) locates Ireland within the Late Female Mobilization grouping, while admitting that Ireland's earlier female franchise belies this location. The analysis of Shaver and Bradshaw (1995) reveals that Ireland favours the traditional model over a range of incomes, while ranking towards the end within the dual-earner model, especially when childcare costs are considered.

In the context of comparative social policy analysis, the usefulness of the gender perspective in the analysis of Lewis and others is undeniable, when such substantive issues as female labour force participation and childcare provision, ignored in other analyses, are considered. These approaches capture the patriarchal and conservative elements of Ireland's welfare regime. However, whether Lewis's approach is too exclusively gender-based is arguable. This contributes to the disregard, for instance, of the great differences between Ireland and Britain. While they may indeed share certain women-unfriendly policies, the contributory factors towards discrimination are very different for both countries, although both involve conservative elements. Ireland's traditional Catholic con-servative influence, which Leibfried's Latin Rim model captures, and Britain's 'laggardly' nature in this regard buttressed by a New Right conservative political ideology throughout the 1980s, deserve distinction from each other. This 'intellectual impasse' is addressed further in Sainsbury (1994), where the contributors to this volume acknowledge the challenges of a synthesis of mainstream, gender-blind analyses, like Esping-Andersen's and feminist theories, which tend to concentrate solely on the experiences of women to counterbalance the former. The result would be a welcome analysis of how welfare states affect both women and men, she claims. Daly (1994: 117) calls for analysis which would reflect the 'circuits of redistribution for both men and women as indi-viduals and members of families', a call which has not yet been answered.

Recent Debate on Irish Social Policy in a Comparative Context

Other writers have discussed Ireland within a comparative context, often within the comparative social policy frameworks that have been developed. These include O'Connell and Rottman (1992), Korpi (1992), and Cousins (1997). While brief treatment here cannot do justice to these contributions, some salient points will be briefly discussed below.

O'Connell and Rottman (1992: 207) consider the application of the general theories of welfare state development to Ireland, that is, the logic of industrialism, the social-democratic and the state-centred approaches. They conclude that while no single approach provides a satisfactory account of the Irish case, the state-centred approach, which subsumes political factors, framed to attract the support of the middle classes and facilitated by a period of economic expansion, best explains the 'silent revolution' of the expansion of social rights in Ireland since the 1960s (O' Connell and Rottman, 1992: 205).

Korpi (1992) uses data from a comparative welfare state programme based at the Swedish Institute for Social Research at Stockholm University to compare Irish developments in old-age pensions and sickness insurance, in terms of replacement rates and coverage, during the period 1930 to 1985 with a number of European countries and average European rates. He notes with surprise the absence of corporatism in Irish social insurance, in contrast to continental Europe, and concludes that this has not been fully explained (Korpi, 1992: 32). This is interesting in the light of the influence of corporatism in other areas of policy.

Cousins (1997) offers the most recent and grounded discussion of Ireland in relation to recent comparative social policy research. He uses the case of Ireland to illustrate the deficiencies of existing approaches, by highlighting the factors which have been important in Irish welfare state development. These include Ireland's colonial and post-colonial status, the importance of agriculture and its status as a dependent peripheral country. The criticisms of general approaches to comparative social policy analysis outlined by Cousins include that they are core-centric, adopt a modernization approach and use variables which do not have the same relevance in core and peripheral countries. Cousins (1997: 228) concludes with a warning about the paradoxical problems of not being able to appreciate individual differences within studies of large numbers of nations, nor taking account of the world economic system by considering national data. This remains a considerable challenge.

As stated above, Kennelly and O'Shea (1998) also extol the virtues of comparison and reproduce European Union Social Protection expenditure figures as a percentage of GDP, which, as discussed in relation to the work of Jones (1985) above, is of limited value. The authors then consider various typologies, including those of Esping-Andersen (1990) and Leibfried (1992), to identify four regimes of welfare state provision: the Scandinavian or Social Democratic model, the Continental or 'social capitalism' model, the liberal Anglo-Saxon model and the Latin Rim countries (Kennelly and O'Shea, 1998: 201). They do not attempt to locate Ireland, or any other country within this framework, although their chapter does provide a useful overview of the main policy developments in Ireland in recent years.

AN EVALUATION OF COMPARATIVE METHODS AND FINDINGS

Ringen's (1991) beguilingly titled article 'Do welfare states come in types?' was and remains a valuable contribution to the debate. He examines the Scandinavian countries, since he suggests that if any welfare states are going to be similar, we would expect them to be the Scandinavian ones. Using inequality and redistribution indicators he makes this comparison and concludes that 'there is no such thing as a Scandinavian model', continuing that he is not 'convinced that the whole question of typologies is very fruitful' (Ringen, 1991: 40). We may be better off regarding welfare states as individually unique. Ringen then wisely directs us back to Titmuss's 'The Social Division of Welfare' (1976) which first expanded our ideas of welfare to include fiscal and occupational measures but which seems to be regularly forgotten, not least in comparative social policy analysis.

Why this search for types of welfare states? Popper's (1968: 47) suggestion that 'our expectation of finding a regularity, is connected with the inborn propensity to look out for regularities, or with a need to find regularities. . .', may help explain this quest for clusters. This search for regularity we see brought us to tidy, or at least pseudo-tidy, conclusions, for example that there are three 'worlds' of welfare capitalism. Popper (1968: 61) answers this claim with the conclusion that 'it can be shown that what is usually called the simplicity of a theory is associated with its logical improbability'. Here, the 'hybrids, anomalies' (Taylor-Gooby, 1991: 97) and Esping-Andersen's admission that there was 'no single pure case' sound familiar. Popper's (1968: 49) warning that 'events which do not yield to these attempts [to regularize], we are inclined to treat as a kind of "background noise"; and we stick to our expectations even when they are inadequate and we ought to accept defeat' may apply to these countries which do not fit within our typologies.

The importance of the variables that are chosen has been clear throughout this discussion. Variable selection has crucial implications for the outcome of the analysis. This can be so, according to Popper (1968: 48), because

> in constructing an induction machine we, the architects of the machine, must decide a priori what constitutes its world; what things are to be taken as similar or equal; and what kind of laws we wish the machine to be able to discover in its world . . . The machine will have its inborn selection principles.

Therefore, observation is always selective, 'it needs a chosen object, a definite task, an interest, a point of view, a problem'(Popper, 1968: 48). Although Popper is referring to scientific methods of observation and hypotheses, his theory is shown to be equally applicable to the 'pseudo-scientific' approach of Esping-Andersen. Indeed Popper (1978: 17) proposes a unity of method; that is to say, 'the view that all theoretical or generalizing sciences make use of the same [deductive] methods, whether they are natural sciences or social sciences'. Losing sight of these selection principles can also lead to the self-justifying fallacy whereby the theories espoused 'appeared to be able to explain practically everything that happened within the fields to which they referred.' 'Once your eyes were thus opened you saw confirming instances everywhere: the world was full of verifications of the theory. Whatever happened always confirmed it', Popper (1968: 34–5) proposes. A hint of this can be found in Esping-Andersen's (1990: 137) analysis of the 'Distribution Regimes in the Power Structure'. Here he examined the impact of political variables on welfare regimes. The results, he claims, give 'substantial comfort to our theoretical argument'.

Bradshaw and Wallace (1990: 154) argue that the case study may be the preferred strategy in some instances, since case studies are not generally atheoretical but help inform general theory 'illuminating phenomena that challenge scholarly consensus on a particular issue'. On the other hand, Ragin warns that 'discourse that is too case-oriented can atomize comparative social science, where every case may seem too different to be compared with any other' (Ragin, 1990: 3). Since one of the primary goals of comparative social science is to make general statements about relationships, this requires the use of concepts which are most easily represented through observable variables, he admits. Ragin (1990: 1) concludes that 'good comparative social science balances emphasis on cases and emphasis on variables', and recommends a synthetic approach which encompasses both emphases. This is good advice for social policy comparativists.

CURRENT CONCERNS: GLOBALIZATION
AND WELFARE REGIMES

Globalization is described by Scholte (1996) as 'what might be summarily characterized as the world becoming a single place'. (See Kofman and Youngs (1996) for further critical debate on this subject.) Recent social policy publications have highlighted the importance of globalization and its consideration for social policy analysis, and this can be seen to be particularly important in relation to comparative social policy analysis. For example, Kloosterman (1994: 187) suggests that the 'logic of post-industrialism' is perhaps too insistent to allow three separate worlds of welfare capitalism. Cox (1998) argues that our consideration of concep-tions of social rights, universality and solidarity as the basis for the welfare state are being challenged by recent welfare reforms which have placed more emphasis on cost-cutting austerity measures, individual responsibility and the duties of citizenship, actuarial reforms in pension schemes, decentralization and the relative power of different clientele interests. Therefore the standard notion of the welfare state, from Marshall and Titmuss, which has informed comparative work to date may not be useful in light of these changes.

George (1998) claims that governments across Europe have been pursuing policies that are largely similar in that they are leading towards the containment and retrenchment of state welfare. George (1998: 31) concludes that the effects of globalization on future developments of the welfare state are serious in a variety of ways: the threat of Newly Industrializing Countries (NICs) and their cheaper labour costs, the internationalization of capital and the reduction of the power of the state in relation to these globalizing influences. George claims that all European welfare states will be moving in a residual direction, regardless of political ideology, because of this hostile economic environment.

Rhodes (1996) reviews recent debates about globalization and European welfare states. International relations, including international political economy can contribute to our understanding in this regard. Internationalization has helped to undermine the traditional welfare agenda of the social democratic left (Rhodes, 1996: 307). Regime theory in itself may be insufficient for a full understanding of contemporary developments, Rhodes (1996: 311) argues, although it will offer insights into the contradictions and stress points of various welfare arrangements. Rhodes re-examines the models of Esping-Andersen, in light of recent changes highlighting the international pressures on each and the response to this. This is a welcome update, though Ireland is not mentioned in relation to any category. Rhodes (1996: 318) concludes that, across all regime types, the net result 'has been progress towards a leaner, meaner, although arguably more efficient welfare state'.

CONCLUSION

The case of Ireland has been considered within the various comparative frameworks described above. This is useful insofar as Ireland appears to be an incongruous, even irreconcilable, case. The question as to whether it could be accommodated by the various models described was addressed. This reveals that while we do gain some insight into different elements of Irish social policy with the help of these comparative approaches, Ireland is seen to cut across types which have been identified. In this respect, Jones's (1985) analysis was an early but welcome development of the social spending league-table approach. Esping-Andersen's (1990) approach does not accommodate Ireland very easily within its framework. Castles and Mitchell (1993) include variables within their typology which do capture important elements of Irish social policy. Leibfried's (1992) analysis introduces the important Latin Rim elements, which does have some relevance for Ireland, being less Latin, understandably, than her southern relations. Lewis (1992) identifies the similarities with the UK in terms of gender impacts but this analysis hides a lot of causal factors. Cousins (1997: 232) concludes by suggesting that his findings 'suggest not that Ireland is in some way exceptional, nor that it falls into a fourth, fifth or sixth World of Welfare but rather that there are more worlds than we have dreamt of'. In an article reviewing comparative social policy work, Pierson (1995: 201) suggested that 'close scrutiny reveals the uniqueness of all welfare regimes' and advised that 'perhaps we have simply to accept that no one study or even series of studies can deliver all the things we are looking for in a comparative understanding of welfare regimes'. As Cousins (1997: 232) observes, and as has been shown above, different countries attach themselves to different families depending on the particular issue being examined.

If comparative study of social policy is not to be simply a frill around the social policy cake, of interest to the particularly energetic or the slightly eccentric, as Higgins (1981: 158) warned, but an important methodological tool for exploring key issues in social policy, then there are important issues which must be addressed. It appears that typologies derived from variable-based analysis, heavily dependent on quantitative data, are of limited value in understanding the complexity of welfare states. The case of Ireland conclusively illustrates this. This suggests that a synthetic approach as espoused by Ragin (1990) may be more useful. It may be 'more appropriate to acknowledge that the complexity of the mix between regime types is likely to increase', than to ask whether regimes are converging or diverging, as Cochrane (1993: 9) suggests. This seems to be at odds, however, with the projections for the far-reaching effects of globalization discussed above, an emerging area of study of crucial importance to social policy analysts. This chapter will conclude, as Cochrane did, that typologies merely 'provide a starting-point from which the significance of differences can be explored more fully', and proposes that this exploration is the challenge facing students of social policy, not just the energetic or eccentric.

NOTE

The author would like to thank Professor David Piachaud of the London School of Economics and Political Science for his invaluable assistance during earlier work on this topic.

SUGGESTED READING

Old favourites include Higgins (1981) and Jones (1985) as these two provide the early calls for comparisons and remain as useful reminders. Recommended reading for those who think in types must be Ringen's (1991) article 'Do welfare states come in types?' Readings on Ireland in relation to comparative social policy analysis should include O'Connell and Rottman (1992), MacLaughlin (1993) and Cousins (1997). Recent debates on globalization and social policy can be best followed in Rhodes (1996), though clearly this debate will have to be followed as it develops.

REFERENCES

Bonoli, G. (1997) 'Classifying Welfare States: a Two Dimension Approach', *Journal of Social Policy*, 26 (3): 351–72.

Bradshaw, Y. and M. Wallace (1990) 'Informing Generality and Explaining Uniqueness: The Place of Case Studies in Comparative Research', pp. 154–71 in C. Ragin (ed.), *Issues and Alternatives in Comparative Social Research*. Leiden: E.J. Brill.

Cahill, M. (1994) *The New Social Policy*. Oxford: Blackwell.

Castles, F. and D. Mitchell (1993) 'Worlds of Welfare and Families of Nations', pp. 93–118 in F. Castles (ed.), *Families of Nations*. Dartmouth: Aldershot.

Cochrane, A. (1993) 'Comparative Approaches and Social Policy', pp. 1–18 in A. Cochrane and J. Clarke (eds), *Comparing Welfare States Britain in an International Context*. London: Sage.

Cook, G. and A. McCashin (1992) 'Inequality, Litigation and Policy Resolution Gender Dependence in Social Security and Personal Income Tax in the Republic of Ireland', Paper presented at York University *Conference on Social Security 50 years after Beveridge*, September 1992.

Cousins, M. (1997) 'Ireland's Place in the Worlds of Welfare Capitalism', *Journal of European Social Policy*, 7(3): 223–35.

Cox, R. H. (1998) 'The Consequences of Welfare Reform How Conceptions of Social Rights are Changing', *Journal of Social Policy*, 27 (1): 1–16.

Daly, M. (1994) 'Comparing Welfare States: Towards a Gender-Friendly Approach', pp. 101–17 in Diane Sainsbury (ed.), *Gendering Welfare States*. London: Sage.

Deacon, B. (ed.) (1992) 'East European Welfare: Past, Present and Future in Comparative Context', pp. 1–31 in B. Deacon, M. Castle-Kanerova, N. Manning, F. Millard, E. Orosz, J. Szalai and A. Vidinova (eds) *The New Eastern Europe: Social Policy Past, Present and Future*. London: Sage.

Esping-Andersen, G. (1990) *The Three Worlds of Welfare Capitalism*. Oxford: Polity.

Esping-Andersen, G. (1997) 'Hybrid or Unique: The Japanese Welfare State Between Europe and America', *Journal of European Social Policy*, 7 (3): 179–89.

George, V. (1998) 'Political Ideology, Globalization and Welfare Futures in Europe', *Journal of Social Policy*, 27(1): 17–36.

Ginsberg, N. (1992) *Divisions of Welfare: A Critical Introduction to Comparative Social Policy*. London: Sage.

Heidenheimer, A., H. Heclo and C. T. Adams (1975) *Comparative Public Policy; The Politics of Social Choice in Europe and America*. London: The MacMillan Press.

Higgins, J. (1981) *States of Welfare, Comparative Analysis in Social Policy*. Oxford: Basil Blackwell.

Hill, M. (1996) *Social Policy: A Comparative Analysis*. London: Prentice Hall/ Harvester Wheatsheaf.

Jones, C. (1985) *Patterns of Social Policy An Introduction to Comparative Analysis*. London: Tavistock Publications.

Kangas, O. (1994) 'The Merging of Welfare Models?', *Journal of European Social Policy*, 4 (2): 79–94.

Kemeny, J. (1995) 'Theories of Power in the Three Worlds of Welfare Capitalism', *Journal of European Social Policy*, 5 (2): 87–96.

Kennelly, B. and E. O'Shea (1998) 'The Welfare State in Ireland', pp. 193–220 in S. Healy and B. Reynolds (eds) *Social Policy in Ireland, Principles, Practice and Problems*. Dublin: Oak Tree Press.

Kloosterman, R. (1994) 'Three Worlds of Welfare Capitalism? The Welfare State and the Post-Industrial Trajectory in the Netherlands after 1980', *West European Politics*, 17 (4): 166–89.

Kofman, E. and G. Youngs (1996): *Globalization: Theory and Practice*. London: Pinter.

Korpi, W. (1992) *Welfare State Development in Europe since 1930: Ireland in a Comparative Perspective*, Twenty-third Geary Lecture. Dublin: Economic and Social Research Institute.

Kraus, F. (1981) 'The Historical Development of Income Inequality in Western Europe and the United States', pp. 187–238 in P. Flora and A. Heidenheimer (eds), *The Development of Welfare States in Europe and America*. New Brunswick: Transaction Books.

Kwon, H-J. (1997) 'Beyond European Welfare Regimes: Comparative Perspectives on East Asian Welfare Systems', *Journal of Social Policy*, 26 (4): 467–84.

Langan, M. and I. Ostner (1991) 'Gender and Welfare towards a Comparative Framework', pp. 127–50 in G. Room (ed.), *Towards a European Welfare State*. Bristol: University of Bristol School for Advanced Urban Studies

Leibfried, S. (1993) 'Towards a European Welfare State?', pp. 133–56, in C. Jones (ed.), *New Perspectives on the Welfare State*. London: Routledge.

Lewis, J. (1992) 'Gender and the Development of Welfare Regimes', *Journal of European Social Policy*, 2 (3): 159–73.

McLaughlin, E. (1993) 'Ireland Catholic Corporatism', pp. 205–37, in A. Cochrane and J. Clarke (eds), *Comparing Welfare States Britain in an International Context*. London: Sage.

O.E.C.D. (1984) 'Social Expenditure Erosion or Evolution?, *O.E.C.D. Observer*, 126 (January): 3–6.

O'Connell, P. and D. Rottman (1992) 'The Irish Welfare State in Comparative Perspective', pp. 205–39 in J.H. Goldthorpe and C.T. Whelan (eds), *The Development of Industrial Society in Ireland*, Proceedings of the British Academy 79. Oxford: Oxford University Press.

Olsson Hort, S. (1993) 'The Swedish Model', pp. 214–36 in J. Berghman and B. Cantillon, *The European Face of Social Security*. Aldershot: Avebury.

Peillon, M. (1994) 'Placing Ireland in a Comparative Perspective', *Economic and Social Review*, 25 (2): 179–95.

Pierson, C. (1995) 'Comparing Welfare States', *Wes: European Politics*, 18 (1): 197–203.

Popper, K. (1968) *Conjectures and Refutations*. London: Routledge.

Popper, K. (1978) 'The Unity of Method', Reading 3, in J. Bynner and K. Stribley, (eds), *Social Research Principles and Procedures*. London: Longman.

Ragin, C. (1987) *The Comparative Method Moving beyond Qualitative and Quantitative Strategies*. Berkeley: University of California Press.

Ragin, C. (1990) 'Introduction: The Problem of Balancing Discourse on Cases and Variables in Comparative Social Science', pp. 1–8 in C. Ragin (ed.), *Issues and Alternatives in Comparative Social Research*. Leiden: E.J. Brill.

Ragin, C. (1994) *Constructing Social Research: The Unity and Diversity of Method*. California: Thousand Oaks.

Rhodes, M. (1996) 'Globalization and West European Welfare States: A Critical Review of Recent Debates', *Journal of European Social Policy*, 6 (4): 305–27.

Ringen, S. (1991) 'Do Welfare States Come in Types?', pp. 31–42 in P. Saunders and D. Encel (eds), *Social Policy in Australia: Options for the 1990s*, SPRC Reports and Proceedings No. 96, Social Policy Research Centre, University of New South Wales.

Room, G. (1991) 'Social Policy and the European Commission', *Social Policy and Administration*, 25 (3): 175–83.

Room, G. (1995) 'Poverty in Europe Competing Paradigms of Analysis', *Policy and Politics*, 23 (2): 103–13.

Sainsbury, D. (ed.) (1994) *Gendering Welfare States*. London: Sage.

Scholte, J. A. (1996) 'Beyond the Buzzword: Towards a Critical Theory of Globalization', pp. 43–57 in E. Kofman and G. Youngs (eds), *Globalization: Theory and Practice*. London: Pinter

Shaver, S. and J. Bradshaw (1995) 'The Recognition of Wifely Labour by Welfare States', *Social Policy and Administration*, 29 (1): 10–25.

Siaroff, A. (1994) 'Work, Welfare and Gender Equality A New Typology', pp. 82–100 in D. Sainsbury (ed.), *Gendering Welfare States*. London: Sage.

Spicker, P. (1995) *Social Policy: Themes and Approaches*. London: Prentice Hall/Harvester Wheatsheaf.

Taylor-Gooby, P. (1991) 'Welfare State Regimes and Welfare Citizenship', *Journal of European Social Policy*, 1 (2): 93–105.

Therborn, G. and J. Roebroek (1986) 'The Irreversible Welfare State: Its Recent Maturation, Its Encounter with the Economic Crisis and Its Future Prospects', *International Journal of Health Services*, 16 (3): 319–38.

Titmuss, R. (1974) *Social Policy*. London: Allen & Unwin.

Titmuss, R. (1976) 'The Social Division of Welfare', pp. 34–55 in R. Titmuss, *Essays on 'The Welfare State'*. London: Allen & Unwin.

Walker, A. (1992) 'The Persistence of Poverty under Welfare States and the Prospects for its Abolition', *International Journal of Health Services*, 22 (1): 1–17.

Weber, M. (1949) *The Methodology of the Social Sciences*. New York: The Free Press.

Whyte, J. (1974) Ireland Politics without Social Bases', pp. 619–52 in R. Rose (ed.), *Electoral Behaviour: A Comparative Handbook*. New York: Free Press.

Wilensky, H.L. (1975) *The Welfare State and Equality*. Berkeley: University of California Press.

6

The Impact of the European Union on Irish Social Policy Development in Relation to Social Exclusion

Sylda Langford

INTRODUCTION

In a European Union (EU)[1] context the term 'social policy' covers a wide range of issues including issues in the area of labour law and working conditions, equality, aspects of employment and vocational training and social security. In the traditional theoretical sense, the term social policy is taken to mean the study of the social services and the welfare state (see, for example, Spicker, 1995: 3–7). While acknowledging the current limited scope of European Community social policy as defined traditionally, it can be argued that by widening the perspective of social policy to embrace broader issues such as social exclusion and unemployment, a broader framework for EU social policy can be elaborated. Much of what is usually referred to as EU social policy bears little relationship to welfare as it is generally understood in the welfare regimes of the EU Member States. As Cochrane and Clarke (1993: 253–61) point out, this is often missed in popular discussions of the EU because of frequent references to the 'social dimension' in EU policies. In attempting to examine the impact of the EU on Irish social policy development since Ireland became a member of the European Community in 1973, this chapter focuses on one specific area of the broader social policy perspective – namely social exclusion – being an area with which the writer has direct experience within the Irish context and also being an area where the EU has made a very significant contribution to the development of policies and programmes and to the understanding of the concept.

In the early days of the European Economic Community, the main focus was on economic policy (Atkinson, 1997). Indeed, some Member States were opposed to community involvement in social policy as they were opposed to possible cash transfers to poorer countries for social protection purposes. Consequently the Community's organs were provided with limited powers in the social policy area. Social policy was a means towards achieving other objectives, largely economic, such as removing barriers to labour mobility and ensuring that differences in the costs of social protection did not prevent competition in the supply of goods.

In the 1970s, the social dimension of the European Community began to emerge more strongly as an issue in its own right. The Social Action Programme accepted by Council in 1974 recognized that the European Community had an important role to play in the formation of social policy and included a commitment to implement, in cooperation with Member States, specific measures to combat poverty. This led, in July 1975, to the first of three European Anti-Poverty Programmes. These programmes were a series of demonstration and pilot projects designed to identify good practice and potential problems in tackling poverty. They were intended to build small-scale, grassroots projects towards larger prototype projects operating at the level of mainstream agencies. The experience gained and the resultant policy lessons were to be put into practice in mainstream policy initiatives in the Member States. The legal competence for the programmes was Article 235,[2] which is a type of 'catch-all' article designed to facilitate innovative measures.

EUROPEAN ANTI-POVERTY PROGRAMMES

The first European Anti-Poverty Programme covered the period 1975–80 and it financed a series of trans-national studies and some 50 local projects across Europe. This programme facilitated an assessment of the dimensions of poverty. It also brought about the beginnings of a questioning of the prevailing philosophies and approaches to poverty and created a degree of tension in official circles. The main value of the first programme was that it put poverty firmly on the European Community agenda for the first time.

In 1981, the European Commission published an evaluation report containing a widely publicized estimate of the number of poor people in the European Community. In 1983, the Commission consulted widely with public and private authorities involved with the problems of poverty and this resulted in agreement on the policy themes and population groupings to be targeted for priority actions under future European Anti-Poverty Programmes. When a second European Anti-Poverty

Programme was under way, it emphasized the need to undertake specific and concrete activities based on joint themes of research and innovation. This programme operated from 1985 to 1989. In Ireland it had a total of nine projects with a locally based self-help focus. In addition, the Community part funded a major survey on poverty in Ireland undertaken by the Economic and Social Research Institute. The poverty surveys raised the profile of the EU in social policy and helped to influence the policies of national governments in relation to poverty. The outcome of the evaluation of the second programme was the important acknowledgement of the structural causes underlying the existence of poverty and recognition that its persistence was incompatible with the aims of the Treaty of Rome (1957). This growing awareness of the structural causes of poverty was reflected in the introduction of the concept of social cohesion into the European Union Structural Funds.[3]

Following the Single European Act (1988), the Structural Funds were reorganized with a view to ensuring effective coordination with the goal of economic and social cohesion. This reform involved the use of Community Support Frameworks (CSF), each representing a coherent multi-annual programme agreed between the Commission and national authorities, identifying development priorities and effectively programming the funding to be provided from the Structural Funds as well as from national resources. The first CSF covered the period 1989–93. As an Objective 1 region,[4] Ireland benefited from the greatly increased funding allocated to the Structural Funds, following their reform, for the period 1989–93. While the Structural Funds can broadly be interpreted as a type of welfare in a social policy context, this welfare is defined in terms of a contribution to economic success. Partnership and participation were promoted as operating principles of the Structural Funds in 1989.

Poverty was now viewed as a structural problem. At the same time, the social dimension was receiving more attention generally in the European Community. In 1989 the Commission put forward a draft of the Community Charter of Fundamental Social Rights of Workers which was adopted in modified form at the Strasbourg European Council in December 1989 by all the Member States, with the exception of the United Kingdom. (The opposition of the United Kingdom at the Maastricht European Council (December 1991) led to the Social Chapter, as such, being excluded from the final Treaty on European Union (1992), but there was an attached Social Protocol.[5] Most Member States regarded this as a very unsatisfactory situation but felt that there had been no option but to accept it at Maastricht. Following the election on 1 May 1997, the new British Government decided to end the UK opt out and to accept that the provisions of the Social Agreement should apply to all fifteen Member States.)

The cumulative understanding of poverty gained through the previous two anti-poverty programmes resulted in a third Anti-Poverty Programme from 1989 until 1994 which focused on social exclusion and marginalization. The third Anti-Poverty Programme identified the poor in the European Community countries as those people with insecure jobs and low incomes; bad and insecure housing; shorter life expectancy and poorer health and education than those of other citizens; those who live in badly planned neighbourhoods or isolated rural areas and who are recipients of services, public or private, which tend to be poorer in quality than those in richer neighbourhoods. Most are unemployed or low paid urban dwellers, with large families to support; many are old people, marginal farmers or ethnic minorities. Inadequate income results in their exclusion by a so-called 'glass ceiling' from the benefits and opportunities that are taken as the norm in a developed society. They are the customers for whom it is not worth opening a bank or a decent shop, the tenants and patients from whom no profit can be made; the electorate whose demands can be disregarded without electoral disaster. In effect, their circumstances are such as to render them socially excluded from what is considered to be the norm in society (Department of Social Welfare, 1995). The third Anti-Poverty Programme therefore introduced the concept of social exclusion into EU social policy.

With such a comprehensive analysis of poverty, it was clear that no single programme or service would by itself be capable of combating poverty. Therefore the third programme concerned itself with the management of the economy and opportunities for work, with education and training, with the distribution of earnings and tax burdens, with social security and health care, with housing and the quality of the environment. In short, it dealt with every aspect of society, private as well as public, and the distribution impacts made upon society.

Given the analysis of poverty on which the third programme was based, its implementation followed logically from this analysis. A basic requirement of the third programme was that its implementation should be local and based on key principles. These principles were that the programme should include:

- multidimensionality, i.e. a comprehensive set of actions were to be taken, ranging across several sectors and coordinated through an area-based integrated plan;

- participation, i.e. the least privileged groups were to be enabled to take part in decisions affecting them;

- partnership, i.e. structures were to be established to combine the efforts of key players in combating exclusion.

Combating exclusion under the third programme meant addressing causes of poverty rather than dealing with its symptoms. It meant that the actions required were not to be confined to one or two Government departments or agencies and it meant that agencies had to collaborate actively through partnership structures.

Third Anti-Poverty Programme in Ireland

Ireland had three projects funded under the third programme. FORUM was an area-based project in north-west Connemara covering a disadvantaged rural area in a peripheral region. People Action Against Unemployment Limited (PAUL) was an area-based project in Limerick, an area typifying the problems of a deprived urban area of local authority housing and high unemployment; Pavee Point (Dublin Travellers' Education and Development Group) was concerned with the social exclusion of Travellers as a specific minority group.

The lessons for policy makers in Ireland from the third programme are set out in the final report of the Irish Research and Development Unit which was one of nine units appointed by the Commission to provide continuous assessments of progress (Mernagh and Commins, 1994). The issues which emerged were:

- In tackling social exclusion, it is essential at the outset to undertake adequate baseline research and analysis of the forms of exclusion affecting the project area and the target groups most affected.
- The second policy lesson was the importance of targeting. Unless disadvantaged groups are made the target of social and economic programmes, the likelihood of their being able to benefit fully from social and economic development is doubtful.
- Meaningful partnership requires having appropriate partners and ensuring that the process of partnership is continuously nurtured.
- Participation in partnership, especially for statutory representatives, should not be seen as an incidental or insignificant activity to be delegated to one person who is left to carry on as best they can. Partnership activity has to be given the necessary time, it has to be backed-up by institutional commitment and the actions of a project should not be divorced from the normal agenda of the agency partner.
- Mechanisms at national level need to be adequate to ensure that programmes have a supportive context. More concrete commitments

to the programme might have been forthcoming from key agencies if, at the commencement of the third programme, there had been an inter-agency group at national level which facilitated dialogue about the programme, guaranteed institutional support, lent status and credibility to the programme and facilitated solving problems of coordination at local level.

Fourth Anti-Poverty Programme

A proposed fourth Anti-Poverty Programme failed to get unanimous agreement in the Council, as it was vetoed by Germany in 1995. Doubts were also raised about how far there was a clear legal basis for such actions in the Treaty and doubts were raised in relation to the principle of subsidiarity. Article 3b of the Treaty on European Union states that

> . . . the Community shall take actions, in accordance with the principle of subsidiarity, only if and insofar as the objectives of the proposed action cannot be sufficiently achieved by the Member States and can therefore, by reason of the scale or effects of the proposed action, be better achieved by the Community.

The implication of Germany's arguments was, in principle, that having back-to-back Anti-Poverty Programmes was a movement away from what was allowable under Article 235 and under the principle of subsidiarity. Once the demonstration stage of the Programmes had ended, it was argued that it was up to Member States to tackle social exclusion in their mainstream programmes and apply the policy lessons of demonstration projects.

However, the Treaty of Amsterdam, which, if ratified by Member States during 1998–99, through a new Article 118(2) as amended by the new Treaty, will now contain a provision giving increased competence on social exclusion. The text in the new Treaty results from a proposal which Ireland put forward during its presidency of the European Union in 1996. With the amendments made by the new Treaty, the EU Treaty will now, for the first time, contain an explicit legal basis for action on social exclusion. (The EC Treaty refers to the Treaty establishing the European Community. The EU Treaty refers to the Treaty on European Union, colloquially referred to as the Maastricht Treaty.) This will permit the Council to adopt measures to encourage cooperation between Member States to combat social exclusion through initiatives aimed at improving knowledge, evaluating experiences and promoting innovative approaches and exchanges of information and best practices. In putting its proposal forward for the insertion of social exclusion in the

Treaty, Ireland argued that such incentive measures could be very beneficial but need not necessarily involve large additional financial costs. Unanimity in the Council will no longer be necessary for the adoption of social exclusion measures. Voting will in future be by qualified majority in the Council.

Permeation of the Concepts of Anti-Poverty Programmes into Social Policy

The EU Anti-Poverty Programmes were highly significant for social policy in that they shifted the focus away from a simplistic concept of poverty to the more complex one of social exclusion. They led to an acceptance that exclusion processes go beyond unemployment and/or low incomes. While unemployment is perhaps the major factor in causing social exclusion, others such as housing, lack of training and education, illiteracy, health problems and lack of access to justice also influence the ability of a significant number of people in Europe to take up the economic and social opportunities available to those in the mainstream.

In Ireland the projects of the third Anti-Poverty Programme led to specific changes in certain Government Programmes and to new approaches. For instance, as Mernagh and Commins (1994: 180) point out, the PAUL project in Limerick influenced thinking behind the setting-up of the Community Employment Scheme and the specific requirements of participants on these schemes for retention of secondary benefits.[6] PAUL's work also gave new insights into the needs of lone parents and problems of indebtedness. The policy decisions taken on the basis of these insights are reflected in the various improvements in the social security provisions for lone parents and in the development of the Money Advice and Budgeting Programme funded by the Department of Social, Community and Family Affairs. The Community Development Programme funded by that Department was initiated as a result of the policy lessons of the second Anti-Poverty Programme. The Combat Poverty Agency, which is now a centre of expertise in the area of social exclusion, is an outcome of the first Anti-Poverty Programme. The National Committee on Pilot Schemes to Combat Poverty, established to coordinate the first programme, was established under statute in 1986 as the Combat Poverty Agency.

At the same time as the Anti-Poverty Programmes were experimenting with the principles of partnership and participation in local area-based projects, these same principles were also being tested in other projects in Ireland. In 1988–90, a Pilot Programme for Integrated Rural Development (IRD) experimented with a bottom-up approach to rural development and was followed by the EU LEADER Community Initiative in 1991.[7] LEADER 1 was the first EU supported local area-based rural development in Ireland.

In 1990, the negotiated social partnership agreement, the Programme for Economic and Social Progress (PESP, 1990–93), initiated an experimental new approach to long-term unemployment. Partnership companies were established on a pilot basis in twelve disadvantaged areas in order to design and implement a more coordinated and multidimensional approach to social exclusion.

The indirect effects of the Anti-Poverty Programmes, and indeed other experimental programmes, were evident in the White Paper on European Social Policy, *Growth, Competitiveness and Employment* (European Commission, 1993). This was produced out of concern that in the twelve Member States 17 million people were out of work, approximately 11 per cent of the population (based on 1988 figures). Three times that number of people were considered to be poor. The White Paper concluded that the ideal society has five components. It is healthy, open, decentralized, competitive and based on solidarity. An important feature in the White Paper was the acknowledgement of the growing importance of local level action and of decentralization of economic activity. This awareness at Commission level had influenced the setting-up of the first Community Support Framework covering the period 1989–93.

The White Paper acknowledged that pockets of poverty and social exclusion will remain and therefore the actions of the Structural Funds must focus on taking back on board those who had fallen overboard when the economic tide lifted all boats. The White Paper was a landmark in social policy terms, as it stated clearly for the first time that economic growth does not automatically eliminate poverty and social exclusion and can result in even greater inequalities between those who benefit from the growth and those who do not, by reason of being excluded structurally. Up to this point, the prevailing theory was that an economic 'rising tide would lift all boats'.

The lessons of the European Anti-Poverty Programmes clearly impacted on the thinking of European Commission policy makers, as elements of the policy lessons can be identified at different levels. Before 1985, the Regulations on the Structural Funds contained provisions for developing the indigenous potential of local areas. These included 'soft' measures as well as capital investment. In the reform of the Structural Funds in 1988 this was developed further when the Global Grants, which particularly promote local and indigenous development, were introduced.

In the 1993 reform of the Structural Funds for the period 1994–99, the European Social Fund (ESF) Regulations were amended and the theme of social exclusion was added. The European Social Fund became more social and there was much of the same language in the Regulations for the ESF as in the third European Anti-Poverty Programme.

Again in the Community Initiative Programmes, which are funded from the Structural Funds, the influence of the European Anti-Poverty Programmes can be identified, as they include measures to combat poverty and exclusion. In the Community Initiative Programmes, the Commission draws up guidelines for using the funds in certain areas where problems are emerging, or are in existence, and which the Commission considers need to be addressed at the level of the Union, via national programmes set up in close cooperation with the Commission, such as URBAN, LEADER, INTERREG, EMPLOYMENT.

The Commission, for example, drew up a strategy on urban poverty, known as URBAN, for selected areas of cities suffering from urban deprivation, social exclusion and attendant problems. The cities had to have a population of at least 100,000. The actions undertaken should be integrated in that they should cover business infrastructure, physical environment, training and equality in order to give a balanced development. The purpose of the actions was to demonstrate that it is possible to make a quantum leap in tackling urban poverty and deprivation by the development of these neighbourhood areas in cities. The URBAN projects are demonstration projects along the lines of the Anti-Poverty Programmes, but on a large scale. At least ten million ECUs were allocated to each selected area. In Ireland three projects were selected: Northside of Cork City, West Tallaght/Clondalkin and Finglas/Ballymun/Darndale in Dublin.

Social Exclusion within the Community Support Frameworks (CSF) and National Development Plan 1994–99

Since 1988, the Structural Funds have been implemented on the basis of an innovative policy approach based on the four principles of concentration, partnership, programming and additionality. (The principle of additionality is to ensure that financing from Community funds is not used to replace national financial aid.) The political priority granted to economic and social cohesion is reflected in the Community priorities for the structural policies. The Structural Funds are a leading instrument for the reduction of disparities and for the promotion of growth and employment across the Union. Measured at the European Union level, the inequalities between individual regions and countries are substantial. The EU procedure to measure this inequality is to compare countries and regions on the basis of income per head measured as Gross Domestic

Product (GDP). When defining the least developed countries and regions where the Structural Funds must have maximum impact, the level of income is used to decide whether areas should benefit as priority areas, i.e. the Objective 1 regions. The criterion set to benefit from Objective 1 status is that there must be an average regional income per head below 75 per cent of the community average.

The Structural Funds are a recognition that, while market forces and the entrepreneurial spirit are essential, social solidarity and mutual support are vital complements to them, not only for social reasons but because they create extra jobs and income, which in turn promote competitive development and sustainable growth. Safeguarding and creating sustainable jobs are therefore the underlying priority for all activities financed by the Structural Funds. As a consequence of this underlying priority, programmes, initiatives and projects targeted at social exclusion and poverty may be supported by Structural Funds only where there is a clear linkage to employment. Hence, the measures proposed for support from the ESF under the Operational Programme for Human Resources Development (HRDOP) extend from in-company training and advanced training for graduates targeted on the needs of the economy, to measures designed to reintegrate the socially excluded into the labour market. Under this Operational Programme assistance is being provided to a number of socially and/or economically disadvantaged groups. Emphasis is being placed, for example, on the long-term unemployed, schools and pupils in designated disadvantaged areas, people with disabilities and ex-offenders. The objective is to assist those who are socially excluded to improve their prospects of obtaining employment or worthwhile alternatives to unemployment. These measures (e.g. Vocational Training Opportunity Scheme (VTOS), Community Employment (CE), Occupational Integration of People with Disabilities, Home/School/ Community Liaison Scheme, Youthstart, Support for Children Experiencing Difficulty in School, Early School Leavers, Community Training, Promotion of Equal Opportunities and, since the Mid-Term Review of the CSF, Childcare Facilities) are designed to meet the education, training and employment needs of different groups within Irish society, many of whom have been marginalized and excluded, with the twin objective of enabling them to contribute ultimately to enhanced economic development thereby ensuring economic and social sustainability, and, ultimately, to social cohesion across the European Union.

The Irish Government submitted the National Development Plan for the period 1994–99 to the Commission in October 1993. The Plan was considered to provide a sufficient basis for the preparation of the Community Support Framework. The CSF constitutes an agreement between the Commission and the Government of Ireland on the purposes and priorities for the use of approximately IR£4.54 billion provided by the Structural Funds in Ireland in the period 1994–99. The experience gained in Ireland under a number of initiatives concerned with disadvantage, including the third European Anti-Poverty Programme, is acknowledged in the text of the National Development Plan. The measures in the CSF are financed by the EU to between 50–75 per cent of the cost with co-funding from the Exchequer. The four funds which finance the nine Operational Programmes in the CSF are set out in Figure 1.

Figure 1 CSF: Structure of Spending 1994–99

Fund	Sectors	Operational Programmes
ERDF	Productive (ERDF, ESF, EAGGF, FIFG)	Industrial Development Agriculture,
ESF		Rural Development and Forestry Fisheries
EAGGF	Infrastructure (ERDF)	Tourism Transport Economic Infrastructure Environmental Services
FIFG	Human Resources (90% ESF, 10% ERDF) Local Development (ERDF, ESF, EAGGF)	Human Resources Development Local Urban and Rural Development

There are three categories of financial assistance under the Structural Funds. These are: the Community Support Framework (90 per cent of Structural Funds); Community Initiatives (nine per cent) for measures of special interest to the European Community and initiated by the Commission; and Innovative Measures (one per cent) for exploring new ways of achieving the objectives of the Structural Funds and again undertaken on the initiative of the Commission. Of the 13 Community Initiatives, six are of particular relevance to social exclusion – EMPLOYMENT (NOW, Horizon, Youthstart, Integra), ADAPT, URBAN, Special Programme for Peace and Reconciliation in Northern

Ireland and the Border Counties, LEADER II and INTERREG II. Of the Innovative measures, those funded under Article 6 of the ESF are of relevance to social exclusion, while Article 10 of the ERDF also offers possibilities for tackling social exclusion through innovative measures in regional policy.

Institutional Impacts of the EU Programmes

The principles and themes of the Anti-Poverty Programmes and social cohesion objectives of the CSFs have also impacted on Ireland at levels other than funding programmes. The language, concepts and analysis of EU social policy have permeated, vertically and horizontally, through Irish social institutions. Certain institutional arrangements have been put in place which reflect the value put by the Irish Government on participation, partnership and multidimensionality as a means of tackling social exclusion. For example in 1993, the government established the National Economic and Social Forum (NESF) to develop economic and social policy initiatives, particularly on unemployment and to contribute to the formation of a national consensus on social and economic matters (see Chapter 8, pp. 139–54). Its membership is made up of three broad strands. The first strand represents the Government and the Oireachtas, while the second is made up of representatives of employer, trade union and farming interests. The third strand represents women, youth, the unemployed, the disadvantaged, older people, people with disabilities, and environmental interests. The third strand had previously been outside the national partnership arrangements and their inclusion in the NESF was an acknowledgement by the government of the desirability to have those who are socially excluded represented at national policy forums. The NESF has published a range of reports and opinions across a wide spectrum of social and economic policies. In December 1997, the government decided, in principle, to establish the NESF on a statutory basis.

The National Economic and Social Council (NESC) was established in 1973 to provide a forum for discussion of the principles relating to the efficient development of the national economy and the achievement of social justice, and to advise the Government on their application. Over one hundred reports on a wide variety of economic and social topics have been published by the Council. Since the mid-1980s, the Council has published a series of strategy reports which have identified interrelated policy measures which are essential to economic development and the broadening of social inclusion. These reports have provided the framework for negotiation of the national agreements between government and social partners over the past decade. Membership of the Council comprised representatives of employers, trade unions, farmers and civil servants. The NESC was the initial driving force behind negotiated economic and social governance whereby the Government and the social partners negotiate national agreements since 1987. Since the concept of social exclusion began to permeate into social policy there have been calls for the widening of the membership of the NESC to include representation from the socially excluded sector. During 1998, representation on the NESC was broadened when two members of the Community Platform and a representative from the Conference of Religious of Ireland (CORI), National Women's Council of Ireland (NWCI) and the National Youth Council of Ireland (NYCI) joined the other partners to represent the socially excluded.

Following on the United Nations World Summit on poverty in Copenhagen in 1995, the Irish Government developed a National Anti-Poverty Strategy (NAPS) with a view to mainstreaming anti-poverty policy in Ireland. The objective of the NAPS was to factor in a consciousness of poverty into all public policy decisions so that social exclusion did not remain merely a fact of social policy. Instead, an effort was to be made to shape public policies so that they prevent rather than remedy poverty and social exclusion.

The NAPS is a ten-year strategy (see Chapter 16, pp. 293–316) which was developed through an inclusive process which drew the social partners, voluntary and community groups and Government departments together to represent the views of all those who are excluded from participation in the benefits of Irish economic growth. The NAPS contains proposals to tackle five key areas causing social exclusion, which are educational disadvantage, income inadequacy, unemployment, urban poverty and rural poverty, and stressed the need for strong institutional structures at different levels to underpin the strategy. The overall objective of the NAPS is to reduce by 50 per cent the numbers defined as poor by the year 2007. The institutional mechanisms for advancing the strategy are a Cabinet Sub-Committee on Social Inclusion chaired by the Taoiseach, an Interdepartmental Policy Committee, and monitoring and evaluation by the NESF and the Combat Poverty Agency.

In October 1996, the Government continued the process of tackling social inclusion by increasing the number of representative bodies for the negotiation of national agreements to include organizations and groups which address problems caused by unemployment and social exclusion. The inclusion of these organizations and groups at this level came about as a result of sustained lobbying by them over the years for a place at the national negotiating table. The social partnership arrangements of previous national agreements were reconfigured into four pillars, i.e. employers, trade unions, farmers and community/voluntary organizations. The 'fourth pillar' represents the interests of the socially excluded and corresponds to the 'third strand' of the NESF. Those representing the interests of the socially excluded are now effectively at the centre of the public policy-making domain. The national agreement *Partnership 2000, for Inclusion, Employment and Competitiveness* (1996) covers the period 1997–99 and its contents is evidence of the extent to which the concepts of partnership participation and multidimensionality have permeated Irish social policy. For the first time (see Chapter 9, pp. 155–77), through Partnership 2000, social exclusion is defined in national social policy:

> Social exclusion can be succinctly described as cumulative marginalisation, from production (unemployment), from consumption (income poverty), from social networks (community, family and neighbours), from decision making and from an adequate quality of life (Government of Ireland, 1996: 17).

Partnership 2000 represents a strategic approach to the deepening of partnership, to action for greater social inclusion and to action towards a new focus on equality. In addition, mechanisms for monitoring progress on social exclusion commitments in the programme have been enhanced by the creation of the 'fourth pillar' which is now positioned to monitor outcomes at the quarterly monitoring meetings of Partnership 2000. Partnership 2000 also contains commitments to implement the NAPS and to tackle the key problems it identified. The process of Partnership 2000 reflects the principles of the third Anti-Poverty Programmes, that is, partnership (all social partners involved), participation (all participate in drawing up an agreed strategic plan and in quarterly monitoring) and multidimensionality (the plan embraced economic growth and social cohesion from the national level to sectoral, community and enterprise level).

FUTURE EU DEVELOPMENTS LIKELY TO IMPACT ON SOCIAL EXCLUSION

Territorial Employment Pacts

Four Territorial Employment Pacts have been established by the Government to participate in a new EU-wide initiative to combat unemployment, set to run up to the end of 1999. The Dublin Region, Limerick City, Westmeath and Dundalk/Drogheda were nominated among 100 regions of greatest need to form a European Network of Employment Pacts in line with the European Commission's communication Actions for Employment in Europe – a Confidence Pact. The areas selected reflect a mix of a regional focus, major urban centres of population and rural areas. The underlying principle of the Pacts is to add value to the wide range of local and national initiatives already in place to enhance the employment prospects of the long-term unemployed. Action Plans have been prepared for each of the Pact areas and the resources needed to implement action plans will be drawn from a combination of public and private contributions, including existing Operational Programmes and Initiatives. These plans are currently awaiting Commission approval, after which the implementation phase will commence. Proposals for greater coordination between local government and local development within the Local Urban and Rural Development (LURD) OP in the context of a planned renewed system of local government will be enhanced by the involvement of both constituencies in the Pacts (see Department of the Environment, 1996).[8]

Amsterdam Treaty

The Amsterdam Treaty sets as objectives for the Community and Member States:

> the promotion of employment, improved living and working conditions, so as to make possible their harmonisation while the improvement is being maintained, proper social protection, dialogue between management and labour, the development of human resources with a view to lasting high employment and the combating of exclusion.

The new Treaty also contains a provision on social exclusion to refer to the situation of persons who are not merely unemployed but marginalized and living in poverty through deprivation of various kinds, including family breakdown, substance abuse and homelessness and who, because of their situation, are excluded from the work force and from social and community networks. The amendment on social exclusion is in effect the insertion into the EC Treaty of the language of the third Anti-Poverty Programme (Government of Ireland, 1998: 84).

In adopting the new Treaty, the Member States also made a number of Declarations, including a Declaration in relation to people with a disability, to the effect that in drawing up measures in relation to the internal market, the Community institutions are to take account of the needs of such persons.[9] The EC Treaty, as amended by the new Treaty, requires the Commission to draw up a report each year on progress in achieving the objectives set out for Social Policy, including the demographic situation in the Community. The Commission is to forward this Report to the European Parliament, the Council and the Economic and

Social Committee. The Parliament may also invite the Commission to report on particular problems in relation to social development.

The new Treaty also inserts a new Title dealing with the question of employment into the EC Treaty immediately after Title VI which deals with economic and monetary policy. At present there are 18 million people unemployed in the EU and the Amsterdam Treaty sets the unemployment issue as one of the Union's priorities. Before the Treaty each Member State looked after its employment policy separately. The new Treaty seeks to reinforce the coordination of national employment policies and foresees the establishment of common guidelines which can, in due course, lead to recommendations to Member States. Following the adoption of the Guidelines by the Council of Ministers in December 1997, there is now a requirement on Member States to incorporate the guidelines into National Employment Action Plans (NEAPS) and to give practical effect to them in the form of national objectives which are to be quantified wherever possible and appropriate. The implementation of the guidelines will be regularly monitored under a common procedure for assessing results each year, commencing with the Cardiff European Council in June 1998. A progress report on actions taken by Member States will feed into the December Summit each year. The Commission may present updated guidelines and, if necessary, propose recommendations to individual Member States. Built upon the four 'pillars' (employability, entrepreneurship, adaptability and equal opportunities) which form the basis of the strategy, the guidelines set out a number of specific targets for Member States to achieve in order to increase employment levels on a lasting basis. These are: tackling youth unemployment and preventing long-term unemployment; transition from passive measures to active measures; encouraging a partnership approach; easing the transition from school to work; exploiting the opportunities for job creation; modernizing work organization; supporting adaptability in enterprises; tackling gender gaps; reconciling work and family life; facilitating integration into the labour market; and promoting the integration of people with disabilities into working life.

The Amsterdam Summit, in June 1997, also agreed that the provisions of the new Employment title should be made effective immediately, and called an Extraordinary European Council to discuss the employment situation. The Heads of State and Government gathered at the Luxembourg Jobs Summit in November 1997 expressed their political will to define and adhere to a comprehensive strategy for employment. This involved the pursuit of sound macroeconomic policies, proper functioning of the Single Market and reform of the labour market based on a number of agreed priorities as expressed in the guidelines for Member States' Employment Policies, 1998.

This type of approach to coordinate national employment policies draws directly on the experience built up by the EU in multilateral surveillance of economic policies, a method that proved particularly successful in the case of economic convergence. The aim is to achieve a convergence process of Member States' employment policies and to create for employment the same resolve as that applying to economic policy, so that targets can be jointly set, verified and regularly updated. The Employment Strategy is based on the conviction that employment is the most effective instrument for eradicating poverty and social exclusion.

Structural Funds (2000–2006)

The Draft Regulations on the Structural Funds (2000–2006) were published by the European Commission on the 18 March, 1998 (*Working Document on the General Regulation on the Structural Funds*, version of January 1998). These set out the broad priorities, procedures and guidelines that will dictate EU funding post 1999.

The Structural Funds are being simplified, with three objectives instead of six and three Community Initiatives instead of 13. The Commission is mainstreaming employment, environment and equality concerns in its programmes and national governments must involve local communities and social partners in planning and monitoring projects. At least one per cent of ESF funding will go to local groups as major Social Fund projects will involve direct payments, although small, to local community groups through non-governmental intermediary funding bodies (this approach in the Special Programme for Peace and Reconciliation in Northern Ireland and the Border Counties led to a flourishing of grassroots community and local development during the 1994–99 period). The Commission has initiated a major decentralization of decision making – decentralization in a community framework – with the Commission no longer as co-manager but as guarantor of the strategic choices agreed in partnership. The Commission will no longer vet every national project, but will agree a strategic approach with Member States, letting them take the day-to-day decisions.

In relation to the eligible projects which can be funded post 1999, it is clear that the broad categories of expenditure that the ERDF and ESF will be able to co-finance remain largely unchanged. However, the draft Regulations indicate that more attention will be given to local services so as to provide instruments better adapted to innovation in the field of business investment and local development and employment initiatives. This could be of particular value for encouraging indigenous development.

A high priority will be attached to programmes that have a strong EU dimension. The overall thrust of the approach of the post-1999 Social Fund is to look for policy rather than programme or project additionality, and to seek to identify in what way Member States are proposing to use ESF money to further develop, improve or totally change their employment and human resource policies in line with the employment guidelines provided for in the Amsterdam Treaty. Therefore, it can be expected that the ESF will co-finance measures identified in the Government's National Employment Action Plan (NEAP). The role of the ESF within the revised Structural Funds takes as its starting point the new Employment Chapter in the Amsterdam Treaty and ESF activity will be based on five policy areas: active labour market policies to fight unemployment; promoting social exclusion; lifelong education and training systems to promote employability; anticipating and facilitating economic and social change; equal opportunities for men and women.

It is clear from the policy objectives set out for the ERDF and the ESF that the Community Support Framework and National Development Plan for 2000–2006 could have a major impact on tackling social exclusion in Ireland in the early years of the twenty-first century.

CONCLUSION

In this Chapter the impact of the EU on Irish social policy development between Ireland's entry to the EC in 1973 and the publication in 1998 of the Draft Regulations for the Structural Funds (2000–2006) was examined in the area of social exclusion, within the framework of the EU Anti-Poverty Programmes and the Structural Funds. The gradual permeation of a highly integrated EU economic policy by social policy principles which emanated from the three demonstration EU Anti-Poverty Programmes and other similar initiatives was outlined. It traces how the close links between unemployment, especially long-term unemployment, and social exclusion led to social cohesion being made a priority objective of the European Community alongside economic growth. This is especially the case where unemployment is transmitted across the generations and is reinforced by being concentrated in particular areas. Having made the linkages between long-term unemployment and social exclusion, EU economic policy gradually targeted the problems associated with long-term unemployment, which are low levels of education, low levels of skills, early school leaving, school dropouts, inequality in access to the labour market, urban black spots, areas of rural disadvantage and membership of minority groups such as Travellers and people with disabilities. The financial instruments for advancing EU economic and social policy were therefore used to target social exclusion from 1988, with the reform of the Structural Funds. As the National Development Plan 1994–99 formed the basis for the Community Support Framework 1994–99 Ireland's objectives in relation to social exclusion became the EU policy objectives for Ireland.

The chapter outlined how Ireland faced the challenge posed in moving towards a social policy system based on the principles of participation, partnership and multidimensionality and how it was assisted in doing so by the EU. In the process, a democratization of structures took place as evidenced in the creation of the NESF and the widening of the membership of the NESC and the social partner arrangements for negotiating national agreements to include representation of groups addressing social exclusion. Within these structures, at national level and others at regional and local level, the principles of the EU Anti-Poverty programmes were internalized.

The role of the EU in assisting Ireland to tackle social exclusion was not only about the transfer of funds but about what the funds reinforced (McCarthy, 1997). Engagement with the EU resulted in Ireland adopting a disciplined programmatic approach to tackling unemployment and social exclusion. This required the EU and national authorities to be specific about what the obstacles were and how the programmes would alleviate them. Ireland produced a National Development Plan which showed how the Structural Funds would meet the plan's strategic objectives. This strategic framework was broken down further into sectoral and operational programmes. The operational programmes comprised both local urban and rural development, i.e. plans go from the broad strategic level to the sectoral, to operational programmes, to measures. Engagement with the EU also resulted in Ireland adopting a systematic process involving participation, monitoring and evaluation. This allowed for funds to be transferred from under-performing projects to other areas. The results from this strategic/programmatic approach, together with the monitoring and evaluation, were fed back into domestic policy. At the same time, arising from the partnership approach at national level, which emerged to deal with the scale of Ireland's economic challenge in the mid-1980s, a sensible income strategy that was consistent with the macroeconomic environment became possible. This resulted in the increase in wages being kept below productivity growth which in turn resulted in employment growth, structural reforms and greater efficiency. Finally, engagement with the EU resulted in consistency across programmes in tackling unemployment and social exclusion. The resultant internal strategic framework, which had a wide degree of ownership by social partners, helped the negotiation of agreements with the EU and the EU agreements in turn reinforced the internal strategy.

The impact of the EU on Irish social policy development, both vertical and horizontal, can be summarized as follows. Unemployment and the social exclusion associated with it became a major focus in national programmes and were reflected in plans with the EU. Across Ireland there was an almost nationwide programme of locally driven projects tackling unemployment and social exclusion funded by the EU. The process and framework of the European Community support was internalized in Irish social policy and institutions. Social exclusion was taken a step further with the formulation of the National Anti-Poverty Strategy which details how government policy can tackle poverty. Ireland benefited from the use of the programmatic framework and discipline promoted by the EU and from the cultural learning of participating in European forums in discussing legitimate options for programme design.

While progress has been made in Ireland, as evidenced in the labour force growth, this has been possible only through a concerted programme of direct interventions to provide work opportunities in the social economy and to subsidize the return to employment or self-employment. The numbers involved in these programmes were equivalent to 75 per cent of the numbers recorded as long-term unemployment (ILO basis) in April 1997.

Because of the linkage between unemployment and social exclusion, it will require an ongoing targeted strategy across a range of departments and agencies to combat social exclusion. This challenge is at the heart of Partnership 2000, the current national programme agreed between the Government and the social partners. Partnership 2000 provides a framework for the development of Ireland's employment system and for tackling social exclusion, including the priorities for the investment of EU Structural Funds, both under the current Community Support Framework and in the next Financial Perspective, arising from Agenda 2000 (1997) and the recently published Draft Regulations for the Structural Funds (2000–2006).

The challenges to include people who have been left behind in our economic and social development through poverty and social exclusion will be with Ireland and its European partners for the foreseeable future. The National Employment Action Plans, the National Anti-Poverty Strategy (1997), the current and future National Development Plans and Community Support Frameworks, the Amsterdam Treaty when ratified, the current national agreement Partnership 2000 and any future national agreements will be the instruments for eliminating social exclusion and for ensuring that the benefits of economic growth are used to promote a more cohesive and inclusive society.

This chapter has shown that the EU has had and continues to have a major impact on Irish social policy in the area of social exclusion by targeted use of structural funds and other Community instruments and in playing a supporting role by encouraging best practices and facilitating cooperation in the fight against social exclusion in the context of unemployment. This is in contrast with the views expressed by Cochrane and Clarke (1993: 257): 'At best it is possible to identify the seeds of welfarism in the operation of [EC] programmes with other ambitions and in the form of rather minor welfare programmes.' Perhaps the differing view can be accounted for by Ireland's position as an Objective 1 region which results in active engagement with the EU.[10]

While the focus of this chapter has been on the impact of the EU, it should be noted that the surge in economic and social development in recent years has not been due solely to the receipt of EU funds. The growth also had roots in enlightened policies on industrial promotion, education and taxation, amongst others. This enhanced economic growth has produced increased funds for government over the past few years in excess of the annual estimates, almost on a par with annual EU transfers. With the predicted diminution in EU funding post 2003, it will be critical, if we are to achieve our objectives of economic and social cohesion, that the same strategic and disciplined approach be applied to the expenditure of national funds as had been applied to EU funding over recent years.

NOTES

1 The terms European Union, European Community, the EU, and the Community are used interchangeably and refer to the 15 Member States of the European Union.

2 Treaties are organized in numbered *Articles*. Articles may be grouped together in *Chapters*. A *Title* is, in principle, a larger subdivision of a Treaty which may contain a number of articles or even chapters – though it may also be as short as a single article. A Treaty may also have various *Sections*.

3 The Community's Structural Funds are:

   • The European Regional Development Fund (ERDF) which aims to reduce the gaps in development between the Community's regions and provides support for productive investment, the creation or moderation of infrastructure and measures that generate economic development, transport, industry, communications etc;

- The European Social Fund (ESF) which has the task of improving employment prospects in the Community and aims to tackle unemployment and exclusion through training and human resource development; and

- The Guidance Section of the European Agricultural Guidance and Guarantee Fund (EAGGF) which assists in part-financing national agricultural aid schemes and in developing and diversifying the Community's rural areas.

These were joined in 1993 by the Financial Instruments for Fisheries Guidance (FIFG) which assists in the restructuring of the fisheries sector. The Cohesion Fund was established to assist the poorer Member States – Ireland, Greece, Spain and Portugal – to meet the Maastricht criteria for a single currency. It supports transport and environmental projects.

4 The Structural Funds concentrate on a limited number of priority objectives. For the period 1994–99 there were seven priority objectives. Objective 1 was 'promoting the development and structural adjustment of regions whose development is lagging behind'. The condition for eligibility under Objective 1 was: regions whose per capita GDP, on the basis of the figures for the previous three years, was less than 75 per cent of the Community average. In Objective 1 regions, EU funding must account for at least 50 per cent of public expenditure on the measures and may not exceed 75 per cent of the total cost of the measures, except for Member States covered by the Cohesion Fund, where it may rise to a maximum of 80 per cent in the outermost regions.

5 A *Protocol* has exactly the same legal status as the Treaty to which it is attached. It can be thought of as analogous to a PS to a letter or, in legal terms, a codicil to a will. Once the new Treaty enters into force the Protocol is to be read for the future as legally part of the Treaty to which they are attached.

6 Secondary benefits are those benefits to which a person is entitled while in receipt of certain social insurance and social assistance payments and to which entitlement is retained while engaged in Community Employment Schemes, Back to Work Allowance Schemes and Area Allowance Schemes in accordance with certain criteria, e.g. rent/mortgage allowance, medical card, differential rent, fuel allowance, footwear and clothing scheme, butter vouchers.

7 For details on the many different European Union sources of funding, see *European Funding in Ireland: Your Guide* published in 1995 by the Communicating Europe Task Force, which is a partnership between the Irish Government and the European Commission Representation in Ireland.

8 A Task Force on Integration of Local Government and Local Development Systems has been established by the Government. It is chaired by the Minister for the Environment and Local Government and held its first meeting on 11 June 1998. The Task Force was given three months to report to Cabinet as to how an integrated approach to local government and local development, with an emphasis on participation and partnership, can be put in place by the end of 1999. In the course of its work, the Task Force held discussions with the four pillars of Partnership 2000. It reported to government in September 1998 and the implementation of the Task Force's recommendations are currently underway. The Task Force will remain in place to oversee and monitor the implementation process.

9 A Declaration is not part of a Treaty and is not legally binding. It is a statement of the political intentions of those who sign the Treaty in question. Unlike a Protocol, it does not have a legal status equivalent to the provisions of a Treaty. Declarations express the intentions of the Member States and have political rather than legal force. A Declaration which is adopted by all the Member States jointly carries greater weight than one made to express their national positions by one or two or three Member States only.

10 Under the current round of Structural Funds, Objective 1 funding for the Community as a whole averages 169.5 ECU per capita, while Objective 2 funding intensity averages 41.9 ECU per capita.

RECOMMENDED READING

Recommended reading on poverty within an EU perspective includes Atkinson (1997), Department of Social Welfare (1995) and Mernagh and Commins (1994). Recommended reading on social exclusion includes Government of Ireland (1996), Kirby and Jacobson (1998), Sabel (1996) and Walsh, Craig, McCafferty (1998). Recommended reading on Structural Funds includes European Commission (1994), European Commission (1996), Economic and Social Research Institute (1997) and Institute of European Affairs (1999).

REFERENCES

Atkinson, A.B. (1997) 'Poverty in Ireland and Anti-Poverty Strategy: A European Perspective', pp. 9–37, in A.W. Gray (ed.), *International Perspectives on the Irish Economy*. Dublin: Indecon Policy Series.

Burden, T. (1998) *Social Policy and Welfare: A Clear Guide*. London: Pluto Press.

Cochrane, A. and J. Clarke (eds) (1993) *Comparing Welfare States: Britain in International Context*. London: Sage.

Department of the Environment (1996) *Better Local Government: A Programme for Change*. Dublin: Stationery Office.

Department of the Environment and Local Government (1998) *Report of the Task Force on Integration of Local Government and Local Development Systems*. Dublin: Stationery Office.

Department of Social Welfare (1995) *Putting Poverty 3 into Policy*. Ballyconnell, Co. Cavan Conference Proceedings.

Economic and Social Research Institute (1997) *EU Structural Funds in Ireland: A Mid-Term Evaluation of the CSF 1994–99*. Dublin: Economic and Social Research Institute.

Economic and Social Research Institute (1999) *National Investment Priorities for the Period 2000–2006*. Dublin: Economic and Social Research Institute.

European Commission (1993) *Growth, Competitiveness, Employment: The Challenges and Ways Forward into the 21st Century*. Luxembourg: Office for Official Publications of the European Communities.

European Commission (1994) *Ireland Community Support Framework 1994–99: EC Structural Funds*. Luxembourg: Office for Official Publications of the European Communities.

European Commission (1994) *European Social Policy: A Way Forward for the Union*. Luxembourg: Directorate General for Employment, Industrial Relations and Social Affairs.

European Commission (1996) *Structural Funds and Cohesion Fund 1994–99 Regulations and Commentary*. Luxembourg: Office for Official Publications of the European Communities.

European Commission (1997) *Agenda 2000: For a Stronger and Wider Union*. Luxembourg: Office for Official Publications of the European Communities.

European Commission (1998) *Draft Regulations for the Structural Funds 2000–2006*. Luxembourg: Office for Official Publications of the European Communities.

Government of Ireland (1995) *Operational Programme for Human Resources Development 1994–99*. Dublin: Stationery Office.

Government of Ireland (1996) *Partnership 2000, for Inclusion, Employment and Competitiveness*. Dublin: Stationery Office.

Government of Ireland (1997) *Sharing in Progress: National Anti-Poverty Strategy*. Dublin: Stationery Office.

Government of Ireland (1998) *Treaty of Amsterdam White Paper*. Dublin: Stationery Office.

Healy, S. and B. Reynolds (eds) (1998) *Social Policy in Ireland: Principles, Practice and Problems*. Dublin: CORI.

Healy, S. and B. Reynolds (eds) (1999) *Social Partnership in a New Century*. Dublin: CORI.

Institute of European Affairs (1999) *Agenda 2000: Implications for Ireland*. Dublin: IEA.

Kirby, P. and D. Jacobson (eds) (1998) *In the Shadow of the Tiger: New Approaches to Combating Social Exclusion*. Dublin: Community Office/DCU Press.

McCarthy, D. (1997) Assistant Secretary of the Department of the Taoiseach, in-house seminar of the Irish Aid Advisory Committee (IAAC), Dublin: Department of Foreign Affairs, 27 November 1997.

Mernagh, M. and P. Commins (1994) *Final Report of the Third EU Poverty Programme*. Dublin: The Irish Research and Development Unit, South Inner City Community Development Association.

National Anti-Poverty Strategy (1997) *Sharing in Progress: National Anti-Poverty Strategy*. Dublin: Stationery Office.

Sabel, C. (1996) *Ireland: Local Partnership and Social Innovation*. Paris: OECD.

Spicker, P. (1995) *Social Policy: Themes and Approaches*. Hemel Hempstead: Prentice Hall/Harvester Wheatsheaf.

Walsh, J., S. Craig and D. McCafferty (1998) *Local Partnerships for Social Inclusion?* Dublin: Oak Tree Press/Combat Poverty Agency.

7

Employment Equality Since Accession to the European Union

Anne Doyle

INTRODUCTION

This chapter describes the complex and interrelated aspects of employment equality. It begins by exploring women and the labour force, before going on to look at gender equality in Europe and the influence of the European Court of Justice. Finally it explores gender equality in Ireland after accession to the European Economic Community.

WOMEN AND THE LABOUR FORCE BEFORE ACCESSION

Women's Participation in the Labour Force

On 1 January 1973, when Ireland acceded to membership of the European Economic Community (EEC), women were economically dependent because of the pattern of their working lives. Characteristically women worked until marriage and either left the workforce at that point or in the child rearing period thereafter, for reasons outlined elsewhere (see Conroy Jackson, 1993; Cousins, 1996). This pattern was somewhat less dominant in a few sectors of the economy such as cleaning services, where women tended to remain working longer, probably for strong social and financial reasons. However, the overall trend was for women's paid employment to be seen as a stopgap between school and marriage.

Table 1 shows that women's participation in the labour force in 1971 was much lower than it is today. The participation rate was especially low in the case of married women. Labour force statistics record that women made up 26 per cent of the labour force, compared with men who comprised the remaining 74 per cent (*Census of the Population of Ireland*, 1971 V: 148–53). More significantly, women's participation in the labour market was overwhelmingly confined to the first 10–15 years of working life. For women in the age cohort 20–29, the participation rate in the labour force was recorded at 51 per cent. For women in the age cohort 40–59, the participation rate in the labour force was recorded at 20.5 per cent. The equivalent participation rates for men in those age cohorts were 92.5 per cent and 96 per cent, respectively.

Table 1. Women's Participation in the Labour Force

	Men as % of total labour force	Women as % of total labour force	Married women's participation in the labour force (as % of total labour force)
1971[1]	74	26	3.5
1998[2]	69	44	19

[1] Source: *Census of Population of Ireland 1971*, V: 144–5, 148–53.
[2] Source: *Quarterly National Household Survey*, March–May 1998.

Women's Remuneration

Women who were in gainful employment in 1971 usually received lower pay than men, even when they were doing equal work or work of equal value. Women's average hourly industrial (manufacturing) earnings were £0.34, as compared with men's average hourly industrial (manufacturing) earnings, which were £0.61 (*Quarterly Industrial Inquiry*, September 1971). Accordingly, women's average hourly industrial earnings amounted to approximately 56 per cent of men's average hourly industrial earnings. Some of the difference in women's and men's earnings can be accounted for by differences in the length of work experience and consequential differences in skill levels and supervisory roles. However, it is almost certain that some of the differences were the result of policies and practices embedded in a labour market which treated women's employment and remuneration differently from men's.

The Public Service – A Case in Point

In 1972, the civil service, local authorities, the health sector and state-sponsored bodies all operated policies and practices which limited women's participation in the labour force. In general, a marriage bar applied in those employments, whereby women were obliged to resign on marriage. A gratuity (one year's pay) was usually paid on resignation for marriage, in lieu of accrued pension entitlement. In addition, public service

employers paid different wage and salary rates to women and men
employees, even when both were employed to do identical work. The
differential was of the order of 20 per cent and was based either on sex-
differentiated or marriage-differentiated scales of pay. Since a marriage
bar generally applied in the case of women, only married men were in a
position to avail of the married scales of pay.

There were a range of public service jobs which were not available
to women. Women were admitted to work in the Garda Siochána (police
force) in 1959, but the number of women in the force was small: 12 in
1959, rising to 35 in 1977. Women were not admitted to join the army
or air corps until 1980 (cadets) and 1981 (non-commissioned officers
(NCOs)), and the naval service until 1995 (cadets) and 1996 (NCOs).
Women's participation in the public service was, in the main, confined
to lower levels in the hierarchy and women who remained in public
service employment seldom reached the top, or even middle-ranking,
positions in their chosen career. Table 2 sets out the position of women
in the General Service structure of the civil service, which is the administrative stream in that employment, just prior to entry to the EEC, and
in 1996, for comparison.

Table 2. Women's Employment in the Civil Service

	% of Posts in Grade held by Women 1972[1]	% of Posts in Grade held by Women 1996[2]
Secretary	Nil	4
Assistant Secretary	Nil	6
Principal Officer	1	13
Assistant Principal Officer	4	24
Administrative Officer	17	36
Higher Executive Officer	13	36
Executive Officer	41	48
Staff Officer	60	75
Clerical Officer	63	79
Clerical Assistant	99	82

[1] Source: Ross, M.(1986) *Employment in the Public Domain in Recent Decades.* Dublin: ESRI
  (Paper No.127)
[2] Source: Department of Finance

GENDER EQUALITY IN EUROPE

Gender Equality in Europe before Ireland's Accession

Article 119 of the Treaty of the European Economic Community (EEC) dealt specifically with one aspect of equality between the sexes. The Article provided for equal pay for women and men for equal work. The terms of the Article treat it as an economic issue that would differentially affect competition within the Community, if some Member States could rely on cheap female labour in the production of goods and services.

Article 119 had been in the Treaty since its ratification in 1957. A Resolution of the Council of the EEC, in December 1961, sought the phased abolition of all pay discrimination on grounds of sex, by 31 December 1964. This objective was not achieved in the timeframe originally envisaged (*Fifth Report on Equal Pay*, 31 December 1968), and in the early 1970s a level of divergence from the principle of equal pay persisted. However, in the early 1970s, when Ireland joined the EEC, a social revolution for women was taking place within the Community. Some of the first intimations of 'Social Europe' were about to become evident.

Anti-Discrimination Directives, 1975–86

The 1970s saw the beginning of a serious drive by the Commission to place the economic equality of women firmly on the agenda of the Council and through the Council on the agenda of every member state. Between the years 1975 and 1986, five anti-discrimination Directives were adopted by the Council. The thrust of the policy in the Directives broke new ground. Between them, they provided a floor of rights that would support the economic equality of women in employment and in social welfare provision. As well as supporting social change towards equal opportunities for women and men, the Directives were underpinned by a philosophical aspiration towards the harmonisation of working and living conditions throughout the Community.

Member States were obliged to transpose these Directives into national law and to provide to citizens effective means of redress if the rights guaranteed in the Directives were infringed. The Directives provided rights to:

• Equal pay for work of equal value (Council Directive, 10.2.1975, 75/117/EEC);

• Equal treatment for women and men in relation to employment (Council Directive 9.2.1976, 76/207/EEC);

- Equal treatment for women and men in the area of social security payments (Council Directive 19.12.1978, 79/7/EEC);

- Equal treatment for women and men in occupational social security schemes (Council Directive 24.7.1986, 86/378/EEC); and

- Equal treatment for self-employed women and men (Council Directive 11.12.1986, 86/613/EEC).

As transposition of these legal instruments into national law proceeded, policies for equality of opportunity found themselves an enduring place on the political agenda of the Community.

Equality Directives, 1992–97

Two other equal opportunities Directives have been proposed by the Commission, both in response to specific concerns. These are the *Directive on the Burden of Proof* (Council Directive 15.12.1997, 97/80/EC) and the draft *Positive Action Directive* (Commission Proposal for a Council Directive 27.3.1996, COM (96) 93 final). The *Directive on the Burden of Proof* provides for a shift in the evidential burden of proof in equality cases and seems to have arisen from a concern to ensure common minimum procedures for establishing a prima facie case under equality law in every member state. The Directive is to be transposed into the law of member states by 1 January 2001. The draft *Directive on Positive Action* owes its origins to the judgement of the European Court of Justice in the Kalanke case (Eckhard Kalanke v Freie-Hansestadt Bremen (C–450/93) [1995]). The draft Directive sought to codify and support arrangements for future positive action measures and those already in place in member states. The draft Directive was not adopted and uncertainty about the legal basis for positive action measures was eventually resolved in the context of the Amsterdam Treaty.

Equal Opportunities Policies

Policy Initiatives (1982–2000)

In 1982, the Commission established a permanent Advisory Committee on Equal Opportunities for Women and Men (Decision of Commission, 9 December 1982, 82/43/EEC). The Committee is composed of representatives from each Member State. Since its inception, the Committee prepared and promulgated four equal opportunities programmes. The first programme (1982–85) focused on strengthening individual rights and counteracting obstacles to equal opportunities for women, particularly relating to constraints based on the traditional segregation of gender roles in society (Council Resolution, 12 July 1982). The second action programme (1986–90) identified actions to improve the employment opportunities of women, particularly employment at an equal level with men in areas of new technology and the more equal sharing of family responsibilities (Second Council Resolution, 24.7.1986, 86/C203/02). The third medium-term action programme (1991–95) focused on the implementation and development of legislation, the integration of women into the labour market and improving the status of women in society (Council Resolution, 21.5.91, 91/C142/01). The most recent medium-term action programme (1996–2000) is concerned to advance the mainstreaming of equality issues (Council Decision, 22.12.95 95/593/EC) (See Section on Mainstreaming, p. 120). The benefits of these programmes have not been as directly evident to Member State nationals as the Directives have been. Instead, the impact of the programmes has been mediated through Commission policy and through support for Member State initiatives and orientation as regards gender equality.

Funding Initiatives, 1989–2000

In the context of the Community Support Framework generally, there has been a formal requirement for all funding to be congruent with existing EU policies. Indeed, the Framework (1989–93) made specific the need to consider 'training and infrastructure requirements which facilitate labour force participation by women with children'. The Framework (1994–99) envisaged that each operational programme it funded would impact on the development of equal opportunities and provide care facilities both for the children and other dependants of trainees. With some exceptions, the aspirations of mainline programmes did not translate in any tangible way to substantial support for the development of equal opportunities through the actual expenditure of European Social Funds. Other avenues of funding, such as Fonds European pour l'Orientation et Garantie Agricole (FEOGA) and European Regional Development Fund (ERDF), have lent even more tenuous support to equal opportunities aspirations.

The New Opportunities for Women (NOW) Programme was proposed by the Commission in 1990, and projects funded by the programme came on-stream in 1992. NOW is one of a number of Community Initiatives which sought, on an experimental basis and in a modest way, to influence action in Member States in a manner that directly accords with Commission policies. NOW was an early initiative through which the Commission provided financial support for equal opportunities demonstration projects that meet certain Commission-determined criteria in the areas of training and employment.

These projects would almost certainly not have taken place were it not for EU support both at policy and financial level. Indeed, the requirement that projects be additional to any actions normally funded by the Member State was an important criterion for eligibility. The opportunities provided by these projects enabled women, who may have been deskilled, to retrain and seek paid employment. Presumably, too, the projects may have had a value in raising an awareness of their rights among the women who participated in them.

The draft proposals for the Community Support Framework (2000–2006) seek to put equal opportunities more firmly on the agenda of those seeking to secure EU funding for national objectives. The approach is supported by the emphasis on mainstreaming as a significant means of advancing equal opportunities policies and on addressing infra-structural requirements of implementing policies for the reconciliation of work and family life.

Mainstreaming (1996 onwards)

In 1996 the Commission issued a communication entitled 'Incorporating Equal Opportunities for women and men into all Community policies and activities' (COM (96) 67 final). The communication represents a policy reorientation away from isolated initiatives focused on women, such as the action programmes outlined above, to a more integrative approach called 'mainstreaming'. Mainstreaming can be described as a system in which

> each and every service carries a responsibility for analysing the implications for women and men respectively (gender impact assessment) of their policies and activities and for amending their policies where necessary. Policy proposals need to be checked at the various levels of the decision-making process in order to ascertain that the gender dimension has been duly taken into account (gender proofing) (Progress Report from the Commission on the follow-up of the Communication 'Incorporating Equal Opportunities for Women and Men into All Community Policies and Activities' (COM (1998) 122 Final, p.10, para 1.26)).

A key outcome of that communication has been the mainstreaming of equal opportunities for women and men in the Community Support Framework (2000–2006) draft General Regulations.

Labour Market Policies

Until the 1990s, proactive measures to encourage women's participation in the labour force may be traced through a few Council Resolutions. In 1994, the Heads of Government of the EU member states, meeting in Essen, established employment equality as one of three labour market priorities for the Union. In 1997, the Heads of Government, meeting in Luxembourg, agreed guidelines for employment under four headings: employability, entrepreneurship, adaptability and equal opportunities. These guidelines provide a blueprint for the development of action plans for employment in each member state. These developments have not substantially influenced Irish equal opportunities initiatives to date. However, Ireland's Employment Action Plan for 1998 (Department of Enterprise, Trade and Employment, 1998) seeks, in response to the equality dimension of the guidelines, to support the employment of women and to develop women's vertical and horizontal integration into the labour market.

Family-Friendly Policies after Accession (1992–96)

Once equal treatment legislation had been in place in member states for some years, it became increasingly obvious that serious barriers to the achievement of equal opportunities persisted, some of which lay embedded in a broader social milieu. One significant policy option identified to surmount these barriers is the implementation of measures to facilitate the reconciliation of work and family life. Two clear areas of initiative evolved from this policy option:

- A Recommendation on Childcare, 1992 (Council Recommendation 31.3.92, 92/241/EEC), and
- A Directive on Parental Leave, 1996 (Council Directive 3.6.96, 96/34/EC).

In addition, a Directive providing for the introduction of measures to encourage improvements in the safety and health at work of pregnant workers and workers who have recently given birth or are breastfeeding was adopted in 1992 (Council Directive 19.10.92, 92/85/EEC).

European Parliament

The Women's Rights Committee of the European Parliament has helped to maintain and enhance interest in, and action for, the equality agenda at the level of the Council and Commission. Through the

Opinion procedures, Parliament has provided a valuable and often alternative view on aspects of the work of the Council and Commission. Procedural changes in the Social Charter of the Maastricht Treaty and the Amsterdam Treaty have given a strengthened voice to Parliament in many areas of Treaty competence, including the social sphere. The Parliament, which is directly elected by EU Member State nationals, may generally be expected to inject a liberalising influence, in contrast to the more mainstream tendencies of the Council which is comprised of the political representatives of the governments of the member states. Experience of the new procedures is in its infancy and the actual impact of the procedures will be seen over time.

The Maastricht and Amsterdam Treaties

As we have seen, the Treaty of the European Economic Community, to which Ireland acceded in 1973, provided for equal pay for equal work at Article 119. The Single European Act (1983) made no change to the gender equality dimension of the constitution of the Community. The Maastricht Treaty (1992), in the context of the Social Charter (which did not then apply to the UK), made some changes of a predominantly procedural nature, which affected the way employment and other social initiatives might be processed. A stronger role was secured for the social partners as regards initiatives arising under the Charter. The Parental Leave Directive was the first measure to be agreed under the social protocol of the Maastricht Treaty. Negotiations for the Amsterdam Treaty (1998) resulted in a significant expansion in the terms of Article 119. The Article was expanded to empower the Council to adopt measures to ensure the application of the principle of equal treatment of women and men in matters connected with employment and occupation, and specifically to allow member states to take positive action measures to redress existing inequalities between the sexes. The Article also retains provision for the principle of equal pay, with slight amendment. In addition, a new Article 13 (replacing old Article 6) extends the competence of the EU to take action on discrimination based on sex, racial or ethnic origin, religion or belief, disability, age or sexual orientation. Prompt action by the Commission in proposing measures under the new Treaty competence can be expected.

INFLUENCES OF THE EUROPEAN COURT OF JUSTICE

European Court of Justice

The Equal Pay and Equal Treatment Directives provide a core of economic rights and, even if left to narrow interpretation by a conservative judiciary, might have been expected to work reasonably well to advance equality between women and men. In the event, the European Court of Justice (ECJ) has, through sometimes spirited and far-reaching judgements, ensured an interpretation of the legislation that would have regard both to the letter and to the spirit of the Directives. Key judgements, particularly from the mid-1980s onwards, have confirmed a broad interpretation of indirect discrimination, and determined that discrimination on grounds of pregnancy amounts to discrimination on grounds of sex, and set parameters for lawful positive action measures.

ECJ Case Law

Indirect Discrimination

EU anti-discrimination legislation outlaws both direct and indirect discrimination (see Prechal and Burrows, 1990: 71–7, 106–7; Blakemore and Drake, 1996). Discrimination is direct when it is based overtly on the ground protected by the legislation. A job advertisement which 'seeks a man to manage a new business . . .' is directly discriminatory on the grounds of sex. Indirect discrimination is more subtle and occurs when discrimination is based on a characteristic that is linked to the discriminatory ground. The characteristic may appear neutral on the face of it, but, in practice, discrimination based on the characteristic impacts disproportionately on members of the disadvantaged group. Indirect discrimination may be justified if there are objective reasons for the discrimination. For example, a maximum height requirement for airline crew may discriminate against tall men, but may be justifiable because of limited headroom in the cabin.

As another example, in one important judgement (Dr Pamela Mary Enderby v Frenchay Health Authority (C–127/92) [1993]), the European Court of Justice held that differences between pay of paramedics in the health services (a speech therapist and a pharmacist) could not be justified on grounds of different collective bargaining outcomes. The Court indicated that consideration must fall to be given to whether the collective bargaining outcomes were themselves linked to sex-differentiated industrial relations procedures and settlements. However, pay differences based on genuine labour market scarcity might justify indirect discrimination in pay.

Discrimination and Pregnancy

The dictum that biology is destiny tended to apply with particular force in the case of pregnant employees. Until the late 1980s, there is evidence that the recruitment and dismissal of pregnant employees were regarded, in some jurisdictions, in a qualitatively different way to the recruitment and dismissal of an employee on grounds of sex. The case law appears to have developed in three phases. The initial phase can be seen in UK case law (Turley v Allders Department Stores Limited (1980) IRLR 4) where, in 1980, it was held that because there was no masculine equivalent to pregnancy, there could be no comparatively disadvantageous treatment of women as a result of pregnancy and, therefore, no discrimination. In the second phase, Irish case law (An Foras Forbatha v Geraghty Williams EEC/1981, DEE4/1982) determined that discrimination on grounds of pregnancy was indirect discrimination. Accordingly, arguments relating to the disbenefits involved in recruiting or retaining a pregnant employee in employment could be accepted as objective justification for the discrimination. Finally, in an important judgement given in 1990 (Elizabeth Johanna Pacifica Dekker v VJV Centrum (C–177/88) [1990]), the European Court of Justice ruled in a way that would force an end to behaviour marked by prejudice against pregnant employees. The Court judged that discrimination against a pregnant employee amounted to direct discrimination. As such, the discrimination was automatically outlawed and no test of objective justification, which might have saved the behaviour from unlawfulness, fell to be considered by the Court. This judgement had profound consequences, both in its analysis and understanding of the issues and for its practical impact on the working lives of women. Each woman availing of maternity leave at some point in her working life was now a potential net beneficiary of this EU-wide development in the rule of law.

Discrimination and Part-time Workers

Historically, the position had been that the majority of part-time workers were women and that these jobs, in general, were low paid. The practice of employers over the years has been to withhold from part-time employees, levels of pay and benefits which are the pro-rata equivalents of those of full-time employees. These practices have had, in the aggregate, a disproportionate impact on the pay and conditions of women employees. Hourly rates of pay for part-time employees have been less than those for full-time employees, even when engaged on like work, and there is a history of no access, or limited access, for part-time workers to pensions and other benefits.

Traditional arguments supporting the less beneficial treatment of part-time workers were based on costs of employing part-time workers, their more tenuous relationship to the enterprise, and the relative value to the employer of part-time employees compared with core (full-time) employees. Against this backdrop, the European Court of Justice began to establish that unequal treatment of part-time workers could amount to unlawful indirect discrimination, where that treatment impacted disproportionately on one sex. In pivotal judgements, over the years 1986 to 1998, the European Court of Justice pointed firmly to the need to ensure that differences in the treatment of full and part-time employees, in such areas as pay and pensions, did not discriminate indirectly against women employees (Bilka Kaufhaus GmbH v Karin Weber von Hartz (C–170/84) [1986]; Union of Commercial and Clerical Employees, Denmark v Danish Employers Association, acting on behalf of Danfoss (C–109/88 [1989]; Helga Nimz v Freie Hansestadt Hamburg (C–184/89) [1991]; Hellen Gerster v Freistadt Bayern (C–1/95) [1997]); Kathleen Hill and Ann Stapleton v the Revenue Commissioners and the Department of Finance (C–243/95) [1998].

Positive Action Measures

The most influential EU issue of the 1990s, in terms of equality of opportunity for women and men, was probably the question of positive action. The accession of Sweden and Finland brought into the EU perspectives on equal opportunities which were more proactive than those in the EU generally. At about the same time, some German Länder put in place positive action measures aimed to improve the balance of the sexes at all levels in local government employment. These measures which involved, on the face of it, discrimination against men, had the objective of securing equality of opportunities for women.

The positive action measures concerned gave rise to two judgements (Eckhard Kalanke v Freie Hansestadt Bremen (C–450/93) [1995] and Hellmut Marschall v Land Nordrhein, Westfalen (C–409/95) [1997]) by the European Court of Justice. Both measures provided for the appointment of a member of the under-represented sex to fill a vacant post where there was available a member of that sex who was equally qualified with members of the other sex, and the post arose in a grade or level that comprised 50 per cent or more of the other sex. The difference between the two measures lay in the degree of discretion to depart from the rule, where the individual circumstances of the candidate of the other sex warranted it. The Court found that the measure that provided the degree of discretion in relation to the candidate of the other sex (before the

Court in the Marschall case) was acceptable under EU law, while the other measure (before the Court in the Kalanke case), which did not provide that degree of discretion, was not permissible under EU law.

These cases seem to mark a coming of age of equal opportunities policies in the European Union. The Equal Treatment Directive had been in place for twenty years, but nothing like an equal distribution of the job opportunities, particularly higher level job opportunities, had been secured by women. The nature of the measures found acceptable under EU law are modest when viewed in comparison with US positive discrimination measures. US measures have applied on a strict quota basis and operated whether or not members of the disadvantaged group are equally qualified with other candidates. While the principle of positive action has been established under EU law, the absence of any broad level of application of the principle in either public or private sector employments, outside Sweden and Finland, is noteworthy.

GENDER EQUALITY IN IRELAND AFTER ACCESSION

National Agenda for Change

The Report of the Commission on the Status of Women was presented to the Government in December 1972. The Commission had been established two years earlier with the following terms of reference:

> To examine and report on the status of women in Irish society, to make recommendations as to the steps necessary to ensure the participation of women on equal terms and conditions with men in the political, social, cultural and economic life of the country.

The recommendations of the Commission identified a programme for change that remains relevant in some respects to this day. In the employment sphere, the Commission made key recommendations which might be summarised as follows:

• Implementation of a policy of equal pay for equal work or work of equal value

• Establishment of a permanent structure to work to eliminate sex discrimination in employment

• Abolition of the marriage bar in employment

• Provision for twelve weeks maternity leave

• Prohibition of advertisements expressly seeking female or male employees (except where sex is a bona fide occupational qualification)

• Provision for childcare including physical infrastructure.

In the years that followed, many of these recommendations were implemented and some were not, but the factors that led to implementation, prompt or otherwise, had as much to do with Ireland's accession to the EU, and its requirements, as with the importance with which the recommendations of the Commission on the Status of Women were viewed.

Equal Pay

The Anti-Discrimination (Pay) Act, 1974, gave effect to the key economic recommendations of the Commission on the Status of Women – equal pay for equal work or work of equal value. The Act also transposed into Irish law the terms of the Directive on Equal Pay. The Act came into operation on 31 December 1975, six weeks in advance of the latest date for transposition provided in the Directive.

The Act established means of redress through new statute-based equal pay officers in the Labour Court and for the award of compensation in successful cases of up to three years arrears of pay and for equal pay from a current date. In the first year after enactment (1976), 51 cases were referred to equal pay officers. The number of referrals was higher in each subsequent year, until 1980 when 107 cases were referred for investigation. Of the recommendations issued in those years, almost three out of four were successful, or partially successful. Many more cases were settled outside the formal redress machinery (Labour Court Annual Reports, 1976–80; Employment Equality Agency, 1977–80). Cases for equal pay were established through a comparative job evaluation of the work of the claimant and that of a cited actual co-worker or cited actual co-workers.

The Anti-Discrimination (Pay) Act, 1974 may be credited, to a considerable degree, with the success in narrowing of the male/female wage differential which took place over the years 1976 to 1982. In that period the differential between women's and men's pay reduced by an average of more than one per cent per year. By way of comparison, the differential narrowed by only three percentage points over the preceding twenty years and has not narrowed appreciably since 1982 at all. As Table 3 shows, a significant divergence between male and female earnings remains today.

Reasons for the Persisting Gap

Table 3 shows the significant improvements that have taken place in women's pay rates since 1971. Statistics for March 1998 give women's average hourly industrial (manufacturing) earnings as £5.79, and men's

Table 3

Year	Women's average hourly earnings	Men's average hourly earnings	Women's average hourly earnings as a % of men's average hourly earnings
1971[1]	£0.34	£0.61	56%
1998[2]	£5.79	£7.74	75%

[1] *Quarterly Industrial Inquiry*, Statistics for September 1971.
[2] *Industrial Earnings and Hours Worked*, Statistics for March 1998.

average hourly industrial (manufacturing) earnings as £7.74 (*Industrial Earnings and Hours Worked*, CSO, January 1999). Based on these figures, the average hourly industrial earnings of women are 75 per cent of equivalent male earnings. Some of the difference may be attributed to such factors as the higher percentage of women in the younger age ranges of the labour force, the fact that men are less likely to take time out of the labour market compared with women, and the segregation of women in traditionally female occupations and sectors of the economy, which have historically been low paid.

An Economic and Social Research Institute (ESRI) study (Callan and Wren, 1994) confirmed an average 20 percentage points differential between female and male hourly earnings for all employees. The research identified a number of factors that may account for some of the difference observed. These include the hourly wage rates for full and part-time jobs, the latter being predominantly taken up by women; overtime working and shift premia which are more often a feature of male employment, and trades union membership – more men are trades union members than women and trades union members tend to command higher wages than non-trades union members.

Having controlled for variables such as educational qualifications, labour market experience and time spent out of the labour market, the ESRI study found that average female wage rates would be over 10 per cent higher on average, if the variables were remunerated in the case of women in the same way as they were for men. Further research on the factors influencing the differential is being undertaken in the context of Partnership 2000.

A further important issue is the continuing impact on wage rates of past discrimination against women in terms of training, recruitment to well-paid jobs, promotion and other career opportunities. Any continuing level of discrimination in these respects, though now unlawful, will perpetuate the wage gap.

National Minimum Wage

Allied to the issue of unequal pay, but conceptually distinct from it, is the issue of low pay. In July 1997, the government established a commission to report on the options for a national minimum wage. The commission reported to government in April 1998, recommending the setting of a national minimum wage. Implementation of the recommendation would be likely to benefit many more women than men, because women are more often in receipt of low wages and are more often in poverty, despite having paid work.

Equal Pay and Pensions

The right to equal pay and pensions was established in Ireland more than a decade in advance of European Court of Justice case law in the area. Recognition of occupational pensions as part of pay was accepted in Irish case law as far back as 1977 (Linson v ASTMS EP1/1997 and DEP2/77). The case established the principles of equal entry ages and retirement ages for both sexes in occupational pensions schemes. The following year, the question of survivor's benefits was tackled (Department of the Public Service v Robinson DEP7/1979). The claim succeeded and subsequently public service pensions schemes were amended to conform with the decision. It is interesting to note that this latter case was taken by former President, then Senator, Mary Robinson, in order to secure access to the Oireachtas Members' Scheme in respect of her spouse.

This area of case law is one indication that in those earlier years, the Labour Court showed considerable acumen and independence in establishing rights in this complex and new area of endeavour. It was not until the 1990s that a series of pensions-related European Court of Justice judgements established such rights clearly under EU law (Douglas Harvey Barber v Guardian Royal Exchange Assurance Group (C–262/88) [1990]; Coloroll Pension Trustees Ltd v James Richard Russell and Others (C–200/91) [1994]; Anna Adriaantje Vroege v NCIV Instituut voor Volkshuisvesting BV and Stichting Pensioenfonds NCIV (C–57/93) [1994]; Geertruida Catharina Fisscher v Voorhuis Hengelo BV and Stichting Bedrijfspensioenfonds voor de Detailhandel (C–128/93) [1994]). In Ireland, at least, these judgements merely confirmed a process of equalization of pensions provision that had been taking shape over the preceding fifteen years. The Pensions Act, 1990, transposed the terms of the Directive on Occupational Social Security into national law. The scope of the pensions equality provisions in Part IV of that Act is conceptually broader than in the Anti-Discrimination (Pay) Act, 1974. However, the bulk of the pensions-related principles, enumerated by statute law in that Act, had already been established in case law under existing equality legislation.

Equal Treatment

The Employment Equality Act, 1977, transposed the Equal Treatment Directive into Irish law. Unlike the Anti-Discrimination (Pay) Act, 1974, the Employment Equality Act, 1977, is not based on a recommendation of the Commission on the Status of Women, December 1972. However, the legislation was the vehicle for realizing two key recommendations of the Commission: abolition of the marriage bar (in the private sector) and the outlawing of discriminatory job advertisements.

The Act outlaws discrimination in employment on grounds of sex and same-sex discrimination on grounds of marital status. Discrimination, in the context of the Act, is taken to occur where a person of one sex is treated less favourably than a person of the other sex. The central focus of the Act is discrimination by employers against employees or prospective employees. The Act specifically outlaws any discrimination in relation to access to employment, conditions of employment, training, work experience and promotion. The Act also outlaws discrimination in a wide range of employment-related fields, including discrimination by trades unions and professional bodies, discrimination in collective agreements, discriminatory employment-related advertising, and discrimination by vocational training institutions. The Act provided for the establishment of the Employment Equality Agency. In addition, the Act established an enhanced redress mechanism compared with that already established under the Anti-Discrimination (Pay) Act, 1974. The Act made provision for the appointment of equality officers in the Labour Court to investigate claims for redress under the Act and the Anti-Discrimination (Pay) Act, 1974, and to make a recommendation for resolution of the claims. Provision was made for an appeal to the Labour Court on the facts and to the High Court on a point of law. Compensation up to a ceiling of two years pay was allowable in successful cases and equal treatment could be ordered from a current date.

Employment Equality Agency

The Employment Equality Agency was established to provide a permanent locus for advancing equal opportunities in employment. The Agency was charged with the dual tasks of working towards the elimination of discrimination and of promoting equality. The Agency consists of a chairperson and ten ordinary members. Four members of the Agency are direct nominees, two each from employers (Irish Business and Employers Confederation, IBEC), and employee organisations (Irish Congress of Trade Unions, ICTU). The remaining six members of the Agency are nominated by the Minister, and three of these members are chosen from women's organisations. The Agency provides information about and promotes awareness of equality legislation through, for example, its telephone enquiry services, information literature, and directly through the media. The Agency also provides advice to individual employees as well as to trades unions, employers, legal professionals and others about equality issues.

The Agency is empowered to give assistance to people who may have been the subject of discrimination if a case involves an important matter of principle, or where it is not reasonable to expect a person to present their case adequately without assistance from the Agency. The Agency monitors recruitment advertising to ensure that it is not discriminatory. Where a discriminatory advertisement is found to have been published, the Agency seeks to ensure that the position is re-advertised in a non-discriminatory manner and that no appointment is made as a result of the original discriminatory advertisement. In 1989, there were 78 discriminatory advertisements recorded by the Agency. By 1993, the number of discriminatory advertisements had dropped to 38. In addition, the Agency has a range of powers of a statutory and investigative nature. The Agency publishes a report of its activities annually.

Sexual Harassment

An important equality issue is the question of how acceptable or comfortable an employee, or category of employee, is made to feel in a particular working environment. Having gained access to particular employments, or to specific areas or levels of work within an employment, some women are confronted with a social barrier to equal participation because of a hostile work environment. By the mid-1980s, Ireland had begun to tackle, through case law, the presenting problem in this context, which had become known as 'sexual harassment'.

Sexual harassment may be described as any unwelcome act, request or conduct that could reasonably be regarded as sexually offensive, humiliating or intimidating (Commission Recommendation of 27 November 1991 on the protection of the dignity of women and men at work (92/C27/04)). The behaviour can range from the display of offensive posters and sexually explicit gestures, to actual sexual assault. The solicitation of sexual favours in return for advancement or other benefits at work is also regarded as sexual harassment. Sexual harassment can result in serious stress at work, a diminution in work performance and, in some cases, may result in an employee having to leave a job.

Despite the clear impact of sexual harassment on the availability of equal opportunities in practice, the Equal Treatment Directive did not expressly outlaw it. EU Member States generally made no specific legal provision for redress for individuals who suffer sexual harassment. The redress machinery in Ireland was unusual among Member States, together with that of the United Kingdom, in finding in employment equality legislation an implicit right to a sexual harassment-free environment.

In 1985, the Labour Court made a determination in their first sexual harassment case (A Garage Proprietor v A Worker EEO2/85). The case involved an employer who subjected a young woman employee to unwanted verbal advances, sexually explicit derogatory remarks and actual physical sexual abuse, leading her to resign from the employment. The Court, in its determination, stated that 'freedom from sexual harassment is a condition of work which an employee of either sex is entitled to expect', and indicated that the Court would 'treat any denial of that freedom as discrimination within the terms of the Employment Equality Act, 1997'. This case involved sexual harassment by the employer himself. In subsequent cases, the Labour Court established the liability of the employer for sexual harassment by another employee or by a client of the business. The key cases were supported by the Employment Equality Agency in a very worthwhile use of its statutory powers.

In the light of such proactive Irish case law, it is perhaps unsurprising that a Council Resolution (29 May 1990, 90/C157/02), which marked the first EU-wide attempt to deal with sexual harassment in the workplace, was sponsored by the Irish presidency of the EU in 1990. The Resolution was followed in 1991 by a Commission Recommendation and Code of Practice (27 November 1991, 92/C27/04) in the area. The Employment Equality Agency published a Code of Practice on Sexual Harassment in 1994, which adapted the EC Code of Practice to meet Irish circumstances, including the backdrop of substantial case law.

In 1994, the High Court cast doubt on aspects of existing case law, especially as regards the liability of the employer for sexual harassment by an employee (The Health Board v B. C. and the Labour Court 1991, No. 6855p) [1994]). The Employment Equality Act, 1998, clarified the statutory liability of the employer and defined and specifically outlawed sexual harassment. These legislative provisions are unique, so far, in the national law of EU Member States.

Family-Friendly Policies

Maternity Leave

The *Report of the Commission on the Status of Women* (December 1972) recommended that pregnant employees should be entitled to a minimum of twelve weeks maternity leave and an additional four weeks optional maternity leave. There seems to have been a certain resistance to the full implementation of this proposal. In 1978, six years after the initial recommendation, the Minister for Labour undertook to examine the implications of providing a statutory entitlement to maternity leave. The Maternity Protection of Employees Act, 1981, was the result of those deliberations. The basic entitlement provided in that Act, 14 weeks maternity leave, with the option of four weeks additional maternity leave, were in line with the Commission's recommendation and with International Labour Organisation (ILO) standards. The Maternity Protection Act, 1994, repealed and re-enacted provisions analogous to those in the 1981 Act with regard to leave. The Act also transposed into Irish law the requirements of Directive 92/85/EEC adopted by Council in 1992. The Act gives specific protection to pregnant workers and women who have recently given birth or are breastfeeding. The legislation required an assessment to be made of workplace health and safety risks and the removal of the risk, the arrangement of other suitable work, and, if neither of these options proved possible, the provision of health and safety leave.

Adoptive Leave

The Budget Statement of the Minister for Finance on 29 January 1992 promised statutory maternity leave for adoptive mothers, analogous to that provided to natural mothers under the Maternity Protection of Employees Act, 1981. The Adoptive Leave Act, 1995, gave legislative effect to that commitment. The decision to confine, in general, the automatic grant of adoptive leave to the female adopting parent gave rise to public debate. The view was that leave should be available to either adopting parent, since adoption, unlike maternity, is unconnected with the biological processes of giving birth and breastfeeding. The Act addressed the anomaly in the way adoptive mothers were treated, compared with natural mothers. Broad proposals to put in place a framework of law to facilitate workers, of both sexes, to combine work and family responsibilities were to follow in the Parental Leave Act, 1998.

Parental Leave

The Parental Leave Act, 1998 transposes the EU Directive on Parental Leave (Council Directive 3.6.96, 96/34/EC). The Act provides for fourteen weeks unpaid leave for both women and men to look after young children. The leave applies in respect of children born or adopted on or after 3 June 1996. Leave may be granted in respect of each child under the age of five years, except in the case of an adopted child where a higher age limit applies. The Act also provides for a limited amount of paid leave (known as *force majeure* leave) for urgent family reasons related to the illness or injury of family members.

Childcare

The Report of the Commission on the Status of Women (December 1972) recommended the development of a national infrastructure for childcare to facilitate working women. This recommendation was not implemented.

In both 1981 and 1990, the then Ministers for Labour established working parties to examine and report on the options for childcare facilities for working parents. The reports of the working parties were published in 1983 and 1994 respectively. Both reports made recommendations for the advancement of childcare provisions based on detailed examinations of the then current issues and requirements. Recommendations of the 1983 report, such as the need for regulation of day care facilities and the role of the health services in childcare provision, are reflected in the Childcare Act, 1991, which dealt primarily with children at risk. Following the 1994 report, small levels of public funding (*c.* £800,000 per annum) for childcare infrastructure were provided through Area Development Management (ADM) in the years 1994–97. (ADM is an intermediary company with charitable status established by the Irish Government and the EU to support local social and economic development in Ireland.) In the mid-term review of the Community Support Framework (1994–99), some European Regional Development Fund (ERDF) finance was provided for childcare development in the years 1998 and 1999. Total funding commitments increased to approximately £2.6m in 1998 and to approximately £4.5m in 1999.

In the last years of the twentieth century, the pressures to develop a childcare infrastructure in Ireland seem to be mounting, against the backdrop of labour market shortages evident in a boom economy, increasing numbers of married women in the labour force, and more long-term labour force shortages forecast, linked with our ageing demographic profile.

In 1996, Partnership 2000 committed the Government to developing a strategy to integrate the different strands of the current arrangements for the delivery of childcare services. An Expert Working Group was established under Partnership 2000 to devise a National Framework for the Development of the Childcare Sector. The Group submitted a final report to the Partnership in February 1999. An interdepartmental committee is in the process of evaluating, costing and prioritising childcare proposals before reporting to Government later in the year.

Second Commission on the Status of Women

Twenty years after the establishment of the First Commission on the Status of Women, in 1970, the Government established the Second Commission on the Status of Women (1993). Among its recommendations which pertain to women and work are the need for a national minimum wage, enhanced employment equality legislation, protection against sexual harassment, and childcare provision. Many of these recommendations, as this chapter has indicated, have been, or are, in the course of being implemented.

Employment Equality and Equal Status Legislation

Proposals for amendment of the Employment Equality Act, 1977, and the Anti-Discrimination (Pay) Act, 1974, were published in 1987, but no legislative action followed. The Programme for Government (1993) committed the Government to the enactment of employment equality and equal status legislation to prohibit discrimination on nine distinct grounds: gender, marital and family status, sexual orientation, religion, age, disability, race, and membership of the Traveller community.

The Employment Equality Bill, 1996 and the Equal Status Bill, 1997 gave legislative effect to these broad-ranging proposals. In 1997, both Bills were referred, in their entirety, to the Supreme Court by the President (in an Article 26 reference under the Constitution) and were found to be unconstitutional by that Court. Apart from two relatively technical points found to be unconstitutional, the Supreme Court found that the provisions in the 1996 Bill which required an employer to pay the costs of providing 'a reasonable accommodation' to an employee with a disability amounted to an unjust attack on the property rights of the employer and as such were unconstitutional.

Employment Equality Act, 1998

The Employment Equality Act, 1998, amended to take account of the judgement of the Supreme Court, was enacted on 18 June 1998. The target date for implementation of the Act is 1 September 1999. The Act outlaws discrimination on the nine grounds listed above. The following paragraphs outline the provisions of the Act as they relate to gender equality.

The Act repeals the Employment Equality Act, 1977, and the Anti-Discrimination (Pay) Act, 1974, and enacts broadly analogous provisions. For the first time in Irish gender equality law, the Act specifically outlaws sexual harassment (as already described, pp. 131–2), allows Irish employers to put in place positive action measures for equal opportunities, and brings the Defence Forces within the scope of the legislation.

The Act provides a new infrastructure for equality (both employment equality and equal status). It replaces the Employment Equality Agency with an Equality Authority with enhanced powers, including powers to prepare statutory codes of practice and to undertake equality reviews and action plans. The Act also provides for the establishment of a new office of Director of Equality Investigations, to hear cases for redress under the legislation at first instance. The equality officers of the Labour Relations Commission will become part of the Director's office on repeal of the existing statutes (see Industrial Relations Act, 1990, section 37). There is provision for appeal to the Labour Court on the facts and to the High Court on a point of law. Alternatively, persons who consider that they have been discriminated against on grounds of gender, and are seeking compensation beyond that which may be awarded by the Director, may apply to the Circuit Court, which is empowered to make an a ward without ceiling in appropriate cases. These arrangements arise from European Court of Justice case law requirements (M H Marshall v Southampton and South West Hampshire Area Health Authority (C–271/91) [1993]).

CONCLUSIONS

It is more than twenty years since the principle of equal pay for equal work and the right not to be discriminated against on grounds of sex have been established in statute law. The establishment of these legal rights has undoubtedly been critical to equal opportunities development. The legislation and related changes in organizational and personal behaviour have probably been the most significant single force in fostering a wider acceptance of the principle of equality between the sexes. The challenges for the future relate, in the main, to the full application of equal opportunities policies.

Obvious and quantifiable evidence remains that women and men continue to experience different treatment at work. The substantial case law in relation to sexual harassment is one illustration of this point. Of particular importance, too, are the differences between the sexes in how each combines work and family life. Recent policy initiatives to develop a national infrastructure for childcare and enact parental leave legislation will be of particular benefit to working women. More fundamentally, the differences in the treatment of women and men at work may be charted in two interrelated labour-market phenomena – the male/female wage differential and vertical and horizontal segregation in the labour market.

Two emerging strands of policy, mainstreaming and positive action measures, are likely to be the focus of future action to address inequality. Positive action measures, targeted directly to compensate women and other groups for existing disadvantage, remain largely untried in this country. The Employment Equality Act, 1998 will allow their wider use for the first time in relation to sex discrimination. The specific provision for such measures in the Amsterdam Treaty and the clarity of recently emerging ECJ case law in the area may encourage an examination of the benefits of positive action initiatives both here and in other member states. Mainstreaming, the other emerging trend, involves the proofing of public policy decisions, schemes and expenditure to ensure that public policy does not reinforce existing disadvantage.

Commonly, positive action and mainstreaming are regarded as alternative policy options. There is some merit in regarding them as complementary aspects of a single equal opportunities agenda. One is focused and honed to address specific identifiable disadvantage, the other is grounded in the need to ensure that public policy decisions are at minimum neutral in their impact on disadvantaged groups. One of these options, or a complementary use of both, seem set to chart the immediate future of equal opportunities development in the EU in the coming years.

EU and national equal opportunities policy has been concerned primarily with equality between the sexes in the world of work. The work environment is a reflection of the wider society and so moves towards a more equal society will in turn increase the potential for full equality in the labour force. At the same time, the economic independence which work provides has, and continues to have, a bearing on women's status and influence outside the work environment.

RECOMMENDED READING

Callan, T. (1991) 'Male-Female Wage Differentials in Ireland', *Economic and Social Review*, 23: 55–72.

Curtin, D. (1988) *Irish Employment Equality Law*. Dublin: Round Hall Press Monographs.

Employment Equality Agency. *Annual Reports of the Employment Equality Agency 1994–97*. Dublin: EEA.

Second Commission on the Status of Women. *Report to Government* (January 1993). Dublin: Stationery Office, pp.91–131, 391–449.

Working Group on Childcare Facilities for Working Parents. *Report to the Minister for Equality and Law Reform* (February 1994). Dublin: Stationery Office.

REFERENCES

Blakemore, K. and R. Drake (1996) *Understanding Equal Opportunity Policies*. London: Prentice Hall/Harvester Wheatsheaf.

Callan, T. (1991) 'Male-Female Wage Differentials in Ireland', *Economic and Social Review*, 23: 55–72.

Callan, T. and A. Wren (1994) *Male/Female Wage Differentials: Analysis and Policy Issues*. Dublin: ESRI (General Research Series Paper No.163).

Commission on the Status of Women (1972) *Report to the Minister for Finance*. Dublin: Stationery Office.

Conroy Jackson, P. (1993) 'Managing Mothers: The Case of Ireland', pp. 72–91 in J. Lewis, (ed.), *Women and Social Policies in Europe: Work, Family and the State*. New York: Edward Elgar.

Cousins, M. (1996) *Pathways to Employment for Women Returning to Paid Work*. Dublin: Employment Equality Agency.

Curtin, D. (1988) *Irish Employment Equality Law*. Dublin: Round Hall.

Employment Equality Agency (1994–97) *Annual Reports*. Dublin: EEA.

Department of Enterprise, Trade and Employment (1998) *Ireland: Employment Action Plan*. Dublin: Stationery Office.

National Minimum Wage Commission (1998) *Report to the Minister for Enterprise, Trade and Employment*. Dublin: Stationery Office.

Partnership 2000 for Inclusion, Employment and Competitiveness (1996) Dublin: Stationery Office.

Prechal, S. and N. Burrows (1990) *Gender Discrimination Law of the European Community*. Aldershot: Dartmouth.

Ross, M. (1986) *Employment in the Public Domain in Recent Decades* (Paper No.127). Dublin: Economic and Social Research Institute.

Second Commission on the Status of Women (1993) *Report to the Government*. Dublin: Stationery Office.

Working Group on Childcare Facilities for Working Parents (1983) *Report to the Minister for Labour*. Dublin: Stationery Office.

Working Group on Childcare Facilities for Working Parents (1994) *Report to the Minister for Equality and Law Reform*. Dublin: Stationery Office.

Working Group on Childcare (1999) *National Childcare Strategy: Report of the Partnership 2000 Expert Working Group on Childcare*. Dublin: Stationery Office.

8

The Policy Process

Catherine Earley

INTRODUCTION

This chapter examines the complexities of the policy-making process as it applies to social policy in Ireland. At the outset, it will discuss what is meant by the term social policy. The first section describes the process of policy making, and the second section discusses some of the important factors which have a bearing on the development of social policies in Ireland. These include, among others, social values, norms and culture, the Constitution, Ireland's membership of the European Union, and the role of pressure groups, including the media and the Roman Catholic Church.

It should be made clear at this point that the emphasis in this chapter is on the process involved in the formation of social policy. The impact of policies are not, therefore, considered, except insofar as they have a bearing on the demands for changing social policy. This should not be taken to imply that an evaluation of existing policy is not a useful exercise (see Chapter 17, pp. 317–34). It means merely that it is not the focus of our attention here. Our attention is directed not towards the effect of policies; rather it is concerned with how those policies were arrived at in the first place. An understanding of this process is valuable for two reasons. The first is because an awareness of how and why existing policies developed provides a useful starting point for evaluating those policies. Secondly, knowledge of how the policy process works is crucial for those who wish to engage in contributing to that process.

THE POLICY-MAKING PROCESS

The process of developing social policy is a complicated and untidy one, and reaching some understanding of how the policy process works is almost as complex a task as the process itself. In order to make sense of it, it is useful to have a theoretical framework within which to locate not only the factors which influence the policy process, but also the process itself. There is a considerable body of literature on theoretical models of policy making (see O'Halpin, 1993 and Galligan, 1998 for valuable discussion on this). No one model, however, provides a totally comprehensive explanation of the policy process. The framework used here is based on systems theory. While a brief description is included here of the use of systems theory as a tool in understanding the policy process, readers are advised to refer to Hall et al. (1975: 24–40) for a more comprehensive explanation.

Systems theory, as it applies to the policy-making process, starts from the premise that human society consists of a series of systems and sub-systems, each interdependent upon and related to the other. One of the most important of these in any society is the political system, which is where the process of political activity, that leads ultimately to policy decisions, occurs. It should be noted here that systems theory perceives the political system not as a set of institutions, but rather as a set of behaviours or processes. There are, in any society, a great number of needs to be met from relatively scarce resources. Some of these needs are translated by key members of society, or by groups, or, indeed, by society as a whole, into demands for political action. These demands are directed at the political system, and can thus be seen as *inputs* into it. Demands can therefore be perceived as the raw materials of the political system. The number of demands presented to the system will usually be too great for the system to meet all of them, and so they must be reduced or regulated within the system. Some demands, as they are considered by the system, will not be met; others will be turned into issues for political resolution. It is on these issues that decisions will be made, and these decisions will then be directed back into society by the political system. Thus they become *outputs* from that system. Essentially, these outputs are what are usually called policies. In essence, therefore, the progress of demands for change through the political system can be characterized as the process of policy making.

The political system is the focus of demands for policy change. There are three aspects of the nature of demand which are important to mention here. The first and most important is that the efficiency with which the political system responds to the demands directed to it will have a bearing on that system's capacity to survive through time. The second is that demands for change can be generated either within the political system itself, or within the society it governs. Finally, the resources required to respond to demands will never be enough to meet all of them, and thus the system must find a way of controlling or regulating the flow of demands through it. The term resources, as used in this context, applies not only to those required to meet demands, but also those required to process them. This implies that the policy-making system must itself have resources – personnel, information, and structures, for example – to analyse and decide upon demands for change. There are those (Lee, 1989; Barrington, 1987) who have raised the question as to whether or not one of the blockages to policy development in Ireland is a lack of these very resources.

In order to cope with the range and number of demands for action on policy issues, all societies must develop mechanisms for regulating the level and flow of demands directed towards the political system. If this does not happen, then support within society for the political system will fall, and the system may face the danger of collapse. One of the most important of these mechanisms is known as *gatekeeping*. If the entry of a demand into the political system can be visualized as the start of a pathway or channel along which it will move to the point of political resolution, then it is also possible to perceive the notion of gateways along the channels through which the demands must pass. It is then possible to go further and visualize these gateways being controlled by gatekeepers, who are responsible for deciding which demands will proceed further and which will not. Gatekeepers exist widely in any society; they can be either individuals, in groups, or institutions who have the knowledge, or the influence, or both, to determine not only which wants will be converted into demands, but also how far those demands will progress once they are in the system. Thus they exist both in society generally, and within the political system itself. Any individual or group which is involved in an attempt to persuade government to introduce new social policies, or modify existing ones, is effectively engaged in the process of gatekeeping. Hence pressure groups seeking change in specific policies, trade unions or employer organizations, individual TDs seeking to further the interests of their constituents, all act as gatekeepers. But so also do civil servants and others who act as advisers to government.

Gatekeepers have considerable power and responsibility to influence the course of the policy process. Not only will they be involved in determining what wants or needs will be translated into demands for political action, they will also operate within the political system itself. Within the system, it is the gatekeepers who will decide which demands will progress to the point where they become issues for policy resolution and which will not. However, gatekeepers do not act in a vacuum; their activities will be constrained by the second set of mechanisms which are used to regulate the flow of demands through the political system. These are known broadly as cultural mechanisms, and they include all those influences in society which determine which demands are valid matters for political decision and which are not. Central social values and norms are extremely important elements of the cultural mechanisms which shape not only the demands articulated, but also the fate of those demands. It is important to remember in considering the role of cultural mechanisms in the policy process that these are not static. Rather they change and evolve through time. The history of social policy is littered with instances of demands for policy change which fell on deaf ears or met with opposition in particular times, only to succeed when the cultural or value climate changed. Policies directed towards the treatment of single mothers and their children provide a clear example of this. The influence of social values on the process of policy making will be discussed in more detail below (pp. 144–6).

The perceived effectiveness of existing social policies will also play a role in the creation of demands for policy change. The interlinkage between social policy and other aspects of government policy was discussed earlier; what is at issue here is the linkage which exists between various aspects of social policies and the way in which these give rise to demands for change in policies. For example, recent governments in Ireland have developed a series of policies aimed at easing the path of unemployed people back into the workforce. These have included job-creation schemes, training schemes and incentives, and changes in the relationship between earned income, taxation and social security. A number of separate government departments or agencies are involved in these developments, with the result that the ensuing set of policies does not appear to form a coherent whole. For example, an unemployed man seeking to return to paid employment will have to consider the various schemes for which he might be eligible; how any income from employment will compare with that to which he is entitled from social security; what, if any, impact it will have on any income his wife or partner may have; and what the implications are for his entitlement to secondary benefits, of which the medical card and rent allowance are the most significant. In addition, if he is not married to his partner, a whole new set of factors will need to be considered. The net result of all this is that policies aimed at returning people to work have become extremely complex, both to access and to administer. This has led to demands from a variety of organizations to modify or adapt these policies so that they are more compatible with each other and easier to administer.

Although systems theory perceives the political process as a set of behaviours rather than a set of institutions, the human beings that indulge in those behaviours inevitably establish institutions in order to accomplish their tasks. We know these institutions as government departments, the Oireachtas and the civil service. It is these institutions, together with others, which are responsible for the processing of demands for social policy change and making decisions thereon. In recent years in Ireland, the lines between the central institutions of political activity and the wider society have become somewhat blurred. This is due in part to decisions made to establish different forms of negotiation with those who have an interest, for whatever reason, in contributing to the policy process. The roles of farming and employer organizations and of trade unions have become more central to the policy process, through the establishment of what is known as a partnership process. This has resulted in recent years in the production of a number of agreements, the latest being *Partnership 2000* (1996). These agreements have become central features of government policy, and while the emphasis may be on matters like wage and salary levels, they nevertheless have very significant implications for social policy (see Chapter 9, pp. 155–77)

Institutions such as the National Economic and Social Forum, and the National Economic and Social Council, upon which all the social partners are represented, also indicate that the nature of the policy-making process in Ireland is undergoing considerable change at present. It must nevertheless be clear that the power to make decisions upon which policy is based remains with government. While these new institutions play an important role in policy making, they are not the only factors which contribute to the creation of demands for policy change or the acceptance of policy decisions once they have been formulated. Thus it is necessary to turn to consider some of the more important of these.

FACTORS INFLUENCING POLICY DEVELOPMENT

As stated earlier, social policy change does not occur in a vacuum. Furthermore, the success of any demand for policy change will often depend on the context within which it is made, on the individuals or groups backing the demand, and on the resources available to meet it. It is proposed here to outline some of the factors which influence the development of social policies in Ireland. Of necessity, this discussion will be brief, but a list of further reading at the end of this chapter will direct the interested reader to further investigation of this fascinating topic. It should be noted here that no inference should be drawn from the order in which the factors influencing social policies are discussed – the degree of importance of all or any of these factors will vary with different elements of policy and over time.

Social Policy and Social Values

The role of social values and culture in determining the shape and nature of social policies is enormous. There is space here only to provide a brief overview of how these are interlinked. For further reading on this issue, see Breen et al. (1990), Goldthorpe and Whelan (1992), Whelan (1994) and Galligan (1998). It should be clear that the development of social policy does not happen in a vacuum. Rather, it is ideologically and culturally specific. By that is meant that the society within which and for which such policies are developed will have an important bearing on their nature and shape. Part of the reason for that linkage is because social values will play an important role in determining which demands for change are perceived as valid issues for political resolution and which are not. But we should also bear in mind that these social values are not static, rather they change and adapt over time. Thus demands for social policy action which would have been out of the question in former times may well be perceived as valid today. Moreover, the manner in which social values evolve will be linked to other aspects of society. The clearest example of this in the Irish context is the degree to which Irish society has been modernized and urbanized in the past thirty years or so, and the impact which that shift has had on social values (see Powell, 1992: 269–328) for further discussion on the impact on modernization on social policy in Ireland). Those born since 1960 often do not have an appreciation of quite how much Irish society has changed in their lifetimes, for they do not remember that period about which Chubb (1982) was able to comment on the rural nature of Irish society, and the predominance of rural values, even up to the 1960s. This is hardly surprising, given that it was only in 1966 that for the first time the proportion of the population living in towns exceeded 50 per cent (Brown, 1985: 18). This same generation is usually surprised to learn that the ban on married women working in the public service was lifted as recently as 1973. These examples serve to illustrate just how much Irish society has changed in the latter half of this century, and this change has had inevitable effects both on social values and on the demands made on public social policy.

One clear example of this is the changing status and role of women in Ireland (see Chapter 13, pp. 231–53), which is best illustrated by the change in the pattern of married women in the paid labour force. Most recent figures appear to indicate that the proportion of married women as a percentage of all women in the labour force increased from a mere 6.8 per cent in 1951, to almost 50 per cent by 1996 (Galligan, 1998: 32). This has significant implications for many aspects of Irish social policy. In the context of this discussion, it should be clear that a social change of this magnitude will in itself affect the nature of demands for policy change in this area.

Another example of the impact of the changing nature of society on demands for social policy change can be drawn from changing attitudes to poverty. In the nineteenth century, the poor were generally divided into 'the deserving' and the 'undeserving' and dealt with accordingly by government policy (See Burke (1987) and Powell (1992)). But notions of citizenship and rights have changed radically over the past hundred years or so, and thus the idea of confining state support to those who are somehow defined as 'deserving' is quite foreign today. That is not to say, incidentally, that the idea of dividing poor people into deserving or undeserving has totally disappeared from the popular mind, merely that it is no longer politically acceptable as a basis on which to determine public policy. Indeed, it is interesting to note that the terms 'poverty' and 'the poor' have been replaced in recent years by the term 'social exclusion' (see, for example, recent reports issued by the Combat Poverty Agency and the National Economic and Social Forum; see also Ó Cinnéide, 1993).

Another more recent example of the influence of social values and norms on social policy development is evident in the issue of family planning legislation. All forms of what used to be known as artificial contraception were banned in Ireland from the 1930s. To most people in Ireland this was acceptable, or at the very least it could be said that this was an issue upon which there appeared to be no public demand for change. Thus any government which attempted to implement a policy on family planning in the 1930s, or even later, would have found it difficult if not impossible to do so. Indeed, John Kelly, a former Attorney-General and noted constitutional expert, commented, in discussing the Magee case, that 'nothing is more certain than that the Supreme Court of 1950, let alone 1940, . . . would have thrown her case out' (Kelly, 1988: 212). (The case referred to concerned Mrs Magee, who challenged the constitutionality of those sections of the Criminal Amendment Act, 1935 which banned the importation of contraceptives.) However, a change in social attitudes, the impact of the women's movement, a decline in the role of the Roman Catholic Church as a major player in the development of government policy, and increasing industrialization and urbanization from the late 1960s on led, in turn, to a change in the cultural and ideological climate which made possible the changes which occurred on this issue in the past twenty years or so (see Chapter 3, pp. 33–50). The main point from this discussion is that any analysis of the process of policy making, and most especially with regard to social policy, must take account of the context and culture within which that process is carried out. Social values will play a part both in defining demands for social policy change, and in how those demands are dealt with by those who have the task of progressing them through the policy-making process.

Social Policy and the Constitution

In considering the factors which influence the policy process in Ireland, one of the most important to be borne in mind is the existence of a written constitution. This is partly because the Constitution contains many statements which have a bearing on those aspects of Irish life to which social policies are relevant. (For detailed discussion on the Constitution and its impact on state policy in Ireland see, among others, Litton (1987), Powell (1992), Gallagher (1993)). Two of the aspects of the Constitution which have a bearing on the development of social policy are discussed here. The first is that all legislation extant in Ireland must be consistent with the Constitution. This means that governments may be constrained in the policies they can introduce by the tenets of the Constitution. For example, a change in the Constitution was required before legislation providing for the dissolution of marriage could be introduced. In addition, there have been instances where the provisions of the Constitution have led to difficulties for government in changing policy in a desired direction. One of the reasons why it took so long to modernize legislation concerning the care of children was the fear that any such legislation might be repugnant to the constitutional provisions in relation to the sovereignty of the family. More recently, the proposed employment equality legislation introduced by the coalition government in 1997 was found to be inconsistent with the Constitution, and the legislation required redrafting. Since much social policy is implemented by way of legislation, this is an extremely important factor which must be taken into account in the development of any policy which requires the backing of legislation.

The second feature of the Constitution which has an impact on the formation of social policy is that it is open to any citizen of the Republic of Ireland to challenge the constitutionality of any existing legislation, even where this had been in existence before the passage of the Constitution in 1937. A considerable amount of social policy change has occurred in the last thirty years or so by individual citizens undertaking such a challenge and succeeding, leading to a consequent requirement for changes in the law. The Magee case has already been referred to. The Murphy case of 1980 led to significant changes in the treatment of married women in the income tax code; the Hyland case of 1988 forced the government of the day to change the manner in which it has implemented a European Union directive on the treatment of men and women in social security.

Challenging the constitutionality of existing legislation is a clumsy way of implementing social policy change, for undertaking such a challenge carries no guarantee of success, as a number of people have found to their cost. For example, the Nicolau case of 1966, which challenged the constitutionality of the Adoption Act, 1953, failed to establish the rights of unmarried fathers to be consulted before the adoption of a child born outside marriage, and the case taken by David Norris, challenging the constitutionality of legislation which criminalized homosexual activity between consenting adults, also failed. He subsequently took his case to the European Court of Human Rights and won. Nevertheless, it has proved a useful tool on occasion in ensuring that the Constitution has played a significant part in developing social policy. It is worth remembering in this context the words of a former Minister for Education that our constitutional courts have played a large part in the process of 'dragging Ireland kicking and screaming into the twentieth century' (Scannell, 1988: 62).

The Constitution provides the citizens of this country with powerful protections. It has also provided some citizens with opportunities over the past three decades for the possibility of making an impact on the policy process. On the other hand, it has also imposed constraints on governments wishing to introduce policy change. However, in both guises, it forms an important part of the context within which social policy change occurs.

Social Policy and the European Union

Ireland became a member of what was then known as the European Economic Community in 1974. Although it was primarily concerned with matters economic, it has nevertheless had – and continues to have – an impact on the process of social policy development in this country, as in all other Member States. In considering this impact, it is important to note that the legislation of the European Union has the force of law in this country. The impact of the EU is manifold on social policy development in Ireland (Ó Cinnéide, 1993) (see Chapter 5, pp. 70–89, and Chapter 7, pp. 114–38). The impact will be discussed here in two illustrations. The first relates to the fact that the EU has moved in the past ten years beyond being an institution concerned primarily with economic issues, and has concerned itself increasingly with questions which have a direct bearing on social policy. These include the rights of employees in the workplace, the free movement of peoples, equality between men and women in social security law, and the right of citizens of Member States to access services such as health care in countries other than those in which they normally reside. One of the consequences for Ireland of this activity is the obligation of this state to ensure that the tenets of the EU are implemented. Pressure from the EU, for example, was one of the most important factors which led to the introduction of equal pay for work of equal value in 1974. It was also pressure from the EU which led to changes in the social security system resulting in greater equality of treatment between men and women in Ireland (see Chapter 7, pp. 114–38).

The obligation of the Irish Government to ensure that all Irish citizens have the rights guaranteed to them by the various Treaties which underpin the EU is one important way in which the EU has had an impact on Irish social policy development. A second significant aspect of our membership is the resources which are available to develop some aspects of social policy. For example, it was funds from Europe which provided the wherewithal in part to fund the variety of programmes which have been developed in recent years with the aim of dealing with poverty and social exclusion (see Chapter 6, pp. 90–113). Financial help from Europe has also played a crucial role in the development of industrial training in Ireland, and this in turn has an impact on the capacity of those without jobs to acquire the skills necessary to obtain employment.

However, there is another aspect to the influence of the EU on the development of social policy in Ireland which must be noted. The requirement to comply with EU policy on social policy related issues means that the Irish government is less free than it was in the past to determine its own social policy agenda. This in turn means that some demands for social policy change will remain further down the policy agenda than they might otherwise be. In addition, accessing funds from the EU usually means that some contribution to the same policies must be made by the Irish state. While this may well increase the funds available for the development of some aspects of social policy, it may also mean that there are fewer resources available to fund those policies which lie outside the remit of the EU.

The influence of the EU on the process of social policy formation in Ireland is considerable. This influence has both positive and negative aspects. Whether the balance between these two is to Ireland's benefit is left to the reader to decide.

The Policy Process and Pressure Groups

Pressure groups, or interest groups, come in a great variety of shapes, sizes and interests. (For a useful discussion of the role of pressure groups in Ireland, see Coakley and Gallagher, 1993.) They may represent the interests of specific groups of people, for example the trade unions, which represent the interests primarily of their members. They may be focused on specific aspects of social policy activity, as is the case for instance with the so called 'pro-life' organizations which have been active in the past fifteen years or so and which have campaigned to ensure that legal abortion would not be introduced in Ireland. They may be groups which have attempted to influence policy as an activity that is secondary to other activities, for example the Catholic Church, whose primary activities lie in quite another sphere, but whose activities in regard to influencing government policy cannot be dismissed. Finally, there are groups or institutions whose role as pressure groups are not always expressed as such, but who nevertheless can on occasion play a significant role in affecting the course of social policy formation. Chief among these are the media, in all its manifestations, and political parties. What pressure groups share, regardless of their size or focus, is an interest in influencing the course of policy change. The role of pressure groups in shaping both the demands for social policy change and the progress of those demands once they are within the political system is considerable. They act primarily, therefore, as gatekeepers in the policy process.

Clearly, some pressure groups will have more influence than others. The level of influence they can bring to bear on the policy process depends upon a wide variety of factors, including their specific area of interest, their skills at communicating their views and the support afforded their demands in society as a whole. Finally, the degree to which pressure groups can attach themselves to the central policy-making system will play a part in determining their effectiveness in influencing the policy process. One clear example of that in the recent past is that of the trade union movement, which has become an significant player in the development of economic and social policy in Ireland through its involvement in a partnership with government, employers, farmers and other groups as in, for example, Partnership 2000 and its predecessors.

Two pressure groups need consideration in somewhat more detail in the context of the policy formation process in Ireland – the Catholic Church and the media. While neither of these has pressure group activity as its prime function, they nevertheless could be described as having considerable roles to play both in the articulation of demands for policy change, and in the outcome of the policy process.

The Roman Catholic Church has for generations had a very powerful influence on the nature and shape of social policy in Ireland. The literature on the role of the Church in this context is extensive. The standard historical work is Whyte (1980); Inglis (1998) and Lee (1989) are also worth consulting. The influence of the Church happened for a number of reasons, including the adherence of so many Irish people to its beliefs and tenets, and the power afforded by Irish society generally and by successive governments to those who led the Church. Moreover, the role which the Church played in the delivery of a variety of social services, especially education and health care, meant that in the past the Church had not only influence, but power in the general area of social policy. However, the pace of change in Ireland, the recent scandals within the Church and the rate at which formal adherence to the Church is declining make it more difficult now than was the case in the past to assess its current role in the policy process. Inglis's description, for example, of the Church as a 'power bloc that operates mainly in the social and moral spheres of Irish life, but which also has a major influence on political and economic life' (1987: 6) is difficult to sustain as we approach the end of the twentieth century. However, we should be cautious about assuming that the decline in formal adherence to the Church is necessarily matched by an equal decline in its influence. While it is almost impossible that the Church today should have the influence it had, for example, over the Mother and Child Scheme in the late 1940s and early 1950s (Browne, 1986; Barrington, 1987), it must not be forgotten that the value system of the majority of Irish people today is still rooted in Catholicism. This means that any influence the Church attempts to exert on the policy process is likely at least to be taken into account by those with whom the responsibility lies for policy decisions. It might, perhaps, be fair to conclude that although the power of the Church to influence social policy which it possessed in the past has waned considerably, it nevertheless remains a pressure group of some influence in the shaping of social policy today. This is especially the case with regard to health care and education, not least because the Church continues to have a major role in the delivery of these services. To take a rather extreme example, it would be difficult to imagine the introduction of abortion facilities into a hospital run by nuns, as so many still are in Ireland.

The role of the media as a pressure group in the policy process is an interesting and not always positive one. The media, particularly the printed media, can play a key role in garnering support for some demands for policy change because, as O'Halpin has pointed out, the media 'are very important in forming public perceptions on policy issues because they are the principal means by which the public obtains news and analysis of national . . . affairs.' (1993: 203). Moreover, our system of 'clientist' government gives an added impetus to the role of the media in influencing the policy process (see Coakley and Gallagher (1993) for a discussion of 'clientism' in Irish politics). The media can also be involved in agenda-setting, in that there is a possibility that demands for policy change which become the focus of media attention may move up the list of priorities ahead of other, perhaps equally valid, issues, which do not, for whatever reason, acquire the same notice. We should be aware of the dangers of the media as an influence in setting the agenda in relation to social policy. Its own agenda is to sell newspapers, or acquire more viewers or listeners. There is therefore an inclination to choose issues which will do just that, and to present them in an overly simplistic fashion. Moreover, there is also the danger that the government of the day, especially when its majority is small, becomes reactive rather than proactive in setting a policy agenda and in the formation of social policy.

The Policy Process and Information

One factor which has the potential to have a powerful effect on the social policy process and which has thus far received little attention in the literature is information, or, more precisely, information technology. The development and availability of computers have begun to have an impact on analysing existing policy, and assessing the possible impact of proposed policies. As Henman has pointed out, 'if policy analysts are to fully appreciate the processes of policy making and the implications of policy, technology must be included in the analysis' (1997: 338). Technology has the capacity to play an increasing role on the evaluation of existing policies, and in their delivery. It also has the capacity to predict more accurately implications of a variety of potential social policy changes. Henman concludes that this means that not only must technology be therefore included in the factors which have an impact on the policy process, but that this impact should not be regarded as neutral (1997: 338).

A rather different way in which information may have the capacity to have an impact on the future development of social policy areas is the recent introduction in Ireland of the Freedom of Information Act, 1996. This legislation imposes upon all branches of government the obligation to make accessible all the legislation and other criteria which are used in the administration of the social services. Much of the publicity surrounding the passage of this legislation concerned the rights of individuals to gain access to any files held on them by government departments. However, the release into the public domain of information concerning the administration on the social services must, inevitably, have an impact in the future on the capacity of both individuals and pressure groups to become more active in the evaluation of existing policies, and defining demands for new ones. It is too early yet to predict precisely what that impact will be, but its potential cannot be ignored.

The elements listed here of those factors which influence the nature and shape of social policy in Ireland are by no means exhaustive. Moreover, it has been possible only to mention in outline the degree of influence which they possess. What is important to bear in mind is that they play an important part at several stages in the policy process, most notably in articulating demands for change, and in determining the success or failure of those demands as they progress through the policy process.

CONCLUSION

The process involved in the development of social policy in Ireland is complex, untidy, and fascinating to study. It starts from the creation of demands within society, or within the political system itself, and involves a complicated web of people, institutions and events. The model chosen here to try to make sense of this process is based on systems theory. Others may find different models more satisfactory in trying to come to grips with what is essentially an intricate and convoluted process. In reaching some understanding of how this process operates, and who the actors within it are, it is important to remember that this is not an academic exercise. The social policies developed and administered by the state have an impact on all citizens, usually for good, sometimes for ill, and the student of social policy has an obligation to reach some understanding of how the process works, and what contribution they can make to it.

RECOMMENDED READING

For those interested in the theoretical aspects of policy making, Hall et al. (1975), O'Halpin (1993) and Galligan (1998) constitute useful references. The range of literature on social values and the process of policy making in the Irish context is extensive: Chubb (1982), Breen et al. (1990), Goldthorpe and Whelan (1992), Whelan (1994) and Galligan (1998) are especially recommended. Those interested in the role of the Constitution and policy making are referred to Litton (1982), Powell (1992) and Gallagher (1993). The influence of the Catholic Church on the policy-making process, especially in a historical context, is discussed in Whyte (1980), Inglis (1998) and Lee (1989).

REFERENCES

Barrington, R. (1987) *Health, Medicine and Politics*. Dublin: Institute of Public Administration.

Breen, R., D. Hannan, D. Rothman and C. Whelan (1990) *Understanding Contemporary Ireland*. Dublin: Gill & Macmillan.

Brown, T. (1985) *Ireland, A Social and Cultural History*. London: Fontana.

Browne, N. (1986) *Against the Tide*. Dublin: Gill & Macmillan.

Burke, H. (1987) *The People and the Poor Law*. Dublin: Women's Educational Bureau.

Chubb, B. (1982) *The Government and Politics of Ireland*. Dublin: Gill & Macmillan.

Coakley, J. and M. Gallagher (eds) (1993) *Politics in the Republic of Ireland*. Dublin: Folens.

Constitution of Ireland (1937) Dublin: Government Publications.

Cousins, M. (1995). *The Irish Social Welfare System: Law and Social Policy*. Dublin: Round Hall Press.

Gallagher, M. (1993) 'The Constitution', in J. Coakley and M. Gallagher (eds), *Politics in the Republic of Ireland*. Dublin: Folens.

Galligan, Y. (1998) *Women and Politics in Contemporary Ireland*. London: Pinter.

Goldthorpe, J.H. and C. T. Whelan (eds) (1992) *The Development of Industrial Society in Ireland*. Oxford: Oxford University Press.

Hall, P., H. Land, R. Parker and A. Webb (1975) *Change, Choice and Conflict in Social Policy*. London: Heineman.

Henman, P. (1997) 'Computer technology – a Political Player in Social Policy', *Journal of Social Policy*, 26 (3) 323–40.

Inglis, T. (1997) *Moral Monopoly: The Catholic Church in Modern Irish Society*. Dublin: Gill & Macmillan.

Inglis T. (1998) *Moral Monopoly: The Rise and Fall of the Catholic Church in Modern Ireland*. 2nd edition. Dublin: University College Dublin Press.

Kelly, J. (1988) 'The Constitution: Law and Manifesto', in F. Litton (ed.), *The Constitution of Ireland*. Dublin: Institute of Public Administration.

Lee, J. (1989) *Ireland, 1912–1985*. Cambridge: Cambridge University Press.

Litton, F. (ed.) (1982) *Unequal Achievement: the Irish Experience, 1957–1982*. Dublin: Institute of Public Administration.

Litton, F. (ed.) (1987) *The Constitution of Ireland, 1937–1987*. Report No.5. Dublin: Institute of Public Administration.

National Economic and Social Council (1975) *An Approach to Social Policy*. Dublin: Stationery Office.

Ó Cinnéide, S. (ed.) (1993) *Social Europe: EC Social Policy and Ireland*. Dublin: Institute of European Affairs.

O'Halpin, E. (1993) 'Policy Making', in J. Coakley and M. Gallagher (eds), *Politics in the Republic of Ireland*. Dublin: Folens.

Partnership 2000 for Inclusion, Employment and Competitiveness (1996) Dublin: Stationery Office.

Powell, F. (1992) *The Politics of Irish Social Policy, 1600–1990*. Lampeter: Edward Mellon Press.

Scannell, Y. (1988). 'The Constitution and the Role of Women', in B. Farrell (ed.), *De Valera's Constitution and Ours*. Dublin: Gill & Macmillan

Whelan, C. T. (ed.) (1994) *Values and Social Change in Ireland*. Dublin: Gill &
    Macmillan.
Whyte, J.H. (1980) *Church and State in Modern Ireland, 1923–1979*. Dublin: Gill &
    Macmillan.

9

Social Partnership in Ireland: Emergence and Process

Michael Rush

INTRODUCTION

Understanding the organization of welfare regimes in capitalist societies involves paying attention to a range of social processes and practices (O'Brien and Penna, 1998; Mishra, 1990; Kemeny, 1995). The organization of welfare in Ireland is increasingly being influenced by the concept and adopted strategy of social partnership within a corporatist framework. This chapter will describe the emergence of this influence, by tracing the social processes and practices in Ireland from the 1950s. It will then outline existing Irish social partnership structures and provide an evaluation of these structures. The role of community development, local policy networks, local government and trade unions within social partnership will conclude the chapter.

THE NATIONAL ECONOMIC AND SOCIAL COUNCIL: TOWARDS A 'SOCIAL' POLICY REGIME FOR IRELAND IN EUROPE

From a situation of despair and crisis in the mid-1980s, Ireland has been developing a model of economic and social governance based on social partnership – at first, since 1987, at the national level (Sabel, 1996; O'Donnell and Thomas, 1998), and more recently at the local level since 1991 (Craig, 1994; Sabel, 1996). At the national level, the National Economic and Social Council (NESC) is the mechanism or body where Irish social partners (academics, government advisors, civil servants, trade unionists and business, farming and community and voluntary interests) create strategies for economic and social policy in Ireland. More recently the efforts of the NESC have been supported by the creation of the National Economic and Social Forum (NESF) in 1993. The membership of the NESF was the first to be widened so that Irish 'social partners' now include Catholic and Protestant church interests and voluntary and community organizations.

In recognition of the key role of the NESC (a role which will be returned to later in this chapter, p. 163), it is worth noting a report which was commissioned in May 1987, the year the current phase of social partnership was initiated. The report's main concern was the implications of Ireland's membership of the European Community. The following quotation from *Ireland in the European Community, Performance, Prospects and Strategy* (NESC, 1989: 509) illustrates Ireland's burgeoning commitment to developing national and European social policy regimes:

> The levels of economic growth required to significantly improve employ-
> ment levels – both in Ireland and in the Community as a whole – will
> require a suitable regime of co-ordinated macroeconomic policies. Such a
> regime because of its potentially beneficial effects on growth, and hence
> employment levels, would constitute a 'social' policy.

One of four main elements of the 'regime' is the 'removal of major inequities in society' and one of the two key requirements of the 'regime' is:

> continued consensus among the social partners, at the national level, and
> at the level of the firm, to ensure a swift and flexible response that is most
> conducive to the objective of fuller employment, higher living standards
> and a better social framework. (NESC, 1989: 557)

In the late 1980s the development of social policy at the national and local levels, through social partnership, was mainly restricted to the considerations and mechanisms of economic and employment growth and the organization of work and (predominantly male) paid employment. In the 1990s there has been a phased inclusion of religious, voluntary and community interests and the expansion of the 'local' to include local government and local development considerations. The expansion of social partnership to bring further employment and economic growth has brought debates on mainstream social policy issues such as income maintenance strategies, the provision of essential public services and reform of local government to the centre of social partnership debates and the modernization of Irish social policy. Elaboration on these debates and discussions in relation to employment, gender, social exclusion and the commodification of care labour, and an understanding of why Ireland is, according to the OECD (Sabel 1996), at the forefront of 'democratic experimentalism' requires a review of its modernization process.

THE HISTORICAL CONTEXT OF SOCIAL PARTNERSHIP

Free Market Stability and Social Polarization 1950s–1990s

A modernizing core 'elite' or post–colonial cadre had been forming in Ireland since before the 1940s which consisted of senior civil servants, academic government advisors and a small number of politicians (Breen et al., 1990: 16). The result of their deliberations was the *Programme for Economic Expansion* (1958), which followed the report *Economic Development* (Department of Finance, 1958). The report and the subsequent programme came at a time when there had been serious doubt as to whether political independence had been a failure. National self–doubt was a legacy of the decades of emigration, slow economic growth, slow job creation and the failure of protectionism and self–sufficiency (Whittaker, 1986; Breen et al., 1990). From 1958 the state facilitated foreign investment broke with protectionism and initiated a commitment to free trade with Western Europe. The fulfilment of these actions was full accession to the European Community in 1973 and progress away from residualism and towards corporatism with regard to industrial relations (Breen et al., 1990:150). Breen et al. concluded that, despite the depth of transformation in Ireland since the 1950s, stability rather than change prevailed, with class polarization and distinction being stoutly maintained in the face of successful economic development.

Education, Expansion of Statutory Employment and Exclusions

The distribution of educational disadvantage has been significant in the shaping of society in Ireland since the 1960s. Farm families responded to declining employment opportunities with high participation rates in education as a route to white collar occupations; urban low–income families especially in Dublin have failed to do so (NESC, 1996: 9). The expansion of the state from the 1960s was accompanied by the creation of 110,000 jobs for the more advantaged employee categories within the public sector, virtually all of them in Dublin.

From the 1960s to the late 1980s the size and capacity of the state infrastructure increased considerably, augmented by state–sponsored bodies. The state's responsibility for those families excluded from the development of the free market economy was restricted mainly to income maintenance. It was the development of the market economy and the maintenance of stable industrial relations which dominated tripartite government programmes in the 1960s and 1970s with the state acting as facilitator in the negotiation of national wage agreements. Employment or improvements for the excluded classes was never really a serious option (Breen et al. 1990: 158).

Opposition within the Modernization Process

The main opposition to the processes of social exclusion and the uneven distribution of slow economic growth, social instability and polarization, came from the political left, some of the Catholic clergy, urban and rural community development organizations and feminist interests. Many of these organizations had developed during the 1970s and early 1980s in response to series of crises: heroin usage, poor housing conditions, unemployment, household poverty, rural migration (Kelleher and Whelan, 1990) and control over women's economic, social and reproductive rights (Kelleher and Whelan, 1990; Conroy Jackson, 1993; Yeates, 1995; McLaughlin and Rodgers, 1997).

A radical agenda or manifesto for much of this opposition was established in 1971 with the Kilkenny Poverty Conference organized by the Catholic Bishops' Council for Social Welfare which provided the transcripts for the seminal *One Million Poor* (Kennedy et al., 1972). The contemporary and historical recognition of significance of the Kilkenny Poverty Conference, and perhaps more importantly the contemporary understanding of the unsustainability of market driven social policy, is articulated by McCarthy (1998: 39):

> In this context a crisis of the state began to emerge. The economic levers that appeared to be reliably at the disposal of the state were no longer delivering growth, employment and stability. On the contrary, particularly in the wake of the oil crisis in the 1970s, we were getting problems of stagnation in countries at different stages of the economic cycle. The particular problem that we saw in Ireland was that trying to spend our way out of an international recession very rapidly proved to be pointless because we set off a very unstable situation. The social counterpart of this was evidence, perhaps not so much from Ireland (although we had the Kilkenny Poverty Conference) indicating a problem of deeper inequality.

Rather than embracing community development and church criticisms and solutions, it has been argued that the state responded piecemeal to alternative approaches and solutions in the absence of any coherent public policies to tackle poverty and social exclusion (Ó Cinnéide and Walsh, 1990: 333).

Long-Term Unemployment

The background to the programmes of the 1950s and 1980s was overall doubt and specifically economic failure. In contrast, the background to the 1990s is the unevenness of the distribution of medium-term economic success. There have been four key and interdependent areas of success since the 1960s: strong economic growth, the change from an agricultural to a modern industrial economy, an increase in living standards and the attraction of inward investment, all in a matter of four decades. The key issue in the early 1990s became the limited impact of successful modernization on unemployment, particularly long term unemployment (NESC, 1990; NESC, 1996: 3).

It was argued that the uneven distribution of success within society and the failure to impact significantly on long-term unemployment over generations since the 1950s had led to the situation of an underclass being reproduced through educational and training systems and sustained through social welfare provision (Breen et al., 1990: 158). This interpretation has been developed and argued over the 1990s, primarily by Nolan and Callan (1994) who suggest that concepts of an urban underclass are not central to an understanding of Irish poverty but that the concept of cumulative urban disadvantages did merit a policy response.

This interpretation has been supported and developed by Curtin et al. (1996: 72) who argued that deprivation in Ireland is a spatially pervasive phenomenon which affected almost every part of the country, and is clustered in particular areas, particularly in the urban areas of Dublin, Galway, Limerick, Cork, Waterford and Drogheda, and the rural areas of Donegal, Mayo, the border areas of Leitrim, Cavan and Monaghan with pockets of deprivation in Roscommon, North Kerry and Clare.

The dismissal by Nolan and Callan (1994) of the relevance of the concept of the underclass to Ireland supports studies showing that the long-term unemployed and other socially excluded individuals, in spite of their social exclusion, continue to orient themselves towards and to hold mainstream values (Anderson and Larsen, 1995a: 175).

Anderson and Larsen have supported the contention that the idealized male model of lifetime permanent employment is implicit in the underclass concept. The concept overlooks the gender restructuring of paid employment in the post-war period (Bagguley and Mann, 1992: 123). The underclass debate, particularly the focus on one-parent families, has been illustrated as an anti-feminist backlash with severe implications for social policy and gender equality (Faludi, 1992; Morris, 1994; Anderson and Larsen, 1995a).

However, when dismissing the concept of the underclass as unhelpful, Nolan and Callan (1994) were also questioning the relevance of the Area-Based Partnerships as a spatial selective response to long-term unemployment and poverty. The problem addressed by Nolan and Callan is that when unemployment is used as the only indicator of deprivation, then key deprived areas including those with low educational attainment and small farmers might be missed. Area-based approaches now take cognizance of a range of demographic deprivation indicators (Haase, 1998), rather than relying on material deprivation indicators or long-term unemployment administrative data.

The implicit criticism of area-based responses implies among other things a dichotomy between universal and selective policy. The suggestion of a dichotomy between universalism and selectivity has dominated a great deal of sociological study of welfare regimes, and serves to marginalize area-based and community development responses. The experience gained by academics, community development activists and statutory agencies from their experiences in the Poverty III programme has led to suggestions that this dichotomy needs to be questioned and critically re-examined (Anderson and Larsen, 1995a: 176).

Nationally Negotiated Programmes since 1987 and Long-Term Modernization

The limitations of long term modernization in Ireland have been identified throughout the 1990s. Key examples of the limitations include: the weakness of income support for households in the child rearing stages of family production (Breen et al., 1990: 97); the strains on the conventional institutional arrangements of family or household, particularly in urban areas of deprivation, (Breen et al., 1990: 121); housing policy and the atrophization of local government (Sabel, 1996: 37); the failure of children from low-income urban households to participate within the education system (NESC, 1996: 9), particularly within Dublin, resulting in early school leaving, problems of literacy, the risk of unemployment and long-term unemployment itself (NESC, 1990; Nolan and Callan, 1994; Task Force on Long Term Unemployment, Office of the Tánaiste, 1995; NESF, 1995). The major difficulty facing the modernization process, according to the NESC, was the increase in the labour force during the 1980s and the resulting rise in the dependency ratio (NESC, 1996: 3). However as late as 1992 only 43.5 per cent of the Irish adult population were in paid employment, with two-thirds of all women and one-third of all men without any paid occupation (Drudy, 1995: 307).

The limitations of modernization remain acute in Ireland in the late 1990s. Continuity and success is implicit in the portrayal of the modernization process since the 1960s by the NESC (1996: 1–11). It is therefore critical to recall the circumstances which led to the partnership approach in the late 1980s. These circumstances are illustrated by Sabel (1996: 39):

> The dilemma was this: by the mid-1980s explosive growth of the public debt gave rise to credible fears that the Irish government could default on its obligations. . . At a decade's distance, it is sometimes hard for the

Irish themselves to recall the urgency of the macroeconomic crisis of the mid-1980s.

The emergence of a process of Irish social partnership in 1987 was preceded by unsuccessful attempts at national agreements in the years between 1970 and 1981, and minimal state involvement between 1981 and 1987. In fact as late as 1988 it was considered that the chances of inclusionary bargaining agreements in Ireland were slim (Hardiman, 1988; Sabel, 1996). Breen et al. (1990: 179) concluded that the trade union movement in Ireland was insufficiently organized both at national and company level to move the country into a neo-corporatist approach where labour quiescence is exchanged for low levels of unemployment. However from the 1960s the state had been gradually moving away from a residual role in relation to industrial relations and a variety of bodies were established which included trade union and employer representation (Breen et al., 1990: 162; O'Donnell and Thomas, 1998: 117). One signal of a change in the nature of the Irish trade union movement was the establishment in 1985 of the Centres for the Unemployed in areas of high unemployment which gave the trade unions a responsibility beyond sectional interests (Sabel, 1996: 41).

The question has been posed whether social partnership since 1987 represents a 'distinct phase' and whether the success of social partnership requires a re-examination of the requirements for effective concertation, i.e. working together (O'Donnell and Thomas, 1998: 118). The establishment of the Centres for the Unemployed and their area-based approach could be included within such a re-examination. In relation to the success of social partnership, it has been measured through its contribution – however difficult to quantify – to improvement in public finances, lower inflation, collective bargaining agreements, economic growth, employment growth, manufacturing output and export growth (Sabel, 1996). In relation to local social partnership arrangements pressure from, and the growth of, community development, religious and feminist groups throughout the 1970s and 1980s would also need re-appraising.

In terms of continuity, the period since 1987 can be seen as a rapid acceleration in the modernization of Ireland. In relation to change there are distinct differences in terms of objectives and process:

Changes in Objectives

- The introduction of the objectives of social inclusion and social equality.
- A contribution to the development of European social and economic policy.

Changes in Process

- The creation of the National Economic and Social Council in 1973 to replace the previous role of the Department of Finance in 1958 .

- The introduction of tripartartite corporatism in 1987 to replace the post-colonial core elite of 1957.

- The creation of the National Economic and Social Forum in 1993.

- The extension of social partnership beyond tripartism through the incorporation of religious, voluntary and community interests.

- The extension of social partnership to the local level and the widening of the local agenda beyond purely commercial considerations.

The Department of the Taoiseach provides the negotiating skills which are critical to extending pluralism of discourse nationally, and the Four Pillars of social partnership (described in the next section), to arrive at a consensus.

IRISH PARTNERSHIP STRUCTURES

Nationally Agreed Programmes since 1987

Four programmes have been nationally agreed since 1987:

The Programme for National Recovery (PNR) 1987–90,
The Programme for Economic and Social Progress (PESP) 1990–93,
The Programme for Competitiveness and Work (PCW) 1994–96
The Partnership 2000 Agreement 1997–2000.

Each programme has been preceded by a report by the National Economic and Social Council (NESC):

Strategy for Development (1986)
A Strategy for the Nineties (1990)
A Strategy for Competitiveness, Growth and Employment (1993)
Strategy into the Twenty-First Century (1996)

These reports and programmes mark a qualitative development on previous programmes since the publication of *Economic Expansion* (1958) and *The Programme for Economic Expansion* (1958), both in terms of participation and content. Social inclusion is part of the agenda of social partnership which seeks to reverse the social exclusion and social polarization which has resulted in Ireland from modernization.

The Four Pillars of National Social Partnership

There are now four 'pillars' of representation within national partnership mechanisms. These are (*a*) the farming organizations, (*b*) the trade unions, (*c*) the community and voluntary organizations, and (*d*) the employer and business organizations. For a detailed and comprehensive discussion of the role and composition of the four pillars, see O'Donnell and Thomas (1998).

The Four Pillars of the Social Partnership

1 *Farming Organizations*
   Irish Farming Organisation (IFA)
   Irish Creamery and Milk Suppliers Association (ICSMA)
   Macra na Feirme
   Irish Co-operative Society (ICOS)
2 *Trade Unions*
   Irish Congress of Trade Unions (ICTU)
3 *Community and Voluntary Organizations*
   Irish National Organisation of the Unemployed (INOU)
   National Women's Council of Ireland (NWCI)
   National Youth Council of Ireland (NYCI)
   Committee of Religious Superiors (CORI)
   Centres for the Unemployed (ICTU-recognized)
   Society of St Vincent de Paul
   Protestant Aid
   Community Platform
4 *Employer and Business Organizations*
   Irish Business and Employers' Confederation (IBEC)
   Construction Industry Federation (CIF)
   Chambers of Commerce of Ireland (CCI)
   Irish Tourist Industry Confederation (ITIC)
   Irish Exporters Association (IEA)
   Small Firms Association (SFA)

The National Economic and Social Council (NESC) and the National Economic and Social Forum (NESF)

The National Economic and Social Council (NESC), established in 1973, provides a forum for discussion on economic development and social justice and advises the government through the Department of the Taoiseach. The NESC has widened its membership through the appointment of government nominees. NESC highlighted the importance of civic associations, community groups and voluntary associations in areas of sport, culture, voluntary action, self-help groups and other areas as key sources for the capacities required for successful economic and social life in the modern world (NESC, 1996: 11).

The National Economic and Social Forum was established in 1993 and included the traditional social partners, trade unions, farming organizations and employers, but also the community and voluntary sector and the main political parties. The NESF widened the process of partnership considerably. Its role was to develop economic and social policy with a particular brief to tackle long-term unemployment. The experience gained by the community representatives and the Catholic Church through their participation on the NESF brought them into the national partnership discussions by the time the Partnership 2000 agreement was being framed. Participation by the employer and business organizations was also widened to include new representative organizations.

Central Review Committee (CRC), Area Development Management (ADM), Area Based Partnerships (ABPs), Partnerships for Local Action Network (PLANET), Strategic Management Initiative (SMI)

The Programme for National Recovery (PNR) in 1987 called for the establishment of the Central Review Committee (CRC) to ensure cooperation between the state and the social partners in monitoring implementation of the programme. In order to enter into tripartite arrangements, the trade unions had accepted reductions in public spending and agreed to moderate wage demands. It was agreed there would be no cuts in social welfare payments. Participation on the CRC led the trade unions and the state to look for new areas of activity for social partnership arrangements. In response to the NESC's influential *Strategy for the Nineties* which highlighted unemployment as the most critical issue to be addressed, the Programme for Economic and Social Progress (1990–93) called for the establishment of twelve pilot Area Based Partnerships (ABPs) as an area based response to long-term unemployment. There are now 38 such ABPs which are local partnership companies. They broke with national tripartism mechanisms through the involvement of community of civic representation, alongside the state and the social partners. Prior to the establishment of the Area Based Partnerships, many partnerships were established in the late 1980s. The first partnerships to involve local marginalized groups were set up as social integration projects under the Poverty III Programme from 1989–94. The accepted narrative for the establishment of the Area Based partnerships locates their origins at the national level of social partnership, with NESC, the PESP, trade unions and the Department of the Taoiseach (Sabel, 1996: 41). An alternative narrative is that pressure on central mechanisms of social partnership and government came throughout the 1980s from the community sector for participatory approaches to local development, which were enhanced by experiences of partnership in Poverty III and the directives of the European Commission. However, even the alternative narratives recognize the key role of the trade union movement at the national level (Turok et al., 1998).

Area Development Management (ADM) is a private company with partnership representation which was established to service the area-based Partnerships. ADM facilitates a number of working groups at the national level through which the local Area Based Partnerships seek to learn from each other's experiences and inform the national policy process, along with national social partners. Extending social partnership to the local level is regarded as a particularly innovative feature of 'democratic experimentalism' (Sabel, 1996: 43). Partnerships for Local Action Network (PLANET) is the organization which has been formed by the 38 local area partnerships to come together at national level.

The Strategic Management Initiative (SMI) is a state initiative within each government department and across all department structures and processes, to develop and implement a programme of change to achieve an excellent service by the civil service for the government and the public, as customers and clients at all levels.

Measuring Success or Failure

Area-based policies and the targeting of assistance through the identification of the District Electoral Divisions (DEDs) with the highest levels of unemployment can form an element within any overall strategy to address poverty in Ireland (Nolan and Callan, 1994: 237). The width and breadth of the focus of such policies determine what percentage of the poor are being targeted, and what percentage of the non-poor also fall within the boundaries of the focus. The implicit suggestion is that widening the focus of policies could weaken their targeting nature, although it has been suggested that the spreading of area based partnerships throughout the country is a rational response to the fact that poverty is not spatially concentrated. Area Development Management (ADM) has been commended by Haase for their systematic targeting of the most disadvantaged areas based on 13 indicators of deprivation within District Electoral Divisions, developed by Haase himself and produced as a map of overall affluence and deprivation in Ireland. It has been claimed that:

the Irish Partnership initiative is one of the most advanced in utilising census based and geographical information systems to inform systematically urban and rural policies to combat unemployment and social exclusion. (Haase, 1998: 30)

Ireland, however, appears to be following to some extent the dominant paradigm of the 1990s by attempting to address spatial exclusion, in a way which is imperceptible to the wider public and to some extent through the offer of assistance and protection to active labour market participants (Offe, 1991: 138; Taylor, 1995: 37).

Degrees of poverty are determined mainly by the tax and social welfare systems, job availability and, to a limited degree, low pay. Since the development of the current phase of Partnership in Ireland and the Programme approach to policy in Ireland, there has been a sharp rise in the numbers falling below 60 per cent income poverty lines, to approximately one-third of all households in the Republic, while those suffering from basic deprivation has fallen from 16 per cent to 15 per cent (Callan et al., 1996: 80). There has been a fall in unemployment live register figures from 282,897 in June 1996, to 228, 937 in June 1998 – a fall of approximately 20 per cent. This is a significant fall and one which has to qualify the pessimism of Taylor (1995: 44):

> And yet the most optimistic observers appear resigned to the fact that growth rates in excess of 5% will be insufficient to reduce significantly the current levels of unemployment. It seems quite clear that along with most of its western European counterparts, high levels of unemployment will remain a semi-permanent feature of the Irish economy.

To what extent these falls are impacting on participation on the numerous labour market programmes is not clear, nor is it clear how many long-term unemployed persons reappear on the live register as short-term unemployed, following such participation.

COMMUNITY DEVELOPMENT AND SOCIAL PARTNERHSIP EXPERIENCE

Participation and Community Development

The term community is increasingly appearing as a feature of the structures and/or aims of public administration (Mayo, 1994). Community development has re-emerged in Ireland from the 1970s and has been used to describe the activist-driven response to urban planning, rural development, unemployment and meeting social needs, particularly those of children and young people (Conroy, 1997). The process has contributed to the growth of area-based women's organizations (Commins,

1979; Keunstler, 1979; Lavan, 1981, Kelleher and Whelan, 1990; Ó Cinnéide and Walsh, 1990; Frazer, 1992; O'Cearbhaill, 1991; Conroy Jackson, 1993; Area Development Management, 1994; Lloyd, 1998).

The growth of the role of community development within Irish public administration and social policy has been in the context of six key developments: the growth of the health boards' community care programme since the 1970s; the relegation of the Social Service Councils (Faughnan, 1990; Ó Cinnéide and Walsh, 1990); urban activism and the Save the West Campaigns in the 1960s and 1970s; the community anti-poverty projects, established after pressure from the Labour Party and the Catholic Church, which resulted in the establishment of the national Pilot Schemes to Combat Poverty and the Combat Povety Agency (Mernagh, 1981; Ó Cinnéide and Walsh, 1990); the establishment of the Community Development Projects funded by the Department of Social Welfare from the late 1980s (Craig, 1994); the introduction of the Area Based Partnerships in 1991 (Cullen, 1994); and the significant growth of labour market programmes, especially Community Employment since 1993 (WRC, 1996).

NESC (1996: 65) has suggested that partnership could be deepened and widened without its effectiveness being undermined. The current national agreement for the first time included the voluntary and community sector in negotiations. The Community Platform is the largest of the non-religious social partners within the 'social pillar'. The Community Platform was established by the Community Workers Co-op (CWC). Although it has been suggested that participation in the national structures of partnership has been an empowering process for the community sector and its representatives (not least through the development of sophisticated negotiation skills), there are fears that the state's agenda does not include empowerment and sustainability of the community sector (Crowley, 1998; Zappone, 1998). Although the experience gained on the ground by women through the provision and management of local community services is positive, women are not reflected within the partnership hierarchy. An inclusive way of working or any attempt by men to release power is also absent. Relationships on the ground, however, revealed the gender imbalance within the statutory sector (McEvoy, 1998). It has been suggested in relation to these debates that the state may need to comprehend that the development agenda goes beyond a consumerist approach and contains a vision for a sustainable and equitable society (Kirby, 1998: 89).

For the first time, the main voices of state criticism or opposition from the 1970s and 1980s, the Catholic clergy and the voluntary and community organizations, are included in (non-wage) national programme

negotiations. Although the Catholic clergy and the community development sector were effectively voices of opposition throughout the
modernization period, their opposition was arguably a result of their
marginalization. Since the mid-1980s, the majority of these groups have
been involved in programme delivery and a degree of concertation.

Marginalization can result in invisibility as in the case of one of
Ireland's most pioneering community development organizations, Muintir
na Tíre. During the late 1950s and early 1960s, Muintir na Tíre played a
major role in the evolution of community development in Ireland. By
the early 1990s it was recognized that the voice of Muintir na Tíre was
in danger of being lost without the appropriate funding being fought for
or negotiated (Devereux, 1993). Muintir played a pioneering role in its
advocacy of community participation in the planning of state agency
delivery of public services (Thomason and Leaper, 1963: 16).

Muintir na Tíre made a significant contribution to the provision of a
rural infrastructure, including schemes for electrification, water schemes
and the building of community halls. Their methods were essentially
conservative with the leadership being drawn from the clergy, teaching
and medical professions. Muintir attempted to play down class antagonisms
in favour of getting things done (Kelleher and Whelan, 1990). Community
development in Ireland was a collaborative project which only through
marginalization became a voice of discontent and opposition.

The Charlestown Committee, the Gaeltacht Civil Rights Movement
and the Save the West movements of the 1960s had the support of
organizations such as Macra na Feirme and the Catholic clergy. These
campaigns suggested alternatives to government developmental policies
and demanded the right of local community groups to choose and
implement their own local development plans.

Infrastructures for Participation and Action

Lloyd (1996: 18) has proposed a three-stage (local/community) development process which depends on the development of networks and
participative structures. An area in stage one has few projects to link and
no Community Development Projects. In stage one areas, there is a
need to work together to form projects.

In stage two, there are Community Development Projects (through
the Department of Social Community and Family Affairs) in place and
therefore stage two is more about enhancing the level of activity in an
area. This is the time to build networks, develop new substantial projects
with a large range of beneficiaries and develop large-scale proposals. As
networks grow, so does the volume of work carried out. Networks are

by no means exclusively open only to the sector, otherwise they will be limited in terms of linkages and synergy.

The third stage is where the sector has at its disposal sufficient economic and cultural capital to begin to infleunce the overall agenda. It can look at enterprise, job creation and structures which contribute to social disadvantage. Now the sector can push the agenda upwards towards central government. At this stage the area has developed a local area (policy) network.

These types of structures, while perhaps fragile, are not easily going to disappear and it would seem that at the level of the local authority they are welcomed for the purposes of their capacity in terms of depth of consultation and mobilization. It has been suggested that there are limitations to the extent that local community networks can influence national policy when compared, for example, to farmers' organizations (Curtin and Varley, 1995). Local networks responded well to the local anti-heroin activists and helped significantly in acquiring a central response; however it is at the local authority level that they are primarily engaged.

These community structures are emerging at the local level with greater turnover of leadership. However, these are local area-based structures and their recognition so far has been confined to the statutory bodies at the local level and local authorities. At the core of the new Irish 'democratic experimentalism' are the area-based partnerships (Sabel, 1995). But at their core are the local area and interest based networks which provide their context (Lloyd, 1996; Watt, 1996).

The structures or mechanisms for local collaboration and participation operate under a variety of names, forums, networks and are at different stages of development (Lloyd, 1996; Watt, 1996). However, whereas some structures will be established and perhaps resourced by partnership bodies to support the partnership body itself, the only effective ones will be those which operate within an autonomous context and for whom participation on partnership bodies at the local level and the national level is a necessary longer-term strategic distraction from their everyday activity, in a similar fashion to the pillars at national level (Lynham, 1996).

Importantly, Lynham has highlighted the responsibility of other sectors to support and work cooperatively with the community sector in the delivery of the Local Development Programme and the wider community development process. From an OECD perspective, a key purpose of Area Based Partnerships is 'the strategy of bringing the lower levels of the specialised bureaucracies into the area-based partnership structure' (Sabel, 1996: 42).

Concerns have been expressed that representational participation may not ensure participation by the most marginalized and that, rather than being complementary, it is increasingly the tensions between representation and participation that are of interest (Crickley, 1996: 11; 1998). Crickley sets out the difficult balancing act for community groups, firstly to build a strong community sector with parity of esteem as equal stakeholders in the shaping of Irish society, and secondly to take community development further by reverting to the idea of community action, which implies collaborative and practical effort and endeavour, rather than charity or dependence on statutory bodies. A similar approach has been articulated as 'Post Industrial Solidarity' by Anderson and Larsen (1995b: 206).

Local Policy Networks

Policy Networks are particularly suited to 'corporatist concertation' which involves a plurality of organizations, usually with opposing interests, which manage their conflicts and coordinate their actions with those of the government according to the national economy (Lehmbruch, 1984: 62). Stable concertation and the effective management of the conflict between capital and labour require that only a few major interests are recognized as legitimate and incorporated into policy-making instruments, while other institutions are denied access. In Ireland the experiment is to broaden concertation or working together beyond corporatism, as the following quotation from Crowley shows (1998: 75):

> Participation by the [community] sector therefore, should be based on a mobilisation of the voice of those experiencing poverty and exclusion and this is another challenge faced by the sector. This challenge should not be confused with a focus on the user involvement which is often promoted by the state, in its search for customer driven social policy.

This type of approach to development has been articulated as utilizing 'indigenous technical knowledge' (Brokensha et al., 1980; Chambers, 1993). More recently the concept of 'neighbourhood solidarity chains' has been introduced in a similar context (Van Rees, 1991). McCarthy (1998: 40) has suggested that there was never an ideological commitment to the welfare state in Ireland, but that it evolved pragmatically as part of 'the general modernisation programme' and that equally addressing the problems that emerged caused no ideological tensions between left and right as in other countries. McCarthy believes that there was a willingness in Ireland to combine its place within the global economy with the advantages of being a small country in terms of flexibility and the capacity to mobilize action.

Local Government and Local and Community Development

The NESC regards the local development experience as having largely bypassed the local government system and suggests that even with reform, local government alone will be unable to meet the needs of local populations on a self-contained basis without maintaining partnership arrangements and the encouragement of participative democracy. Lloyd, in a comparative analysis of Irish and Swedish local government systems (1998: 24), has argued that a complete overhaul of local government is required prior to any integration of local development mechanisms and infrastructures. The NESC (1996: 60) has highlighted the agenda for local government reform and the related development of a 'wider range of public services'.

The reality for Ireland is that as late as the 1990s levels of excluded or discouraged labour remained unacceptably high. In terms of extending public services and establishing new ones, a correlation has been made between the administrative category of the long-term unemployed (and the encouragement of the use of Community Employment) and the following specific areas of work:

> Environment Improvements
> Layout of Local Authority Estates
> Tenant Estate Management
> Community Creche and Childcare Facilities
> Community Sports and Leisure Facilities
> Community based Arts and Culture Projects
> Community based School Projects at pre-school, primary and second level
> Community care, including the care of the elderly
> Community based assistance and respite for people with a disability
> (Office of the Tánaiste, 1995: 123).

Social Partnership and the policy environment in relation to excluded labour in Ireland has been criticized by Taylor (1995).

If the range of public services is to be widened, as is proposed by NESC, access to 'real' public-sector jobs or jobs for the delivery of services to the public 'whatever agency delivers them' (NESC, 1996: 61) and universal access to these mainstream services (including by the disadvantaged) are perhaps two different debates.

NESC (1996: 11) has suggested that community life and voluntary associations are a critical social resource and that Ireland has 'displayed considerable vitality in the continuation, formation and vibrancy of associations in sport, culture, voluntary action, self-help and other areas.'

The potential for commodification in these areas without disrupting the positive fabrics of Irish society and the replacement of 'community' or services for the poor with 'quality' and universal services lie at the heart of the modernization and partnership debate.

Increasingly, social policy theorists are moving away from the Poor Law mentality where the socially excluded were considered 'drop-outs' and increasingly they view them as 'pushed-outs' (Anderson and Larsen, 1995b: 218). Spatially segregated groups of disadvantaged people, often in public sector housing, constitute a minority of the 'pushed-outs'. Employment in new public services should be open to all, as should access to the services. Constructing a civic environment which can demand this precludes a return to the residual centralism of the past and, on the contrary, demands the complex (albeit urban) pluralist and inclusive approach adopted by Connolly (1997: 84).

> This would require a new approach to community and local development which places the primacy and control of residents and their organisations above the needs of the statutory and voluntary professional interests and the return on private investment in urban areas.

Trade Unions and Social Welfare Productivity Agreements

Theorists have conceptualized social welfare systems in terms of social well-being, institutional relationships to secure collective welfare and an inclusive discourse in relation to the conceptualization of welfare (O'Brien and Penna, 1998: 7). Welfare systems and public administration generally are increasingly being influenced by the productive dynamics of contemporary capitalism.

McCarthy (1998: 48) and NESC (1996: 60) have suggested that the best of local government and local development need to be brought into proximity without harming either. This would mean a move away from 'democratic experimentalism' in the production and delivery of local welfare services and towards mainstreaming in some form or other.

Issues in relation to terms and conditions of workers, quality of services, the relationship between production and wages, productivity agreements, and local labour clauses, all fall within the traditional preserve of the trade union movement. This could signal a requirement on their part to deepen and widen trade union participation and ensure experimentalism does not end up mainstreaming the erosion of workers' occupational protection systems. A flexible, innovative, autonomous and productive workforce within the local development and local government environs will fail to deliver solidarity with excluded labour and social disadvantage, without organizing itself in the traditional representative bodies of the trade union movement.

CONCLUSION

It has been illustrated in this chapter that Ireland since the Revolution of 1958 (Breen, 1990: 38) has gone through a relatively 'organic' modernization process involving a series of modifications in the administration and type of its welfare regime, from residual state centralism 1958–87 (Breen et al., 1990: 16; McCarthy, 1998: 42) towards conservative corporatism 1987–93 (Conroy, 1993), and further from 1993 to participative local and national social partnership or, more critically, 'convivial corporatism'. The proposals of the NESC (1998: 60) for an extension of services to the public, or public services in the more traditional sense, suggest a movement away from the legacy of austerity of the mid-1980s, towards a form of universalist social welfare services system through the development of a social corporatist approach. If the phase from 1958 to 1987 included the development of state-led services, the phase since 1987 has been characterized by subsidiarity and the incorporation and transformation of associational organizations and community activism into delivery of welfare services on an ad hoc, non-ideologically or predetermined basis. The future of welfare in Ireland and the relationship of the welfare society and the welfare state are still very much an ideological, if more secular, open question.

RECOMMENDED READING

Breen, R. et al. (1990) *Understanding Contemporary Ireland: State Class and Development in the Republic of Ireland*. London: Macmillan.

Craig, S. (1994) *Progress through Partnership, Final Evaluation Report of the PESP Pilot Initiative on Long Term Unemployment*. Dublin: Combat Poverty Agency.

Kirby, P. and D. Jacobson (eds) (1998) *In the Shadow of the Tiger*. Dublin: Dublin City University.

Lloyd, A. (1998) 'Nordic Substance and Celtic Mist: A comparison of Local Democracy in Sweden and Ireland', pp. 15–26 in *Local Development in Ireland; Policy Implications for the Future*. Dublin: CWC.

O'Donnell, R. and D. Thomas (1998) 'Partnership and Policy Making', in S. Healy and B. Reynolds (eds), *Social Policy in Ireland*. Dublin: Oak Tree Press.

Sabel, C. (1996) *Ireland: Local Partnerships and Social Innovation*. Paris: OECD.

Taylor, G. (1995) 'The Politics of Conviviality: Voluntary Workfare and the Right to Useful Unemployment', *Administration*, 43 (3): 36–56

Whittaker, T.K. (1986) 'Economic Development, 1958–85', in K.A. Kennedy (ed.), *Ireland in Transition*. Cork: Mercier Press.

REFERENCES

Anderson, J. and J.E. Larsen (1995a) 'The Underclass Debate: A Spreading Disease', in N. Mortensen (ed.), *Social Integration and Marginalisation*. Fredovikstery: Samfundslitteratur.

Anderson, J. and J.E. Larsen (1995b) 'Post Industrial Solidarity: Future Challenges and Poverty III Lessons', in N. Mortensen (ed.) *Social Integration and Marginalisation*. Fredovikstery: Samfundslitteratur.

Area Development Management (1994) *Local Community Development*, Number 1. Dublin: ADM.

Bagguley, P. and K. Mann (1992) 'Idle Thieving Bastards: Scholarly Representations of the Underclass', *Work, Employment and Society*, 6 (1):

Breen, R., D. Hannan, D. Rothman and C. Whelan (1990) *Understanding Contemporary Ireland: State Class and Development in the Republic of Ireland*. London: Macmillan.

Brokensha, D., D.M. Warren and O. Werner (eds) (1980) *Indigenous Knowledge Systems and Development*. Lanham: University Press of America.

Callan, T., B. Nolan, B.J. Whelan, C.T. Whelan and J. Williams (1996) *Poverty in the 1990s: Evidence from the 1994 Living in Ireland Survey*. Dublin: Oak Tree Press.

Chambers, R. (1993) *Challenging the Professions: Frontiers of Rural Development*. London: Intermediate Technology Publications.

Commins, P. (1979) *Co-operation and Community Development in the West of Ireland*. Paper to International Seminar on Marginal Regions, July–August 3, Trinity College, Dublin.

Connolly, D. (1997) 'Developing Dublin's Inner City: Who Benefits?'. Unpublished dissertation, Trinity College Dublin.

Conroy, P. (1997) 'The Household Economy Meets the Social Economy', pp. 6–8 in C. Lawlor and J. Hedges (eds), *Recognising the Social Economy*. Dublin: AWF.

Conroy Jackson, P. (1993) 'Managing the Mothers: The Case of Ireland', pp. 72–91 in J. Lewis (ed.), *Women and Social Policies in Europe: Work, Family and the State*. Aldershot: Edward Elgar.

Craig, S. (1994) *Progress through Partnership: Final Evaluation Report of the PESP Pilot Initiative on Long Term Unemployment*. Dublin: Combat Poverty Agency.

Crickley, S. (1996) 'Community Development in the 1990s, in *Proceedings of the Community Development Forum*, Kilkenny, 1996. Dublin: ADM.

Crickley, S. (1998) 'Local Development and Local Governance', pp. 7–14 in *Challenges for the Future in Local Development in Ireland: Policy Implications for the Future*. Dublin: CWC.

Crowley, N. (1998) 'Partnership 2000: Empowerment or Co-option', pp. 69–81 in P. Kirby and D. Jacobson (eds), *In the Shadow of the Tiger*. Dublin: Dublin City University.

Cullen, B. (1994) *A Programme in the making: A Review of the Community Development Programme*. Dublin: Combat Poverty Agency.

Curtin, C., T. Haase and H. Tovey (1996) *Poverty in Rural Ireland: A Political Economy Perspective*. Dublin: Combat Poverty Agency.

Curtin, C. and T. Varley (1995) 'Community Action and the State', pp. 379–409 in P. Clancy et al. (eds), *Irish Society: Sociological Perspectives*. Dublin: Institute of Public Administration.

Department of the Environment (1996) *Better Local Government: A Programme for Change.* Dublin: Stationery Office.

Department of Finance (1958) *Economic Development.* Department: Stationery Office.

Devereux, E. (1993) 'The Lonely Furrow: Muintir na Tíre and Irish Community Development', *Community Development Journal*, 28 (1): 43–54.

Drudy, S. (1995) 'Class Society, Inequality and the De-classed', pp. 295–323 in P. Clancy et al. (eds), *Irish Society: Sociological Perspectives.* Dublin: Institute of Public Administration.

Esping-Andersen, G. (1990) *The Three Worlds of Welfare Capitalism.* Oxford: Polity, Blackwell.

Faludi, S. (1992) *Backlash: The Undeclared War against Women.* London: Chatto & Windus.

Faughnan, P. (1990) *Partners in Progress: The Role of the NGOs–Voluntary Organisations in the Social Services Field.* Dublin: Social Science Research Centre, UCD.

Frazer, H. (1992) 'Partnership and Integrated Development', in *Consensus or Censorship? Community Work in Partnership with the State. Co-options* (Journal of the Community Workers' Co-operative) Spring 1992.

Haase, T. (1998) 'The Distribution of Poverty and the Partnerships Response', pp. 18–31in P. Kirby and D. Jacobson (eds), *In the Shadow of the Tiger.* Dublin: Dublin City University Press.

Hardiman, N. (1988) *Pay Politics and Economic Performance in Ireland 1970–87.* Oxford: Clarendon Press.

Kearney, N. (1981) 'Poverty and Social Work', in *One Million Poor? The Challenge of Irish Inequality.* Dublin: Turoe Press.

Kelleher, P. and M. Whelan (1990) *Dublin Communities in Action: A Study of Six Community Projects.* Dublin: Community Action Network/Combat Poverty Agency.

Kemeny, J. (1995) 'Theories of Power in the Three Worlds of Welfare Capitalism', *Journal of European Social Policy*, 4 (2): 87–96.

Kennedy, S. et al. (1972) *One Million Poor? The Challenge of Irish Inequality.* Dublin: Turoe Press.

Keunstler, P. (1979) 'Review of Community of Community Development: The International Experience', in *Summer School Report: Community Development through Popular Participation.* Dublin: Overseas Institute for Community Development (Combat Poverty Agency).

Kirby, P. (1998) 'Issues Raised and Agenda for Action', pp. 82–90 in P. Kirby and D. Jacobson (eds), *In the Shadow of the Tiger.* Dublin: Dublin City University Press.

Lavan, A. (1981) *Social Need and Community Social Services: Voluntary and Social Co-operation in Tallaght.* Dublin: Tallaght Welfare Society.

Lehmbruch, G. (1984) 'Concertation and the Structure of Corporatist Networks', in J.H. Goldthorpe (ed.), *Order and Conflict in Contemporary Society.* Oxford: Clarendon Press.

Lewis, J. (1992) 'Gender and the Development of Welfare Regimes', *Journal of European Social Policy*, 2 (3): 159–73.

Lloyd, A. (1996) 'The Role of the Community Coordinator/Link Worker', pp. 16–18 in *Proceedings of the Community Development Forum*, Kilkenny 1996. Dublin: ADM.

Lloyd, A. (1998) 'Nordic Substance and Celtic Mist: A comparison of Local Democracy in Sweden and Ireland', pp. 15–26 in *Local Development in Ireland; Policy Implications for the Future*. Dublin: CWC.

Lynham, S. (1996) 'Community Development within the Local Development Programme', in *Proceedings of the Community Development Forum*, Kilkenny 1996. Dublin: ADM.

Lynch, K. and E. McLaughlin (1997) 'Caring Labour and Love Labour', pp. 250–94 in P. Clancy et al. (eds), *Irish Society: Sociological Perspectives*. Dublin: Institute of Public Administration.

McCarthy, D. (1998) 'the Genesis and Evolution of the Irish State's Commitment to Social Partnership', in P. Kirby and D. Jacobson (eds), *In the Shadow of the Tiger*. Dublin: Dublin City University Press.

McEvoy, M. (1998) 'Gender Equality in the Partnerships: Controlling Power', pp. 59–68 in P. Kirby and D. Jacobson (eds), *In the Shadow of the Tiger*. Dublin: Dublin City University Press.

McLaughlin, E. and P. Rodgers (1997) 'Single Mothers in the Republic of Ireland', pp. 45–80 in S. Duncan and R. Edwards (eds), *Single Mothers in an International context: Mothers or Workers*. London: UCL Press.

Mayo, M. (1994) *Communities and Caring: The Mixed Economy of Welfare*. Basingstoke: Macmillan.

Mernagh, M. (1981) 'Combat Poverty: The Experience and the Challenge (1975–1980), in *Conference on Poverty*, 1981, Papers of the Kilkenny Conference, 6–8 November 1981, Dublin: Council for Social Welfare (committee of the Catholic Bishops' Council).

Mishra, R. (1990) *The Welfare State in Capitalist Society: Policies of Retrenchment and Maintenance in Europe, North America and Australia*. Hertfordshire: Harvester Wheatsheaf.

Morris, L. (1994) *Dangerous Classes: The Underclass and Social Citizenship*. London: Routledge.

NESC (1986) *Strategy for Development*. Dublin: NESC.

NESC (1989) *Ireland in the European Community: Performance, Prospects and Strategy*. Dublin: NESC.

NESC (1990) *A Strategy for the Nineties*. Dublin: NESC.

NESC (1993) *A Strategy for Competitiveness, Growth and Employment*. Dublin: NESC.

NESC (1996) *A Strategy into the 21st Century*. Dublin: NESC.

NESF (1995) *Ending Long-term Unemployment*. Report no. 4. Dublin: NESF.

Nolan, B. and T. Callan (eds) (1994) *Poverty and Policy in Ireland*. Dublin: Gill & Macmillan.

O'Brien, M. and S. Penna (1998) *Theorising Welfare: Enlightenment and Modern Society*. London: Sage.

O'Cearbhaill, D. (1991) 'Help or Hindrance: The Impact of Local Administrative and Political Structure on Neighbourhood Development in Ireland', *Community Development Journal*, 26 (2): 139–46.

Ó Cinnéide, S. and J. Walsh (1990) 'Multiplications and Divisions: Trends in Community Development in Ireland since the 1960s', *Community Development Journal*, 25 (4): 326–36.

O'Donnell, R. and D. Thomas (1998) 'Partnership and Policy Making', pp. 117–46 in S. Healy and B. Reynolds (eds), *Social Policy in Ireland*. Dublin: Oak Tree Press.

Offe, C. (1991) 'Smooth Consolidation In the West German Welfare State: Structural Change, Fiscal Policies and Populist Politics', pp. 124–46 in F. Piven (ed.), *Labour Parties in Post Industrial Society*. Cambridge: Polity Press.

Office of the Tánaiste (1995) *Report of the Task Force on Long-term Unemployment*. Dublin: Stationery Office.

Partnership 2000 Agreement (1996) Dublin: Stationery Office.

Programme for Competitiveness and Work (1993) Dublin: Stationery Office

Programme for Economic and Social Progress (1990) Dublin: Stationery Office.

Programme for Economic Expansion (1958). Dublin: Stationery Office.

Programme for National Recovery (1987). Dublin: Stationery Office.

Sabel, C. (1996) *Ireland: Local Partnerships and Social Innovation*. Paris: OECD.

Taylor, G. (1995) 'The Politics of Conviviality: Voluntary Workfare and the Right to Useful Unemployment', *Administration*, 43 (3): 36–56.

Thomason, G.A. and R.A.B. Leaper (1963) 'Organising the Community', Report and Paper of the European Study Group on Organising Resources for Community Development, Gormanstown, Co. Meath, July 1962. Tipperary: Muintir na Tíre.

Toomey, D. (1996) 'Chasing the Dragon: Issue Networks and Drug Policy in Dublin', Unpublished dissertation submitted to Department of Political Science and Sociology, University College Galway.

Turok, I. S. O'Suichrú and F. Friedhelm (1998) *Inclusive Cities: Building Local Capacity for Development*. Draft Report for the European Commission, DG XVI and Glasgow Development Agency, in association with the European Urban Institute.

Van Rees, W. (ed.) (1991) *A Survey of Contemporary Community Development in Europe*. The Hague: Opbouwteksten.

Watt, P. (1996) 'Strategies to Enhance Community Participation', in *Proceedings of the Community Development Forum*. Kilkenny, 1996. Dublin: ADM.

WRC (1996) 'Jobs and the Long-Term Unemployed', *Integra Review*. Issue 2 (Winter): 7–8.

Whittaker, T.K. (1986) 'Economic Development, 1958–85', pp. 10–18 in K.A. Kennedy (ed.), *Ireland in Transition*. Cork: Mercier Press.

Wilenski, H. and C. Lebeaux (1958) *Industrial Society and Social Welfare*. New York: Russell Sage.

Yeates, N. (1995) 'Unequal Status, Unequal Treatment: The Gender Structuring of Welfare: Ireland', WERC discussion Paper, Labour Mobility Programme, DG XII, Commission of European Community.

Zappone, K. (1998) 'Top Down or Bottom Up: The Involvement of the Community Sector in Partnership', pp. 50–8 in P. Kirby and D. Jacobson (eds), *In the Shadow of the Tiger*. Dublin: Dublin City University Press.

10
Public Consultation and Participation in Policy Making

Rachel Iredale

Consultation is an exchange between citizens and their government, between those who make policy and people affected by policy choices. Consultation is, above all, a technique for some measure of public involvement in government action. Its precise form will be shaped by the problem at hand and by the willingness of decision makers to open up their processes (Davis, 1997: 31).

INTRODUCTION

In general there are competing blocks of interest involved in a pluralistic policy process, with no single one having dominant control over the state which is assumed to be an independent entity. This competition provides the prime guarantee against a concentration of power. Many societies aspire to this pluralistic policy process, but in reality most western democracies are heavily influenced by those interests with resources, such as capital or cultural influence. Policy adoption then becomes the outcome of the way in which control, power and influence can be exerted (see Chapter 8, pp. 139–54). The Catholic Church and the medical profession have historically played key roles in the development of Irish social policy. Other influences on the policy process in Ireland have included a strong voluntary sector, the social partners and the European Union.

Since the 1960s terms like 'citizen involvement' and 'public consultation' have begun to feature strongly in political discussions across Western Europe about how best to optimize the policy-making process, how to obtain legitimacy for decisions and how to involve citizens in mobilizing general support for particular social policies (see Chapter 3, pp. 33–50 and Chapter 9, pp. 155–77). In general, these discussions seemed to be an indicator of the disturbed relations between governments and the general public in advanced industrialized western democracies.

Evidence was also available about the dislike of formalized stylized forms of contemporary democracy, such as voting; the concern about the fragile trust the general public had in representative democracy, and the lack of accountability in public services (Coakley and Gallagher, 1992).

THE DEMOCRATIC DEFICIT

Conventional processes of public decision making largely rely on the work of elected representatives, while conventional structures for public debate place great emphasis upon professional institutions and organized interest groups. Coote and Lenaghan (1997:1) note that in many democratic societies:

> the distances between the electorate and their elected representatives can be very great. The distance is perceived both horizontally (the geographical distance between localities and increasingly centralised government), and vertically (multiple layers of decision-making, reinforced by a culture of secrecy, through which information and consent must be filtered).

As a consequence, many are now concerned with what is frequently referred to as the 'democratic deficit', and numerous innovative methods for overcoming this deficit have begun to emerge in order to open up more possibilities for public consultation in policy making, and to encourage 'active citizenship' (Stewart et al., 1994: 4). Recently, there has been a real drive towards increasing public consultation in political and social decision making both in Ireland and elsewhere (Davis, 1997). This drive has led to government efforts to make more information available to the public, to listen to a wider range of interests, to obtain better information from affected parties, and to be more responsive to what is heard. Including public consultation in the policy process is likely to produce better social policies that lead not only to improved services, but also to identifying and addressing problems that are important to people. Increasing public consultation is justified because it is a democratic goal in itself and because it allows the citizens of a country to be informed of, and empowered about, issues that concern their everyday lives.

Public consultation exercises can, however, be limited in the sense that the government retains control over the decision-making process. Arnstein (1969) has argued that some consultations aim only to manipulate public opinion, and that others are mere demonstrations in tokenism. Often they involve only people who clearly understand the issues involved. The crucial difference between public consultation and public participation is that the latter entails a real shift in authority and control over the decision making to the citizens involved. Consultation can enhance representative democracy if conducted properly, but participation challenges it.

CONSULTATION WITH SERVICE USERS AND USER GROUPS

Social policies are generally seen to exist to provide for the patient, client or citizen, but this has not always been sufficiently emphasized in the past. Examples of successfully integrating lay knowledge into the different stages of the policy process are rare. However, a trend of inviting users to collaborate with service providers has emerged which is occurring within a context of fundamental and far-reaching change in social policy and social work practice in Ireland, for example, the consultation process which resulted from the Department of Health *Developing a Policy on Women's Health* (1995b).

The provision of public services is based on two assumptions – first of all, that they will be targeted to those who need them most and, secondly, that they will be used by the groups at whom they are targeted. However, there may be a contradiction between what users want and what user-based services are likely to offer, as they are based on two distinct political ideologies. The former focuses on assertive self-advocacy and empowerment of users. Having a direct say in the planning, organization and delivery of services allows users to gain greater control over their lives. With the latter agenda there is an emphasis on consumer choice, with a shift to more diversity in the supply of services. This is a consumerist approach that emphasizes improving efficiency and effectiveness, and is similar to trying to improve consumer satisfaction with other goods in a market situation. However, if services are perceived to be irrelevant, are failing to meet need or are unresponsive to users, low utilization is the likely effect which, in turn, will have implications for health and social gain in society.

Obtaining the user perspective is becoming evident in many aspects of Irish policy making. Initiatives that promote user involvement in decision making are currently being developed by government, for example in tackling long-term unemployment (through the Area Development Management (ADM) Ltd), and poverty (National Anti-Poverty Strategy (NAPS)). The attractiveness of the user perspective is undeniable but it is essential to involve users of services at every stage of the decision-making process. This includes:

• obtaining all relevant information from users
• exploring whether needs are being met
• planning policies together

- involving users in the implementation of these policies
- obtaining their opinion when services are being evaluated
- identifying problems that remain to be addressed

Perhaps some of the best examples of public consultation with users come from the field of health policy where a stated intention of the Department of Health (1994: 27) is to 'reorientate the decision-making process towards more open and explicit choice mechanisms which take account not only of detailed information and analysis, but which also strive to reflect the public's preferences to whatever degree is possible'.

Research on users of the health services can take many forms. For example, there are studies which give a statistical indication of what large numbers of people think about health care in this country and what could be done to improve it (Wiley and Merriman, 1996). Much of this research focuses on patient satisfaction or views on experiences of the health services. In the Health Strategy it was stated that health boards would be required to evaluate patient satisfaction with general aspects of the health services, such as waiting times and the manner in which services are delivered, by making use of consumer surveys and other measurement techniques (Department of Health, 1994: 39).

Despite the fact that many health policy documents attach increasing importance to seeking out and acting upon the views of users about the healthcare services provided in this country (Department of Health 1995a, 1995b; Department of Health and Children, 1997), the reality remains that these aspirations are only just beginning to be followed through. Over the past decade research that takes account of the experiences of patients themselves has fuelled some changes. For example, the Charter of Rights for Hospital Patients was an early indication that hospital services in this country were re-orientating towards greater consumer responsiveness. Further charters relating to children, pregnancy, the elderly, and people with mental and physical disabilities are promised for the future. The development of these charters is an expression of an increasing view that public services are there to serve the public, and that the public are 'customers', with a set of legitimate expectations in relation to service standards.

Women's health is one area where user involvement is debated extensively and policies are beginning to emerge to reflect this mood. The involvement of the National Women's Council (NWCI) in the wake of the publication of the 1995 discussion document on Women's Health led to the development of a nationwide consultation process, the recommendations of which were to be translated into *A Plan for Women's Health*. When the plan was published in 1997, there was in fact much criticism of the failure of the Department of Health to do so (Personal communications with NWCI, 1997). One positive response, however, was the establishment of the Women's Health Council in 1997, to meet demands by women for increased representation and consultation in the health services (NWCI, 1998). It is representative of a wide range of interests concerned with women's health in Ireland. In addition, health boards are establishing structures for consulting women on health issues and will prepare a regional plan for women's health to implement the commitments of the national plan and the issues identified during the consultative process over the period 1997–99. Health boards will also review their staff training and development programmes to include sensitivity training in relation to attitudes towards women clients and patients, thereby creating a women-friendly service (Department of Health, 1997).

Shaping a Healthier Future (1994: 27) stated that 'the Department of Health will initiate detailed research into possible approaches to identifying the public's preferences between competing priorities'. But how do we know what the public want? How do the general public choose between priorities? Do their opinions change over time? Quantitative research needs to be matched with research that asks people to participate actively in decisions about issues which intimately affect their lives. This necessitates a systematic qualitative analysis of what the general public think and feel about the current and future operation of all aspects of the public health care system.

Although increasing user-involvement is generally felt to be a good thing, problems may also ensue. For example, user representatives may become incorporated into existing power processes and may lose touch with ordinary users. There may be a tendency to focus on particular types of issues or services to the detriment of others that are less popular (e.g. cervical screening, as opposed to senile dementia). Another problem with user-involvement includes the fact that decision makers often feel users are more concerned with the quality of services than anything else and fail to appreciate governance and management issues (Forbes and Sashidharan, 1997). Furthermore, there has been an uncritical approach to the definition of users. User is synonymous with someone who utilizes a service, but to conflate the different experiences of disparate groups of people under the catch-all category 'user' may be meaningless and mis-leading. Some groups may find themselves over- or under-represented, and although different groups may all have the same need for a particular service, such needs are never uniform and can be influenced by age, gender, race and level of ability.

Lay Expertise

Developing a decision-making culture that is both evidence based and inclusive requires more qualitative research with ordinary members of the public. Davis (1997), building on the work of Arnstein (1969), has described a continuum of public involvement types and instruments that are typically used by decision makers, depending on what needs to be achieved. This continuum ranges from simply informing people through government promotion campaigns to empowering the lay populace to take control of decisions which affect them directly. This typology of traditional types is given in Table 1:

Table 1.   Types of Public Involvement

Information	Consultation	Partnership	Delegation	Control
• surveys	• interest/user groups	• advisory committees	• public inquiries	• referenda
• information campaigns	• public hearings	• policy communities		

Davis (1997: 35) claims that surveys and information campaigns have a role to play in the policy process, but they 'will not satisfy those looking for more meaningful interaction'. Likewise partnerships with advisory committees and existing policy communities provide some measure of joint decision making, but they serve only to explore particular issues and can become entrenched in the very processes that they seek to remain outside. The National Economic and Social Forum (NESF) is an innovative example of a partnership that includes people traditionally outside of the advisory committee process. According to Davis (1997: 36) the intention behind delegation 'is to ensure policy options are formulated at arms length from partisan politics' and to 'shift policy responsibility to an institution or process outside political control'. This method is used frequently by the Irish government, typically for contentious issues, e.g. the Hepatitis C Inquiry. In Davis's continuum, referenda are the only method used to involve the public in making decisions directly.

In considering ways of involving the public more in policy making, it is important to remember that the public has a dual relationship with those responsible for making the decisions. They are both service users and citizens and in each capacity they may have different interests. Coote and Lenaghan (1997: 5) argue that 'too often, public involvement exercises confuse the patient/user and the citizen. Consulting the public is taken to mean consulting relevant user groups, so that individuals and groups who are not current users, but who may use the service in the future, or who do not use it although they need it, are excluded from the process.'

It is relatively easy to identify service users or to consult with existing user groups on policy issues. Similarly, it is relatively straightforward to conduct an information campaign or delegate power to a set of representatives nominated by government. It is more difficult, however, to reach those who remain silent, invisible or excluded. What is needed therefore, are new ways of drawing the ordinary citizen into the decision-making process and giving them control over the decisions made. Many authors writing about the concept of citizenship tend to focus on the conception of the social citizen as a rights-claimer; rarely are the duties of citizenship specified (see Chapter 11, pp. 195–209). Although the concept of citizenship is often used as a shorthand reference for the values which are thought to underlie the modern welfare state (Parker, 1975), the inclusive nature of citizenship may need to be stressed further.

Most citizens would probably want to be consulted on major issues, even though they might be cynical about their ability to influence government decisions. Unfortunately, the extent to which the public should become involved in determining social policies is sometimes questioned by policy makers. It could be argued that members of the public have an inadequate understanding of social and political issues and that they are ill-equipped to understand the complex issues that surround such debates. However, there are positive indications from some new models of public involvement that ordinary members of the public are both able and willing to participate in decision making, given the time, opportunity and support to do so (Stewart et al., 1994; Coote and Lenaghan, 1997).

What then are the most suitable ways of enabling the public to participate directly in policy decisions? It is not feasible to hold a referendum on every issue (it would be costly and time-consuming) and the number of people who could be asked for their opinion on a policy issue is potentially enormous. Political representatives and bodies like the health boards and local authorities continue to make and take decisions on our behalf. However, health boards in Ireland are not elected – even though the majority are city/county councillors – and in their capacity as health board members, they are only indirectly accountable to the people, while local authorities are often elected on a very low turnout. The limited role of local government in this country may account for low voter turnout. According to the *Institute of Public Administration*

Yearbook (1996), recent figures for local government election turn-out have been 63.6 per cent in 1979, 58.2 per cent in 1985 and 55.1 per cent in 1991.

It can be argued, however, that it is neither desirable nor realistic to expect that existing structures of representative democracy will be replaced immediately by participative democracy. What is needed is more informed decision making and a wider engagement with the lay populace in decisions which affect them. By trying to incorporate lay expertise into the policy-making process, the short term interests of politicians, which may be directed only as far as the next election, and the long-term interests of citizens can be reconciled to the benefit of the society as a whole.

What characterizes many of the new methods of public participation is the time available for deliberation and scrutiny of the issue. They also aim specifically to involve groups traditionally outside the consultative process, including women, young people, the elderly, the unemployed, people with a disability and those from socio-economically deprived areas. As a result they create a sense of ownership over the issue at stake. Some of these techniques for public participation in policy making include focus groups, planning cells, deliberative opinion polls, consensus conferences and Citizens' Juries.

Focus Groups

Focus groups are becoming one of the most widely used qualitative research tools in the social sciences (Stewart and Shamdasanai, 1990). A focus group involves a selected group of six to ten people being led through a list of topics by a facilitator over a period of one or two hours. Focus groups are quicker and cheaper than individual interviews; they allow direct interaction with participants; they can explore the values and beliefs which underlie the opinions offered during the course of the group; and they result in large amounts of rich data expressed in the respondents' own words. The major strength of focus groups is the way in which the group dynamic operates and members of the group stimulate each other to explore reactions to the common experience and to generate new ideas.

Focus groups are particularly useful when there are power differences between the participants and the decision makers or professionals, when the everyday use of language and culture of particular groups is of interest, and when one wants to explore the degree of consensus on a given topic (Krueger, 1994). They can be used for a variety of purposes, such as to:

- complement other research methods
- stimulate dialogue with citizens
- identify good practice
- explore survey results further
- facilitate participation
- empower citizens
- pinpoint priorities
- understand the views, attitudes and expectations of the public.

Focus groups are now increasingly being used in the UK and the US by political parties and participants are drawn not just from party members, but also from the general public. (The monarchy in the UK is making use of focus groups to discover how best to improve its public image.) Other examples where focus groups are being used to facilitate decision making include finding out how to make use of wasteland in a locality, to pilot new information services, and to examine how well community-care policies are working and whether their impact is contingent upon particular areas (Morgan, 1997).

The benefits to participants of being in a focus group should not be underestimated. Focus groups allow participants the opportunity to be involved in decision-making processes, to be valued as experts and to be given the chance to work collaboratively with researchers and policy makers. The groups can be empowering, can raise consciousness and can become a forum for change, both before, during and after the focus group itself (Johnson, 1996).

Planning Cells

A new participatory instrument called the *Plannungzelle* (planning cell) has been developing in Germany since the 1970s, through the work of Peter Dienel's research centre for 'Citizens' Participation and Planning Procedures'. Dienel (1978: 74) defines the planning cell as a 'group of citizens who have been randomly selected and they are granted leave from their workday obligations for a limited period of time in order to work out solutions for given, soluble planning problems' with the assistance of experts who provide information and advice. The intention behind these planning cells is to improve the efficiency of decision making in the planning process, and to offer new possibilities of political participation by the citizen.

About 25 people voluntarily participate in each planning cell, working full-time as public consultants for between two and five days. Often a number of planning cells run simultaneously – using the same experts and the same evidence – to see if different decisions are made. Dienel has organized planning cells, commissioned by local and regional governments, to deal with issues as diverse as urban renewal, national energy policies, planning recreation parks and the criteria for the testing of consumer goods. This model of public participation has also been used by his research centre in Spain, the Netherlands and Palestine.

Deliberative Opinion Polls

In the early 1970s, Granada TV in England began bringing together groups of randomly selected people in what they called the 'Election 500'. Since then the deliberative opinion poll pioneered by James Fishkin in the US has evolved. It is premised on the notion that 'ordinary citizens, when immersed in the relevant materials, can deal with difficult intellectual questions' (Fishkin, 1991: 9).

A deliberative opinion poll is a way of involving statistically significant numbers of the general public in an extended, informed debate which leads to a vote or series of votes. A sample of voters is brought to a single site for two days to listen to expert evidence and discuss the issue at stake. Participants' opinions are polled both before and after the event. Fishkin (1991: 81) claims 'an ordinary opinion poll models what the electorate thinks, given how little it knows. A deliberative opinion poll models what the electorate *would* think if, hypothetically, it could be immersed in intensive deliberative processes'. Although deliberative opinion polls are used frequently in the UK by the mass media (for example by the TV station Channel Four), they have not yet been commissioned by any official organization (Coote and Lenaghan, 1997), nor have they been used in Ireland yet.

Consensus Conferences

The word 'consensus' refers to a general agreement or collective opinion and the consensus conference is another method whereby the public have an opportunity to become informed and deliberate over an extended period of time in a controlled environment. The intention behind a consensus conference is to give a voice to lay people whose interests are principally those of the concerned citizen.

Although the method has its origins in the US, the Danish Board of Technology took up the concept in the 1980s to describe a new form of technology assessment that involved a panel of lay people in dialogue with a panel of experts. At a consensus conference a group of 15–20 lay people question the experts about a controversial subject (usually scientific or technological), assess the experts' responses, reach a consensus about the subject and report its conclusions. Consensus conferences have been used to address such subjects as food irradiation and transgenic animals in Denmark and they have also become popular in the Netherlands since 1993. The only consensus conference to be held in the UK was sponsored by the Science Museum in 1994 and focused on plant biotechnology (Joss and Durant, 1994; see http://www.open.gov.uk/scmus/finalrep.htm). The distinctive feature of all of these initiatives is that the lay public are the main actors throughout, from deciding on the questions to be addressed, to selecting the experts and reaching the conclusions.

Citizens' Juries

One component of most western democracies has been a fair and balanced legal system. The jury process was first introduced in the Middle Ages when jurors were required to make decisions on the basis of their personal knowledge of affairs in their localities. The belief that the jury system provided a unique guarantee of justice led not only to its inclusion in the American Constitution, but also to its introduction into many European systems of law. However, the jury system has only existed in its modern form for three centuries or so, and the members of a jury are now a group of independent citizens. They typically have no personal or selfish interest in the case before them, and their decisions are made solely on the basis of the evidence presented in court.

One of the most innovative forms of public participation is the Citizens' Jury which is based on the model used in legal trials. Although the American model of Citizens' Juries was developed by the millionaire Ned Crosby, founder of the Jefferson Centre for New Democratic Processes in Minneapolis in the early 1970s, it did not come to the UK until 1996. A Citizens' Jury is typically held for a period of four to five days in which a group of twelve to sixteen randomly selected jurors question expert witnesses, deliberate on a question or series of questions and present their recommendations. Again, they are based on the premise that ordinary people given enough opportunity, time, support and resources are eminently capable of arriving at complex decisions about policy matters.

What is distinctive about a Citizens' Jury – as with the other methods of public participation – is the fact that it involves ordinary members of the public, not in their capacity as users of services or members of a particular interest group, but in their capacity as citizens. According to the Institute for Public Policy Research (1996:1) the members of a

Citizens' Jury 'are not merely a resource to be mined by researchers, nor actors in a public relations exercise. They are citizens engaged in a serious civic task who become lay experts as well as competent and confident decision makers'.

A Citizens' Jury differs from an ordinary legal trial in that much more interaction among jurors, and particularly between jurors and witnesses, takes place. Jurors engage in group work and discussions and have considerable opportunity to cross-examine witnesses themselves after they have presented their evidence. Over a period of four days, ten to fifteen witnesses may be called. Fifteen minutes are usually allowed for each witness session followed by 45 minutes or so for questions. The jury deliberates over the evidence together and in small groups before reaching any decisions. With the help of a moderator, a number of recommendations are agreed and presented to whichever decision-making body has commissioned the Citizens' Jury.

Arguments in favour of the jury method in general include that it is a safeguard of liberty, it can be an essential check on injustice and that it is the best means for establishing the truth. Arguments in favour of Citizens' Juries reflect these points, and also emphasize improving reflexivity, fostering notions of active citizenship and providing the public perspective on topical issues. Critics of Citizens' Juries generally tend to emphasize expense, lack of representativeness, and that jurors may lack the ability to understand all the evidence. These criticisms have been addressed elsewhere (Iredale and Longley, 1998).

Citizens' Juries are an innovative way of conducting an informed dialogue with the public which is useful for both elected authorities and unelected public-interest bodies. Although there has not yet been a Citizens' Jury in the Republic of Ireland, there has been one in Northern Ireland on the future of health and social services. The kinds of social policy issues that Citizens' Juries have been used for in England with health authorities and local government include the closure of hospitals, services for drug addicts, and the use of public space in an inner city area (Institute for Public Policy Research, 1996). The author has recently organized the first Citizens' Jury in Wales on the topic of genetic testing for common disorders in the NHS (Welsh Institute for Health and Social Care, 1998).

IMPROVING PUBLIC INVOLVEMENT

In recent years there have been numerous indications that Ireland is modernizing, evidenced for example by the election of Mary Robinson and Mary McAleese as successive Presidents. Other indications of a liberalization of attitudes and a relaxation of traditional values include the decriminalization of homosexuality in 1995, the Supreme Court's decision on the right to die and the introduction of divorce in 1997. New social situations, rapid technological progress, the globalization of trade and changing demographic trends have forced Ireland to develop in ways similar to other western democracies. The evidence from Europe and the US demonstrates that there are a myriad of ways to approach improving democracy in Ireland.

Public consultation initiatives have already begun in earnest, especially in relation to health, housing and education policy. However, little has emerged in terms of direct public participation in decision making. Democratic reforms will not succeed simply by putting power into the hands of the people, if they result in efficiency of decision making, reasonableness and the workability of policies being sacrificed (Crosby, 1996). Nor will they succeed if we simply rely on an authentic voice of the people arising spontaneously in response to perceived injustices or intolerable situations. Democratic reform cannot be built on such rare events. It has become necessary to put genuine public participation firmly onto the agenda.

Any new model of public participation must be able to command public confidence. There needs to be a well chosen group of people to provide input into the policy-making process, representative of the wider population, and care must be taken not to exclude certain groups. Regardless of whether the method chosen is a Citizens' Jury, a deliberative opinion poll or a consensus conference, Crosby (1996) has argued that the group must be seen by the broader society to be legitimate, be well-informed, have enough time to consider all the issues, have a good climate for deliberation, and be trustworthy. The author's experience with focus group research and Citizens' Juries is that participants move beyond their own particular interests and concerns, and adopt a broader perspective that is representative of the community at large – the equivalent of Rawls's 'veil of ignorance' (Rawls, 1972).

It might be feasible to use a series of focus groups or a Citizens' Jury to gauge how much demand there would be to move towards the provision of a national basic income as part of a new policy approach to tackle poverty, unemployment and social exclusion. The Conference of Religious of Ireland (CORI) (1996) has argued that traditional measures of progress, such as GNP or GDP, should be replaced with more comprehensive and integrated indicators which acknowledge, inter alia, the right of all to participation in decisions which impact on them. CORI (1996) claims that full citizenship is not merely about political rights, such as the right to vote and the right to be treated equally before the law. It also incorporates social rights, such as the right to work, to an adequate income and to participation in society.

Public participation enhances accountability, and makes the planning process more transparent. Accountability is by nature retrospective, with one party accounting to another for a particular decision, course of action or expenditure already completed. This contrasts significantly with the prospective nature of planning. Some decision makers are themselves calling for public participation to be improved, and there is scope for the government to make use of innovative public consultation exercises at the White Paper stage. For example, one of the priorities that had to be addressed in the White Paper on Science and Technology (November 1996) was improved public perception of science and technology. In an article in *The Irish Times* (14 November 1996) Pat Rabbitte TD, then Minister for Science and Technology, wrote:

> public policy formation is about setting and achieving objectives, it is not about scattering taxpayers' money to all and sundry. It is about long-term planning and about a vision of how Ireland's economic prosperity and social development will be shaped. As with any vision, there is room for debate, informed discussion and differing points of view. Is there anyone out there?

Europe's future may lie in the creation of a Citizens' Europe, which must therefore have both the support of its citizens and a civil dialogue. Padraig Flynn, member of the European Commission with responsibility for Employment, Industrial Relations and Social Affairs, frequently argues that a civil dialogue must be developed across Europe that will inform the political dialogue with Member States and the social dialogue with employers and trade unions. Given that public policy is increasingly made at a European level, it is important that ordinary members of the public retain some sense of having a say in affairs that concern them. The Irish government was forced to change some of the wording for the Amsterdam Treaty referendum (Eighteenth Amendment of the Constitution Bill, 1998) after strong criticism about the fact that it would allow the government to implement radical measures without first consulting the electorate. This was paradoxical given that the intention of the Amsterdam Treaty was to make Europe more democratic. Fortunately, the referendum on the Amsterdam Treaty held in May 1998 – necessary to ratify the Treaty before 1 January 1999 – brought control back directly to the people (see Chapter 6, pp. 90–113).

Research on public involvement in other countries has resulted in a number of important questions being raised, which will also have to be addressed in this country. Some of these questions include what mechanisms exist to balance the various views obtained during the decision-making process with reference to: the distortion of views as a result of soliciting public opinion; whether the presentation of information is in a form accessible to the public; the extent to which public involvement raises expectations unreasonably and the extent to which issues are not being sufficiently addressed by policy makers.

According to Hogwood and Gunn (1984), an issue is likely to reach the political agenda only if one or more of the following circumstances apply – (*a*) the issue has reached crisis proportions and can no longer be ignored; (*b*) it has an emotive aspect or a human interest angle; (*c*) it might raise questions about power and legitimacy in society, and (*d*) the issue is fashionable in some way. There are many issues missing from the policy agenda as Ireland approaches the twenty-first century that meet these criteria, e.g. environmental pollution, human-assisted reproduction, genetic engineering, BSE and other food scares, and the future of the European Union. All of these issues will benefit from an informed public debate and ensuring that the values and preferences of the lay populace influence future policy plans and strategies.

CONCLUSION

There are real anxieties about the low levels of communication and trust between those making decisions on behalf of the public and the general public themselves. Improving public consultation and participation in public policy making forms part of a broader debate in western societies, not just in relation to social policy, but also in regard to a wider range of issues.

Giddens (1991) has suggested that social reflexivity is perhaps becoming the defining hallmark in the risk society of late modernity. Individuals are no longer passive agents duped by hegemonic ideologies or mere receptacles for biased, mediated information. Although there may be considerable differences between the perspectives of the ordinary citizen and the policy professional, it is necessary for the so-called experts to accept the legitimacy of the public voice and allow ordinary citizens to join in the dialogue on issues that affect us all. The evidence from other countries shows that the general public are eminently capable of making decisions on complex policy issues if given the time, opportunity, resources and support to do so.

As Ireland enters the twenty-first century, informed citizen consultation and participation will be a defining element, with new approaches required to deal effectively with local, national and international issues. Regardless of whichever option to improve public involvement is chosen, the general public must have enough information to enable them to participate effectively. This information should pertain not only to the particular issue or service being addressed, but also to the nature of the decision-making process. Focus groups, deliberative opinion polls, consensus conferences and Citizens' Juries are not intended to replace completely other forms of public involvement, but must complement elections, referendums, opinion polls, and public meetings. Any of these initiatives – singularly or together – can encourage debate, achieve more democratic accountability, and create a sense of ownership over social policy amongst all Irish citizens.

RECOMMENDED READING

Coote, A. and J. Lenaghan (1997) *Citizens' Juries: Theory into Practice.* London: Institute for Public Policy Research.

Davis, G. (1997) 'Rethinking Policy Making: A New Role for Consultation?', *Administration*, 45 (3): 26–47.

Department of Health and Children (1997) *Customer Service Action Plan 1998–1999.* Dublin: Stationery Office.

REFERENCES

Arnstein, S. (1969) 'A Ladder of Citizen Participation', *Journal of the American Institute of Planners*, 35 (4): 216–24.

Coakley, J. and M. Gallagher (1992) *Politics in the Republic of Ireland.* Galway: PSAI Press.

Conference of Religious of Ireland (1996) *Progress, Values and Social Policy.* Dublin: Conference of Religious of Ireland.

Coote, A. and J. Lenaghan (1997) *Citizens' Juries: Theory into Practice.* London: Institute for Public Policy Research.

Cousins, M. (1997) 'Ireland's Place in the Worlds of Welfare Capitalism', *Journal of European Social Policy*, 17 (3): 223–35.

Crosby, N. (1996) *How Should We Live Together? The Philosophical Underpinnings of the Citizens' Jury Process.* Unpublished Paper: Centre for New Democratic Processes.

Curry, J. (1998) *Irish Social Services.* 3rd edition. Dublin: Institute of Public Administration.

Davis, G. (1997) 'Rethinking Policy Making: A New Role for Consultation?', *Administration*, 45 (3): 26–47.

Department of Enterprise and Employment (1996) *White Paper on Science and Technology.* Dublin: Stationery Office.

Department of Health (1994) *Shaping a Healthier Future. A Strategy for Effective Healthcare in the 1990s.* Dublin: Stationery Office.

Department of Health (1995a) *A Health Promotion Strategy: Making the Healthier Choice the Easier Choice.* Dublin: Stationery Office.

Department of Health (1995b) *Developing a Policy for Women's Health – A Discussion Document*. Dublin: Stationery Office.

Department of Health (1997) *A Plan for Women's Health*. Dublin: Stationery Office.

Department of Health and Children (1997) *Customer Service Action Plan 1998–99*. Dublin: Stationery Office.

Dienel, P. (1978) *Plannungszelle*. Opladen: West Deutsche Verlag.

Fishkin, J. S. (1991) *Democracy and Deliberation: New Directions for Democratic Form*. New Haven: Yale University Press.

Forbes, J. and S.P. Sashidharan (1997) 'User Involvement in Services; Incorporation or Challenge?', *British Journal of Social Work*, 27: 481–98.

Giddens, A. (1991) *Modernity and Self-Identity: Self and Society in the Late Modern Age*. Cambridge: Polity.

Hannon, P. (1992) *Church, State, Morality and the Law*. Dublin: Gill & Macmillan.

Hogwood, B.W. and L.A. Gunn (1984) *Policy Analysis for the Real World*, Oxford: Oxford University Press.

Institute for Public Policy Research (1996) *Citizens' Juries: Towards Best Practice*. London: Institute for Public Policy Research.

Iredale, R. and M. Longley (1998) 'Public Perspectives of the New Genetics: The Citizens' Jury Experiment', in R. Chadwick (ed.), *Genetic Information: Acquisition, Access and Control*, London: Plenum Press.

Johnson, A. (1996) '"It's Good to Talk": The Focus Group and the Sociological Imagination', *The Sociological Review*, 44 (3): 517–38.

Joss, S. and J. Durant (1994) *Consensus Conferences: A Review of the Danish, Dutch and UK Approaches to this Special Form of Technology Assessment, and an Assessment of the Options for a Proposed Swiss Consensus Conference*. London: Science Museum.

Krueger, R.A. (1994) *Focus Groups: A Practical Guide for Applied Research*. 2nd edition. California: Sage.

Morgan, D.L. (1997) *Focus Groups as Qualitative Research*. 2nd edition. Qualitative Research Methods Series Vol. 16. California: Sage.

National Anti-Poverty Strategy. (1996) *Sharing in Progress*. Dublin: Stationery Office.

National Economic and Social Forum (1997) *A Framework for Partnership: Enriching Strategic Consensus Through Partnership*. Report No.19. Dublin: Stationery Office.

National Women's Council of Ireland (1997) 'Women's Health Process at National and Regional Level', *In Focus* (March).

Parker, J. (1975) *Social Policy and Citizenship*. London: Macmillan.

Rawls, J. (1972) *A Theory of Justice*. Oxford: Oxford University Press.

Stewart, D.W. and P.N. Shamdasanai (1990) *Focus Groups: Theory and Practice*. London: Sage.

Stewart, J., E. Kendall and A. Coote (1994) *Citizens' Juries*. London: Institute for Public Policy Research.

Welsh Institute for Health and Social Care (1998) *Report of the Citizens' Jury on Genetic Testing for Common Disorders*. Cardiff: Welsh Institute for Health and Social Care.

Whyte, J.H. (1980) *Church and State in Modern Ireland 1923–1979*. Dublin: Gill & Macmillan.

Wiley, M.M. and B. Merriman (1996) *Women and Health Care in Ireland. Knowledge, Attitudes and Behaviour*. Dublin: Oak Tree Press.

11
Citizenship and Irish Social Policy

Jennifer D'Arcy

There is said to be concord in a state when the citizens agree about their interests, adopt the same policy, and put their common resolve into effect.

(Aristotle, *Ethics*, Book IX)

INTRODUCTION

The 1990s have seen citizenship re-emerge as a crucial concept in social policy discourse. In Ireland, the Department of Social Welfare (1997) has become engaged in debates concerning active citizenship in an attempt to establish a paradigm to facilitate the development of community and voluntary activity. The relationship between the individual and society is one of mutual dependence. Lewis (1997: 104) views citizenship as a concept 'which provides a way of constructing competing understandings about the relations between the people, the state and welfare'. Lister (1998: 2) argues that the philosophy of citizenship has provided a means of reconciling the collectivist tradition of the left with notions of individual rights and responsibilities, recognizing that the alternative to the political credo of the New Right cannot discard the individual to which the latter directed its appeal. Citizenship, in recent times, has become an indispensable concept which provides a framework for the discussion of social rights, welfare issues, social identity and political participation. This chapter investigates the concept of citizenship with particular reference to social welfare and Irish social policy.

DEFINING CITIZENSHIP

Citizenship is embedded in membership of and participation within a community in society. Important to any discussion of citizenship are the rights and duties integral to the concept which are often seen as reciprocal.

Citizenship throughout its history has always been involved in contesting public and private interests. It has always depended upon society's ability to promise and give what has been needed by individuals and their families. Marshall defines citizenship as 'a status bestowed on those who are full members of a community. All who possess the status are equal with respect to the rights and duties with which the status is endowed' (Marshall and Bottomore, 1992: 18). Held (1991: 20) claims that citizenship is linked to community through membership, participation, rights and duties, arguing that 'if citizenship entails membership in the community and membership in the community implies forms of social participation, then citizenship is above all about the involvement of people in the community in which they live'.

Two significant traditions in understanding citizenship are discussed by Healy and Reynolds (1998: 12–13). First of all, the liberal political tradition defines citizenship in terms of rights. This could be termed the modern idea of citizenship which reaches back to the New Liberalism movement of the early twentieth century in whose hands it became a key term for defining the conditions for all members of the society to take a full and productive role in the nation's life. This tradition sees civil and political rights as the means by which social policy guarantees the freedom and formal equality of individuals. Contemporary discussions of citizenship take as their source the work of Marshall (1950). In this work he characterizes the process of modernization over the past three hundred years as the history of the general expansion of citizenship, in relation to the rights of citizens, and a growth in the number of those entitled to citizen status. The second tradition of citizenship identified by Healy and Reynolds (1998) is the civic republicanism approach advocated by Aristotle. This approach adopts the view of citizenship as pertaining to obligations. Individuals are obliged by duty to participate politically. This tradition also emphasizes the social obligations of the individual. Healy and Reynolds offer the example of work – that is, that active citizens must be willing to work and be actively seeking work.

The issue of citizenship is characterized by Lister (1998: 13) as being one of both rights and obligations and argues that 'at heart, what is at issue in the mainstream debates is the balance between rights and obligations and the nature of each'. The emphasis on social rights as central to citizenship Healy and Reynolds (1998: 13) argue is often ignored and downplayed today and has been replaced with a greater emphasis on duty and obligation. The Department of Social Welfare (1997: 25) Green Paper on the community and voluntary sector illustrates this, offering an understanding of citizenship based on the duties and roles each person or community must play in their future. The Green Paper sees this as active citizenship, an extension of formal citizenship, which extends democratic society from being one of basic civil, political, social and economic rights to one epitomized by democratic participation and responsibility. The concept of the active citizen draws on a combination of both the liberal and civic republican tradition by emphasizing both rights and duties.

The importance of the citizen as actor is identified by Lister (1998: 38). She argues that:

> to act as a citizen requires first a sense of agency, the belief that one can act, acting as a citizen especially collectively in turn fosters that sense of agency. This agency is not simply about the capacity to choose and act but it is also about a conscious capacity which is important to the individual's self identity.

Thus, for individuals to truly partake of their rights to citizenship, they must not only be aware of their rights as dictated by the liberal tradition, they also have an obligation to participate actively within society to ensure those rights.

Marshall's Theory of Citizenship

Marshall (1950) divides citizenship into three types of rights: civil, political and social, which he claims developed during the eighteenth, nineteenth and twentieth centuries respectively. Civil rights involve the freedom of individuals to live where they choose, freedom of speech and religion, the right to own property and the right to equal justice before the law. These rights were not fully established in most European countries until the late eighteenth century/early nineteenth century. The development of civil rights is closely linked to the developments of judicial instruments. The main instrument for enforcing these civil rights is the court system. Political rights are concerned with the right to vote and to organize. Political rights entail the right to elect and be elected. These rights had to be struggled for and different groups within society received these rights at different times, given governments' reluctance to recognize universal franchise.

Finally, Marshall identifies social rights as being the prerogative or right of each individual to enjoy a certain minimum standard of welfare. These rights include adequate health care, housing, education and social security. With the decrease in *laissez-faire* policies in the early twentieth century, followed by an increase in market intervention through taxation, and provision of a minimum wage and social services, social rights have been brought into citizenship. Marshall (1965) saw the extension of social citizenship as a process directed towards the modification of the 'whole pattern of social inequality' within capitalist society. George and Page (1995: 107) argue that the central theme to be found in Marshall's work is that the collectivist social services contribute to the maintenance and enhancement of social welfare so long as such interventions do not subvert the system of competitive markets.

Rights and the Irish Constitution

It is useful to examine the Irish Constitution (Bunreacht na hÉireann) for evidence of the enshrinement of the rights described by Marshall. Civil rights, defined by Marshall as the foundation for political and in turn social rights, are outlined within the Constitution from Articles 40.1 to Articles 44.6. These Articles define the fundamental civil rights pertaining to the Irish citizen and include that:

> All citizens shall, as human persons, be held equal before the law [Article 40.1].

> The state guarantees in its laws to respect, and as far as practicable, by its laws to defend and vindicate the personal rights of the citizen [Article 40.3.1].

> The state guarantees liberty for the exercise of the following rights, subject to public order and morality: the right of the citizen to express freely their convictions and opinions; the right of the citizen to assemble peaceably and without arms; the right of the citizen to form associations and unions [Article 40.6.1].

> Laws regulating the manner in which the right of forming associations and unions and the right of free assembly may be exercised shall contain no political, religious or class discrimination [Article 40.6.2].

Within the civil rights postulated by Bunreacht na hÉireann, the right to organize has been established [Article 40.6.2]. Marshall views the right to organize and to vote (political rights) as essential to the realization of social rights. The right to vote is outlined in Article 16.1.2.

> All citizens, and, such other persons in the state as may be determined by law, without distinction of sex who have reached the age of eighteen years who are not disqualified by law and comply with the provisions of law relating to the election of members of Dáil Éireann, shall have the right to vote at an election for members of Dáil Éireann.

The right to vote and to organize is seen by Marshall as an important instrument in achieving social rights. Barbalet (1988: 9) has argued that when citizenship comes to incorporate political rights a conflict emerges.

This is discussed by Marshall (1950) and exemplified by the case of trade unionism. Marshall (1950: 94) claims that the right to form associations and to organize collectively, through a trade union, for example, established 'the claim that they, as citizens, were entitled to certain social rights'.

The 1937 Constitution goes on to make provisions for issues relating to social policy in Article 45, which include that:

> The state shall strive to promote the welfare of the whole people by securing and protecting as effectively as it may a social order in which justice and charity shall inform all the institutions of the national life [Article 45.1].

> The state shall, in particular, direct its policy toward securing:
> . . . That the citizen (all of whom, men and women equally, have the right to an adequate means of livelihood) may through their occupations find the means of making reasonable provision for their domestic needs [Article 45.2].

> The state pledges itself to safeguard with especial care the economic interests of the weaker sections of the community, and, where necessary, to contribute to the support of the infirm, the widow, the orphan, and the aged [Article 45.4].

In his treatment of the development of citizenship, Marshall equates social rights with social policy. Social rights by their nature have a direct relationship with social policy: 'they imply an absolute right to a certain standard of civilization which is conditional only on the discharge of the general duties of citizenship' (Marshall, 1950: 94). Therefore, an onus is placed upon the state to accommodate the delivery of social rights to its citizens. For the state, this entails ensuring a degree of economic security. As a result of the state's obligations in this regard, Barbalet (1988) claims that 'it is in this vein that a necessary association of social rights and social policy is implicit'. However he also discusses the problematic relationship between social policy and social rights. He argues that the practice of social policy may undermine the qualities individuals require in order to recognize and exercise rights. This is particularly so in a welfare state where the delivery of social services tends to operate in ways which emphasize the dependent status of their client, where, for example, women are categorized as dependants under the Irish social welfare code. Barbalet goes on to argue that in a society stratified by social class in which socialization and experience differentially equip people from different class backgrounds, it is likely that those most in need of social services are least likely to receive them as rights.

Critiques of Marshall's Theory of Citizenship

During the late 1950s and early 1960s, *Citizenship and Social Class* (Marshall, 1950) had a considerable influence on sociological thought. In recent times the claim for a revival of citizenship has renewed interest in Marshall's work.

Rees (1994) identifies two theories of citizenship in the writings of Marshall, with the view put forward in earlier work differing from that implied in later work. In Marshall's earlier work, Rees observes that he was more concerned with discussing the concept of citizenship and the relationship with the capitalist class system with little attention being paid to the emerging concept of national citizenship. He argues that Marshall came to restrict the undertanding of citizenship to the political sphere, thereby enforcing a conventional liberal view. However, he suggests a paradox emerging in much of Marshall's later work and contends that there is a strong view of citizenship attributed to Marshall which he may never have held and which Rees argues was relinquished in the later writings. Rees argues that in Marshall's later work, for example in *The Right to Welfare and Other Essays,* citizenship is viewed as national membership and as a body of obligations. Marshall is concerned with the reality of social rights, discretion versus enforceable entitlements, i.e. selectivity versus universal entitlements. Rees contends that Marshall's later theoretical discussion of citizenship progressed beyond looking at the relationship between citizenship and the class system to looking at the concept of citizenship as a bearer of its own inequalities.

Barbalet (1988) criticizes Marshall's proposition that social rights can be rights of citizenship on three grounds. First, citizenship rights are rights of participation in a common national community; social rights may be required for the practice of citizenship insofar as they enable such participation. Secondly, citizenship rights are necessarily universal; social rights on the other hand are only ever meaningful when they are substantive, and substantive rights can never be universal. Finally, social rights are always conditional upon an administrative and professional infrastructure and ultimately upon a fiscal basis. Thus they might be better described not as rights but as conditional opportunities.

In an article on citizenship and routes to welfare in old age, Twine (1992) criticizes another controversial aspect of Marshall's work. He accuses Marshall of confusing rights with opportunities, offering the example of security in retirement. Twine argues that Marshall neglected the civil opportunity route. The civil opportunity route to secure retirement for older people could come about through employment, carrying the eventual enjoyment of a good occupational pension. He maintains that, as long as civil opportunity takes precedence over social rights, those absent from the labour market may experience poverty in their pre-retirement life course and consequently in their old age. He points out that this is particularly true for women, and despite attempts to provide equal opportunities for women, the risk of this occurring is strengthened by governments encouraging the civil route to welfare above the social route.

Stewart (1995) looks at the evolutionary nature of Marshall's work, arguing that it gives a sense of irreversibility to the institutionalization of rights. He highlights the recent developments in Britain which question Marshall's approach, for example, right wing ideologies and their effect on welfare. He examines discussions about the meaningfulness of particular combinations of citizenship rights relating them to the empowerment of equally autonomous individuals, arguing that 'the central thrust of much of the study of social stratification, for example, has been to demonstrate the manner in which patterns of social inequality in the form of class, sex and race serve to give many formal rights only a literal meaning' (Stewart, 1995: 72).

It is generally accepted that the post war construction of welfare enormously extended the range of state support for welfare. However, while Britain experienced this vast expansion of state-supported welfare based on a strong ideological philosophy evident in *The Beveridge Report* (Beveridge, 1942), the development of state welfare in Ireland took place in a piecemeal fashion, responding to needs as they arose. Within Britain itself, the development of welfare fell short of establishing universal access; benefits were conditional rather than unconditional. In the case of married women, access was as dependants rather than as citizens in their own right. This has led O' Connor (1993) and Lister (1998) to contest the 'universalism' of citizenship, seeing it as deeply circumscribed, a highly conditional universalism which assumes a family-based social and economic structure.

Held (1989) argues that citizenship has always meant a certain reciprocity of rights against and duties towards the community. If citizenship entails membership in the community and membership implies forms of social participation, then it is misleading to think of citizenship primarily in relationship to class or the capitalist relations of production. Held goes on to argue that citizenship is concerned with the involvement of people in a community in which they live; and people have been barred from citizenship on grounds of gender, race and age among many other factors.

> To analyse citizenship as if it were a matter of the inclusion or exclusion of social classes is to eclipse from view a variety of dimensions of

social life which have been central to the struggle over citizenship. (Held, 1989: 199)

Held calls for a reconsideration of the debate about citizenship initiated by Marshall, considering it in need of elaboration and modification.

Differentiated Citizenship

Marshall has effectively, throughout his analysis, avoided addressing the understanding of the differentiated experience of citizenship encountered by groups within society. However debates concerning participation and empowerment have focused upon addressing these issues. Barbalet (1988:1) claims that

> [t]he issue of who can practise citizenship and on what terms is not only a matter of the legal scope of citizenship and the formal nature of the rights entailed in it. It is also a matter of the non-political capacities of citizens which derive from the social resources they command and to which they have access.

The 1990s have seen the emergence of debates challenging the existing paradigm of rights and entitlement to citizenship. These debates have relied, to some extent, upon European concerns with race and social exclusion (Comité des Sages, 1996). Over the last two decades, the issue of Travellers in Irish society has raised concerns about ethnicity and culture within society. Mac Gréil (1996: 324) addresses the issue of ethnicity, Travellers and social policy. The housing policy of assimilation (i.e. Travellers ceasing to live their nomadic lifestyle and settling into the 'settled' community) is questionable on the basis of how well it respects the civil rights and the ethnicity of the Travelling Community. Mac Gréil calls for a pluralist approach to the Travelling Community, which he sees as preserving and promoting the cultural differences between the Travellers and the settled community, affording them equal access to cultural, economic and social amenities. A pluralist policy based upon equal treatment and a focus on participation and empowerment, would address the challenges to full citizenship posed by a postmodern society (Turner, 1994; Mac Gréil, 1996).

Currently, Ireland is facing the issue of refugees and asylum seekers, forcing the government to rethink the conditions of citizenship. The issue of refugee status poses questions about citizenship rights and entitlements. Refugees have differentiated citizenship: for example, asylum seekers are denied the right to engage in employment while awaiting refugee status. Solomos and Back (1996: 214) argue for the reconceptualization of citizenship in the context of multi-cultural societies. They identify the need for protection of the rights of minorities and the need to facilitate minority groups and propose the development of extensive notions of citizenship and democracy which include those minorities that are excluded on racial and ethnic criteria.

Rees (1994) claims that Marshall's analysis of citizenship never addressed in any significant detail the problems posed by the enactment and enforcement of rights to women, which push deep into areas that Marshall did not consider, such as family and relationships. This issue is discussed at great length by those concerned with the feminist perspective of citizenship, seeking to revisit general theoretical understandings of citizenship (see chapter 13, pp. 231–53). Walby (1994) argues that the absence of gender analysis in Marshall's conceptualization of citizenship causes problems for the understanding of citizenship. She emphasizes the importance of the private and public spheres, seeing them as being of critical concern to the position of women as citizens within society. She contends that aspects of civil citizenship for women are largely contingent upon success in obtaining political citizenship. Walby views this as being more important than has often been considered in analyses of changes in gender relations, since she regards it as the basis of the transformation from private to public patriarchy. She suggests that social citizenship for women is incompatible with, and unobtainable under, women's confinement to the family.

In Pascall's (1986) view, a feminist approach should mean more than putting women into the picture. It means criticizing and renewing conceptual apparatus and understanding social policy as part of a wider process. While Marshall remarks on the importance of women's suffrage and its implementation in the twentieth century, he does not analyse the development of citizenship rights from women's perspectives. The historical sequence of women's citizenship rights differs from the one Marshall describes for men. Nowhere does he analyse the problematic relationship between citizenship and dependency in the family as he does between citizenship and social class. The status of married women as dependants has often been supported and entrenched by the very social rights that are seen to epitomize citizenship. (For further discussion of citizenship and gender see also O'Connor (1993); Lister (1991); Vogel (1994); and Williams (1989)).

CITIZENSHIP, SOCIAL WELFARE AND GENDER IN IRELAND

Silver (1995: 8) argues that 'the history and values of a particular state tend to be embedded in the public and private institutions that define the parameters of social membership'. In the process of providing payments, the social security system treats people in certain and unequal

ways. The basis for this treatment is derived from the interpretation of
the Constitution of Ireland (Government of Ireland, 1937). The traditional
view of the role of women in society is exemplified in Article 42:2.1
which states that 'in particular, the state recognizes that by her life within
the home, woman gives to the state, a support without which the
common good cannot be achieved'. Bunreacht na hÉireann goes on to
add that 'the state shall therefore endeavour to ensure that mothers shall
not be obliged by economic necessity to engage in labour to the neglect
of their duties in the home' [Article 41.2.2]. The dominant perception of
women in Ireland was built upon this framework. Women were placed
securely within the home and by its own declaration the state would
make every effort to keep them from entering the public sphere.
McLaughlin claims that the Constitution 'outlined a series of social
policy principles which were intended to re-establish and reinforce
traditional gender relations by removing women from public life' (1993:
210). Hussey (1993: 418) notes that 'no woman took part in the deliberations during the writing of the Constitution'. However, as Ward (1995)
indicates, women did object to its content.

The basis for the civil, political and social rights of women are
curtailed and limited by the conservative Catholic ethos postulated within
the Constitution and permeating throughout society, thus affecting
women's participation within the public sphere. The Report of the
Constitution Review Group (1996) disclosed the following statistics:
women comprise 50.3% of Ireland's population, 99% of homeworkers
and just 36% of the total employed labour force. The same statistics
revealed that women are overwhelmingly represented in low paid, low
status employment, comprising 72% of all part-time workers and 85%
of the lowest paid part-time workers.

Ginsburg (1979: 26) argues that 'the social security system not only
reflects but strengthens the subordinate position of women as domestic
workers inside the family and wage workers outside the family'. The
Irish welfare state has succeeded in defining a position for women
situated within the home and depriving them access to the public sphere,
hence hindering their access to equal rights as citizens. An analysis of
social welfare law in Ireland by Donnelly (1993) observes that no other
field of law contains so many explicit references to gender. This can be
seen through such entitlements as those of single women, deserted
wives, unmarried mothers, widows and widowers. Donnelly claims that
'this resort to gender as a basis for social welfare payments is grounded
upon the historical reality of a society which discriminates against women
in terms of employment thereby consigning them to an inferior economic
position' (Donnelly, 1993: 90).

Social welfare inequalities stem, according to Sohrab (1994), at least in part from the limited recognition in social security systems of unpaid caring in establishing entitlement to social security benefits. Moroney (1976: 213) argues that, by presenting traditional family responsibilities for dependants and the division of labour between the sexes and between generations as normal or natural, the state supports and sustains these relationships without being intrusive. Thus, they preserve the illusion that the family is a private domain. Women and families continue to bear the social costs of dependency and the privatisation of family life protects 'normal' inequalities between family members and constrains the demand on public services. Qureshi and Walker (1989: 27) argue that the state operates a dual role in terms of care; it may provide support where it is necessary, but its main concern is to ensure the continuance of the prime responsibility of the family for support and care of its own members – the responsibility for which predominantly falls on women. The implications of caring for women are further articulated by Twine (1992), who points out that, because women have traditionally substituted paid labour for unpaid labour in the home, they are being denied what he describes as 'the civil opportunity route to welfare'.

Citizenship, Participation and Social Policy

Debates concerning citizenship have more recently been embroiled in arguments about participation and empowerment. For participation to be possible, a political agenda is needed in which civil and social rights are incorporated (Croft and Beresford, 1996; Powell and Guerin, 1997). The 1970s gave birth to new social movements struggling for participatory democracy and for social equality and justice. Alternative models of working and of organization are now developing at local, national and international level (see chapter 9, pp. 155–77). Why is there a desire for participatory democracy? Spicker (1996) believes that the only source that individuals have for voicing their demands is through their social relationships and social networks. He believes that the ability to use this source represents freedom in the collective sense. The responsibility to participate as a member in society is integral to the civic republican view of citizenship (Held, 1989; Taylor, 1996; Lister, 1998).

The new debates surrounding citizenship in social policy, which emerged in the late 1980s, are largely concerned with inclusion. Croft and Beresford (1996: 180) claim that the 'idea of citizenship is now being used as a way of highlighting people's exclusions and of giving force to arguments and campaigns for their involvement'. In the opinion of Taylor (1996), citizenship as a legal entitlement entails not just the formal membership of a nation state, but also a whole array of socio-economic and ideological practices connected to nationalism. He believes that these practices amount to processes of exclusion and inclusion of particular groups and categories of individuals. He states that these have included women, racialized groups, children and lesbian women and gay men.

According to Taylor, the first step that must be taken is to recognize the rights of marginalized or excluded groups to demand their own forms of collective action needed to achieve their needs. He argues that citizenship theory has to be able to allow those autonomous movements the right to challenge the state and market structures of power. Croft and Beresford (1996) assert that participation 'reflects the democratic ethos of our society, encourages people's independence and self determination, and is consistent with people's human and civil rights' (Curtin and Varley, 1995; Croft and Beresford, 1996; Taylor 1992, 1996; Comité des Sages, 1996).

CONCLUSION: CITIZENSHIP – PRESENT AND FUTURE

The concept of citizenship according to Rees (1985, 1994) may have a dual effect of being both exclusionary and inclusionary, a view echoed by Silver (1995). It has been suggested by Kymlicka and Norman (1994) that the unwillingness of liberal theorists to depart from the concept of citizenship (as defined by Marshall) may derive from the recognition that citizenship is not just a legal status defined by rights and responsibilities but also an identity. Citizenship is an expression of one's membership within a political community. Grasping this concept allows liberal theorists to strengthen the idea of civic community. Kymlicka and Norman (1994) search for an adequate understanding of citizenship, balancing both rights and obligations. Cairns and Williams (1985:43) argue that we need 'a fuller, richer and yet more subtle understanding of citizenship because what the state needs from the citizenry cannot be secured by coercion, but only cooperation and self restraint in the exercise of private power'. Concerns are emerging for people's participation and inclusion within society. Theoretical discussion has developed in order to re-define the rights, responsibilities and status of citizens with the aim of facilitating this participation.

Feminist perspectives have concentrated largely on the relationship of women to the private and public sphere, focusing on women's lack of participation within the public sphere. Previous attempts to meet citizenship rights led to a marginalization of those excluded from the 'collective' nature of state welfare provision on the one hand and of those unable to compete as market consumers on the other. Pateman (1989:129) contends that for women to enter the public sphere will require radical changes in both the private and public spheres:

> liberal principles cannot simply be universalised to extend to women in the public sphere without raising an acute problem about the patriarchal structure of private life . . . the spheres are integrally related and women's full membership in public life is impossible without changes in the domestic sphere.

Reconceptualizations of citizenship must address the deeper basis of social power, demanding that the needs of individuals be accommodated. To facilitate this, the needs of individuals for access to the necessary conditions and resources to enable them to achieve autonomy and self-determination must be addressed. Taylor (1996: 163) argues that conceptualizations of citizenship must address the internal division of labour and the processes of exclusion of 'racialized' groups, allowing citizenship to become a genuinely liberatory, internationalist and anti-nationalist concept.

RECOMMENDED READING

Barbalet, J. M. (1994) 'Theories of Citizenship', pp. 1–14 in J.M. Barbalet (cd.), *Citizenship, Rights, Struggles and Class Inequality*. Milton Keynes: Open University Press.

Lister, R. (1998) *Citizenship: Feminist Perspectives*. London: Macmillan.

Marshall, T. H. (1950) *Citizenship and Social Class and Other Essays*. Cambridge: Cambridge University Press.

Marshall, T. H. (1981) *The Right to Welfare and Other Essays*. London: Heinemann.

Rees, A. M. (1985) *T. H. Marshall's Social Policy in the Twentieth Century*. London: Hutchinson.

Van Steenbergen, B. (ed.) (1994) *The Condition of Citizenship*. London: Sage.

REFERENCES

Barbalet, J. M. (1988) *Citizenship*. London: Open University Press.

Barbalet, J. M. (1994) 'Theories of Citizenship', pp. 1–14 in J.M. Barbalet (ed.), *Citizenship, Rights, Struggles and Class Inequality*. Milton Keynes: Open University Press.

Beveridge, W. (1942) *Social Insurance and Allied Services*. London: HMSO.

Cairns, A. and C. Williams (1985) *Constitutionalism, Citizenship and Society in Canada*. Toronto: University of Toronto Press.

Comité des Sages (1996) *For a Europe of Civic and Social Rights*, Chaired by Maria de Lourd. Luxembourg: Office for Official Publications for European Union.

Constitution Review Group (1996) *Report*. Dublin: Stationery Office.

Croft, S. and P. Beresford (1996) 'The Politics of Participation', pp. 175–98 in D. Taylor (ed.), *Critical Social Policy: A Reader*. London: Sage.

Curtin, C. and T. Varley (1995) 'Community Action and the State', pp. 379–409 in P. Clancy et al. (eds), *Irish Society: Sociological Perspectives*. Dublin: Institute of Public Administration.

Department of Social Welfare (1997) *Supporting Voluntary Activity: A Green Paper on the Community and Voluntary Sector and its Relationship with the State*. Dublin: Stationery Office.

Donnelly, A. (1993) 'Social Welfare Law', pp. 90–108 in A.Connelly (ed.), *Gender and the Law in Ireland*. Dublin: Oak Tree Press.

George, V. and R. Page (1995) *Modern Thinkers on Welfare*. Hertfordshire: Prentice Hall /Harvester Wheatsheaf.

Ginsburg, N. (1979) *Class, Capital and Social Policy*. London: Macmillan.

Government of Ireland (1937) *Bunreacht na hÉireann/Constitution of Ireland*. Dublin: Stationery Office.

Healy, S. and B. Reynolds (eds) (1998) *Social Policy in Ireland: Principles, Practice and Problems*. Dublin: Oak Tree Press.

Held, D. (1989) *Political Theory and the Modern State: Essays on State, Power and Democracy*. Cambridge: Polity.

Held, D. (1991) 'Between State and Civil Society: Citizenship', pp.19–25 in G. Andrews (ed.), *Citizenship*. London: Lawrence & Wishart.

Hussey, G. (1993) *Ireland Today; Anatomy of a Changing State*. Dublin: Townhouse & Viking.

Kymlicka, W. and W. Norman (1994) 'Return of the Citizen: A Survey of Recent Work on Citizenship Theory', *Ethics*, 104: 352–81.

Lewis, J. (1997) *Lone Mothers in European Welfare Regimes: Shifting Policy Logistics*. London: Jessica Kingsley.

Lister, R. (1991) 'Citizenship Engendered', *Journal of Critical Social Policy*, 32: 65–71.

Lister, R. (1998) *Citizenship: Feminist Perspectives*. London: Macmillan.

Mac Gréil, M. (1996) *Prejudice in Ireland Revisited*. Maynooth: Survey and Research Unit, St Patrick's College.

Marshall, T. H. (1950) *Citizenship and Social Class and Other Essays*. Cambridge: Cambridge University Press.

Marshall, T.H. (1965) 'The Right to Welfare', *Sociological Review*, 13 (3).

Marshall, T.H. (1981) *The Right to Welfare and Other Essays*. London: Heinemann Educational Books.

Marshall,T.H. and T. Bottomore (1992) *Citizenship and Social Class*. London: Pluto Press.

McLaughlin, E. (1993) 'Ireland: Catholic Corporatism', pp. 205–37 in A. Cochrane and J. Clarke (eds), *Comparing Welfare States: Britain in International Context*. London: Sage.

Moroney, R.M. (1976) *The Family and the State*. London: Longman.

O'Connor, J. (1993) 'Gender, Class and Citizenship in the Comparative Analysis of Welfare State Regimes: Theoretical and Methodological Issues', *British Journal of Sociology*, 44: 501–18.

Pascall, G. (1986) *Social Policy: A Feminist Analysis*. London: Tavistock.

Pateman, C. (1989) *The Disorder of Women*. Cambridge: Polity.

Powell, F. and D. Guerin (1997) *Civil Society and Social Policy*. Dublin: A & A Farmar.

Qureshi, H. and A. Walker (1989) *The Caring Relationship*. London: Macmillan.

Rees, A. M. (1985) *T.H. Marshall's Social Policy in the Twentieth Century*. London: Hutchinson.

Rees, A. M. (1994) 'The Other Marshall', *Journal of Social Policy*, 24 (3): 341–62.

Silver, H. (1995) 'Social Exclusion, Social Inclusion', *Democratic Dialogue* 2: 7–31.

Solomos, J. and L. Back (1996) *Racism and Society*. London: Macmillan.

Sohrab, J.A. (1994) 'An Overview of the Equality Directive on Social Security and its Implementation in Four Social Security Systems', *Journal of European Social Policy*, 4: 263–76.

Spicker, P. (1996) 'Understanding Particularism', pp. 220–34 in D. Taylor (ed.), *Critical Social Policy: A Reader*. London: Sage.

Stewart, A. (1995) 'Two Conceptions of Citizenship', *British Journal of Sociology*, 46(1): 63–78.

Taylor, D. (1992) 'A Big Idea for the Nineties: The Rise in Citizens' Charters', *Critical Social Policy*, 33: 87–94.

Taylor, D. (1996) 'Citizenship and Social Power', pp.156–67 in D. Taylor (ed.), *Critical Social Policy: A Reader*. London: Sage.

Turner, B. (1994) 'Post Modern Culture/Post Modern Citizen', pp.153–168 in B. Van Steenbergen (ed.), *The Condition of Citizenship*. London: Sage.

Twine, F. (1992) 'Citizenship, Opportunities, Rights and Routes to Welfare in Old Age', *Journal of Social Policy*, 21(2): 165–75.

Van Steenbergen, B. (ed.) (1994) *The Condition of Citizenship*. London: Sage.

Vogel, U. (1994) 'Marriage and the Boundaries of Citizenship', pp.76–89 in B. Van Steenbergen (ed.), *The Condition of Citizenship*. London: Sage.

Walby, S. (1994) 'Is Citizenship Gendered?', *Sociology*, 28 (2): 379–95.

Ward (1995) *Unmanageable Revolutionaries: Women and Irish Nationalism*. London: Pluto Press.

Williams, F. (1989) *Social Policy, A Critical Introduction*. Cambridge: Polity.

12
Poverty in Ireland

Helen Johnston[1]

INTRODUCTION

In the words of the Irish National Anti-Poverty Strategy *Sharing in Progress* (Government of Ireland, 1997: 2):

> Tackling poverty and social exclusion is one of the major challenges facing Irish society. It will involve ensuring that the impact of the very rapid economic, social and demographic changes reduces social inequalities and social polarisation. It will mean ensuring that the benefits of sound economic management and growth are distributed fairly and, in particular, are used to tackle the underlying causes of poverty and social exclusion. Investing in tackling poverty is in the interests of us all. As well as causing much misery and hardship, failure to do so would ultimately impose huge social and economic costs on society and curtail economic growth and the development of a more cohesive society.

Poverty is therefore of concern at individual, household, community and societal level. It is of concern at local, regional and national level. It is of concern for economic, social and political reasons.

This chapter will examine how poverty is defined, how it is measured and will then go on to describe the extent and nature and experience of poverty in Ireland. In order to tackle poverty it is important to understand its causes and consequences. Finally anti-poverty policy will be briefly highlighted.

POVERTY: DEFINING THE CONCEPT

A great deal has been written about the definitions and understanding of poverty, social exclusion and inequality. One thing all commentators are agreed upon is that these are complex and difficult concepts to define. There are a number of reasons why one would want to define poverty. These include:

- having a broad understanding of what poverty is;
- being able to measure poverty in order to enumerate and describe the poor; and
- having a basis for introducing and implementing anti-poverty policies.

For some people the term poverty brings to mind the image of what is commonly referred to as absolute poverty. Absolute poverty is often used to describe outright destitution, the struggle to survive, not having enough food to stay alive, not having enough clean water to avoid dehydration or infection by life threatening diseases, or not having shelter from the elements; that is, people do not have the basic physical require-ments of food, water, clothing and shelter (Government of Ireland, 1997: 29). The term 'absolute poverty' is usually applied to developing countries.

In Ireland, while few people die of hunger, it can be argued that there are still some people subject to absolute poverty. These people are unable to house, clothe or feed themselves. However, in the developed world, including Ireland, poverty is understood in a relative way rather than an absolute way. Relative poverty is described with reference to the prevailing socio-economic conditions of the society in question. This state was defined by Townsend in 1979 as follows:

> Individuals, families and groups in the population can be said to be in poverty when they lack the resources to obtain the type of diet, participate in the activities and have the living conditions and amenities which are customary, or at least widely encouraged, or approved, in the societies to which they belong. Their resources are so seriously below those commanded by the average individual or family that they are, in effect, excluded from ordinary living patterns, customs and activities (Townsend, 1979: 31).

Using this definition poverty is defined in relation to the prevailing societal norms and in this sense is relative rather than absolute. Thus, an understanding of relative poverty recognizes that poverty involves isolation, powerlessness and exclusion from participation in the normal activities of society as well as lack of money. Relative poverty recognizes that the unequal distribution of resources and opportunities contributes to poverty. Such an understanding of poverty recognizes that people have social, emotional and cultural needs as well as physical needs. It is recognized that relative poverty is multi-dimensional, dynamic and impacts on individuals, households and communities (Government of Ireland, 1997: 2).

Based on this understanding of poverty the Irish Government, in its National Anti-Poverty Strategy (NAPS), has defined poverty as:

> People are living in poverty, if their income and resources (material, cultural and social) are so inadequate as to preclude them from having a standard of living which is regarded as acceptable by Irish society generally. As a result of inadequate income and resources people may be excluded and marginalised from participating in activities which are considered the norm for other people in society. (Government of Ireland, 1997: 3).

The term social exclusion has increasingly appeared in the poverty litera-ture in recent years, particularly that originating from Europe. It focuses mainly on relational issues, such as inadequate social participation, lack of social integration and lack of power. It has been argued that the use of the term social exclusion is helpful because it takes account of new and emerging forms of poverty and disadvantage brought about by very rapid economic, social and technological changes. In particular, it helps to increase the understanding of poverty in three respects: by broadening the focus from income/expenditure to multi-dimensional disadvantage; from a moment in time to dynamic analysis; and from the individual or household to the local community in its spatial dimension (Room, 1995: 233–4).

In an interim report on the work of the European Union's Third Poverty Programme in Ireland, Commins (1993) argued that, in order to understand the process of exclusion, there is a need to look at the processes of integration. Commins's interpretation of exclusion is based on a rights approach and he describes social exclusion as the failure of one or more of the following systems:

(a) the democratic and legal system, which promotes civic integration;

(b) the labour market which promotes economic integration;

(c) the welfare state system promoting what may be called social integration;

(d) the family and community system which promotes interpersonal inte-gration. (Commins, 1993: 4).

In this context civic integration means being an equal citizen in a democratic system. Economic integration means having a job, having a valued economic function, being able to pay your way. Social inte-gration means being able to avail yourself of the social services provided by the state. Interpersonal integration means having family and friends, neighbours and social networks to provide care and companionship and moral support when needed. All four systems are important and can be seen as complementary: when one or two are weak the others need to be strong. Where all the systems have failed – the worst situation – we find those who are the most marginalized and most excluded.

Nolan and Whelan (1996), however, argue for the use of the concept of poverty in preference to social exclusion. They argue that people understand what poverty is and that there is a general consensus on what constitutes a minimum acceptable standard of living: the same cannot be said of social exclusion which is not yet a commonly used or understood term and is a concept which is still relatively ill-defined and thus difficult to measure. Nevertheless, they do concede that the use of the term social exclusion could have strategic advantages:

> One could see it as analogous to the emphasis by Scandinavian social scientists on inequality rather than poverty as the core concept: arguably, policies directed to reducing inequalities in those countries were also particularly effective in tackling poverty, at least until recently (Nolan and Whelan, 1996: 195).

The Irish Government has an agreed definition of social exclusion contained in the national agreement *Partnership 2000*. In *Partnership 2000* social exclusion is defined as:

> Cumulative marginalisation: from production (employment), from consumption (income poverty), from social networks (community, family and neighbourhoods), from decision making and from an adequate quality of life. (Government of Ireland, 1996).

In the international literature a range of concepts, definitions and measurements of poverty and social exclusion is in use and there are arguments and preferences for the use of one term over another, for example see Nolan and Whelan, 1996; Room, 1995; Berghman, 1995, Robbins et al., 1994; Commins, 1993; Atkinson, 1987.

The Irish government has considered the issue of poverty and social exclusion at some length and has agreed and adopted definitions of both poverty and social exclusion, as defined earlier in this chapter.

The Measurement of Poverty

Poverty can be measured in a number of different ways: by measuring expenditure or consumption; by using social welfare rates; by asking people what they regard as the minimum resources they would require to make ends meet; by using the prevailing income levels drawn from survey data; by using indicators of deprivation; or by describing the experience of poverty through local surveys, group discussions and case studies. Poverty does not lend itself to measurement by purely scientific or agreed measures. A number of measures are used and the strengths and weaknesses of these measures are documented in Callan et al., 1996a.

Other useful texts on poverty measurement are Nolan and Callan, 1994; Nolan and Whelan, 1996; and Callan et al., 1996b. For summary information, see the National Anti-Poverty Strategy (Government of Ireland, 1997) and Combat Poverty Agency Fact Sheets and Poverty Briefings.

This section outlines some of the main methods by which poverty has been measured.

Budget Standard Approach

One method which uses an expenditure/consumption approach to poverty measurement is the budget standard approach which was used in much of the early poverty research in Britain and is still used in the United States today. Essentially this method involves costing a typical basket of goods and services required for a basic standard of living. A crucial element of this approach is the food element based on an adequate nutritional diet. Weaknesses of this approach are the extent to which judgements are required as to what constitutes a basic standard of living. It cannot be seen therefore as a purely objective approach to measuring poverty. In its favour, however, is that it is easily understood and people can identify with the commodities which make up an adequate standard of living. Examples of the use of a budget standard approach are *The Cost of a Child* (Carney et al., 1994) report published by the Combat Poverty Agency and work done by Bradshaw et al. (1993) in England.

Social Welfare Rates

Another approach to defining and measuring poverty is using rates of income support provided by the social welfare system as a benchmark. The advantages of this approach are that the benchmark is based on actual rates, not the views of 'experts', that the information is readily available and that rates of income support can increase in line with changing standards of living over time. The main disadvantage with this approach is that increasing social welfare rates could lead to an increase in measured poverty levels, as the notional poverty line also rises.

Subjective Poverty Lines

More common measures of poverty are independent of the social welfare system and can provide a benchmark against which the effectiveness of the social welfare system can be assessed. One such approach is the use of subjective poverty lines based on asking people what they would regard as the minimum resources they would require 'to make ends meet' or what income levels they would consider as 'bad', 'very bad' and so on. While this approach is useful in exploring people's views on the adequacy of various income levels it has many shortcomings. Assumptions are involved by the respondents in interpreting the questions, and by the researchers in interpreting the responses. There may also be a variety of responses across the population as different groups may hold quite different views.

Relative Income Poverty Lines

A more popular approach, which is widely used across Europe and the OECD countries, is the use of relative poverty lines based on income levels in society. For example, 'poverty lines' have been 'drawn' at half average income or sixty per cent of average income. The advantages of this approach are that it is based on the concept that people will require, and are entitled to, a minimum level of income to enable them to participate fully in society, and that minimum income will rise as average living standards rise. Being fairly widely used, and employing a relative concept, it allows comparison of poverty levels across countries. It is also transparent, can be readily understood and provides a good starting point for the analysis of poverty, in identifying the relative position and composition of low income groups. Some of the difficulties associated with this approach include the availability of good quality, up-to-date information on which to derive average income, and the arbitrariness with which the cut-off point is decided. The use of relative income poverty lines is also established on a rather narrow base – income levels; the need to broaden this definition is discussed in the next section. Sen (1983) has some concerns about this approach: any improvement in the living standards of low income groups is discounted when it is shared by the rest of the population. Similarly, if the incomes of the population as a whole decline – and those on very low incomes are even worse off – it will not become apparent as an increase in the numbers living in poverty.

Deprivation Indicators

Deprivation indicators are used to identify households which lack an amenity or do not participate in activities which the majority of the population have or participate in. This approach was employed by Townsend (1979) initially and developed by Mack and Lansley (1985) in the UK and in Ireland by the ESRI, see Nolan and Whelan (1996). Essentially people are asked whether or not they have certain items or participate in certain activities and if they do not whether this is because they choose not to or whether it is because they cannot afford them, i.e. 'enforced' lack. Much work has been done to develop appropriate and relevant indicators of deprivation, for example Callan, Nolan and Whelan (1993: 51) have proposed groupings of items as follows:

(*a*) 'basic' life style items such as food and clothing
(*b*) 'housing' and 'household durables' relating to housing quality and facilities
(*c*) 'other' or 'secondary' life style items such as social participation and leisure activities, having a car or telephone.

The advantages of this approach are that it lets us explore a broader concept of poverty and alludes to the multi-dimensional nature of poverty, i.e. someone may be housing poor, but not poor by the other dimensions described. When linked to income poverty it enables us to investigate why a household may be living on a very low income but not suffering from deprivation or why someone may have a relatively high income but lack many of the basic necessities of life or fail to participate in any social contact. Such analysis raises questions of the different dimensions of poverty, changes over time and movements in and out of poverty.

Some of the difficulties of using deprivation indicators relate to the selection of items and the degree of judgement involved. It is also unknown to what extent differences in living patterns may be largely attributable to different preferences rather than the availability of resources.

Experience of Poverty

While national surveys help us to measure the proportion of the population who are living in poverty, such surveys tell us little about what it is actually like to live in poverty. Local surveys, group discussions and case studies can help us to understand the different dimensions of poverty and provide insights into the lives of people living on inadequate incomes, the daily struggle to make ends meet and the experience of leading bleak, restricted and marginalized lives, for example see O'Neill (1992).

THE EXTENT OF POVERTY IN IRELAND

Having described how poverty can be defined and measured, the remainder of this chapter will briefly describe the extent and nature of poverty in Ireland. More detailed information is available in a range of texts, including Government of Ireland (1997), Callan et al. (1996a),

Nolan et al. (1998), Nolan and Watson (1999), Callan et al. (forthcoming), Nolan and Whelan (forthcoming) and Factsheets and Briefings from the Combat Poverty Agency.

Recent information on poverty in Ireland comes from a survey of household income, called the *Living in Ireland Survey* (LIIS), carried out by the Economic and Social Research Institute (ESRI) in 1994.[2] This survey was part of a European-wide study which collected information in each EU state on household income and has continued to collect the same information from similar households each year since then.

In Ireland 4000 households were surveyed in 1994 and within those households nearly 10,000 people were interviewed. The results give a general picture of the extent of income poverty and the experience of deprivation on a national scale and of trends and changes since 1987, the last time a comparable study was conducted.

Using income poverty lines, between 21 per cent and 34 per cent of the population can be said to be living on incomes below 50 per cent to 60 per cent of average disposable income, based on income lines derived from the 1994 data (see Table 1). Fifty per cent to sixty per cent of average disposable income was approximately £64 to £77 per week respectively for a single adult in 1994, and 760,000 to 1.2 million people could be said to be living below these income levels. (The equivalent figures for 1999 are £72 to £87 per week, approximately.)

In interpreting information on levels of poverty in Ireland it is important to note that:

- income is not the only indicator of poverty
- not all persons in a particular income band will be in the same circumstances
- households and people move in and out of poverty over time
- poverty lines do not tell us about how income is shared within households, between men and women, or between adults and children
- national household surveys do not include people who do not live in traditional households such as: Traveller families, people who are homeless, women and children who leave home to seek refuge from violent partners, children in care and others in institutions.

As described in an earlier section, poverty can also be measured using deprivation indicators. Using a combination of income poverty lines and basic deprivation indicators between nine per cent and 15 per cent of the population can be said to be living in poverty, at the 50 per cent and 60 per cent income poverty lines respectively. In this measure the eight basic indicators of deprivation included are:

Table 1. Households and People Affected by Poverty in 1994

	Households	Persons
50 per cent poverty line	18.5	20.7
60 per cent poverty line	34.6	34.0

Source: Derived from Callan et al., 1996a.

Notes

1 This information is based on employing an equivalence scale of 1/.66/.33, which is used to adjust the income of each household to take into account its size and composition. Equivalence scales are based on the principle that adults have greater needs than children and that households can benefit from economies of scale. An equivalence scale of 1/.66/.33 implies a value of 1 is assigned to the first adult in the household; 0.66 to other adults in the household and 0.33 to children in the households. For further discussion on equivalence scales see Callan et al. (1989).

2 A child is defined as under 14 years of age.

3 The well-being of each household is represented by its 'adult equivalent income', which is the total income divided by the number of adult equivalents, as defined by the equivalence scale.

4 Current disposable income per adult equivalent is a measure reflecting net pay from employment or self-employment (after the deduction of income tax and PRSI contribution) as well as social welfare payments, private pensions, and income from investment and property.

5 Mean disposable income averaged over households in the 1994 LIIS was £280. The income per adult equivalent averaged over households was £128.94, using the 1/.66/.33 equivalence scale (£64.47 at the 50% poverty line and £77.36 at the 60% poverty line).

6 In general, the number of persons below poverty lines is higher than the corresponding proportion of households. This indicates that households below poverty lines are somewhat larger than average. The higher proportion of households than persons at the 60% poverty line relates to the high number of single adult elderly households falling below this poverty line. In general, persons are more often used than households to describe the level of poverty.

- debt problems arising from ordinary living expenses
- had a day in the last two weeks without a substantial meal
- had to go without heating during the last year through lack of money

Enforced lack of:

- new clothes
- two pairs of shoes
- warm overcoat
- roast or equivalent once a week
- meal with meat, fish or equivalent every second day.

As is evident from this list these items are very basic and people/ households lacking these items are experiencing fairly severe deprivation. When households lacking at least one of these basic items are combined with the respective income lines the percentage of people falling below these thresholds can be said to be living in persistent poverty.

The focus of the National Anti-Poverty Strategy (NAPS) is on those who are subject to income poverty and do not have any resources on which they can draw i.e. the nine to 15 per cent of the population who in 1994 were found to be persistently poor (see Chapter 16, pp. 293–316).

Examining poverty trends over time shows that, in general, while numbers experiencing relative poverty have increased, numbers experiencing poverty combined with deprivation have fallen slightly as has the depth of poverty. As shown in Table 2 the percentage of people below the 50 per cent and 60 per cent relative poverty lines has increased over the last 20 years. When relative income lines are combined with basic deprivation measures there has been a small reduction in the percentage of households below these lines and experiencing basic deprivation between 1987 and 1994. Thus combining relative income lines with basic deprivation criteria can give a different picture to one using income lines alone. These differences relate to the different types of household experiencing poverty and assists in our understanding of the nature of poverty and the various processes generating it. As well as examining changes in purely relative terms, looking at the numbers falling below income thresholds held constant in real terms since 1987 is also informative. There has been a substantial decline in the numbers below

Table 2. Percentage of the Population in Poverty: 1973 to 1994

	1973 HBS	1980 HBS	1987 ESRI	1994 LIIS
50% line	15%	16%	19%	21%
60% line	25%	27%	30%	34%
50% line + basic deprivation	NA	NA	10%	9%
60% line + basic deprivation	NA	NA	16%	15%

Source: Derived from Callan et al., 1996a.

Notes
1   1973 and 1980 HBS = Household Budget Survey undertaken by the Central Statistics Office
2   1987 ESRI = Household Income, Poverty and Usage of State Services Survey undertaken by the ESRI.
3   1994 LIIS = Living in Ireland Survey undertaken by the ESRI.

thresholds held constant from 1987 indicating that those on the lowest incomes have also benefited from the growth in real average incomes which has taken place over the period. For example, about 20 per cent of persons were below half average income in 1987; by 1994 only eight per cent were below that line uprated by the increases in inflation over the period. Similarly, at the 60 per cent poverty line, about 30 per cent of persons were below the line in 1987; this had fallen to about 20 per cent in 1994.

There has been a consistent fall in the depth of poverty, i.e. how far people fall below the poverty lines, between 1973 and 1994. Government spending on welfare payments over the last ten years has focused primarily on improving the lowest levels of social welfare payments. This has contributed to a reduction in the depth of poverty, even though the increases have not been substantial enough to raise people above the poverty lines.

Who are the Poor in Ireland?

In identifying the composition of the poor it is important to distinguish between those groups of people who account for a substantial proportion of those living in poverty (known as incidence) and other groups of people who may be subjected to a high risk of poverty (known as at risk). That is, it is useful to know which types of household are at high risk of poverty and which account for most of the poor.

Classifying households on the basis of Labour Force Status of the head of household, those headed by an unemployed person were the largest group in poverty in 1994, representing one-third of all households in poverty (33 per cent). Households headed by someone working in the home were the second largest group at 25 per cent (see Callan et al., 1996a). Households headed by an unemployed person also had the highest risk of poverty, followed by households headed by someone with a disability, and households headed by someone working full-time in the home, see Table 3. The increase in poverty risk in households headed by a full-time home worker appears to relate to the increase in risk for single adult households. Many of these households were headed by older women.

Table 4 shows the risk of poverty when households are classified on the basis of their size and composition. The highest risks of poverty were for households comprising a single adult only, a single adult or three or more adults with children, and a couple with three or more children. A significant proportion of the single adult households below the line in 1994 comprised an older person or widow. It should also be noted that some of the three adult households may in fact have referred to single

Table 3. Risks of Poverty by Labour Force Status of the Head of Household, 1987 and 1994

Labour Force Status of the Head of Household	1987	1994
Employee	3%	3%
Self Employed	10%	15%
Farmer	33%	20%
Unemployed	57%	59%
Ill/Disabled	34%	44%
Retired	9%	11%
Home Duties	10%	35%
ALL HOUSEHOLDS	16%	18%

Source: Derived from Callan et al., 1996a.

Notes
1 For definitions see Tables 1 and 2.
2 Risks at the 50% relative poverty line.
3 The classifications used in this table are based on standard labour force survey classifications.

or two parent families with older children (a child was defined as under 14 years by the study, so three or more adults with children may have been single adults or couples with older children). In this context it is important to note that the risk of falling below the 50 per cent poverty line for households comprising a single adult with children rose from about 30 per cent in 1987 to 57 per cent in 1994 and almost all of these were lone parents (mostly mothers). Although lone parents are still a relatively small proportion of the population (less than three per cent of the survey sample) they do face a particularly high risk of poverty.

In terms of the incidence of poor households classified by household type 'other households with children' are the biggest group under the 50 per cent income line at 34 per cent. As stated, this category comprises single adults with children and three or more adults with children, mostly the latter. Single adult households were the second largest group in poverty at 25 per cent at the 50 per cent line. The main changes between 1987 and 1994 in the types of households experiencing poverty were the substantial decline in the risk of poverty for farm households and the increased poverty risk for single adult households, the elderly, households headed by women and households headed by full-time home workers, with a good deal of overlap between these groups. The drop in the number of farm households in poverty was largely because 1986, the

Table 4. Risks of Poverty by Household Type, 1987 and 1994

Household Type	1987	1994
I adult	12%	21%
2 adults	12%	9%
3 or more adults	11%	10%
2 adults, I child	17%	14%
2 adults, 2 children	18%	14%
2 adults, 3 children	21%	22%
2 adults, 4+ children	36%	38%
Others with children	23%	33%
ALL HOUSEHOLDS	17%	18%

Source: Derived from Callan et al., 1996a.

Notes
1   For definitions see Tables I and 2.
2   Risks at the 50% relative poverty line.
3   Child is classified as being under 14 years of age; 'others with children' includes single
    adults with children (most of whom are lone parents) and 3 or more adults with
    children.

year covered by the 1987 survey, was an unusually bad one for farming
and farm incomes substantially improved between 1987 and 1994.
However, the volatility of farming incomes makes it relatively difficult to
be precise about the risk of poverty for farmers based on data collected
only for single years. As mentioned earlier, public policy from 1987 to
1994 gave priority to increasing the lowest social welfare payments. This
has led to a reduction in the depth of poverty but has had little impact
on the overall numbers in poverty at the 50 and 60 per cent poverty
lines. This policy of prioritizing increases in the lowest rates of welfare
also explains the increase in the number of single adult households
comprising an older person or widow experiencing poverty over the
period. Pensions, which were set at a relatively high rate in 1987, increased
more slowly than the lowest social welfare rates and average incomes in
general over the period.

    The findings on the risk of poverty by household type are borne out
in the relatively high levels of child poverty in Ireland. In 1994, between
29 per cent and 40 per cent of children were at risk of poverty (at the 50
per cent and 60 per cent poverty lines respectively), compared to 18 to
32 per cent for adults. Ireland has the second highest rate of child poverty
in the European Union and Irish children are two-thirds more likely to
be in poverty than adults. Unemployment has been identified as the

main reason for the high level of child poverty. Child poverty has increased since 1987 and this is a particularly worrying trend since children who grow up in poverty are more likely in their turn to face a range of social problems, do less well at school and be the future long-term unemployed.

The gender dimension of poverty is also important. Men and women can endure different risks of poverty and poverty can be experienced differently by men and women. The way poverty is measured through national household surveys, by assuming that resources are fairly shared within the household, can mean that the gender dimension of poverty is not always evident, and in particular it can be argued that women's poverty can be hidden. In addition, inequality and discrimination can increase the risk of poverty. An analysis of the 1994 Living in Ireland survey data shows firstly, that the poverty risk of households headed by women was considerably higher than the risk of poverty for households headed by men or couples. Secondly, there is a particularly high overall risk for households headed by women (24 per cent at the 50 per cent poverty line and 53 per cent at the 60 per cent poverty line). This is mainly due to the high proportion of households consisting of an older women living alone among this group. Thirdly, there has been a large increase in poverty risk for households headed by women between 1987 and 1994 compared to the relatively stable situation for households headed by men or couples. Some of these changes are explained by an increased risk of poverty for older people, as discussed earlier.

It has also been shown that the experience of poverty for women may be substantially different from that of men. This may relate to the demands made on women in low income families. For example, Rottman's (1994) study on the distribution of income within Irish households shows that households on the lowest incomes and those relying on social welfare payments display a different pattern of income sharing and financial management to other households. Management systems in low income households tend to give wives the stressful responsibility of managing expenses for food, fuel and housing. O'Neill's (1992) study clearly shows that the burden of poverty often falls on women. Their poverty goes beyond the material deprivation of poverty because of the obstacles to social participation resulting from child-rearing or family responsibilities, because of economic dependence, because of difficulties of struggling to bring up families on low incomes and in poor environments, because of parenting alone, because of barriers in accessing education, training or employment opportunities, because of lack of adequate, accessible or affordable childcare facilities, or because some women are victims of domestic violence. For further information on women and poverty see Daly (1989) and Nolan and Watson (1999).

While national household surveys are useful in the analysis of poverty, they do not include those who do not live in private households. Many people who do not live in private households are among the most vulnerable and marginalized in our society. Other studies have shown that members of the Travelling community and other ethnic minorities have a very high risk of poverty, as well as people who are homeless, some sections of the gay community, refugees and prisoners' families.

Where are the Poor in Ireland?

Poverty affects virtually every part of Ireland. This is because poverty is mainly due to structural causes, such as educational disadvantage, being in the unskilled manual working class and long-term unemployment rather than locational factors per se, although public sector housing has been found to be an important indicator. Nevertheless, 50 per cent of all poor households do not live in local authority housing. Concentrations of disadvantage can be found in some areas throughout the country, particularly in:

• decaying inner city areas;
• large suburban public housing estates and public housing estates on the fringes of rural towns; and
• isolated and underdeveloped rural areas.

Where concentrations of disadvantage occur it has been found that communities suffer from cumulative disadvantage and for such people the cumulative effect intensifies their experience of poverty. For further information see Nolan et al., 1998; Haase, 1999; Curtin et al., 1996; and Nolan and Whelan, 1999.

The Experience of Poverty

In addition to knowing about the numbers of people living in poverty and who they are it is important to understand what it actually means to live in poverty. Much of the current debate about poverty fails to convey the experience and quality of life for low income families. Statistical data and academic reports cannot provide insights into what it is really like to have to live in poverty, to struggle on a daily basis to make ends meet, with little hope of improvement, and to feel excluded from a standard of living experienced by the majority of the population. A range of studies provide insights into the experience of living in poverty. These include: Combat Poverty Agency, 1989, 1991; O'Neill, 1992; Murphy-Lawless, 1992; and Daly and Walsh, 1988.

The key issues emerging from studies of the experience of people living in poverty are the importance of a regular, certain and adequate income and the desire of people to participate in society and to seek the best for their children. This is illustrated by the overriding importance of feeding a family, of providing children with the basic necessities of life and encouraging them to 'get an education', the difficulty of providing for special occasions such as Christmas, Communion and Confirmation, the difficulty of coping with unforeseen expenses and events, and the constant threat of debt. People living in poverty have few choices in life, often suffer ill health and psychological stress, often feel thwarted by the complications of 'the system' and can be denied their basic rights as citizens (Government of Ireland, 1997: 58).

The Causes and Consequences of Poverty

In understanding poverty, and particularly in trying to identify solutions, it is important to try to understand the causes of poverty. The causes of poverty have been clearly identified in the government's National Anti-Poverty Strategy as structural, and related to the principal systems through which resources in society are allocated. In examining the operation of the labour market, unemployment, particularly long-term unemployment, has been shown to be a fundamental cause of poverty; and the experience of unemployment is very unequally shared. The education system can reproduce inequalities and poverty. The tax and social welfare systems have a critical role to play in relation to addressing poverty. The impact of inequality, discrimination, disability and resource distribution within households can reinforce the impact of these other causes of poverty.

The consequences of high levels and concentrations of poverty can lead to a threat to the social fabric of the country and can incur high economic costs. The consequences of poverty include: concentrations of poverty in certain communities; effects on physical health and an increase in psychological distress; an increase in crime; an increasing drug culture; and the alienation of young people.

The causes and consequences of poverty are often inextricably linked. In a worst case scenario this can result in a cycle of poverty. If this cycle of poverty is not broken, some individuals and groups of people will become further marginalized and alienated from the rest of society. This will hold back economic development and subsequently result in increased costs and security risks for the rest of society. In breaking this cycle of poverty attention should be primarily focused on addressing the main structural causes, while not ignoring ameliorative actions. (Government of Ireland, 1997: 6, 7).

Anti-Poverty Policy

Policies to tackle poverty must be based on an understanding of the multi-dimensional nature of poverty. This means involving a wide range of policy areas covering the social and cultural as well as the economic dimensions of people's lives. It calls for the inclusion of tackling poverty in the strategic objectives of all government departments and agencies. It involves tackling the deep-seated underlying structural inequalities that create and perpetuate poverty. Thus, there is a need to ensure that government policies and programmes contribute to achieving a fairer distribution of resources and opportunities in all areas of day to day life and do not create or perpetuate excessive inequalities.

In Ireland there are a number of policies at national and local level seeking to address poverty. These include: the National Anti-Poverty Strategy; the current national agreement *Partnership 2000;* various initiatives in the education system; the Local Employment Service; and the Local Urban and Rural Development Programme, to name a few. Strategically the most important of these is the National Anti-Poverty Strategy, NAPS. The NAPS was launched in 1997 and is set within a ten-year time-frame to 2007. Under the Strategy the government is committed to tackling poverty across all government departments, state agencies and local government. The NAPS has an agreed definition of poverty (referred to earlier) and has set an overall target for poverty reduction in Ireland – *to reduce the 9–15 per cent of the persistently poor in 1994 to 5–10% in 2007.* In the summer of 1998 the Government introduced Poverty Proofing. All government departments now have to assess policies and programmes at design and review stages in relation to the likely impact they will have or have had on poverty and on inequalities which are likely to lead to poverty, with a view to poverty reduction. For further information on the National Anti-Poverty Strategy readers are referred to Chapter 16 (pp. 293–16) for examples of cross-cutting initiatives in public policy.

CONCLUSIONS

Ireland is currently experiencing a period of unprecedented economic growth. The success of the Irish economy in the last decade has been unsurpassed in its history. Ireland has sustained such high levels of economic growth that it has jumped from being one of the poor European Union members to being a middle-range state, with the highest rate of economic growth in the EU.

But, as stated by Sweeney (1998: 15):

Low price rises, a healthy balance of payments and other economic indicators are secondary economic objectives. The three primary objectives in any economy are high growth, full employment and an acceptable distribution of income and wealth. Ireland has been superbly successful in the first objective in recent years, but less so in the other two. Thus the success is tarnished.

Ireland still has unacceptably high levels of poverty and marginalization. We have so far failed to use our new-found wealth to make serious inroads into poverty, to ensure that everyone has enough to live with dignity and participate fully in our society. But, we do now have the resources, and a strategy in place, to address structural inequalities and to really tackle poverty and exclusion. What is required is the acceptance of the need to redistribute some of Ireland's new-found wealth and the will to do so. The choice is to share the benefits of economic growth for a more prosperous, just, peaceful and inclusive society or to promote a culture of survival of the fittest and the entrenchment of a two-tier divided society.

NOTE

1 Helen Johnston works as Head of Research in the Combat Poverty Agency. The views expressed are those of the author and not necessarily those of the Combat Poverty Agency.
2 An analysis of data from the 1997 Living in Ireland survey will be available in the summer of 1999 (see Callan et al., 1999)

RECOMMENDED READING

Key general texts on poverty conceptualization and measurement are Townsend (1979), Room (1995), Piachaud (1987) and Nolan and Callan (1994). For information on the Irish situation Callan et al. (1996) and Government of Ireland (1997) are recommended. For specific poverty issues the following books may be useful for reference. On the spatial distribution of poverty – Nolan et al. (1998), Curtin et al. (1996), Nolan and Whelan (1999), Pringle et al. (1999); on women and poverty – Daly (1989) and Nolan and Watson (1999); on the experience of poverty – O'Neill (1992); on educational disadvantage – Kellaghan et al. (1995) and Breen (1991); on unemployment and poverty – the Task Force on Long-Term Unemployment (1995) and Whelan et al. (1991); on child poverty – Nolan and Farrell (1990) and Carney et al. (1994); on disability and poverty – Combat Poverty Agency, Forum of People with Disabilities and the National Rehabilitation Board (1994) and the Commission on the Status of People with Disabilities (1996); on lone parents and poverty – McCashin (1996) and Millar et al. (1992); on Travellers – the Task Force on the Travelling Community (1995) and Dublin Travellers Education and Development Group (1994); and on homosexuality, discrimination and poverty – GLEN/NEXUS (1995). Good general reference material on poverty and broader economic and social issues are reports from the National Economic and Social Council, National Economic and

Social Forum and the Economic and Social Research Institute. The Combat Poverty Agency carries a wide range of material on poverty, produces a quarterly magazine and has a well-stocked library.

REFERENCES

Atkinson, A.B. (1987) 'On the Measurement of Poverty', *Econometrica*, 55 (4): 749–64.

Berghman, J. (1995) 'Social Exclusion in Europe: Policy Context and Analytical Framework', pp. 10–28 in G. Room (ed), *Beyond the Threshold: The Measurement and Analysis of Social Exclusion*. Bristol: The Policy Press.

Bradshaw, J (ed.) (1993) *Budget Standards of the United Kingdom*. Aldershot: Avebury.

Breen, R., (1991) *Education, Employment and Training in the Youth Labour Market*. General Research Series, Paper No. 152, Dublin: ESRI.

Callan, T., B. Nolan, B.J. Whelan and D.F. Hannan with S. Creighton (1989) *Poverty, Income and Welfare in Ireland*. General Research Series No. 146. Dublin: ESRI.

Callan, T., B. Nolan and C.T. Whelan (1993) 'Resources, Deprivation and the Measurement of Poverty', *Journal of Social Policy*, 22 (2): 141–72.

Callan, T., B. Nolan, B.J. Whelan, C.T. Whelan and J. Williams (1996a) *Poverty in the 1990s: Evidence from the 1994 Living in Ireland Survey*. Dublin: Oak Tree Press.

Callan, T., B. Nolan and C.T. Whelan (1996b) *A Review of the Commission on Social Welfare's Minimum Adequate Income*. Dublin: ESRI.

Callan T., R. Layte, B. Nolan, D. Watson, C.T. Whelan, J. Williams and B. Maitre (1999) *Monitoring Trends in Poverty for the National Anti-Poverty Strategy*. Dublin: ESRI, Combat Poverty Agency and Department of Social Community and Family Affairs.

Callan, T., B. Nolan, D. O'Neill and O. Sweetman (forthcoming) *The Distribution of Income in Ireland*. Dublin: Oak Tree Press.

Carney, C., E. Fitzgerald, G. Kiely and P. Quinn (1994) *The Cost of a Child*. Dublin: Combat Poverty Agency.

Combat Poverty Agency (1989) *Pictures of Poverty*. Dublin: Combat Poverty Agency.

Combat Poverty Agency (1991) *Scheme of Last Resort? A Review of Supplementary Welfare Allowance*. Dublin: Combat Poverty Agency.

Combat Poverty Agency, Forum of People with Disabilities and the National Rehabilitation Board (1994) *Disability, Exclusion and Poverty*. Papers from the National Conference 'Disability, Exclusion and Poverty: A Policy Conference' organized by the Combat Poverty Agency, the Forum of People with Disabilities and the National Rehabilitation Board.

Commins, P. (ed.) (1993) *Combating Exclusion in Ireland 1990–1994: A Midway Report*. Dublin: The European Programme to Foster the Social and Economic Integration of the Least Privileged Groups.

Commission on the Status of People with Disabilities (1996) *A Strategy for Equality*. Dublin: Stationery Office.

Curtin, C., T. Haase and H. Tovey (1996) *Poverty in Rural Ireland: A Political Economy Perspective*. Dublin: Oak Tree Press.

Daly, M. (1989) *Women and Poverty*. Dublin: Attic Press.

Daly, M. and J. Walsh (1988) *Money Lending and Low Income Families*. Dublin: Combat Poverty Agency.

Donnison, D. (1991) *Urban Poverty, the Economy and Public Policy*. Dublin: Combat Poverty Agency.

Dublin Travellers Education and Development Group (1994) *Reach Out: Report by DTEDG on the Poverty 3 Programme 1990–1994* by J O'Connell. Dublin: Pavee Point.

GLEN/NEXUS (1995) *Poverty: Lesbians and Gay Men: The Economic and Social Effects of Discrimination*. Dublin: Combat Poverty Agency.

Government of Ireland (1996) *Partnership 2000 for Inclusion, Employment and Competitiveness*. Dublin: Stationery Office.

Government of Ireland (1997) *Sharing in Progress: National Anti-Poverty Strategy*. Dublin: Stationery Office.

Haase, T. (1999) 'Affluence and Deprivation: A Spatial Analysis based on the 1991 Census of Population', pp. 13–36 in D.G. Pringle, J. Walsh and M. Hennessy (eds), *Poor People, Poor Places: A Geography of Deprivation in Ireland*. Dublin: Oak Tree Press..

Hannan, D.F. and S. Shortall (1991) *The Quality of Their Education: School Leavers' Views of Educational Objectives and Outcomes*. General Research Series, Paper No. 153. Dublin: ESRI.

Ireland (1992) *Urban Crime and Disorder: Report of the Interdepartmental Group*. Dublin: Stationery Office.

Kellaghan, T., S.Weir, S. O hHuallachain and M. Morgan (1995) *Educational Disadvantage in Ireland*. Dublin: Department of Education, Combat Poverty Agency and the Educational Research Centre.

McCashin, A. (1996) *Lone Mothers in Ireland: A Local Study*. Dublin: Oak Tree Press.

Mack, J. and S. Lansley (1985) *Poor Britain*. London: Allen & Unwin.

Millar, J., S. Leeper and C. Davies (1992) *Lone Parents, Poverty and Public Policy in the Republic of Ireland*. Dublin: Combat Poverty Agency.

Murphy-Lawless, J. (1992) *The Adequacy of Income and Family Expenditure*. Dublin: Combat Poverty Agency.

National Economic and Social Council (1988) *Redistribution through State Social Expenditure in the Republic of Ireland: 1973–1980*. Dublin: National Economic and Social Council.

National Economic and Social Council (1990) *A Strategy for the Nineties: Economic Stability and Structural Change*. Dublin: National Economic and Social Council.

National Economic and Social Council (1993) *A Strategy for Competitiveness, Growth and Employment*. Dublin: National Economic and Social Council.

National Economic and Social Council (1994) *New Approaches to Rural Development*. Dublin: National Economic and Social Council.

National Economic and Social Council (1996) *Strategy into the 21st Century*. Dublin: National Economic and Social Council.

National Economic and Social Forum (1994) *Income Maintenance Strategies*. Dublin: National Economic and Social Forum.

National Economic and Social Forum (1994) *Ending Long-Term Unemployment*. Dublin: National Economic and Social Forum.

National Economic and Social Forum (1996) *Equality Proofing Issues*. Dublin: National Economic and Social Forum.

National Economic and Social Forum (1997a) *Early School Leavers and Youth Unemployment*. Dublin: National Economic and Social Forum.

National Economic and Social Forum (1997b) *Rural Renewal – Combating Social Exclusion*. Dublin: National Economic and Social Forum.

Nolan, B. (1991) *The Wealth of Irish Households: What Can We Learn from Survey Data?* Dublin: Combat Poverty Agency.

Nolan, B. (1993) *Low Pay in Ireland*. General Research Series, Paper No. 159. Dublin: ESRI.

Nolan, B. and T. Callan (eds) (1994) *Poverty and Policy in Ireland*. Dublin: Gill & Macmillan.

Nolan, B., T. Callan, C.T. Whelan and J. Williams (1994) *Poverty and Time: Perspectives on the Dynamics of Poverty*. General Research Series, Paper No.166. Dublin: ESRI.

Nolan, B. and B. Farrell (1990) *Child Poverty in Ireland*. Dublin: Combat Poverty Agency.

Nolan, B. and D. Watson (1999) *Women and Poverty*. Dublin: Oak Tree Press.

Nolan, B. and C.T. Whelan (1996) *Resources, Deprivation and Poverty*. Oxford: Oxford University Press.

Nolan, B. and C.T. Whelan (1999) *Loading the Dice? A Study of Cumulative Disadvantage*. Dublin: Oak Tree Press.

Nolan, B., C.T. Whelan and J. Williams (1998) *Where Are Poor Households?The Spatial Distribution of Poverty and Deprivation in Ireland*. Dublin: Oak Tree Press.

O'Neill, C. (1992) *Telling It Like It Is*. Dublin: Combat Poverty Agency.

Piachaud, D. (1987) 'Problems in the Definition and Measurement of Poverty', *Journal of Social Policy*, 16 (2); 147–64.

Pringle, D.G., J. Walsh and M. Hennessy (eds) (1999) *Poor People, Poor Places: A Geography of Poverty and Deprivation in Ireland*. Dublin: Oak Tree Press.

Robbins, D. et al. (1994) *National Policies to Combat Social Exclusion*. (The Third National Report of the European Observatory on Policies to Combat Social Exclusion). Brussels: European Commission.

Room, G. (ed.) (1995) *Beyond the Threshold: The Measurement and Analysis of Social Exclusion*. Bristol: Policy Press.

Rottman, D. B. (1994) *Income Distribution within Irish Households*. Dublin: Combat Poverty Agency.

Sen, A. (1983) 'Poor, Relatively Speaking', *Oxford Economic Papers*, 32 (2): 153–69.

Sweeney, P. (1998) *The Celtic Tiger: Ireland's Economic Miracle Explained*. Dublin: Oak Tree Press.

Task Force on Long-Term Unemployment (1995) *Report of the Task Force on Unemployment*. Dublin: Stationery Office.

Task Force on the Travelling Community (1995) *Report of the Task Force on the Travelling Community*. Dublin: Stationery Office.

Townsend, P. (1979) *Poverty in the United Kingdom*. Harmondsworth: Penguin.

United Nations (1995) *Declaration and Programme of Action of the World Summit for Social Development*. Copenhagen: United Nations, 10 March 1995.

Whelan, C.T., D.F. Hannan and S. Creighton (1991) *Unemployment, Poverty and Psychological Distress*. General Research Series Paper No.150. Dublin: ESRI.

Williams, J. and B.J. Whelan (1993) *The Dynamics of Poverty: Issues in Short-term Poverty Transitions in Ireland*. Dublin: Combat Poverty Agency.

13
Women and Social Policy

Patricia Kennedy

INTRODUCTION

Since its development as social administration in the London School of Economics, social policy as a subject area has been dominated by men and male thinking. It was dominated for many years by Richard Titmuss, the 'founding father' of social policy, around whom there existed a network of universities and government departments, headed by male theorists, including David Donnison, Brian Abel-Smith, Peter Townsend, Robert Pinker, theorists familiar to students of social policy. From the end of the 1960s, the situation began to change and a more critical approach to the study of social policy began to emerge. In particular, structuralist (Mishra, 1977) and feminist (Wilson, 1977) critiques began to appear. Some writers question the degree to which these critiques have become part of the mainstream, including Gillian Pascall (1986), Fiona Williams, (1989, 1997) and Mary McIntosh (1997).

A GENDER DIMENSION

In recent decades Gender Studies as a subject has developed, and writings on gender have become prevalent in many disciplines. Gender Studies examine how issues affect both men and women, both similarly and differently. Gender is viewed as an important variable and this is invaluable when such issues as the family, employment, domestic violence, rape, childcare and equality legislation are examined. Gender Studies is generally viewed as less politically motivated than Women's Studies which places women at the centre of analysis. Women's Studies has developed as a distinct area of study within the major universities.

In Ireland, a rich body of literature on women's experiences within society has developed in the last three decades, coming from a variety of sources, influenced undoubtedly by the women's movement which became more visible, united and active since the 1970s (Coulter, 1993; Smyth, 1993 and O'Connor, 1998). Such studies, shaped by a variety of academic disciplines and theories, have emerged which provide a very valuable insight into the context in which women live their lives in Ireland. Historical accounts such as *Women in Irish Society: The Historical Dimension* (Mac Curtain and Ó Corráin, 1978); *Unmanageable Revolutionaries* (Ward, 1983), and *The Missing Sex: Putting Women into Irish History* (Ward, 1991) provide a historical context from which to launch an investigation into the study of women's issues in Ireland. More broad-based texts like *Gender in Irish Society* (Curtin et al., 1987), *Irish Women's Studies Reader* (Smyth, 1993) and *Women and Irish Society: A Sociological Reader* (Byrne and Leonard, 1997) provide a more sociological analysis of past and current events. Texts like *Understanding Contemporary Ireland* (Breen et al., 1990) have addressed such pertinent issues as the changing status of the family and women's status within society. More specific texts and collections have tackled issues of women's poverty (Daly,1989), lone parents (McCashin, 1993, 1996; Millar et al., 1992; Conroy Jackson, 1993; Conroy, 1997), unmarried mothers (Flanagan and Richardson, 1992), abortion (Smyth, 1992; Mahon et al., 1998), legal issues (Connolly, 1993, Kingston et al.,1997), health (Wiley and Merriman, 1996), and education (Cullen,1987; Smyth,1997). Community-based women's groups, often with the support and guidance of the Combat Poverty Agency, have contributed an invaluable insight into women's life experiences (Daly, 1989; Hayes, 1990; Carney et al., 1994). Some writings which deal specifically with the welfare state include Yeates (1997), Coakley (1997), and Cantillon (1997). Looking at Ireland from a comparative perspective the writings of Lewis (1993, 1997) and McLaughlin (1993) have offered important insights regarding women's situation within different welfare regimes. In recent years there has developed the beginning of a body of critical literature on women's experiences of childbirth (Murphy Lawless, 1991a, 1991b, 1992, 1998; O'Connor 1995; Kennedy, 1997; Kennedy and Murphy Lawless, 1998) and on women as carers (Lynch and McLaughlin, 1995). Many of these texts have drawn on feminist literature as a tool of analysis.

Women's studies in general draws on feminist ideas and perspectives and has crossed all disciplines including the arts, humanities and the natural and social sciences. There has emerged within the discipline of social policy an area referred to as 'women and social policy' which has tended to draw on feminist theory and has been fuelled by women's community activism. This chapter introduces some of the debates which have developed under the guise of 'women and social policy', and in doing so it elucidates gaps in our knowledge of social policy, both social theory and social policies in relation to Ireland.

FEMINIST SOCIAL POLICY

A feminist perspective incorporates power relations into the analysis of social policy, by introducing the concept of patriarchy, which Walby defines as 'a system of social structures and practices in which men dominate, oppress and exploit women' (1990: 20). Feminist theory and the women's movement have influenced social policy. Since the 1970s there has been a re-emergence of feminism (Coulter, 1993) which has been reflected in social policy analysis. Williams (1997) refers to social policy as being concerned with the 'hard end' of women's studies. McIntosh (1996: 14) writes of how feminist critiques of the welfare state began in the 1970s and since then have been 'detailed and sustained' and suggests that in the last two decades there has been 'a decisive shift towards an acceptance of some kind of feminist analysis'(1996: 25).

McIntosh (1996: 17) indicates that it is not enough to critique the welfare state; what is needed is a vision of the new social policy which could replace it, stating pragmatically 'this will mean discussing what sort of welfare state we do want, not just sniping at the existing one and waiting for The Revolution to put it right'. McIntosh states that first of all, it is necessary to develop a feminist presence in all areas where changes in social policy are sought. This has occurred to an extent in Ireland through the representation of the National Women's Council of Ireland (NWCI) on the National Economic and Social Forum (NESF) and as a social partner in, for example, Partnership 2000. Secondly, writing of men's relation to feminist social policy, McIntosh indicates that 'there is never an entirely acceptable stance for outsiders towards a movement of liberation' (1996: 24). She stresses that anyone concerned with social policy must take seriously the issues raised, decide what stand to take on the issues 'and must see the question of women as integral to any analysis of social policy' (1996: 24). In Ireland, the writings of, for example, Cousins (1995) and Cook and McCashin (1997) have taken an important step in this direction in recent years.

Feminism as an Ideology

George and Wilding (1994) explore what is understood by 'an ideology', concluding that it is a view of the world; it offers a critique of existing socio-economic systems; it offers a vision of the future and draws some guidelines as to how to achieve this ideal society. There is much debate regarding definitions of feminism and in recent years there has been an aggressive backlash against feminism (Faludi, 1992). Pascall argues that there is no single feminist social policy 'partly because there is no single feminist theory' (1986: 19). She claims that feminist analysis is primarily about 'putting women in where they have been left out, about keeping women on the stage rather than relegating them to the wings' and she claims that 'such a quest leads to a profound rethinking' (1986: 1). She refers to the need to examine language from a feminist perspective and indicates the value of a feminist methodology, as well as questioning 'subject and area boundaries' (1986: 5).

Williams (1989, 1997) outlines the influence of feminist theory on mainstream social policy since the 1970s. She stresses the centrality of welfare issues to women's lives as consumers and users of welfare services, as well as welfare workers both paid and unpaid (1997: 258). These words echo Dominelli's (1991: 3) observation that women have 'a contradictory relationship with the welfare state', that the welfare state can control women yet can enable women as claimants and as workers to achieve some financial autonomy. Williams (1997: 259) stresses the contradictions which the welfare state embodies: the power to offer women greater freedoms while at the same time having the capacity to constrain, control and restrict women's lives. Williams (1989) traces the development of feminist social policy and the ways in which different issues and perspectives have emerged, looking at new conceptual dimensions generated by feminist work in social policy and the impact of feminism upon new developments within social policy.

George and Wilding (1994) differentiate between three different strands of feminism – liberal, socialist and radical. They argue that feminism has added new insights and another dimension to our analysis of the welfare state, that it has highlighted gender specific consequences of social policy and has drawn attention to a range of social problems such as domestic violence and rape (National Women's Council of Ireland, 1996; Meade, 1997). It has emphasized that the personal is political and put caring work on the public agenda (Lynch and McLaughlin, 1995). It has examined the social relations of welfare providers and users and has added a gender dimension to socialist analysis as well as to the equality debate in social policy which traditionally focused on social class (Coakley, 1997; Yeates, 1997).

Like Pascall (1986), Williams argues that to an extent the development of feminist critiques within social policy mirrors the development of feminist ideas in general. Writing in 1989, Williams identifies six political perspectives which influenced feminist debates during the 1970s and 1980s; these are libertarian feminism, liberal feminism, welfare feminism, radical feminism, Black feminism and Marxist/socialist feminism. Writing in 1997, Williams argues that by the mid-1980s 'a number of shifts took place in both theory and practice' (Williams, 1997:

262): a growing concern with the concept of difference, a move away from seeking equality with men to affirming women's difference from men. At the same time, identity politics became more pertinent, and some feminist writers began to refine thinking around race (Bhavnani and Phoenix, 1994), disability (Morris, 1996), age (Arber and Ginn, 1991), and sexuality (Carabine, 1992; Van Every, 1991). Exploring Williams's (1989, 1997) classification of feminist approaches to social policy offers an invaluable insight into the debates in feminist social policy.

Strands of Feminist Thought

Libertarian feminism, according to Williams, is an 'off-shoot of neo-liberalism'. These theorists view women's oppression as caused by state intervention and see liberty as achievable through the freedom of the market. They maintain the division between the public and the private and tend to ignore social class and racial differences.

Liberal feminists view women's oppression as caused by sex-biased laws. Bryson suggests that 'liberal feminism has seldom been expressed in its pure form' (1992: 159). These theorists view women's oppression as resulting from sex discrimination as well as sex-biased laws. This group would look to the state to implement equality legislation as a means of achieving greater equality. They too maintain the separation between the public and private spheres and can tend to ignore both race and class. The work of Friedan (1986) is often associated with this ideological approach as are campaigns for equal opportunities and equality legislation, for example, in Ireland. Many of the demands of the women's liberation movement of the 1970s could be said to reflect this ideology, for example in the call for equality legislation in relation to employment and education. In Ireland many of the recommendations of the first and the second Commissions on the Status of Women (Commission, 1972; Second Commission, 1993) could be said to reflect this strand of feminist thought.

According to Williams, *welfare feminists* view the institution of motherhood as being devalued. They see women's role as determined by biology and view the welfare state as a potential vehicle of change. They argue that the state should acknowledge the value of motherhood and introduce reforms for mothers and children. Theorists associated with this ideological stance include Dalla Costa and James (1972) and it is associated in Ireland with the campaigns for increased child benefit, and for equal treatment in the social welfare system which have featured strongly in Ireland since the mid-1980s (Coakley, 1997).

Radical feminists are generally viewed as holding an extreme view. They argue that women's oppression is caused by patriarchy and in particular by men's power over women's reproduction and sexuality. They would view the public and private as linked and stress that the personal is political. Associated with this ideological approach are such writers as Firestone (1979), Dworkin (1981), and Daly (1978). They view the welfare state as a patriarchal institution exercising power over women. In Ireland, services which have developed in line with this thinking would include Women's Aid Refuges which have strict policies regarding men and boys.

Socialist/Marxist feminism places the position of women within a socialist analysis of the state. Women's position must be looked at in terms of capitalism, but not only capitalism; patriarchy is also crucial. Socialist feminists (Wilson, 1977; Barrett and McIntosh, 1991) have introduced the concept of social reproduction to the debate. They have placed social reproduction as central to any analysis of the welfare state. Women reproduce the working class on a daily basis and on a generational basis. Social reproduction involves the reproduction of ideas, values and norms. Women form the reserve army of labour and women's low pay reinforces women's dependency within marriage. The family has a central role in the capitalist state. Williams (1989: 60), in an evaluation of socialist feminism, suggests that, from a theoretical viewpoint, there are different approaches within socialist feminism. She summarizes the three broad areas of agreement of these differing approaches as: the importance of understanding men's and women's behaviour as socially constructed; a recognition of the differential as well as shared experiences of oppression of different classes, races, ages and cultures; a belief that the personal is political. The broad areas of disagreement with these differing approaches are, first of all, the extent to which women's liberation can be met without a massive reorganization of the economic and social structures or without the mobilization of women and the working class. Secondly, the relationship between patriarchy and capitalism in the creation of oppression. 'Central to these early analyses was an analysis of the family as the site of oppression with the ideology of familism permeating all areas of state provision and restricting women's role to that of wife and mother' (Williams, 1997: 261). In Ireland, women's activism in the trade union movement reflects some of these principles.

Black feminists such as Bhavnani and Phoenix (1994), Carby (1987) and Hooks (1982, 1984) view oppression as caused by racially structured patriarchal capitalism and argue that the relationship between production and reproduction must be viewed in the context of race and the racial division of labour. While race has become an issue in Ireland in recent years with a large increase in the number of immigrants – particularly refugees and asylum seekers – the largest ethnic group in Ireland,

Travellers, has consistently been subjected to racist attitudes and attacks. The ethos underlying the National Traveller Women's Council and the Primary Health Care for Travellers Project would reflect this strand of feminist thought.

Recognising that there is no one feminist approach, the feminist contribution to social policy has been invaluable in that it 'has added new conceptual dimensions to the study of social policy and reformulation of old concepts' (Williams, 1997: 264). Social policy has gained from a feminist analysis which questions the use of language as well as methodologies. It is some of these issues that the remainder of this chapter will address.

Methodology

Feminist theory has influenced research methods. Social research traditionally tended to emphasize the importance of objectivity, scientific methods and statistical analysis. Feminist research recognizes the importance of the subjective, the personal, giving women a voice, for example in *Women and Poverty*, Daly (1989) uses a variety of sources, including poetry, to indicate women's experiences of poverty. Roberts (1981) claims that the duty of feminist research is threefold. First of all, it must criticize existing social structures and ways of perceiving them. Then, it must introduce corrective mechanisms by providing an alternative viewpoint and data to substantiate it. Finally, it must start to lay a groundwork for a transformation of social science and society.

Feminist research is often interpreted as 'the study of what is missing' (Reinharz, 1992: 162). As Reinharz indicates (1992: 162):

> an early impetus of feminist scholarship was recognising that information was missing about particular women and about women in general. Identifying such exclusions, erasures, and missing information is characteristic of much feminist scholarship . . . of interest to feminist researchers are the ways certain topics came to be missing and the implications of these gaps.

A feminist approach is concerned with analysing texts and questioning the absence of others. Reinharz (1992: 163) suggests that 'feminist content analysis is a study both of texts that exist and texts that do not' and continues on to argue that

> by discovering patterns between existing and missing documents, and with power/gender relations in the society of the time, and by bringing this material to the attention of people today, new ties are made that help explain the current relation between gender and power and give some groups a greater sense of their own history.

Looking, for example, at the subject of pregnancy and labour in Ireland, there have indeed been exclusions, erasures and missing information. Apart from medical research papers (Begley, 1991, 1997), and clinical reports, women's experience of childbirth in Ireland has not been studied *or* analysed, except for some notable exceptions in recent years (Kennedy and Lawless, 1998). This is despite the fact that Ireland, often referred to as 'Mother Ireland' (McLaughlin, 1993; Gray and Ryan, 1997), where motherhood was given a special place in the 1937 Constitution (Article 41.(2)1) and where in excess of 50,000 women each year experience pregnancy, has a dearth of analysis of motherhood.

Reinharz (1992: 213) refers to the use of 'multiple methods' in feminist scholarship. She refers to how 'multi-method research creates the opportunity to put texts or people in contexts, thus providing a richer and far more accurate interpretation'. She indicates that epistemology and methodology are central to feminist research (1992: 1). There is much scholarly debate regarding the methods of feminist research. While feminist writers often employ qualitative methods and stress the importance of biography, this writer agrees with Reinharz that 'feminism is a perspective, not a method' (Reinharz, 1992: 241). Reinharz states that feminism is a perspective which adopts the methods of the discipline in question whereby feminist scholarship uses a discipline for its power turning that power 'to feminist ends' (Reinharz, 1992: 243).

Language

Language is of vital importance in social policy analysis. Language can be used to broaden horizons, to deconstruct structures, to provide and introduce alternatives, to broaden outlooks and, more negatively, to obscure. Lerner states that the process of redefinition involves a threefold challenge which involves: 'correctly defining, deconstructing existing theory and of constructing a new paradigm' (Lerner, 1986: 231). Reinharz (1992: 217) draws our attention to the use of language by feminist writers: 'many feminist researchers have invented words'. She says that feminism has the power to 're-name, re-define, re-shape the world'. She argues that feminists must address the use of language, that they must question and re-examine language. Feminists must explore the 'need for re-definition and the inadequacy of terms for describing the female experience, the status of women in society and the various levels of woman's consciousness present a problem to all feminist thinkers' (Lerner, 1986: xii).

Traditionally, social policy has used language which aggregates people: the family, the community, the household. Feminist writers have begun to deconstruct this language. One important term used widely in social policy is 'lone parent'. But a closer examination shows that lone parent-hood is a very different experience depending on whether one is a lone mother or a lone father. Feminists have deconstructed the family; not all families have two parents; not all families are heterosexual. Feminists have raised questions about the household. What is a household? What happens within that household? Pahl (1990), for example, explores the distribution of income within households which she refers to as 'the black box' and her work has been applied to the Irish case by Rothman (1994). Coakley (1999) has begun to challenge mainstream work on the measurement of poverty by constructing an alternative deprivation index based on mothers' expressed needs. Meade (1997: 344) refers to the issue that has been raised by feminists regarding the language around violence against women:

> Domestic Violence! It almost makes it sound cosy. Like Domestic Science or something. What are we talking about is rape, mental torture and abuse.

Concepts

Feminism has deconstructed and added new dimensions to existing concepts, for example, reproduction, dependency and citizenship.

Reproduction

In social policy there was a traditional emphasis on production and productive labour to the neglect of biological reproduction and social reproduction, that is, the reproduction of ideas, beliefs, values and culture. Feminist writers have focused on the reproduction of poverty, the reproduction of inequalities, for example in relation to standards of health (Jackson and Flanagan, 1993).

Dependency

Feminist theory has influenced how the concept of dependency has been treated in social policy discourse. Feminist writers have highlighted the institutionalization of dependency within the welfare state. In Ireland, for example, a system based on Beveridgean principles has meant that a male breadwinner model has developed where women are expected to depend on a male partner for financial support, and, in the absence of such a partner, depend on a patriarchal state. Feminists writing of the Scandinavian welfare states (Hernes 1987; Siim, 1990) have highlighted the dependency of females in that region on the patriarchal state either as welfare recipients or as workers. Feminists have also highlighted how dependency for a woman generally involves caring for another person (Finch and Groves, 1983). Feminist writers have highlighted the institutionalization of women's caring roles in the professions (Dominelli, 1991). Morris (1996) has highlighted the complexity of caring as an issue for women with disabilities.

Citizenship

Feminist writers have addressed the concept of citizenship. They have further developed Marshall's definition of social citizenship, which has been very much identified with the development of western welfare states, including Ireland (see Chapter 11, pp. 195–209). Orloff (1993) claims that citizenship itself is gendered and that women have not yet obtained full civil and political rights 'and if women do not participate in the formation and administration of policy, social policy for women is unlikely to translate into woman's social citizenship'(1993: 322). However, in Orloff's view, 'gender must be incorporated into the core concepts of research on the welfare state "citizen", "social rights" "claims" "welfare" and the analytic dimensions used to evaluate inputs, content and effects'. She continues on 'Feminist research can thereby incorporate advances in the mainstream literature while transforming it to incorporate gender relations' (1993: 305).

An exploration of feminist writings in the area of comparative social policy will help to clarify the feminist contribution to social policy.

Comparative Approaches

Looking at social policies from a comparative perspective, many writers, including Sainsbury (1994), refer to the tendency of mainstream and feminist writers to remain separate in their contributions to analysis of welfare (see Chapter 5, pp. 70–89). Sainsbury claims there is a need to gender welfare states 'to incorporate gender into the comparative analysis of welfare states – by drawing on a broad spectrum of insights from both feminist and mainstream research' (1994: 1). Sainsbury claims that feminist research paradigms have sought to bring women and gender into the analysis of the welfare state. This research has documented the inequalities between women and men as recipients of welfare, has questioned the interrelationships between the state, the market and the family, acknowledged the role of familial and gender ideologies and has attempted to 'redress gaps in mainstream research' (Sainsbury, 1994: 2). These writers have contributed especially to elucidating issues around women's informal, unpaid work as well as women's marginalized position in the labour market.

Lewis (1992: 160) criticizes Esping-Andersen's (1990) work on welfare regimes for ignoring unpaid labour and argues that the concept of welfare regimes must take into consideration the sphere of unpaid as well as paid work: 'work is defined as paid work and welfare as policies that permit, encourage or discourage the de-commodification of labour'. She acknowledges the value of such an analysis for women: 'the problem of the valuing of the unpaid work that is done primarily by women in providing welfare mainly within the family and in providing those providers social entitlements'(1992: 160). Lewis stresses that the relationship between paid work, unpaid work and welfare is gendered. Esping-Andersen defines de-commodification as 'the degree to which individuals, or families can uphold a socially acceptable standard of living independently of market participation' (1990: 37). Furthermore, Lewis claims that the concepts of de-commodification and dependency have 'a gendered meaning that is rarely acknowledged'(1992: 161). She criticizes Esping-Andersen for his gender blind concept of de-commodification, saying that 'de-commodification for women is likely to result in their carrying out unpaid caring work' (1992: 16).

Lewis (1992) indicates that commodification ensures that human needs and labour power become commodities. A person's well-being depends on her relationship to the cash nexus and the satisfaction of human wants is linked to buying commodities. In this situation, Lewis concludes, purchasing power and redistribution are crucial. At the same time labour power is also a commodity, and so people's right to exist outside the market is at stake. People as workers are commodities and captive to powers beyond their control. They are destroyed by simple events like illness, are replaceable and are easily rendered redundant. Lewis's succinct summary of the perils of commodification ring loud alarm bells for women. To what extent are women dispensable within the patriarchal constraints of the labour market? Women are caught in a bind between the patriarchal employment market, patriarchal healthcare and the patriarchal social welfare systems.

Taylor-Gooby (1991) claims that the relationship is not between paid work and welfare but between paid work, unpaid work and welfare. This set of relationships is gendered. While the gender divisions of paid work have changed with greater numbers of women having entered the labour market, the gendered division of unpaid work has not changed substantially (Kiely, 1995). Clearly, therefore, this discussion reveals that concepts like de-commodification and dependency have a gendered meaning.

Esping-Andersen (1990) claims that de-commodification is a necessary prerequisite for workers' political mobilization. Lewis argues that the worker Esping-Andersen has in mind is the male worker whose mobilization also relies on female support. How possible is it for the pregnant woman or new mother to become politically mobilized? Cousins (1995: 114–15) refers to

> The weakness of a transient category of persons with little organizational representation (pregnant women who are not in employment) in the formation of social policy and highlights the extent to which trade union priorities involve their own members rather than welfare recipients generally (and particularly women who are not in employment).

Lewis has been joined in her criticism of Esping-Andersen by other writers, among them Orloff (1993). Adapting the work of the power resource theorists, Orloff, develops a conceptual framework for examining the gender content of social provision that draws on both feminist and mainstream work. She extends the state-market relations dimension, to consider how states use families for the provision of caring work which she renames the state-market-family dimension in an attempt to account for 'families contributions to welfare and the political importance of the family-state division of welfare labour' (1993: 322).

Orloff broadens the concept of stratification to consider the effects of social provision by the state on gender relations. In particular she questions how the state deals with the issue of labour, both paid and unpaid, as a stratifying factor (1993: 322). Social citizenship, rights and de-commodification, she criticizes for implicit assumptions regarding the sexual division of caring and domestic labour and for ignoring the different effects on men and women. She points out that de-commodification does not apply fully to women workers and that caring work is ignored. Looking at the historical development of welfare states, Orloff draws our attention to the development of *paternalist* welfare states to the detriment of *maternalist* welfare states. This, in turn, has shaped subsequent social policies. Orloff outlines how changes in the extent of paternalism of welfare states can be assessed: firstly, the extent to which the state has taken over the provision of welfare services; secondly, the relative treatment of paid/unpaid workers, raising the question of women's access to paid work and the capacity to form/maintain autonomous households; and thirdly, the bases of people's claims to services (1993: 323).

O'Connor, writing in 1993, suggests that the incorporation of gender into the analysis of welfare regimes entails a reassessment of the conventional definitions of political mobilization and participation and a modification of the concept of de-commodification. She states: 'the concept of de-commodification...must be supplemented by the concept of personal autonomy or insulation from personal and/or public dependence' (1993: 501). 'Personal autonomy', O'Connor claims, 'is central to unravelling the complexity of the relationships amongst state, market and family' (1993: 513).

Lewis (1993) argues that the 'welfare dependency' of a woman is likely to involve caring for another dependant and the greater independence of that other. The unequal division of unpaid work blurs the division between dependent and independent, commodified and de-commodified. Because women conceive, become pregnant, give birth and nurse babies they tend to find themselves in the role as carer for their infants as well as for the elderly and for people with disabilities. This caring role is prescribed for women in Irish society.

THE CASE OF IRELAND

Ireland as a Male Breadwinner-Type State

Lewis, in 1992, presented a theoretical model to incorporate the gender dimension of welfare states. In her three-tiered model of welfare states as weak, modified and strong male breadwinner-type states, Lewis categorizes Ireland as a strong male breadwinner-type state. The strong male breadwinner state, according to Lewis's typology, is characterized by low labour force participation rates for women, a high incidence of part-time work, underdeveloped childcare, poor maternity entitlements and inequality between husbands and wives in relation to social security. This is a useful model from which to begin analysing women's relationship to the labour market and the social welfare system in Ireland, that is, women's role as earner and as carer.

De-commodification: Irish Mothers as Earners and Carers

'If women enter the public sphere as workers then they must do so on equal terms as men.' (Lewis: 1992)

Employment is a general prerequisite to independence. The majority of women in Ireland have traditionally been denied access to paid employment (Daly, 1989; McLaughlin, 1993; Conroy Jackson, 1993; Conroy, 1997; Smyth, 1997). Mothers have had particular difficulty accessing well paid full-time employment for a variety of reasons, many of which are due to Ireland's conservative corporatist tendencies. The emphasis on subsidiarity, Catholic social teaching and lack of childcare have all contributed to women's alienation from the paid labour market. Direct state intervention in the form of legislation has excluded women from the labour market. Conroy (as Conroy Jackson, 1993; Conroy, 1997) presents some of the most salient factors which have hampered mothers' participation in the labour force. These have included the dominant patriarchal ideology which was reflected in social and economic policies. Looking at the period since Independence in 1922, there has been a series of barriers to women's participation in the paid labour force. These have been explicit – for example employment legislation – and more subtle – for example legislation relating to the availability of contraception. Immediately after Independence, legislation was introduced which actively discouraged women's participation in the public service upon marriage. The marriage bar meant women in the public service had to retire on marriage. This was also adopted by private employers and was not abolished until 1973. Some years after Independence, the Irish Constitution of 1937 clearly stated the place of the Irish mother was to be in the home:

Article 41.2 of the Constitution

1   In particular, the State recognizes that by her life within the home, woman gives to the State a support without which the common good cannot be achieved.

2   The State shall therefore, endeavour to ensure that mothers shall not be obliged by economic necessity to engage in labour to the neglect of their duties in the home.

The Constitution reflected the dominant Catholic social teaching of the period, together with a concern about high male unemployment. This ideology was institutionalized in the tax and social welfare systems which aggregated income tax until 1980 and married women could not claim means-tested unemployment assistance until 1986. Continuing disincentives to women's employment include disparities in women's earnings together with inflexible working patterns regarding job sharing, flexitime and work share (NESF, 1996).

While women have been hampered in accessing the labour market, they have also had difficulties in accessing vocational training. Cousins (1996), in his study of women returners whom he defines as 'women who wish to return to the paid labour force after a period of absence due to family responsibilities', highlights some of the difficulties of this particular group in accessing training which would equip them with the necessary skills for participation in the changing labour market. He outlines the practices which have rendered women invisible and have also discriminated against women regarding entry to employment and training schemes. Irish women, and particularly mothers, are underrepresented on the live register as a proportion of those claiming unemployment payments. The live register is an important tool as it determines a person's right to access training schemes which are a gateway to employment. For women who wish to return to the labour market having cared full-time for children or others, or mothers entering the labour market for the first time, access to good quality training is essential.

Since the 1970s there have been some improvements regarding women's labour force status. These are most directly related to Ireland's membership of the European Union (see Chapter 7, pp. 114–38). Factors such as equality legislation, falling birth rate, male unemployment, rising house prices as well as the economic boom which Ireland has enjoyed in the 1990s, ensure that mothers are more likely to seek full-time employment.

Low Labour Participation Rates for Women

It is difficult to estimate statistically women's participation in the labour market as statistics available from both the live register and the labour force surveys do not give a true picture of women's labour force partici-pation (Cousins, 1996). In the 25 years between 1971 and 1996, the number of women at work grew by 212,000, reaching 488,000 in 1996 (Central Statistics Office, 1997). There was a growth rate of 23,000 for males over the same period. Changes have particularly involved married women. In 1971 married women accounted for only 14% of the work-force, whereas in 1996 about half the female workforce was married. In 1996, using ILO statistics, 41.1% of Irish women aged 15 or over were in the labour force. This compares with 58.7% for Denmark (the highest rate in the EU) and 34.6% for Italy (the lowest in the EU) (Labour Force Statistics, 1997).

In 1991, one-quarter of all mothers, one-third of all mothers with one or two dependent children, and over one-fifth of all mothers with three or more dependent children were in the labour force. Overall, slightly more than one-third (36.6%) of mothers were in the labour force in 1996, while about two-fifths (43%) of mothers with one or two dependent children were in the labour force. Only 33.2% of mothers with three or more children were in the labour force (Central Statistics Office, 1997).

A High Incidence of Part-time Work

In 1996, of 507,700 women in the labour force, 111,000 were engaged in part-time work (Central Statistics Office, 1997). Women's high representation among part-time workers is due to the fact that women in

Ireland have to balance their caring responsibilities with paid work while having practically no state support in accessing childcare services.

Underdeveloped Childcare

Women working outside the home need a good standard of accessible, affordable childcare. This has never been available in Ireland. Childcare facilities in Ireland are underdeveloped and there is no tax relief on childcare. Even in the 1990s, few workplace nurseries are in existence (Ditch et al., 1997). An ideology which maintains that childcare provision is a private issue ensures Ireland has one the of lowest levels of public childcare in the EU. Women are therefore constantly faced with having to reconcile paid work, family life and the roles and demands of biological motherhood.

Poor Maternity Entitlements

'Social welfare policies amount to no less than state organization of domestic life.' (Wilson, 1977: 9).

According to Lewis (1993), poor maternity entitlements are a characteristic of strong male breadwinner-type states. Kennedy (1997) outlines the minutiae of maternity entitlements in Ireland. There are four payments relevant to women in relation to maternity. These are: once-off cash payments paid to women around the time of childbirth to assist with the additional financial costs associated with childbirth (means-tested Maternity Grant); payments designed to replace a woman's income while she is absent from the paid labour market on a temporary basis due to childbirth (Maternity Benefit based on insurance record of the woman); Child Benefit (a universal payment); and the exceptional needs payments (ENPs) which exist outside the maternity-related payments (part of the Supplementary Welfare Allowance (SWA) Scheme) to which women often have to turn for essential items like maternity clothes, baby clothes and prams.

The most important of these payments is maternity benefit (introduced under the 1981 Maternity Protection of Employment Act, superseded by the 1994 Maternity Protection Act), as this is the payment designed to replace women's income while they take time out of paid employment to give birth. In Ireland in 1995, there were 48,530 births (Central Statistics Office, 1995), but only 15,655 women received maternity benefit, with a further 52 receiving adoption benefit (Department of Social Welfare, 1995). Thus, the majority of Irish women who give birth do not receive maternity benefit. Cousins, in an account of the historical development of maternity rights in Ireland, indicates that 'developments in the 1980s and 1990s have seen maternity protection being much more closely linked to participation in the paid labour force and the abolition of both maternity grants and allowances for women who are not in employment' (1995: 114–15).

There is no paid parental leave in Ireland, no legal entitlement to paternity leave, and limited maternity leave. Since the introduction of the 1981 Maternity Protection of Employment Act, a woman is entitled to fourteen weeks leave on the birth of her child. Conditions are attached to this leave for determining when the woman must take the time off. Since 1994 (under the Maternity Protection Act) there is also a restricted Health and Safety Leave and Health and Safety Benefit which entitles some women to protective leave from paid employment while pregnant, having recently given birth or are breastfeeding when that employment is considered a risk to the health and safety of the woman and alternative suitable work cannot be provided.

Inequality between Husbands and Wives in Relation to Social Security

Since the Equality Directive of 1986 (see Chapter 7, pp. 117–18), men and women have been legally entitled to equal treatment under the social security system. However, the reality has proved different. Daly (1989), Yeates (1997), Cook and McCashin (1997) and Coakley (1997) write of the inequalities between husbands and wives inherent in the Irish social security system. Daly (1989: 65) refers to the Irish welfare system as 'a system designed by men for men' relating it to the fact that the Irish social welfare system developed around a traditional model of a man's working life. Yeates (1997) traces the development of the system in more detail and suggests that inequality has continually been institu-tionalized, even as recently as 1995 in the guise of the Social Welfare (No. 2) Bill which preceded the Divorce Referendum of that year which failed to move towards the individualization of payments, instead reinforcing women's dependency status.

Women in Ireland have traditionally been entitled to social welfare in their capacities as wives or mothers – as dependants. Men generally claim as individuals, and for their wives and children, whereas women are generally claimed for as dependants, except for lone mothers who claim on their own behalf and on behalf of their children. At the most basic level, women have difficulty accessing benefits, owing to the complexities associated with registering as unemployed (Cousins, 1996). Daly (1989: 58), asking what does it mean to be a dependant, surmises:

If assigned this status, the social welfare system considers that you need less money: the payment for the dependant spouse is only around 60% of that for the main claimant. Two people may be able to live more cheaply than one but why is it that the cheaper payment is most often for the woman? Also, why aren't the same dependency rules applied to any two people forming a household?

Daly (1989: 58) writes of the hardship associated with 'split payments' which she refers to as 'one of the clearest examples of the hardship and discrimination that arises from the assumption of dependency'. Cook and McCashin (1997) suggest that there has been a lack of debate around equity in the social security system in Ireland.

CONCLUSION

This chapter has introduced what has become known as 'women and social policy' in academic discourse. It discussed the contribution of feminist theory to social policy analysis, emphasising that there is no one 'feminist theory' but rather various strands of feminism which straddle the ideological spectrum from right to left. It examined the contribution of feminist theorists writing on social policy from a comparative perspective. To demonstrate the usefulness of such an analysis, it presented Lewis's male breadwinner model and applied this to the Irish situation.

RECOMMENDED READING

Byrne A. and M. Leonard (eds) (1997) *Women and Irish Society: A Sociological Reader.* Belfast: Beyond the Pale.

George V. and P. Wilding (1994) *Welfare and Ideology.* London: Harvester Wheatsheaf.

O'Connor, P. (1998) *Emerging Voices: Women in Contemporary Irish Society.* Dublin: Institute of Public Administration.

Pascall, G (1986) *Social Policy A Feminist Analysis.* London: Tavistock.

Williams, F (1989) *Social Policy a Critical Introduction: Issues of Race, Gender and Class.* Cambridge: Polity Press.

Williams, F (1997) 'Feminism and Social Policy', pp. 258–81 in V. Robinson and D. Richardson (eds), *Introducing Women's Studies.* 2nd edition, London: Macmillan.

REFERENCES

Arber, S. and J. Ginn (1991) *Gender and Later Life: A Sociological Analysis of Resources and Restraints.* London: Sage.

Barrett, M. (1980) *Women's Oppression Today the Marxist/Feminist Encounter.* London: Verso.

Barrett, M. and M. McIntosh (1991) *Women's Oppression Today: The Marxist/ Feminist Encounter*. London: Verser.

Barry, U. (1992) 'Movement Change and Reaction: The Struggle over Reproductive Rights in Ireland', pp. 107–18 in A. Smyth (ed.), *The Abortion Papers*. Dublin: Attic.

Begley, C. M. (1991) 'Post-partum Haemorrhage – Who is at Risk?', *Midwives Chronicle*, 104: 102–6.

Begley C. M. (1997) 'Midwives in the Making: A Longitudinal Study of the Experiences of Student Midwives during their Two Year Training in Ireland', Unpublished PhD thesis, University of Dublin, Trinity College.

Beveridge, W. *Social Insurance and Allied Services*. Cmnd. 6404. London: HMSO.

Bhavnani, K. and A. Phoenix (eds) (1994*) Shifting Identities, Shifting Racisms, a Feminism and Psychology Reader*. London: Sage.

Breen, R., F. Marron, D. Rothman and C. Whelan (1990) *Understanding Contemporary Ireland: State, Class and Development in the Republic of Ireland*. Dublin: Gill & Macmillan.

Bryson, V (1992) *Feminist Political Theory*. London: Macmillan.

Bunreacht na hEireann (Constitution of Ireland) (1937) Dublin: Stationery Office.

Byrne, A. and M. Leonard (eds) (1997) *Women and Irish Society: A Sociological Reader*. Belfast: Beyond the Pale.

Cantillon, S. (1997) 'Women and Poverty: Differences in Living Standards within Households', pp. 196–214 in A. Byrne and M. Leonard (eds), *Women and Irish Society: A Sociological Reader*. Belfast: Beyond the Pale.

Carabine, J. (1992) 'Constructing Women, Women's Sexuality and Social Policy', *Critical Social Policy*, 34: 23–37.

Carby, H. (1987*) Reconstructing Womanhood: The Emergence of the Afro-American Woman Novelist*. New York: Oxford University Press.

Carney, C., E. Fitzgerald, G. Kiely and P. Quinn (1994) *The Cost of a Child: A Report on the Financial Cost of Child-rearing in Ireland*. Dublin: Combat Poverty Agency.

Central Statistics Office (1995) *Vital Statistics*. Dublin: Stationery Office.

Central Statistics Office (1997) *Women in the Workforce: Statistical Release, September 1997*. Dublin and Cork: Central Statistics Office.

Coakley, A. (1997) 'Gendered Citizenship: The Social Construction of Mothers in Ireland', pp. 181–95 in A. Byrne and M. Leonard (eds), *Women and Irish Society: A Sociological Reader*. Belfast: Beyond the Pale.

Coakley, A. (1999) 'The Social Construction of Mothers in Ireland, unpublished PhD thesis', Dublin: University of Dublin, Trinity College.

Commission on the Status of Women (1972) *Report to the Minister for Finance*. Dublin: Stationery Office.

Connolly, A. (ed.) (1993) *Gender and the Law in Ireland*. Dublin: Oak Tree Press.

Conroy, P (1997) 'Lone Mothers: The Case of Ireland', pp. 76–95 in J. Lewis (ed.), *Lone Mothers in European Welfare Regimes, Shifting Policy Logics*. London: Jessica Kingsley.

Conroy Jackson, P. (1993) 'Managing the Mothers: The Care of Ireland', pp. 72–91 in J. Lewis (ed.), *Women and Social Policies in Europe: Work, Family and the State*. Aldershot: Edward Elgar.

Cook, G. and A. McCashin (1997) 'Male breadwinner: A Case Study of Gender and Social Security in the Republic of Ireland', pp. 167–80 in A. Byrne and M. Leonard (eds), *Women and Irish Society: A Sociological Reader*. Belfast: Beyond the Pale.

Coulter, C. (1993) *The Hidden Tradition: Feminism, Women and Nationalism in Ireland*. Cork: Undercurrents Series, Cork University Press.

Cousins, M. (1995) *Social Welfare and the Law in Ireland*. Dublin: Gill & Macmillan.

Cousins, M. (1996) *Pathways to Employment for Women Returning to Paid Work*. Dublin: Employment Equality Agency.

Cullen, M. (1987) *Girls Don't do Honours: Irish Women in Education in the Nineteenth and Twentieth Centuries*. Dublin: Women's Education Bureau.

Curtin, C., P. Jackson and B. O'Connor (1987) *Gender in Irish Society*. Galway: Galway University Press.

Dalla Costa, M.R. and S. James (1972) *The Power of Women and the Subversion of the Community*. London: Falling Wall Press.

Daly, M. (1978), *Gyn/Ecology: The Metaethics of Radical Feminism*. Boston: Beacon Press.

Daly, M. (1989) *Women and Poverty*. Dublin: Attic.

Department of Social Welfare (1995) *Annual Statistics*. Dublin: Stationery Office.

Ditch, J., J. Bradshaw and T. Eardley (1997) *Developments in Family Policy in 1994*. York: European Observatory on National Family Policies, Social Policy Research Unit.

Dominelli, L. (1991) *Women Across Continents*. London: Harvester Wheatsheaf.

Dworkin, A. (1981) *Pornography: Men Possessing Women*. London: The Women's Press.

Esping-Andersen, G. (1990) *The Three Worlds of Welfare Capitalism*. Cambridge: Polity.

Faludi, S. (1992.) *Backlash: The Undeclared War Against Women*. London: Chatto & Windus.

Finch, J. and D. Groves (eds), (1983) *A Labour of Love, Women, Work and Caring*. London: Routledge & Kegan Paul.

Firestone, S. (1979) *The Dialectic of Sex, the Case for Feminist Revolution*. London: Women's Press.

Flanagan, N. and V. Richardson (1992) *Unmarried Mothers: A Sociological Profile*. Dublin: Department of Social Policy and Social Work/Social Work Research Unit, National Maternity Hospital.

Friedan, B. (1986) *The Feminine Mystique*. Harmondsworth: Penguin.

George, V. and P. Wilding (1994) *Welfare and Ideology* London: Harvester Wheatsheaf.

Gray, B. and L. Ryan (1997), '(Dis) locating 'Woman' and Women in Representations of Irish Nationality', pp. 517–34 in A. Byrne and M. Leonard (eds), *Women and Irish Society: A Sociological Reader, A Sociological Reader*. Belfast: Beyond the Pale.

Hayes, L. (1990) *Working for Change, a Study of Three Women's Community Projects*. Dublin: Combat Poverty Agency.

Hernes, H. (1987) 'Women and the Welfare State: The Transition from Private to Public Dependence', in A.S. Sassoon (ed.), *Women and the State*. London: Hutchinson.

Hooks, B. (1982) *Ain't I a Woman , Black Women and Feminism*. London: Pluto.

Hooks, B. (1984) *Feminist Theory from Margin to Centre*. Boston: South End Press.

Hyde, A. (1997) 'Gender Differences in the Responses of Parents to their Daughters Non-Marital Pregnancy', pp. 282–95 in A. Byrne and M. Leonard (eds), *Women and Irish Society: A Sociological Reader*. Belfast: Beyond the Pale.

Jackson, P. and N. Flanagan (1993) *Women and Poverty in the European Community: Issues in the Current Debate*. Dublin: Department of Social Policy and Social Work, UCD.

Kennedy, P. (1997) 'A Comparative Study of Maternity Entitlements in Ireland and Northern Ireland', pp. 311–24 in A. Byrne and M. Leonard (eds), *Women and Irish Society: A Sociological Reader*. Belfast: Beyond the Pale.

Kennedy, P and J. Murphy Lawless (eds) (1998) *Returning Birth to Women: Challenging Policy and Practice*. Dublin: Women's Education and Research Resource Centre, UCD and Centre for Women's Studies, TCD.

Kiely, G. (1995) 'Fathers in Families', pp. 147–58 in I.C. McCarthy (ed.), *Irish Family Studies: Selected Papers*. Dublin: Family Studies Centre, UCD.

Kingston, J., A. Whelan and I. Bacik (1997) *Abortion and the Law*. Dublin: Round Hall Press.

Lerner, G (1986) *The Creation of Patriarchy*. London: Open University Press.

Lewis, J, (1992) 'Gender and the Development of Welfare Regimes', *Journal of European Social Policy*, 2(3): 159–73.

Lewis, J. (ed.) (1993), *Women and Social Policies in Europe: Work, Family and the State*. New York: Edward Elgar.

Lewis, J. (ed.) (1997) *Lone Mothers in European Welfare Regimes, Shifting Policy Logics*. London: Jessica Kingsley.

Lynch, K. and E. McLaughlin (1995) 'Caring Labour and Love Labour', pp. 250–92 in P. Clancy, S. Drudy, K. Lynch and L. O'Dowd (eds), *Irish Society: Sociological Perspectives*. Dublin: Institute of Public Administration.

MacCurtain, M. and D. Ó Corráin, D. (1978) *Women in Irish Society: The Historical Dimension*. Dublin: Arlen House.

Mahon, E., C. Conlon and L. Dillon (1998) *Women and Crisis Pregnancy*. Dublin: Stationery Office.

McCashin, A. (1993) *Lone Parents in the Republic of Ireland: Enumeration, Descriptions and Implications for Social Security*. Broadsheet Series, Paper No. 29, Dublin: Economic and Social Research Institute.

McCashin, A. (1996) *Lone Mothers in Ireland: A local study*. Dublin: Oak Tree Press in association with Combat Poverty Agency.

McIntosh, M, (1996) 'Feminism and Social Policy', pp. 13–26 in D. Taylor (ed.), *Critical Social Policy*. London: Sage.

McLaughlin, E. (1993) 'Ireland: Catholic Corporatism', pp. 205–37 in A. Cochrane and J. Clarke (eds), *Comparing Welfare States: Britain in an International Context*. London: Sage.

Meade, R. (1997) 'Domestic Violence: An Analysis and Response from Community Activists', pp. 342–56 in A. Byrne and M. Leonard (eds), *Women and Irish Society: A Sociological Reader*. Belfast: Beyond the Pale.

Millar, J., S. Leeper and C. Davies (1992) *Lone Parents, Poverty and Public Policy*. Dublin: Combat Poverty Agency.

Mishra, R (1977) *Society and Social Policy*. London: Macmillan.

Morris, J. (1996) '*Us*' and '*Them*'? Feminist Research, Community Care and Disability, pp. 77–94 in D. Taylor (ed.), *Critical Social Policy*. London: Sage.

Murphy-Lawless, J. (1991a) 'Images of 'Poor Women' in the Writings of Irish Men Midwives', in M. MacCurtain and M. O'Dowd (eds), *Women in Early Modern Ireland*. Edinburgh: Edinburgh University Press.

Murphy-Lawless, J. (1991b) 'Piggy in the Middle: The Midwife's Role in Achieving Woman-controlled Childbirth', *Irish Journal of Psychology*, 12 (2): 198–215.

Murphy Lawless, J. (1992), 'The Obstetric View of Feminine Identity: a Nineteenth Century Case History of the Use of Forceps in Ireland', in A. Smyth (ed.), *The Abortion Papers*. Dublin: Attic.

Murphy Lawless, J. (1998) *Reading Birth and Death: A History of Obstetric Thinking*. Cork: Cork University Press.

National Economic and Social Forum (1996) *Jobs Potential of Job Sharing*. Dublin.

National Women's Council of Ireland (1996) *Report of the Working Party on the Legal and Judicial Process for Victims of Sexual and Other Crimes of Violence Against Women and Children*. Dublin: National Women's Council of Ireland.

O'Connor, J (1993) 'Gender, Class and Citizenship in the Comparative Analysis of Welfare State Regimes: Theoretical and Methodological Issues', *British Journal of Sociology*, 44 (3): 501–18.

O'Connor, M (1995) *Birth Tides*. London: Pandora.

O'Connor, P. (1998) *Emerging Voices: Women in Contemporary Irish Society*. Dublin: Institute of Public Administration.

Orloff, A S (1993) 'Gender and the Social Rights of Citizenship: the Comparative Analysis of Gender Relations and Welfare States', *American Sociological Review*, 58 (June): 303–28.

Pahl, J. (1990) 'Household Spending, Personal Spending and the Control of Money in Marriage', *Sociology*, 24 (1): 119–38.

Pascall, G. (1986), *Social Policy: A Feminist Analysis*. London: Tavistock.

Reinharz, S. (1992) *Feminist Methods in Social Research*. Milton Keynes: Open University Press.

Rich, A. (1980) *On Lies, Secrets And Silence, selected prose 1966–1978*. London: Virago.

Rich, A. (1977) *Of Women Born, Motherhood as Experience and Institution*. London: Virago.

Rigal, J. (1997) 'Family Planning for Irish Traveller Women: Gender, Ethnicity and Professionalism at Work', pp. 268–81 in A. Byrne and M. Leonard (eds), *Women and Irish Society: A Sociological Reader*. Belfast: Beyond the Pale.

Roberts, H. (1981) (ed.) *Doing Feminist Research*. London: Routledge & Kegan Paul.

Robinson, V. and D. Richardson (1997) (eds), *Introducing Women's Studies*. London: Macmillan.

Roll, J. (1992), *Lone Parent Families in Europe*. London: Family Policy Studies Centre.

Rothman, D.B. (1994) *Income Distribution within Irish Households: Allocating Resources within Ireland*. (Research Report Series, No.18) Dublin: Combat Poverty Agency.

Sainsbury, D. (ed.) (1994) *Gendering Welfare States*. London: Sage.

Second Commission on the Status of Women (1993). *Report to Government*. Dublin: Stationery Office.

Siim B. (1990) 'Women and the Welfare State: between Public and Private Dependence, a Comparative Approach to Care Work in Denmark and Britain', in C. Ungerson (ed.), *Gender and Caring, Work and Welfare in Britain and Scandinavia*. London: Harvester Wheatsheaf.

Smyth, A. (ed.) (1992) *The Abortion Papers*. Dublin: Attic.

Smyth, A. (ed.) (1993) *Irish Women's Studies Reader*. Dublin: Attic.

Smyth, E. (1997) 'Labour Market Structures and Women's Employment in the Republic of Ireland', pp. 63–80 in A. Byrne and M. Leonard (eds), *Women and Irish Society: A Sociological Reader*. Belfast: Beyond the Pale.

Taylor Gooby, P. (1991) 'Welfare State Regimes and Welfare Citizenship', *Journal of Social Policy*, 20 (1): 93–105.

Valiulis, M.G. and M. O'Dowd (eds) (1997) *Women and Irish History*. Dublin: Wolfhound Press.

Van Every, J. (1991) 'Who is the Family? The Assumptions of British Social Policy', *Critical Social Policy*, 33 (1991/92): 62–75.

Walby, S. (1990) *Theorizing Patriarchy*. Oxford: Blackwell.

Ward, M. (1983) *Unmanageable Revolutionaries, Women and Irish Nationalism*. Dingle: Brandon.

Ward, M. (1991) *The Missing Sex: Putting Women into Irish History*. Dublin: Attic Press.

Wiley, M. and B. Merriman (1996) *Women and Health Care in Ireland: Knowledge, Attitudes and Behaviour*. Dublin: Oak Tree Press in association with Economic and Social Research Institute.

Williams, F. (1989), *Social Policy A Critical Introduction: Issues of Race, Gender and Class*. Cambridge: Polity.

Williams, F. (1997) 'Feminism and Social Policy', pp. 258–81 in V. Robinson and D. Richardson (eds), *Introducing Women's Studies*. 2nd edition. London: Macmillan.

Wilson, E. (1977) *Women and the Welfare State*. London: Tavistock.

Yeates, N. (1997) 'Gender and the Development of the Irish Social Welfare System', pp. 145–66 in A. Byrne and M.Leonard (eds), *Women and Irish Society: A Sociological Reader*. Belfast: Beyond the Pale.

14

The Family and Social Policy

Gabriel Kiely

INTRODUCTION

Family policy as a distinct field within the broader framework of social policy has received increased attention in Ireland, as in other European countries, over the past decade. This is reflected, for example, in Ireland with the restructuring of the Department of Social Welfare in 1997 into a new Department of Social, Community and Family Affairs. This is the first time in the history of the state that a government department included the term 'family' in its title. However, what is meant by family policy and where it fits in Irish social policy is by no means clear. This chapter will address some of the issues involved in defining and locating family policy in the wider context of Irish social policy, including the social and historical background of the policies, current issues in family policy and the relationship between the state and families.

Defining Families

The family is legally defined in Ireland as being based on marriage. This definition is based on a Supreme Court interpretation of Article 41.3.1 of the Constitution (State/Nicholaou v An Bord Uchtála, 1966), which pledges to 'guard with special care the institution of Marriage, on which the Family is founded'. However, this definition is very restrictive and tells us little about families and nothing about family policy. There are several other ways of approaching the definition. For example, families can be described as biological entities, administrative categories and social groups. Biological definitions include only those who are related by blood and are of little use in a policy context, as they exclude from a family group people not related by blood, such as stepchildren and adopted children. Social definitions are those which tend to be used in sociological studies of the family and are largely used by researchers to denote the specific group being studied as identified by the researcher. For example, the classical definition used by Giddens (1989) excludes families composed of adult children and their dependent elderly parents and families of adult siblings living together. He defines 'the family' as 'a group of persons directly linked by kin connections, the adult members of which assume responsibility for caring for children' (Giddens, 1989: 384). In the policy context, administrative definitions are the most relevant as these define the membership of the group termed 'family', who are entitled to specified benefits and protection. For example, the Social Welfare Act (1991) uses an administrative approach by treating cohabiting couples in the same way as married couples with regard to certain social welfare payments. Similarly, the Expert Working Group on the Integration of Tax and Social Welfare, in their report, *Integrating Tax and Social Welfare* (1996: 106), recommends that, in certain situations, cohabiting couples be treated the same as married couples.

The main difficulty with any of these approaches to defining 'the family' is that each of them excludes social groupings which are manifestly families. The lack of a clear definition of what constitutes a family can pose problems in the development and articulation of family policies. One way of overcoming the problem is to avoid defining the family and use the term 'families' instead, thus acknowledging that families are multiple in variety. This is the approach used by the European Observatory on National Family Policies (1990: 11). The use of the term 'families' allows for the inclusion of all social groups that could be described or perceived as being a family. Policy makers must take account of the realities that exist in society. From a family policy perspective this means acknowledging the diversity of families and developing policies that protect all families equally. Any definition of the family of necessity is restrictive and therefore excludes some social groupings that might in another definition be regarded as a family.

Families vs Households

From a policy perspective, a distinction needs to be drawn between families and households. For example, the Household Budget Survey, commonly thought to be a study of families, is a survey of households and not families. The significance of this distinction becomes all the more apparent when the composition of households and families is examined. In Ireland, 89 per cent of the population live in what is termed 'family households', but these households represent only 73 per cent of all households (Eurostat, 1995). The other households are either one-person households or multi-person households composed of persons who are not relatives, such as two friends sharing a flat. Household is essentially a spatial concept, whereas families are kin groups not necessarily sharing a common household. Some households are families, but not all families are households.

Defining the Field of Family Policy

Family policy can be defined as any governmental measure which has consequences, intended or unintended, for families. Family policy therefore refers to objectives concerning the well-being of families and the specific measures taken by government bodies to achieve them (Aldous and Dumon, 1990: 1370). Family policy, however, not only refers to the direct influence of governmental measures on families (and thus to the active intended intervention of the government), but also to the unwanted effect that measures not intended for families have on families (Sels, 1990: 9).

In their classic work on family policy, Kamerman and Kahn (1979) identify three approaches to family policy. The first is when family policy is defined as a 'field' in which certain objectives regarding the family are established and various policies are developed to achieve these goals. This is illustrated, for example, by establishing an objective that children should be protected from abuse and to achieve this objective specific measures such as the Child Care Act (1991) are then implemented. The second approach is where family policy is defined as an 'instrument' of social control (Kamerman and Kahn, 1979: 6). In this situation, society may identify goals which do not have direct relevance to families, but which require some sort of behaviour on the part of families or family members for goal attainment. An example of this is the Carer's Allowance which was introduced in 1990. It is payable to carers on a means-tested basis, who are providing elderly or incapacitated pensioners with full-time care and attention, and thus supporting families in their role as social service providers. The third approach is when family policy is seen as a 'perspective' or criteria for social policy choice (Kamerman and Kahn, 1979: 7). This approach is not currently an explicit element in Irish family policy. However, the proposal put forward by the Commission on the Family in its *Final Report* (1998) for the use of Family Impact Statements, if implemented, would be an example of this approach to family policy.

The European Observatory on National Family Policies in its 1990 *Annual Report* distinguishes between what it describes as the institutionalization of family life (i.e. legislation) on one hand, and social measures supporting family life on the other, as the two main dimensions of family policy. This is similar to the approach used by the Commission on the Family (1998: 3) in which the Commission divides policies under the two broad headings of 'regulation of family matters' and 'resource distribution'. The first of these – regulation of family matters – includes the law on marriage, marital breakdown and family property legislation. The European Observatory (1991: 9) includes all so-called family law as well. The second dimension to family policy, i.e. resource distribution, includes a range of purposes including promoting social equity and supporting minimum standards (Commission on the Family, 1998: 3). The European Observatory (1991: 9) describes these policies as enabling policies insofar as they are geared at enabling family members to more adequate role performance and/or role change, and include material and non-material measures.

Current Issues in Family Policy

Since family policy essentially includes all actions by the state that impinge on families, it is difficult to set boundaries on the aspects of public policy to be included. However, a number of issues have emerged in recent times as key issues in family policy. These include: (*a*) child welfare; (*b*) the integration of work and family roles; (*c*) family income supports; (*d*) regulation of adult relationships; and (*e*) care by family members. This is not an exhaustive list, but it does serve as some indication of where the current debate in family policy tends to be focused. Each of these aspects of family policy can include both dimensions of family policy (regulatory measures and distribution of resources) and each is a substantial policy area in its own right.

Child welfare includes all regulations and provisions dealing with the well-being and protection of children. The traditional focus in family policy on children has been on their vulnerability. But recently, primarily as the result of the UN Convention on the Rights of the Child in 1989, and the Kilkenny Incest Investigation in 1993, there has been an increased emphasis on the rights of children as their position as citizens has become recognized (see 'Children: Status and Policies in Europe', in Ditch et al. (1998: 31–54). The need to balance the rights of the child, the rights of the parents and the position of the state is the focus of current public concern. The courts interpret the Constitution to locate the rights of the child within the family (Kiely and Richardson, 1995: 37). However, the Constitution Review Group Final Report (1996) among its proposals for change make a number of recommendations that would give explicit guarantee in the Constitution for the protection of the rights of children (see Kiely, 1998a).

The integration of work and family roles as an area of family policy is quite extensive. It includes policies and measures which enable fathers and mothers to share childcare tasks, both within and outside the home and which also enable them to fully participate in the paid labour force, such as maternity and paternity leave, childcare services, maternity protection of employees, regulation of part-time and flexible working works, job sharing and career breaks. Equal opportunities legislation is of major importance in the relationship between people's working and home lives, and to an extent is the key to integrating both of these aspects of a person's life. In recent years there has been an increased focus on the role of fathers in families, particularly on their participation in housework and childcare (see Kiely, 1995). This participation is seen as a necessary part of the equation in relation to women's participation in the paid labour force. However, the only policy initiative that includes fathers in this area has been the introduction of parental leave.

Family income supports encompass all fiscal policies including taxation and social welfare that support or hinder families to function as economically viable units, especially with regard to the costs of rearing children and caring for dependent adult members. Households with children, especially large families, face a disproportionate risk of poverty in Ireland, and children are more likely to be in poverty than adults (Carney et al., 1994: xii). State financial support for families in Ireland has therefore been focused primarily on poor families and as such is a major element in an anti-poverty strategy. However, from a family policy perspective, there are many other dimensions involved in family income supports, including horizontal equity, impact on female labour force participation, and intra-family resource distribution (see, for example, Child Benefit Review Committee, 1995).

The regulation of adult relationships includes family legislation and social provisions dealing with marriage, divorce and separation, cohabitation and single parenthood. It also includes fertility, parenthood, pregnancy, abortion, violence and the general regulation of sexual relationships. The regulation (or deregulation in some cases) of adult relationship and the consequent rights, duties and responsibilities of partners have been the focus of much public debate, legislation and more than one referendum in Ireland in recent years.

Care by family members as an area of family policy is concerned with the role played by family members as providers of care for each other and the extent to which state policy and provisions support them in providing this care (Kiely, 1998b). Caretaking is the emotional and physical care given by family members sharing a common household. This caretaking occurs primarily, although not exclusively, across generations.

That is, the care by parents for children, the care of dependent elderly parents by their children, the care by a spouse for a spouse, the care of elderly dependent siblings for each other, and the care by family members of other dependent relatives. This has been a relatively neglected area in Irish family policy, although it has increasingly become one of the key areas of family policy throughout most of Europe. This rise in interest is related to the ageing of the population and to the rise in multi-generational families (see Savage, 1995).

Health, education and housing policies also have family policy dimensions. These are sometimes included in the five categories given above, and not treated separately. The same applies to policies that deal with family stress and difficulties, such as family counselling services. Any categorising of policies is of necessity arbitrary. However, how the various aspects of family policy are organized here reflects the dominant themes as they seem to emerge in various national reports throughout Europe on studies of family policy (see, for example, the annual reports of the European Observatory on National Family Policies).

IRISH FAMILY POLICY

Historical Development of Irish Family Policy

Up until the 1600s, the early Irish Brehon laws regulated many aspects of family life. They dealt with a whole range of family matters including marriage, divorce, offences against women and children, and fosterage (see Kelly, 1988). These laws placed a legal responsibility on the kin group to care for its members.

The first piece of legislation under British rule that comes under the general heading of family policy was the 1634 Act of the Irish Parliament for the Erection of Houses of Correction. The Act placed responsibility on immediate family for the care of family members. Under the Act, a man who deserted his family would be sent to a house of correction. It was not until the 1703 Act of the Irish Parliament, which established St James Street Workhouse and levied a tax for the care of the poor, that responsibility for family members started to shift to the community at large. The next piece of legislation in the category of family policy was the 1838 Irish Poor Law Act. This Act was not family-friendly and it impacted severely on many families. Based on the principle of less eligibility, it required entire families to enter workhouses where family members were segregated by sex, and parents separated from children. The Act also required parents to pay for their children and adult children to pay for elderly parents (Burke, 1987: 49). The 1847 Irish Poor Relief

Extension Act further extended family provision by the state by identifying specific family members and groups as entitled to outdoor relief. By now the state, however reluctantly, had entered the arena of family policy, by recognising that it shared with the family the responsibility of providing for its members.

The end of the nineteenth century and the start of the twentieth century saw rapid development in social legislation and especially in family policy. This included the Workmen's Compensation Act (1887), the Non-Contributory Old Age Pension Act (1908), the Children's Act (1908), and the National Insurance Act (1911), which included among other provisions a maternity benefit (see Chapter 2, pp. 11–32). There was, however, strong opposition from the Catholic hierarchy to many of the provisions of these acts, as the hierarchy espoused the precepts of subsidiarity and non-intervention in the affairs of the family by the state. It was here that the seeds of family policy in Ireland for over the first half of the twentieth century were sown. The state, on the one hand, providing family supports based on a patriarchal conception of the family, and the Catholic Church on the other, while reinforcing this conception, opposing state intervention while trying to uphold the privacy of the family. This approach was based on the so-called social teaching of the Catholic Church, which was articulated in the two papal encyclicals *Rerum Novarum* (1891) and *Quadragesimo Ano* (1931).

The culmination of this approach by church and state to family policy is reflected in the position of the family, as enshrined in the 1937 Irish Constitution, which states:

> The State recognises the family as the natural primary and fundamental unit group of society and as a moral institution possessing inalienable and imprescriptable rights antecedent and superior to all positive law (Article 41.1.1).

> The State therefore guarantees to protect the family in its constitution and authority as the necessary basis of social order and as indispensable to the welfare of the nation and the State (Article 41.1.2).

Irish family policy reinforced the traditional division of labour by sex within the family, with the husband as head of the household and the main provider. His wife and children were defined as dependants and their rights, in the context of social provisions, were derived by virtue of their relationship to him. This was reflected in the 1929 bar on the employment of married women in the public service and in certain other employments such as the banks; the exclusion of women from the social insurance scheme when they got married (1929); and the payment of lower rates of benefits to married women than to non-married women. Bishop Dignan, Chair of the National Health Insurance Society (quoted in Whyte, 1980: 102), writing in 1945 on proposals for an expanded social insurance scheme, stated: 'by the natural and divine law, the father of the family is bound to maintain his home for himself, his wife and his family: no authority, not even the State, can relieve him of this duty and privilege.'

The relationship between the state and families in Ireland up to recent times can be characterized as minimal interventionist, driven by the belief on the part of the state in the absolute privacy of the family. The family unit has traditionally been perceived by society as private and inviolable and this has been reflected in legislation, the provision of social services and social and family policy (Richardson, 1993: 135). The concept of the privatization of the family was also maintained at the level of individual families and was a deep-seated principle within Irish culture, resulting in extreme reluctance to become involved in what is regarded as family business either at the level of individual families or at the level of legislation (Kiely and Richardson, 1995: 157). The most celebrated example of the significance of the social teaching of the Catholic Church on the non-intervention by the state in the affairs of the family is the 'Mother and Child' Scheme proposed in 1949 by the then Minister for Health, Dr Noel Browne. Indeed, the ruling of the Supreme Court in 1994, when it declared the Matrimonial Home Bill (1993) as unconstitutional on the grounds that it was too great an intrusion into the private decision-making of the family, further reflects the role of the concept of privatization of the family in Irish culture right up to present times.

One important development arising from the principle of subsidiarity and the state's reluctance to engage in family policy was the growth of a vibrant and extensive voluntary sector. This grew out of the strong community tradition of self-help with a base in rural Ireland and the major contribution made by religious communities, particularly in the area of provision for disadvantaged and marginalized groups (Kiely and Richardson, 1995: 29). In most cases, voluntary organizations complemented the role of statutory services and in some cases they developed to fill gaps in statutory services. The voluntary sector continues to make a major contribution to all aspects of social service provision and community development. It is a diverse sector which ranges from informal systems of help and support provided by relatives, friends and neighbours, to sophisticated and highly developed service provision.

It was not until the 1960s, with the introduction of a national programme of industrialization, that change in the Irish family and subsequent state involvement in family policy came about. The industrialization process started a dramatic transformation of the family which eventually

ıt a need for new changes in family policy legislation and provision.
ł's entry in 1973 to the then European Economic Community
(___) was in effect the turning point in this process.

The 1970s saw a new direction in family policy, with the removal of
the so-called marriage bar on employment (1972); the introduction of
Deserted Wife's Benefit (1973); the Anti-discrimination (Pay) Act
(1972); the abolition of the old Poor Law and its replacement by a
national means-tested scheme (Supplementary Welfare Allowance) in
1975; the Employment Equality Act (1977); and the Health Act (1979),
which finally legalized family planning services. These changes
represented a new direction in family policy away from the privatization
of the family which was tied to a patriarchal conception of family
structure and life. The new direction, which was in part stimulated by
the Report of the First Commission on the Status of Women (1972) and
Ireland's entry to the EEC focused more on issues of equality.

While the 1980s saw a continuation in the development of family law
and family policy generally, the old issue of the privatization of the
family continued to be a significant theme. This was particularly notice-
able as the issues of sexual morality began to dominate the debate on
family policy. This debate focused principally around contraception,
abortion, divorce and the rights of parents over their children. The other
main concern was the economic plight of many families, especially those
with four or more children and on low income. It was not until the
1990s that family policy emerged as a significant political issue on the
agendas of the political parties and as a major election platform of
successive governments. This is illustrated by the inclusion of family
policy issues in the *Programme for Government* (January 1993) of the Fianna
Fáil and Labour Party coalition government; the policy agreement
between the coalition government of Fine Gael, the Labour Party and
Democratic Left, as expressed in *A Government of Renewal* (December
1994); and in the policy document of the Fianna Fáil and Progressive
Democrats' coalition government, *Agenda 2000* (January 1997).

Current State of Irish Family Policy

Ireland does not have an integrated family policy. One must look to
other policy areas such as social welfare, housing and childcare to
evaluate family policy. However, there are no unifying elements in these
policies regarding the promotion or protection of family life. Indeed, at
times it could be argued that, while many policies and provisions directly
impinge on the family, some take little if any concern for their impact on
the family. There is, however, growing evidence of the state's concern

for the needs of all families, as reflected not only in the policy documents of recent governments, but also in the establishment in 1995 of the Commission on the Family, and the aforementioned restructuring in 1997 of the Department of Social Welfare into a new Department of Social, Community and Family Affairs.

Given the range of family policy provisions introduced in recent years and the proposals for additional family legislation, it would appear that these changes are not merely political rhetoric or simply a matter of political labelling. The state does seem to be responding to changing family needs. In so doing, it is moving away from the old piecemeal approach which was often driven by crisis management and responses to pressure groups. The *Report of the Commission on the Family* (Commission on the Family, 1998) holds out promise for the future. If its recommendations are implemented, Ireland will have joined with other European states who recognize that protecting families and family members requires an active role by the state in the development of explicit family policies.

Report of the Commission on the Family (1998)

In 1995, the then Minister for Social Welfare established the Commission on the Family, with the following brief:

> To examine the effects of legislation and policies and make recommendations to the Government on proposals which strengthen the capacity of families to carry out their functions in a changing economic and social environment (Commission on the Family, 1988: 3)

In 1996, the Commission submitted an interim report to the government (*Strengthening Families for Life*, Commission, 1996), and in May 1998 it presented its final report to the newly constituted Department of Social, Community and Family Affairs.

The *Final Report of the Commission on the Family* (Commission, 1998: 7) begins by pointing out the 'need for coherence and clarity of objectives in relation to family policy needs . . . so that the valid role of the state in supporting family life and in promoting family well-being can be more effective.' In order to achieve these objectives the Commission states that the 'principles that underlie family policy need to be set out clearly' and that there is a 'need to strengthen the institutional framework of family policy'.

The Commission proposed six principles which it described as 'the essential truths about families which should underlie the formulation of policy in relation to families'. These six principles are:

- Recognition that the family unit is a fundamental unit providing stability and well being in our society.

- The unique and essential family function is that of caring and nurturing all its members.

- Continuity and stability are major requirements in family relationships.

- An equality of well-being is recognised between individual family members.

- Family membership confers rights, duties and responsibilities.

- A diversity of family forms and relationships should be recognised. (Commission on the Family, 1998: 7–8)

In order to achieve the overall objective of the principles which is family well-being, the Commission notes that a new approach to family policy formulation based on coordination is needed. It states that 'coordination and collaboration between state and community services at local level where services are delivered would go a long way towards achieving desirable outcomes for families' (Commission on the Family, 1998: 5).

The Commission, in the final chapter of its report, sets out in detail radical new proposals to strengthen the institutional framework for families. Having evaluated various policy options to achieve this objective, the Commission recommends the use of the Strategic Management Initiative, which underpins major public sector reforms and which has been given a statutory basis by the Public Service Management Act (1997) (Commission on the Family, 1998: 635). The Act provides new authority and structures for dealing with areas of critical importance that cross departmental boundaries (see Chapter 16, pp. 293–316). Under the Strategic Management process, the government would identify family well-being as an area of critical importance and to this end the Commission recommends that the Cabinet Subcommittee on Social Inclusion would include in its remit this 'family' objective (p. 636).

To strengthen the institutional framework for families further, the Commission also recommends the establishment of a separate and distinct Family Affairs Unit within the Department of Social, Community and Family Affairs. This unit would have responsibility for coordinating different departments and agencies in the achievement of shared objectives in relation to outcomes for families; to pioneer new approaches to the provision of services for families; to initiate policy responses to new and emerging issues; to evaluate the effects of legislation and policies on families; to promote awareness about new and emerging issues affecting families and to undertake research to inform policy development (Commission on the Family, 1998: 636–7).

Another new initiative proposed by the Commission to strengthen the institutional framework for families is the use of Family Impact Statements. These impact statements would be a means of routinely assessing the impact on families of policies and programmes at all stages of policy development and implementation (p.639). They would highlight awareness of how government affects families, put a focus on supporting and strengthening families in all actions taken by government and facilitate development of a coherent policy approach to families across government departments and services (p.640).

The coordination of all services for families is not an easy task and indeed may not even be possible depending on how family services are defined. The approach to the problem by the Commission is to try to have services coordinated and delivered at a local level. This would involve the transformation of local offices of the Department of Social, Community and Family Affairs into 'one-stop-shops' to provide a gateway to all services for families (p.17).

The Report of the Commission on the Family was the first major report on family policy in Ireland. It is comprehensive in its scope and recommendations and proposes a radical new approach to Irish family policy. The report, while making major policy recommendations, did so within a realistic framework and thereby made the adoption of the recommendations by whatever government happened to be in power a realistic option. However, the extent to which this will occur remains to be seen (see Chapter 16, pp. 311–14).

Individualism and Family Policy

If family policy in the first half of this century can be characterized as driven by the principle of subsidiarity and the privatization of the family, and the period since the 1970s by equality concerns and issues of sexual morality, it would appear that current policy directions are influenced by a rise in the value of individualism. While individualism may well be an integral part of equality, it does not necessarily follow that individualism as a driving principle in family policy leads to equality. To what extent individualism becomes the driving principle in the development of Irish family policy is perhaps the most fundamental question facing family-policy makers.

Family needs and individual needs are not always compatible. Invariably people have to make choices in their private and family lives between these sets of needs. So too must policy makers, and finding a balance in policy measures is not an easy task. Essentially, there are two extreme approaches. One is characterized by traditional family policy in Ireland, where the needs of the family superseded the needs of the individual. The second is the approach espoused in some northern European countries in which the needs of the individual are paramount. Neither approach leads to a satisfactory family outcome; just as unhappy families make unhappy individuals, so too do unhappy individuals make unhappy families.

Individualism is a hallmark of modern capitalist, market-driven societies. However, there is little evidence to show that individualism is a dominant feature within families although the rise in divorce, cohabitation and declining birth rates are claimed to represent such evidence. This argument has validity only if individualism and familism are represented as a dichotomy, with no ground in between. All the indications are that families continue to be a significant source of support and care for most people and that this support and care is provided by family members with little assistance from outside (see Millar and Warman, 1996). It is interesting to note in this context that the latest report of the European Observatory on National Family Policies (Ditch et al., 1998) shows a rise in multi-generation family units and that, contrary to popular belief, there does not appear to be conflict between the interests of different generations. Walker (1998) concludes from his research that high levels of support are provided by children to their ageing parents, which he says suggests that intergenerational solidarity within families remains strong in the European Union.

However, there is still a need to balance the interests of individuals with the needs of families. This is reflected in the move to remove the concept of dependency in the Tax and Social Welfare code and in the Child Care Act 1991 which protects the interests of children. The challenge for the policy makers is to preserve and support the benefits to society provided by the family while ensuring that the rights of individuals are protected.

CONCLUSION

Recent developments in family policy combined with the publication of the *Final Report of the Commission on the Family* (Commission on the Family, 1998) and the establishment of the Department of Social, Community and Family Affairs would indicate that family policy has now taken its place on the Irish political agenda. The old non-interventionist philosophy seems to be now replaced by a more proactive approach to the needs of families. All the indications are that this new direction will be maintained at least for the immediate future.

This does not mean, however, that there is a national consensus on which direction policies should take. There are strong ideological divides on what constitutes the best interest of families, as was apparent in the recent debate leading up to the divorce referendum in 1996. While these debates are likely to continue, they have not resulted in inaction on the part of the state, as was the case in the past.

The hallmark of the current policy direction seems to be permissiveness in the sense that policies allow for choice. In the past, family policies tended to be prescriptive and prohibitive. This new direction therefore reflects the changing nature of families in Ireland, which increasingly are characterized by diversity. Family policies, while guaranteeing the protection of families and family members as required by the Constitution, are also making provision for the protection and support of diverse family types. They are moving in the direction of providing families with choices between meaningful alternatives.

RECOMMENDED READING

Commission on the Family (1998) *Final Report*. Dublin: Stationery Office.
Colgan-McCarthy, I. (1995) *Irish Family Studies: Selected Papers*, Dublin. Family Studies Centre, University College Dublin.
European Observatory on National Family Policies. *Annual Report* for the years 1991 to 1996. Brussels: European Commission.

REFERENCES

Aldous, J. and W. Dumon (1990) 'Family Policy in the 1980's: Controversy and Consensus', *Journal of Marriage and the Family*, 52(4): 1136–51.
Burke, H. (1987) *The People and the Poor Law in Nineteenth Century Ireland*. West Sussex: The Women's Education Bureau.
Carney, C., E. Fitzgerald, G. Kiely and P. Quinn (1994) *The Cost of a Child*. Dublin: Combat Poverty Agency and the Family Studies Centre, University College Dublin.
Child Benefit Review Committee (1995) *Report to the Minister for Social Welfare*. Dublin: Stationery Office.
Commission on the Family (1996) *Interim Report: Strengthening Families for Life*. Dublin: Stationery Office.
Commission on the Family (1998) *Final Report*. Dublin: Stationery Office.
Constitution Review Group (1996) *Report of the Constitution Review Group*. Dublin: Stationery Office.
Ditch, J., H. Barnes, J. Bradshaw and M. Kilkey (1998) *A Synthesis of National Family Policies 1996*. York: European Observatory on National Family Policies, European Commission.
Dumon, W. (ed.) (1990) *Family Policy in EEC Countries*. Leuven: Social Research Institute.

Dumon, W. (1994) *Changing Family Policies in the Member States of the EU*. Brussels: European Observatory on National Family Policies, Commission of the European Communities.

European Observatory on National Family Policies (1991) *Annual Report 1990*. Brussels: Commission of the European Communities.

Eurostat (1995) *Statistics in Focus: Population and Social Conditions*.

Expert Working Group (1996) *Integrating Tax and Social Welfare*. Dublin: Stationery Office.

Giddens, A. (1989) *Sociology*. Cambridge: Polity Press.

Kamerman, S. and A. Kahn (1979) *Family Policy*. New York: Columbia University Press.

Kelly, F. (1988) *A Guide to Early Irish Law*. Dublin: Institute for Advanced Studies.

Kiely, G. (1995) 'Fathers in Families', pp. 113–30 in I. Colgan-McCarthy (ed.), *Irish Family Studies*. Dublin: Family Studies Centre, University College Dublin.

Kiely, G. (1998a) 'Report on Ireland for the Year 1996', in J. Ditch, H. Barnes and J. Bradshaw (eds), *Developments in National Family Policies in 1996*. York: European Observatory on National Family Policies, European Commission.

Kiely, G. (1998b) 'Caregiving within Families', pp. 91–100 in K. Matthijs (ed.), *The Family: Contemporary Perspectives and Challenges*. Leuven: Leuven University Press.

Kiely, G. and V. Richardson (1995) 'Family Policy in Ireland', pp. 27–47 in I. Colgan-McCarthy (ed.), *Irish Family Studies*, Dublin: Family Studies Centre, University College Dublin.

Millar, J. and A. Warman (1996) *Family Obligations in Europe*. London: Family Policy Studies Centre.

Richardson, V. (1993) 'Privatisation of the Family in Ireland and the Principle of Subsidiarity', pp. 135–42 in *Decentralisation and Gearing the Various Policy Levels to the Private-Public Divide*. Proceedings of the Workshop of the EU Observatory on National Family Policies. Bordeaux.

Savage, A. (1995) *Who Will Care?* Dublin: European Foundation for the Development of Living and Working Conditions.

Sels, C. and W. Dumon (1990) 'Family and Population Policy in Belgium', pp. 5–28 in W. Dumon (ed.), *Family Policy in EEC Countries*, Leuven: Social Research Institute.

Walker, A. (1998) 'Ageing Generations and the Family in Europe', paper read at the Conference 'European Family Forum', Athens, 20-22 May.

Whyte, J. (1980) *Church and State in Modern Ireland*. 2nd edition. Dublin: Gill & Macmillan.

15

Financing Social Services

Eithne Fitzgerald

INTRODUCTION

Collective provision of the main social services – social security, health, education, personal social services, subsidized housing – is the hallmark of the modern welfare state. The rationale for collective provision may have various roots: in concepts of social solidarity, citizenship, or equality; in the view that a well-functioning welfare state can underpin economic growth; or in a recognition of market failure, that leaving these services to the private market does not bring socially optimal results.

Directly funded services are the most visible form of the welfare state. A parallel system of state support may be given through tax relief on specific spending items. In Ireland, the principal tax reliefs on private social spending are for mortgage interest, pension contributions, private health insurance, and third-level fees for approved courses. These reliefs are often called *tax expenditures*. State support given in this form is usually subject to far less public scrutiny and public debate than more visible forms of public subsidy.

Social services may be characterized as universal, where everyone is entitled to service, or selective, where entitlement is restricted, usually by means-tests. In Ireland child benefit, free travel for those aged 66 or over, and primary education are universal social services. Free General Practitioner (GP) services to medical card holders, and higher education grants, are selective services. To assess the overall impact of social services in redistributing resources, it is important to look at who pays as well as who benefits, to examine the incidence of any taxes or charges used to fund the service, and at levels of take-up as well as formal entitlement.

COST PRESSURES

There are certain inbuilt cost pressures which put a strain on paying for quality social services. The development of new treatments and improvements in medical technology have led to a consistent upward pressure in the unit cost of medical care. Social services are labour-intensive and, unlike manufacturing, there is little scope to reduce costs through automation or economies of scale. As unit costs fall in other areas of the economy, social services become relatively more expensive to provide. In Ireland, this trend has been accentuated by the tendency for public service pay rates to rise faster than those in the private sector.

For most of Western Europe, an ageing population with higher life expectancy is putting pressure on the cost of funding pensions and health care. A smaller share of the total population in the workforce has to fund a higher number of dependants. Although reports like the OECD Jobs Study (1994) have called for lower taxes on labour – in other words, lower social security contributions in order to encourage jobs, there is limited scope to deliver on this in countries already facing major problems in funding their pension commitments because of rising numbers in the older age groups.

Ireland, after independence, had very high levels of dependency until the early 1990s. Since then, counter to the general European trend, Ireland's dependency ratio has been falling sharply, and will continue to do so into the twenty-first century (Economic and Social Research Institute, 1997). Ireland has an expanding young workforce, an older generation depleted by emigration, and a relatively low birth rate, which fell by one-third between 1980 and 1996. The drop in the birth rate has brought a demographic dividend in the school system, enabling class sizes to be reduced from an unchanged teacher complement. While this change in the demographic pattern has tended to ease pressure in education and social welfare, it has contributed to difficulties in the housing area. An expanded generation in the household-forming age groups adds to pressure on house prices, which in turn increases the demand for social housing from those priced out of the private housing market (Bacon, 1998).

Market Failure

Economic theory argues that, if the right assumptions hold, the market is the best mechanism for allocating ordinary goods and services, like food, clothes, or leisure. If demand exceeds supply for a period, prices rise, and this sends a signal to other suppliers to enter the market. Competition among suppliers should ensure no excess profits are charged or artificial shortages persist. The market reaches an equilibrium at a price where the demand at the going price is fulfilled. Demand in the market is, however, demand backed by cash, and given the unequal distribution of income, social need and market demand are not necessarily equated.

The market is a poor mechanism for allocating social services. There are a number of reasons why the market fails in the case of social services.

Pure Collective Goods

Certain goods, like clean air or policing, are purely collective in character – they cannot be parcelled out and given only to those who are prepared to pay. Public health is a collective good in this sense – if the community as a whole invests in good sanitation, ensures clean air, and controls infectious disease through vaccination, the benefits accrue to all, and not just those who may have paid for the public health programme.

External Benefits

External benefits occur where the return to society as a whole is higher than the return to the individual, and left to the private market alone, there would be under-provision. The return to society as a whole, in terms of cultural and economic development, from a well-educated population is higher than the return to the individual. If poor people can afford only squalid or unsanitary housing, other people suffer from the environmental deterioration, and poorer public health. It is in society's interest to encourage higher participation in education and better standards of low-income housing than people might afford or choose if left to a completely free market, through measures like free or subsidized education, and subsidized housing.

Merit Goods

If provision was left to the market alone and people had to pay full market prices, expensive hospital treatment and a good education for their children would be beyond the reach of many low-income families. In our society, we consider it morally unacceptable that the poor would be left to die because they cannot afford health care, or that the children of poor families would grow up illiterate because their parents cannot afford schooling. In these cases, society provides a basic minimum standard of provision below which it is intended no one need fall, usually delivered in kind through free or subsidized education and health care. Society also considers it morally unacceptable that people would starve because they are unable to afford food. However, direct provision of food aid is normally confined to emergency famine or refugee crises, and, in most Western societies, income-maintenance programmes of social insurance or social assistance guarantee a certain minimum standard of living from which families can budget for food, the US food stamps programme being an exception.

Making Decisions on Another's Behalf

The model of consumer choice in a free market assumes the rational consumer is making decisions for himself or herself. This is not always the reality. In a free market for education, for example, it is parents and not children who decide how much of their budget to allocate to education and how much to other items. (In the case of graduate study this may be reversed, with children, not parents, deciding how the parental budget will be spent.) If it is left to market forces alone some parents, through deprivation or neglect, may under-provide for their children's education.

Supply and Demand Not Independent

The classic economic model assumes consumer sovereignty with supply and demand independent of each other, yet there are cases where it is the supplier, not the consumer, who decides what quantity and quality of service will be bought. Someone who approaches their doctor with a pain in the stomach is in the doctor's hands as to whether the treatment ordered will be a simple antacid syrup or major stomach surgery. The patient is hardly in a position to shop around for a cheaper remedy, a surgeon with lower fees, or a shorter hospital stay.

Imperfect Information

The theory of consumer choice assumes consumers can make rational choices between known alternatives. However, some social needs cannot be readily anticipated or known, and it may be costly and time consuming for consumers to evaluate other complex alternatives. Although the need for pension provision in old age is one of the social needs which is readily foreseeable, people cannot anticipate how long they will live after retirement, what the going rate of inflation will be over the course of their retirement, and whether any retirement lump sum will prove sufficient to met a target standard of living in old age. Evaluating alternative pension and life insurance options is a complex business on which it may be difficult to get disinterested advice.

Risk and Uncertainty

People cannot anticipate what illnesses they will experience over their lifetime, or whether and for how long they may suffer a loss of income in the future through illness, unemployment or the death of a partner. Private sector insurance does provide cover against some of these contingencies, through health insurance and life insurance; there is no actuarial base, however, and no private insurance market against contingencies like future unemployment or marriage breakdown.

People differ considerably in the extent to which they anticipate and plan for the future; those on very tight budgets may be more likely simply to live for the present. Should people who fail to insure or under-insure be denied health treatment? Should people who are a poor risk, for example because of family medical history, be priced out of health cover in an unfettered private market?

From the insurance companies' viewpoint, the private market for insurance suffer two important drawbacks. First is *adverse selection,* the likelihood that a disproportionate number of the bad risks end up on their books. For example, people are more conscious of taking out health insurance when they reach late middle age than in their early twenties, but older people on average are more expensive to provide cover for because of their increased risk of hospitalization. The second drawback is what is called *moral hazard* – the idea that people take fewer precautions once they know they are insured, which raises the average risk level all-round.

Public, Private and Voluntary Sector Provision

While for all these reasons the market fails to deliver the best answer to provision of social services, in many welfare states there is a market fringe providing social services to certain categories as well as mainstream collective provision. Examples would be private sector pension provision, private health insurance and private schooling. In the case of housing, it is the private sector which is dominant, and the public housing sector is the fringe. The strong market ideology of the Thatcher and Reagan years, and the financial strain experienced by welfare states in a period of growing unemployment, rising costs, and rapidly ageing societies have together seen a shift in emphasis develop towards more market-based approaches. The World Bank's Report *Averting the Old Age Crisis* (1994) is substantially modelled on the Chilean pension reform of the 1980s which involved the replacement of the previous state system with one where pensions are funded on an individual personal basis.

Between purely public provision of services, and purely privately financed services, there is a range of intermediate options.

Charitable and religious organizations played a major role in the early development of services like health and education. In Ireland the dominant model of provision of education at primary and secondary level is in schools owned by or vested in religious bodies. Virtually all the current funding, and most of the capital funding, comes from the state, and ownership and control is secured with only a modest financial input from the parishes or religious orders. The hospital and health sector has also a significant degree of voluntary religious ownership, while now almost entirely publicly funded. New services such as rehabilitation training, refuges for victims of domestic violence and rape crisis centres, have been developed by voluntary organizations initially mainly through their own voluntary fund-raising, but there is now a significant share of public funding.

Public finance for social services may be raised either nationally or locally. Education is frequently run by local or regional authorities, and Ireland is unusual in the degree to which education is centrally managed and funded by central government. For example, three-quarters of UK funding for education originated locally in 1992, compared to 0.1 per cent in Ireland (OECD, 1995). While health services are regionally managed in Ireland through the eight health boards, again funding is virtually entirely from central government. Central government grants fund local authority capital spending on housing, and given that 80 per cent of Irish local authority tenants are on welfare, subsidized local authority rents do not cover maintenance and management costs in full, and make no contribution to servicing the capital cost.

Social security systems frequently evolved from sectoral arrangements, and in some European countries significant parts of the social security system are still run on occupational lines, for example in Belgium, France, the Netherlands, and Germany. Social security is thus typically funded through employer and employee contributions, although in Denmark, Sweden and Australia funding from general taxation has been the norm. In France and Belgium, entitlement to health care is primarily through social insurance contributions. In Germany, housing cooperatives sponsored by trade unions and occupational groups have played a broadly similar role to that played by local authority housing in Ireland.

Publicly provided services are not necessarily free at the point of delivery. User charges are common in the health area, with Belgium, France, Ireland, Italy, Luxembourg and Portugal all having provision for contributions by service users, usually those above a certain minimum income (MISSOC, 1996). While public housing may be heavily subsidized it is rarely rent free. Charges for private services may be publicly subsidized, for example private housing rents through Housing Benefit in the UK, and Supplementary Welfare rent supplements in Ireland. Another example is the Drug Refund scheme, where patients can claim back a proportion of what they spent on medicines at private chemists.

Private sector purchases may also be subsidized through the tax system, in what are termed *tax expenditures*. Tax relief on mortgage interest has played an important role in subsidizing owner-occupied housing in both Ireland and the UK. Tax relief on health insurance has long been a feature of the Irish tax code, tax relief on education fees for approved private third-level courses has been in place since 1996, and modest tax relief on private rents was extended to all private tenants in 1995.

Some charitable and voluntary organizations rely purely on their own fund-raising to provide their services. Increasingly in Ireland during the 1980s and 1990s, however, FÁS has become a major indirect financial supporter through funding the Social Employment Scheme – and subsequently Community Employment (CE) – work experience programmes, funding not only work experience places for unemployed people seeking a route back to the job market, but also supervisory jobs in these organizations. Most of the 40,000 CE jobs are in the voluntary sector, a high proportion of them in social service activities. Because Community Employment, in turn, is almost two-thirds funded by savings on social welfare for participants, only those who bring a social welfare saving with them (with the exception of lone parents) qualify to go on the programme.

EU funding, either under mainstream Operational Programmes or EU-led Community Initiatives, has also provided important financial support to voluntary groups pioneering new approaches.

At the other end of the continuum from publicly funded services are services that are privately provided and funded. In Ireland, people in the middle and upper income groups pay for family doctor care (although if medical expenses go above a threshold figure for the year, tax relief may be claimed). Family care remains important in providing personal care for dependent elderly people and people with disabilities.

There has been an active debate around the idea of service vouchers as an alternative to direct provision, a view long espoused on the radical right, but more recently being voiced by consumer groups, such as parents of children with a disability seeking a greater choice for their children. A monopoly on service through public provision, it is argued, may result in the dominance of service providers, and a neglect of the service consumer.

PAYING FOR THE WELFARE STATE

The main sources of funding for social services are

- general taxation (national and local)
- general borrowing
- earmarked taxation
- earmarked borrowing
- tax relief
- occupational welfare, employer-funded
- user charges
- state or agency enterprise activities
- charitable fund-raising
- private spending

In Ireland, the main social services – health, education and social welfare – now account for about two-thirds of current government spending. The pool of general taxation, therefore, largely goes to pay for these services. With the exception of social welfare spending, where earmarked taxes through PRSI contributions play an important role, most current public spending on Irish social services is funded from general taxation. Income from other sources, such as hospital charges, the health levy, and lottery receipts, come to a small fraction of the total. Since 1989, EU Structural Funds have been a significant source of income for the Exchequer, one that will diminish in importance into the twenty-first century.

Chart 1. Main Social Services as share of Government Spending 1997

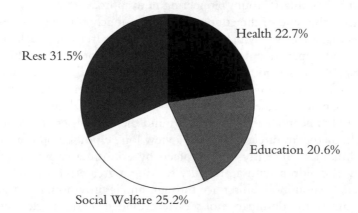

Rest 31.5%

Health 22.7%

Education 20.6%

Social Welfare 25.2%

Source: Department of Finance.

Chart 2. Main Sources of Taxation, 1997

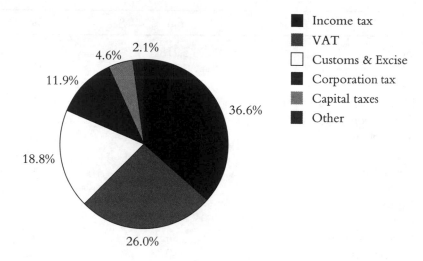

Income tax
VAT
Customs & Excise
Corporation tax
Capital taxes
Other

Source: Department of Finance

Borrowing

In the past, borrowing was a significant source of finance in Ireland for government spending – current as well as capital, although progressively in the 1990s governments have run a current surplus. Most borrowing is of a general kind, and is applied to capital spending, such as roads, education buildings, or hospitals. Local authorities were able to borrow from the Local Loans fund for various purposes, principally housing, and in return remitted loan charges to central government for interest on the sums involved. This has now been replaced by a system of central government capital grants to local authorities for their housing programme.

In 1995, legislation was introduced (Securitisation (Proceeds of Certain Mortgages) Act) which provided for the capitalization of a stream of income from local authorities' housing accounts to central government, for example the repayments on tenant purchase housing. The National Treasury Management Agency borrowed £140m that year, using these repayments as security, in order to fund the payment of Equal Treatment arrears to social welfare recipients.

Table 1. Financing of Central Government 1997

	£m	%
Income tax	5,218	30
VAT	3,718	22
Excise	2,507	15
PRSI	1,945	11
Corporation tax	1,699	10
Stamp duty	429	2
Car tax	100	0.6
Capital tax	225	1
Levies	189	1
Customs	179	1
Lottery	98	0.5
Other non-tax revenue	345	2
Current surplus	604	3.5
TOTAL	17,255	100

Source: Department of Finance

Table 2. Current Gross Government Spending on Social Service 1997

	£m
Education	2,362
Health	2,678
Social welfare	4,567

Source: Estimates for Public Services 1999 (abridged) Table 6

TAXATION

Tax systems are characterized as *progressive* if the higher up the income scale you go, the higher the share you pay. A tax system is *neutral* if people in each income group pay proportional shares. A tax is *regressive* if the lower income group pay a higher share of income than those further up the income scale. Flat rate taxes are regressive in character. A tax of £100 a year tax represents 1% of income for someone earning £10,000 a year, but only 0.25% of income to someone earning £40,000. General expenditure taxes such as Value Added Tax (VAT) are also regressive, because they bear more heavily on those who spend all their income than on those up the income scale who can afford to save a share of income.

Consider the following example. Anne earns £100 a week, and spends it all – there is no margin for saving. If expenditure tax is set at 10%, Anne will pay tax of £10, or 10% of her income. Barry earns £200 a week, spends £180 and saves £20. Barry's expenditure tax comes to £18, or 10% of what he spends. However, this is only 9% of his income, a lower share than Anne pays.

Spending taxes can be targeted at particular categories of expenditure – luxury cars, for example – as a proxy for taxing those who can afford luxury items. More commonly, spending taxes are targeted at goods where the demand is not particularly sensitive to price, such as petrol, drink and tobacco, because total revenue may rise following an increase in duty. Where these items form a higher share of the spending budget of poorer families, the net result is regressive. For example, the health education message that smoking is bad for you has had a much stronger impact among the middle classes than among lower income groups. While taxes on tobacco and cigarettes can be seen on the one hand as a tax on a harmful and polluting activity, on the other hand, because of higher smoking rates in lower income groups, these taxes effectively bear more heavily on the poor.

Income taxes are generally designed to be progressive, with successive slices of income subject to higher rates of tax. For the tax year 1999/2000, the first £14,000 of taxable income for a single person is charged to tax at 24% and the balance of taxable income at 46%. Nominally, that should mean that taxpayers on higher incomes pay a higher share of their incomes in tax. Certain expenditure, however, is deductible against income tax and this can blunt the extent to which the tax system proves to be progressive in practice. Tax relief on mortgage interest, on private health insurance and on pension contributions are some of the most common deductions against taxable income. Generous tax allowances given to encourage particular kinds of investment, for example in providing housing to rent, in urban renewal, in seaside resorts, and in the Business Expansion Scheme (BES), offer particularly attractive tax shelters which are largely availed of by upper income taxpayers.

People in business may be able to organize their affairs to take their return as capital gain rather than income. In 1998/9, capital gains were taxable at 20%, compared to tax rates on earned income of 24% and 46%.

The Revenue Commissioners (1997) surveyed a sample of taxpayers earning over £250,000 a year, to assess the extent to which high income earners are effectively reducing tax bills through availing of such tax reliefs. In 1994/5, one in five was paying an effective tax rate of under 25%; one in nine was paying an effective tax rate of less than 10%, despite a nominal top tax rate that year of 48%, which would have been applied to any taxable income of over £16,400 for a couple. Business deductions, business losses, BES and film investments, and pension contributions were the main vehicles being used to reduce exposure to tax.

The following example illustrates how this can be done. It shows two single taxpayers on £20,000. Taxpayer A has no extra tax allowances over and above the personal and PAYE tax credits. Taxpayer B claims mortgage interest relief of £2,000, health insurance relief of £1,000 (which both apply at the lower tax rate of 24%) and tax relief of £5,000 under the BES scheme which applies at the taxpayer's top marginal rate.

Table 3. Example of How Tax Reliefs Reduce Effective Tax Rates (1999/2000)

	Taxpayer A		Taxpayer B	
Income	£25,000		£25,000	
Taxable @ 24%	£14,000	= £3,360	£14,000	= £3,360
Balance @ 46%	£11,000	= £5,060	£11,000	= £5,060
Gross tax bill	£8,420		£8,420	
Less personal allowance	£4,200	– £1,008	£4,200	– £1,008
Less PAYE allowance	£1,000	– £240	£1,000	– £240
Less mortgage interest	—	—	£2,000	– £480
Less VHI @ 24%	—	—	£1,000	– £240
Less BES @ 46%	—	—	£5,000	– £2,300
Net tax payable		£7,172		£4,152
Effective tax rate	28.7%		16.6%	

Tax Allowances and Tax Credits

Traditionally, the tax system operated on the basis of tax allowances, whereby certain sums were deducted from gross income to arrive at a figure for taxable income. Under this system, a tax allowance of £1,000 would be worth £460 a year in terms of reducing the tax bill of a taxpayer paying at the top tax rate of 46%, and worth only £240 a year to lower income taxpayers paying tax at the 24% rate. A commitment to move to a tax credit system, beginning with the 1999/2000 tax year, is intended to see tax allowances converted into tax credits – in other words, a £1,000 tax credit would be worth exactly the same in terms of reducing the tax bill by £1,000 to someone in the higher or lower tax band.

From April 1999, the system of personal allowances has been standard-rated as the first move towards a tax credit system. The personal tax

allowance for a single person of £4,200 is worth the same to lower-rate
and to top-rate taxpayers, being effectively applied at the 24% rate.
Mortgage interest and tax relief on medical insurance were progressively
changed to a standard rate over the 1994–97 tax years. Other reliefs in
particular business reliefs remain deductible at the taxpayer's top rate of
tax, and are worth almost twice as much to top rate taxpayers as to those
in the lower income tax band.

The significance of tax reliefs as a form of fiscal welfare can be gauged
from the following table which gives estimates of the value in tax
foregone of some of the principal tax reliefs.

Table 4. Estimated Value of Tax Reliefs, 1998

	£m	Estimated nos
Mortgage interest	163.2	415,000
Rent, private tenancies	14.8	84,400
Medical insurance	61.0	442,200
Medical expenses	25.5	76,000
Pension contributions	312	n.a.
Pension fund income	59	n.a.
Third level fees	0.4	1,600
Business reliefs		
BES	41.8	n.a.
Urban renewal	48	n.a.
's.23' for landlords	26.2	n.a.
Film investment	19.1	2,500
Seaside resorts	5	n.a.

Source: Department of Finance, TSG 98/03A

Direct Funding vs Tax Relief

The Department of Finance runs a tight system of spending control,
with a separate section overseeing the spending programme of each
government department. Proposals for new expenditure are expected to
be carefully costed and their impact assessed before receiving approval.
Fiscal welfare, through the tax system, is not subject to similar official
scrutiny, yet tax concessions and public spending are part of the same
continuum. There is no difference in principle between a proposal
which costs £5m in terms of direct spending, and one which costs £5m

in tax foregone, in their impact on the public purse, although it is easier to identify what direct spending is costing. The establishment of the Tax Strategy Group in November 1993, where representatives of government departments and political advisers examine proposals for budget tax changes and Finance Bill proposals, has improved the evaluation on the tax side.

In public debate, those who receive cash benefits, live in public housing or receive hospital care in a public ward are identifiable recipients of public funds. Those who are buying their own homes or who opt for private hospital care are also being subsidized from public funds, but less visibly, through the tax system. A purchaser of an urban renewal apartment may be receiving as large a public subsidy in cash terms as a local authority tenant. While criteria of selectivity and targeting are frequently applied to social spending, the reverse is usually the case in terms of tax subsidies. For example, rent allowances under the Supplementary Welfare Allowance scheme are very tightly targeted at those on low incomes, and are withdrawn pound for pound where income is above the Supplementary Welfare rate, so that an old age pensioner on a higher welfare rate will not qualify for a full rent allowance. There are also strict criteria on accommodation cost, and if a tenant rents a flat which is outside the price range or considered too large for his or her needs, the rent allowance will be cut or withdrawn altogether. In contrast, a house purchaser who trades up the market from a five-bedroom home to a seven-bedroom home can claim mortgage interest relief on the new mortgage and no questions about being over-accommodated will be raised.

Until 1994, mortgage interest relief could be claimed in full at a person's top tax rate; tax relief on £1,000 worth of mortgage interest was worth £480 a year to a top rate (48%) taxpayer, and £270 a year to someone on a lower income paying tax at the 27% rate. Since then, tax relief on mortgage interest and on health insurance has been phased down to apply at the lower rate of tax only. Business reliefs like the BES scheme apply at the top rate of tax and are worth more in cash terms to higher income taxpayers.

FINANCING THE SOCIAL WELFARE SYSTEM

Social security contributions which are levied as a percentage of payroll are the most common form of earmarked taxation used to fund social services. In some EU countries, the social insurance contribution also funds health care. There are different views on the merits of ring-fencing a particular tax for a particular purpose. Economists argue that social security contributions are just another form of tax, a view taken by the

Commission on Taxation (Ireland, 1983). Others see social insurance as an expression of social solidarity, with contributions conferring an entitlement as of right as an alternative to means testing, the view underlying the Beveridge Report (1942).

The higher the share of payroll in a firm's total costs, the higher the social security deductions for both employers and employees. A firm producing in a labour-intensive way will pay higher PRSI contributions than a firm producing a similar output in a capital-intensive way. In this way, economists argue that social security contributions constitute a tax on labour and inhibit employment. Given Ireland's generous corporate tax regime for manufacturing, however, employer's PRSI may often be the only significant contribution to public funds from some companies.

From the point of view of the social security authorities, dedicated funding gives the ability to plan, and some freedom from fighting their corner for resources with the Department of Finance, particularly at a time of strong growth in employment. Given the degree of financial independence it confers, it is hardly surprising that the Department of Social, Community and Family Affairs (formerly the Department of Social Welfare) have strongly opposed cuts in PRSI and have been robust defenders of the present system (Department of Social Welfare, 1996). The health levy, which funds about ten per cent of health spending, is less important as an autonomous source of income.

Social Insurance in Ireland

The Irish social welfare system has two main branches – social insurance, where entitlement to benefits is based on the person's record of social insurance contributions, and social assistance benefits, which are means-tested. Social assistance payments are funded from the general pool of tax revenue, while social insurance is funded by PRSI contributions from employers and insured persons. Originally social insurance was funded on a tripartite basis, with roughly equal shares contributed by employers, workers and the state. The state, while reducing its contribution, is still liable for any unanticipated shortfall, but by 1997 employers were paying over two-thirds, employees and self-employed one-third, and there was no net state contribution. The employer contribution and any state share make social insurance good value for the contributor when related to any comparable private insurance cover. Originally a flat-rate sum, social insurance is now levied on a pay-related basis from employers and insured persons, subject both to an income floor (£100 a week for employees in 1999/2000) and an income ceiling (£25,400 per annum in 1999/2000). In addition, a 2% Health Levy (previously a

Table 5. Financing of Social Welfare Services 1987 and 1997

Social insurance	1987 £m	1987 %	1997 £m	1997 %
Employers	634	47	1,370	71
Employees	307	23	450	23
Self-employed	-	-	124	6
State	405	30	(-6)	-
Other	2		-	
Total social insurance	1,348	100	1,939	100

Source: Statistical Information on Social Welfare 1987, 1997.

Table 6. Financing of Total Social Welfare Services 1987 and 1997

	1987 £m	1987 %	1997 £m	1997 %
Social insurance	1,348	53	1,939	43
Social assistance	1,210	47	2,585	57
Overall total	2,558	100	4,524	100
Financed by state	1,615	63	2,578	57

Source: Statistical Information on Social Welfare, 1987, 1997.

1.25% Health Levy and 1% Employment and Training Levy) is collected as part of the pay-related social insurance (PRSI) system, and remitted to the Department of Health and Children.

There are separate contribution rates for different kinds of employment. Class A applies to most private sector workers, whereas public sector workers recruited before April 1995 pay at a lower rate. The Commission on Social Welfare (1986) had recommended a common rate for employees in both the public and private sectors; nine years later the solution adopted involves effectively phasing-in this recommendation over up to forty years. Following concern about the burden of PRSI payments on people earning too little to pay tax, successive budgets in the 1990s exempted the bottom slice of income from PRSI and levies. PRSI is thus progressive for the very low-income earners, but regressive once the income ceiling has been reached. In 1998, someone earning about £50,000 a year would be liable for the same PRSI contribution paid by someone earning half that sum.

Table 7. Main Classes of PRSI Contribution

Class	Sector	Nos.	Benefits
A	Most private sector	1,009,000	All
B, D	Most public sector	159,000	Widow's pension, Occupational injuries
S	Self-employed	144,000	Old age, widow's pension
J	<£30 a week	79,000	Occupational injuries

Source: Social Insurance Discussion Document, 1996

The interaction of PRSI and two separate levies, several different occupational PRSI classes, income floors and income ceilings, and exemption from levies for those with medical cards, has led to an extremely complicated PRSI system. By 1997, there were 53 separate rates of PRSI contribution.

Pay As You Go vs Funded Pensions

In Ireland, as in most economies, social security pensions have been funded on a pay-as-you-go basis, with the contributions of this generation paying the pensions of the previous generation. This is only sustainable where the size of succeeding generations is in broad balance or where the income of each succeeding generation is growing sufficiently to meet the pension guarantee given to the generation now in retirement. Many economies are now finding that the combination of recession and high unemployment among the working-age population and a rising proportion of pensioners in the population is putting great strain on financing their social security pensions. As a result, some countries have raised pension age and tightened up on contribution conditions to lessen their funding problems.

These funding problems are giving rise to increasing interest in private pension provision, and in funded pensions schemes, where the contributions are not paid out to current pensioners but are invested to meet future liabilities. There is also interest in moving from *defined benefit* schemes, where insured people are guaranteed a certain level of income in retirement, to *defined contribution* schemes, where the contribution is known in advance, but the income in old age may vary depending on the value of the fund at retirement and the return on fund investments. Switching from a pay-as-you-go system to a funded one is not a simple matter. If today's contributions are needed to pay today's pensioners, they are not available to build up a fund for future pension requirements. Making the switch involves an element of double contributions.

EU Structural Funds

The value of EU Structural Funds over the period 1994–99 to the Irish Exchequer is £6065m, amounting to about three per cent of GNP. There are four main categories: the Cohesion Fund which must be spent on either roads or sanitary services; the European Social Fund (ESF) which mainly funds education and training programmes (at post-Junior Certificate level only); the European Regional Development Fund, spent mainly on physical infrastructure; and Community Initiatives, which are EU-designed programmes, many involving the voluntary sector rather than government spending. The Irish government had considerable discretion in choosing the mix of projects and programmes to which the funding would be allocated. In that sense, the availability of these funds has facilitated an overall increase in spending, but the choice as to whether domestic funds or EU funds were allocated to particular programmes is not particularly significant. The main social programmes against which EU funds have been pencilled for the period are education and training under the Human Resources Operational Programme (£1435m over the six years), and local development in disadvantaged areas (£81m) under the Local Development Programme. The Community Initiatives (£368m.) are a series of programmes devised by Brussels, and these have funded social programmes, largely through the voluntary sector, for the disadvantaged and people with a disability (HORIZON), for women (NOW), job training for young people (YOUTHSTART), and development of disadvantaged urban communities (URBAN), most of them pilot projects.

The fact that something is EU-funded may distort the selection of our domestic priorities. For example, in education, it may mean more funds for teacher centres and for third level, because these are the areas that EU funds can be spent on, and less for primary education than we might otherwise choose.

Lottery Funds

Contrary to popular myth, lottery funds are neither very significant nor independent of general government spending. The national lottery raised about £100m in 1997 which, as the Estimates volume shows, is put in with other public spending; most of it is pre-committed either paying for health and welfare programmes run by voluntary agencies which otherwise the state would have to fund out of mainstream revenue, or paying the head-office expenses of national sporting and youth organizations. There is almost no discretionary money involved.

Charges for Services

The main charges for social services are housing rents, hospital charges, and postgraduate fees. The rationale for charges is that the consumer who benefits from the service shares some of the cost, and that consumers are more likely to value a service for which they have paid. They also provide a modest income towards service costs. Rents for local authority housing cover about two-thirds of maintenance and management costs, and do not contribute anything towards servicing the original capital cost; low rental income reflects the fact that four out of five tenants are on welfare. Charges may be seen as deterring excessive use or abuse of a service, although health charges may do little to deter the wealthy hypochondriac. Charges for outpatient services are intended to prevent these expensive services being used as a first port of call by people who should more appropriately see their family doctor.

Voluntary Fundraising

Voluntary organizations typically depend on fund-raising to deliver part or most of their services. For many small organizations, uncertainty from year to year about public funding, and the need to raise funds can absorb a great deal of their energies, diverting energies from what they are trying to achieve and the delivery of their services. Funds raised independently like this give voluntary organizations the freedom to pioneer new ideas and set their own priorities. There is also a risk that some organizations may set service priorities based on what is most marketable from a fund-raising point of view.

Accountability

With public funding of the voluntary sector comes public accountability. In the health area where a sizeable share of services is delivered through voluntary agencies, the laissez-faire approach of the past is increasingly to be replaced, as outlined in the National Health Strategy (Department of Health, 1994), by service contracts where the voluntary body contracts to supply certain services to a certain standard in return for public funding. Organizations receiving a significant share of their budgets from public funds can be liable to audit by the Comptroller and Auditor General who can examine not only the probity of the accounts but also effectiveness and value for money. Such agencies can also be designated, by regulation, to come under the Freedom of Information Act.

REDISTRIBUTION

The overall impact of a social service system depends both on who pays for and who receives services. How the system is financed is only one part of the picture. Who receives the service, and the level of take-up in services nominally open to all is also important. The overall impact depends on how financing and take-up balance out together. That impact may be progressive, it could be broadly neutral, or it may effectively redistribute income and resources upwards.

For example, a system of free education open to all is likely to have a higher take-up by the upper income group who usually have higher participation rates in education, particularly in third-level education, the most expensive level. If that education system is financed by proportional taxation on each income group, the overall net result will be to redistribute income upwards.

Services like education and child benefits redistribute resources towards those with families, and to the younger generation. Health services are disproportionately used by the very elderly, and health care and pensions redistribute resources generally from the working generation to the retired. Social security benefits redistribute income from those at work to those who are out of the workforce because they are retired, ill or unemployed.

Redistribution in Ireland: The Evidence

The Central Statistics Office (1995) carried out calculations on the 1987 Household Budget Survey to estimate the extent to which the Irish system is redistributive. This study estimated the amount of direct tax paid by households, e.g. income tax and PRSI; the amount of indirect tax paid by households, such as VAT and taxes on drink and tobacco; direct cash transfers to households from the state through the social welfare system, child benefits, and housing grants; and the cash value of the utilization of state services such as education, health, and subsidized local authority housing. The overall conclusions were:

- taxes on income (income tax and PRSI) were broadly progressive
- indirect taxes were regressive
- non-cash benefits (health, education and housing) taken together were broadly neutral

- cash transfers – mainly social welfare – were progressive
- there was net redistribution from urban to rural households
- there was net redistribution to the elderly (mainly through health care and pensions), and to larger families

THE BUDGET CYCLE

Budgetary control in Ireland lies with the Department of Finance. Every year, departments draw up their estimate of spending requirements for the coming year, in theory on a 'no policy change' basis, with any new services separately identified. The full-year cost of any budget changes implemented from mid-year must be included. The Department of Finance sets an overall figure for aggregate current spending, and intensive bilateral discussions take place to try and ensure the sums fit within the overall total. That total in turn is influenced by requirements for economic and monetary stability, and the balance between tax changes and expenditure changes planned for the Budget. The published estimates give the spending allocations and targets for the coming year, subject to whatever spending adjustment are made on Budget Day. The main changes announced on Budget Day are the annual social welfare increases and tax changes; occasionally other significant spending changes may be announced as well as relatively minor items ('Budget sweeteners') such as extra grants to specific charities. The annual Finance Act gives effect not only to any tax changes announced in the Budget but may also contain other technical changes with significant revenue implications.

Since 1993, the shape of tax and welfare Budget changes has been prepared in detail by the Tax Strategy Group, who also examine technical proposals for the Finance Bill. The detailed alternative tax packages formed an important part of the discussions on the Programme for Competitiveness and Work in 1995, and both the tax and welfare packages formed a key part of the negotiations on the successor agreement, Partnership 2000.

Budget Policy and European Monetary Union (EMU)

In preparation for EMU entry, participating Governments were required under the terms of the Maastricht Treaty to bring their budget deficits under three per cent, and their debt/GDP ratio in the direction of 60%. For most EU countries experiencing sluggish economic growth, meeting the Maastricht criteria imposed a tight constraint on public spending, and on social spending in particular. In Ireland's case, the period of preparation for EMU-entry coincided with a period of exceptional economic growth. Although some budgetary discipline was required in Ireland to meet the criteria, they were achieved relatively painlessly. The debt/GDP ratio fell primarily because of rapidly rising GDP rather than because of debt reduction.

Within the single currency, Ireland can no longer use revaluation/ devaluation or changes in interest rates to manage economic policy or overcome economic difficulties. The burden of managing economic policy at home and of responding to any economic shocks falls on budgetary policy and incomes policy. Any overheating in the Irish economy has to be managed through appropriate budget and tax policy rather than higher interest rates. When dangerous inflationary pressure builds up, the right economic policy is to increase the budget surplus, withdraw excess spending power from circulation and reduce present or future indebtedness. If the common European interest rate is too high for domestic Irish economic circumstances, it may be appropriate to reduce tax or increase public spending.

Public Sector Pay

The most rapidly growing area of public spending has not been better services for unemployment black-spots, better schools or hospitals, but the growth in public service pay rates fuelled by special pay claims and high overtime for groups like prison officers. Between 1988 and 1997, average earnings of public sector workers grew by 58%, compared to a 37% increase for industrial workers in manufacturing (CSO).

There is a very real trade-off between paying public servants more to do the same job, and delivering more public services – choices which are more stark within an overall ceiling on public spending set by the critical role of fiscal policy in a post-EMU environment.

Ireland is a price-taker on world markets. It is clear that the costs of those goods we export have to be in line with those of competitor countries if we are to retain market share. What is less obvious is that costs in the purely domestic non-traded sectors of the economy also play a crucial role in competitiveness. The costs in these sectors, whether the high insurance costs of a claims culture, the costs of restrictive practices in the legal profession or banking sector, the costs of supporting an expensive prison service, or excessive public pay growth relative to earnings in the private sector feed into the costs for those sectors trading in foreign markets. This is another reason why it is important to restrict the growth in public sector pay levels to those being achieved in the wider economy.

CONCLUSION

The major constraint on bringing about improvements in social services is the cost of implementing change. Utopian theories of welfare reform have foundered on the rocks of the cost and funding problems. The simplicity of the basic income concept, compared to a complicated and inconsistent social welfare system, has run up against the formidable obstacle of the likely cost – £1bn at 1993–94 prices – and a tax rate of 68% to fund it (Callan, O'Donoghue and O'Neill, 1994). Understanding what services cost, how they are financed, what the constraints are and how change might be funded is critical to achieving change.

RECOMMENDED READING

Barr, N. (1993) *The Economics of the Welfare State*. London: Macmillan.

Department of Social Welfare (1996) *Social Insurance Discussion Document*. Dublin: Stationery Office.

Glennester, H. (1997) *Paying for Welfare*. Hemel Hempstead: Harvester Wheatsheaf.

Nolan, B. (1991) *Charging for Public Health Services in Ireland*. Dublin: Economic and Social Research Institute.

REFERENCES AND ADDITIONAL BACKGROUND READING

Alcock, P. (1996) 'Advantage and Disadvantage of Contributory Base in Targeting Benefits – Social Analysis of Insurance Schemes in the UK', *International Social Security Review*, 49 (1): 31–49.

Bacon, P. (1998) *Report on House Prices*. Dublin: Stationery Office.

Barr, N. (1993) *The Economics of the Welfare State*. London: Macmillan.

Beveridge, Sir W. (1942) *Social Insurance and Allied Services*, Cmd 6404. London: HMSO.

Bolderson, H. and D. Mabbett (1996) 'Cost Containment in Complex Social Security Systems' *International Social Security Review*, 49 (1) 3–17.

Callan, T., C. O'Donoghue and C. O'Neill (1994) *Analysis of Basic Income Schemes for Ireland*. Policy Research Series, Paper 21. Dublin: Economic and Social Reserach Institute.

Central Statistics Office (1995) *Redistributive Effects of State Taxes and Benefits on Household Incomes in 1987*.

Commission on Social Welfare (1986) *Report*. Dublin: Stationery Office.

Department of Education and Science. *Tuarascail Staitistiul* (annual)

Department of Finance. *Appropriations Accounts* (annual)

Department of Finance. *Budget book* (annual)

Department of Finance. *Estimates for the Public Service* (annual)

Department of Health (1994) *Shaping a Healthier Future: A Strategy for Effective Healthcare in the 1990s*. Dublin: Stationery Office.

Department of Social, Community and Family Affairs. *Statistical Information on Social Welfare Services* (annual)

Department of Social Welfare (1996) *Social Insurance Discussion Document*. Dublin: Stationery Office.

Department of the Environment. *Annual Bulletin of Housing Statistics* (annual)

Department of the Environment. *Quarterly Bulletin of Housing Statistics*

Department of the Environment. *Returns of Local Taxation* (annual)

Economic and Social Research Institute (1997) *Medium-term Review 1997–2003*. Dublin: ESRI.

Euzeby, A. (1997) 'Social Security: Indispensable Solidarity', *International Social Security Review*, 50 (3): 3–15.

Figueras, J. (1998) *Cost Containment Reforms in Europe,* conference paper to regional meeting of International Social Security Association, Dublin, May 1998. Geneva: ISSA.

Glennester, H. (1997) *Paying for Welfare*. Hemel Hempstead: Harvester Wheatsheaf.

Honohan, P. (ed.) (1997) *EU Structural Funds in Ireland – A Mid-term Evaluation of the CSF*. Dublin: Economic and Social Research Institute.

Ireland (1983) *Report of the Commission on Taxation*. Dublin: Stationery Office.

Ireland (1983, 1984) *Comprehensive Public Expenditure Programmes*; *Comprehensive Public Expenditure Programmes 1984*. Dublin: Stationery Office.

Ireland (1989) *Report of the Commission on Health Funding*. Dublin: Stationery Office.

Ireland (1996) *Integrating Tax and Social Welfare: Expert Working Group Report*. Dublin: Stationery Office.

Kvist, J. and A. Sinfield (1997) 'Comparing Tax Welfare States', *Social Policy Review*, 9: 249–75.

MISSOC (1996) *Social Protection in Member States of the European Union*. Cologne: MISSOC.

NESC 36 (1977) *Universality and Selectivity: Strategies in Social Policy*. Dublin: NESC.

NESC 85 (1988) *Redistribution Through State Social Expenditure in the Republic of Ireland 1973-80*. Dublin: NESC.

Nolan, B. (1991) *Charging for Public Health Services in Ireland*. Dublin: Economic and Social Research Institute.

OECD (1994) *The Jobs Study*. Paris: OECD.

OECD (1995) *Education at a Glance*. Paris: OECD.

Programme for Competitiveness and Work (1994) Dublin: Stationery Office.

Partnership 2000 for Inclusion, Employment and Competitiveness (1996) Dublin: Stationery Office.

Revenue Commissioners (1997) *Effective Tax Rates for High Earning Individuals* (press release).

World Bank (1994) *Averting the Old Age Crisis*. Washington: World Bank.

16

Cross-cutting Initiatives in Public Policy: Some Irish Examples

Deirdre Carroll

INTRODUCTION

The Strategic Management Initiative, the important 'change agenda' initiative under way in the public service in recent years, has set out the road map for the Civil and Public Service of the future. At the heart of that initiative are three aims: excellent service to the customer, maximum contribution to national development and efficient and effective use of our resources.

A key principle of the Initiative is that issues which cross departmental boundaries must be dealt with systematically, on the basis that many vital national issues and desired outcomes can no longer be contained within the remit and skill base of a single department or agency. Indeed, it is now a requirement for all departments that the Strategy Statement which they are obliged to prepare under the Public Service Management Act (1997) should identify and address such cross-departmental issues, as well as the steps to be taken to consult with other relevant departments/ agencies. This requirement reflects a concern, evident over a long term, that there is a need to strengthen the government and the administration's capability to anticipate future problems and opportunities so as to take considered action in good time.

This century has seen a dramatic change in the tasks which governments are expected to perform and there is clearly a well documented trend whereby governments have taken action to improve the organization and management of their institutional machinery in order to make better decisions and achieve better results. Indeed, the general public has become aware that the most serious problems facing modern industrialized societies are interrelated and may only be resolved over a long period of time. This has led to greater public interest in longer-term issues. In this context, government is seen as custodian of the common future, responsible for balancing present demands with those of future generations, and safeguarding, as far as possible, decisions for future choice. As the range of government activities has extended, the need for more effective coordination across departmental boundaries has become more acute, calling for more comprehensive, multidisciplinary planning. Also, improved analytical capacities and increased information have created greater awareness of the complex consequences of policy decisions. Particularly since the recessionary period during the 1970s and early 1980s, governments have taken measures to improve the management of public expenditure and income, and this has given rise to the need for a coherent overview of governmental policies and priorities, within which alternative policies can be systematically compared in terms of their results or outputs as well as of the resource inputs which they require.

Much of this planning activity has taken place under the banner of 'strategic planning', which is usually understood in its broadest sense to cover the complex processes around the higher levels of central government and major departments, through which overall comparative judgements are made regarding national priorities, and strategic policy decisions are formulated and reviewed. Strategic planning for such decisions calls for a broad perspective across the range of governmental activities, and a proper weighing of longer term and short-term consi-derations. A key purpose of this planning has been the exploration of longer-term aspects of socio-economic development, seeking to encourage public discussion of longer-term issues and draw broad conclusions not too constrained by day-to-day considerations. The immediate short-term effects on decisions may be small, but over a period the results of such work may effect considerable changes in policy through gradual changes in governmental and public opinion.

An important role has been played in many countries, including Ireland, by commissions or working groups of civil servants and outside experts, set up by government, with a membership intended to bring together the best range of expertise and opinion. In some cases, the recommendations of such commissions or working groups may fail to be implemented because they cannot exert a sustained influence on policy. On the other hand, it is argued that their recommendations may carry sufficient weight, tempered by realism, to have a serious influence, particularly if they represent a combination of outside experts *and* civil servants. The examples referred to in this chapter will, I hope, help show this to be the case.

In essence, such groups/commissions have met a gap in the policy-making machinery arising from the following:

- Those forced to deal continually with a stream of pressing problems may devote insufficient attention to a wider scene in which there should be overall assessment, anticipation of future emergencies, or indeed emerging key issues, and some review of existing policies which time or poor design has rendered inefficient, or inappropriate.

- The traditional flow of recommendations up departmental channels may need to be supplemented when problems cut across departmental boundaries, or when departmental loyalties or perspectives inhibit the identification of new possibilities or encourage neglect of the adverse side-effects which new or existing programmes may generate.

- Adherence to one commonly used way of altering policies (a little more here, a little less here) will inhibit the adoption of 'bold' new schemes and prolong the life of established schemes after they are seen to be ineffective.

As against that, there are countervailing influences pulling policy making back towards a position of status quo. Rationale for this is often argued as follows:

- In a world of change and widespread freedom and ability to react to change, it is not easy to identify problems beyond the horizon. It is also often difficult to undo policies when those policies, however obsolete or ill-advised, will have built around them vested interests well able to protest at, and obstruct, any subsequent lessening of privileges.

- Departments have assumed their present shape because this has let them concentrate expertise in ways which have been suited to handling a very large part of the business to be done.

- Much of the gradualism in policy making is a means of coping with unforeseeable difficulties before they reach the dimensions of a major problem or crisis stage.

In the real world of day-to-day policy formulation and administration, there is and always will be, a tension between the above forces. The challenge for those involved in managing such tensions is to know when the timing is right for a move into a 'strategic phase'. Often, of course, the choice is made through the pressure of external events and the system is galvanized, sometimes unwillingly, into taking the longer-term strategic view.

This chapter will refer to a number of 'cross-cutting' initiatives in which this author has been involved. Each of them has dealt with issues which, in terms of the earlier discussion, could be described as strategic. These are:

1 *Irish Women: Agenda for Practical Action. Report of the Working Party on Women's Affairs and Family Law Reform.* February 1985 (see pp. 296–9).

2 Child Benefit Review Committee, *Report to the Minister for Social Welfare.* January 1995 (see pp. 299–301).

3 *Report of the Expert Working Group on Integrating Tax and Social Welfare.* June 1996 (see pp. 301–4).

4 *Sharing in Progress. National Anti-Poverty Strategy.* April 1997 (see pp. 304–8).

5 *Securing Retirement Income. National Pensions Policy Initiative Report of the Pensions Board.* May 1998 (see pp. 308–11).

6 *Strengthening Families for Life. Final Report of the Commission on the Family to the Minister for Social, Community and Family Affairs.* June 1998 (see pp. 311–14).

These reports are considered under the following headings :

• The context, including the strategic nature, of the topic being examined.

• The process involved in preparing the report, including level of consultation, involvement of experts etc.

• The impact of the report. In this context, considerations would arise such as: Could it be argued that the report led to changes in public opinion, or indeed has public opinion been mobilized around the concerns identified in the report? Have relevant changes in policies, practices etc. been achieved?

Irish Women: Agenda for Practical Action. Report of the Working Party on Women' s Affairs and Family Law Reform, **February 1985**

The Context

The Working Party was established by the then Taoiseach, Dr Garret FitzGerald. The context for this Report was the rapidly changing role of women in Irish society. The Report noted that important changes were taking place in the role of women and in the contribution they were making to the economic and social life of the community. These changes were associated with more and younger married women in the population, fewer children per marriage, more married women at work, increased mobility of women, greater job opportunities and more diversified education for women. While much progress had already been made in removing basic economic and social discrimination against women, there were, however, a wider range of measures open to society to promote actively greater participation by women in economic and social life. This, the Report stated, required the provision of positive opportunities and facilities to enable women to participate to a far greater extent in the economic and social life of the community. The underlying demographic, educational and labour force trends demonstrated clearly how inappropriate were the then socio-economic structures and why it was necessary to create new opportunities, to mobilize the potential contribution women could make.

The Report put forward an *Agenda for Practical Action* (1985) across a wide range of areas, covering employment, education, the health services, childcare facilities, social welfare, women in rural Ireland, women in the home, single parents, family law reform and other issues such as the appointment of women to state boards. Some of these areas had already been examined in the report of the first Commission on the Status of Women in 1972 and would also be the subject of a Second Commission which reported in January 1993. Thus the context was in a sense a shifting one reflecting changes over two decades during which social change in Ireland was intensified and 'telescoped' into a short historical period. The strategic nature of the subject is evident if one considers the definition of the word 'strategy' as 'the series of steps needed to win a campaign or other major objective'. It does not require lengthy analysis to indicate that the so-called 'women's agenda' and the supporting economic and social change required to advance it, meets this definition! As regards the contribution which the Working Party report made to the long term strategy of achieving change in the 'women's agenda', I will return to this matter under the discussion of its impact.

The Process

The Working Party first met on 7 April 1983 and met an additional six times in plenary session. At its second meeting it was agreed that the Working Party could best make progress by discussing the particular issues raised in appropriate sub-committees. The sub-committees dealt with employment and education, social issues and law reform. In addition there were numerous bilateral contacts to agree specific aspects of the Report. The Working Party took as the starting point for their work the position of women in Irish society as reflected in the 26 submissions it received and in the findings of the Commission on the Status of Women which reported in December 1972, as well as the information and expertise built up since the appointment of a Minister of State for Women's Affairs and Family Law Reform, Nuala Fennell. The preface to the Report states that:

> The subject matter of the Working Party's Report deals directly with or
> indirectly impacts on virtually the entire area of economic and social
> policy. For this reason the Working Party decided that it could not discuss
> in detail each issue in the Report. Rather the Working Party decided that
> Departmental representatives would advise and recommend essentially on
> the matters in their own areas of competence (1985: 8).

The Report also noted that its findings would have to be set in the
context of public expenditure priorities. It also stated that

> the findings of the Working Party represent, in the Working Party's view,
> objectives the Government can accept in the Women's Affairs and Family
> Law Reform areas given their determination to eliminate inequality of
> opportunity in all areas of activity. *Policies can be implemented to achieve those
> objectives both immediately and in the years ahead.* It is a matter for Government
> to decide on the priority of the objectives proposed relative to other
> policy objectives and consequently on the pace at which it will be
> possible to implement them (1985: 9).

Following on the discussion earlier about the definition of 'strategic', it is
clear that the Working Party perceived the agenda it put forward as a
long-term one which would by its very nature take years to implement.

In essence, the Working Party, while being perhaps unusual for its
time in addressing such a wide 'cross-cutting' agenda, followed a predict-
able pattern in which departments advised on policies particular to their
own department's functions and could not commit themselves to the
whole Report which was very wide-ranging. It should be noted also that
there were three reservations, which are referred to in the Report. It
was, in reality, 'early days' for such an attempt and while the Report
managed to analyse and comment on a very broad range of issues on
which there was at that stage very divided opinion in society at large, its
recommendations were in some cases very tentative. In that sense, it
could be argued that it lacked the dynamism which would have come
from the type of open forum which a commission could achieve. On
the other hand, as its title suggests, it put forward a 'practical' agenda
which, with the benefit of hindsight, made much sense.

The Impact

When discussing the impact of the Report, one must, in a sense, draw
intuitively on the evidence here, as it is not possible to state categorically
whether a change would have happened without the benefit of a report.
In addition, the then Office of the Minister of State for Women's Affairs
and Family Law Reform was abolished shortly afterwards and the

Report's findings were not actively monitored in the same way as would be the case for a commission. Anyone familiar with this area however would see a common thread in the types of issues the Report dealt with, right up to the present day and it would be fair to say that substantial changes for the better have occurred in the position of women across the range of economic and social policies. A report prepared by Goodbody Consultants for the National Women's Council of Ireland states for instance (1997: 9) that:

> Progress has been made. There is a much greater recognition now in national and local policy and programmes of the validity and importance of achieving gender equality. There is much greater support, in principle at least, for the objectives of the National Women's Council.

In sum, the impact of the Report is likely to have been of the 'slow burner' variety. Being an entirely civil-service driven working party, it is likely to have pushed to its limits the boundary, at that time, beyond which 'the system' could not envisage change occurring in this area. The considerable analysis and detail provided in the Report provided a fertile landscape from which bolder and more radical plans could be sketched in future.

The Child Benefit Review Committee, *Report to the Minister for Social Welfare*, January 1997

The Context

The Child Benefit Review Committee was established by the Minister for Social Welfare, Dr Michael Woods, TD, in October 1994. From the terms of reference, it is clear that the Committee was working within the context of the Programme for Partnership Government (1993). The terms of reference of the Review Committee requested the Committee to make recommendations that could be considered for the 1995 Budget. While the Report therefore had a clear, short-term objective, it was set in a context where child income support had been the subject of ongoing strategic focus, which drew on evidence about the link between poverty and family size, the impact on labour market incentives of the policy interventions in the child support area and studies on the relative costs of children by age. The Group noted a marked decline in the number of births in Ireland, from 74,000 in 1980 to 49,000 in 1993, and a fall in the fertility rate and the birth rate.

The Group noted that Child Benefit (CB) was one of several measures by the state in the area of child support; that it represents a contribution towards the costs of children, while not meeting the full costs; that means-tested payments (Child Dependant Allowances, Family Income Supplement) represent higher transfers than CB to needy families; that CB is of particular value to mothers with no other direct support and that it is almost invariably spent on the children or on general household expenses. It took the view that Child Benefit fulfilled a number of roles, the most important of which are assistance to all households with children in recognition of the higher costs incurred and the alleviation, without contributing to labour market disincentives, of household poverty associated with children.

The Group did not set a target rate for Child Benefit. Such a target rate could only be set in the context of all of the elements of child income support and would need to have regard to the overall 1995 Budgetary context. It noted, however, the broad emerging consensus in favour of an increase. On the assumption that the relevant funds would be available, the Group recommended an increase in Child Benefit of £5 per month per child, and the extension of the statutory entitlement to Child Benefit up to age 18, except when the young person concerned is in paid employment or an apprenticeship. It also made a number of other general recommendations in the context of child income support.

The Process

The Committee comprised representatives of the relevant government departments and outside experts. It was chaired by a non-civil servant, Dr Finola Kennedy, an economist. It had a short time-scale in which to report and therefore did not seek submissions, although a few interested individuals wrote to the Committee. It drew considerably, as it had been asked to do, on the many studies which had been carried out in this field and noted in particular the ongoing work of the Expert Working Group on the Integration of Tax and Social Welfare.

The Impact

In the 1995 Budget, Child Benefit was increased by £7 per month per child. While budgetary decisions are a matter for government, the fact that the Committee's Report was available at such a strategically appropriate time, that it represented the view of a range of experts, and that a firm basis for moving forward on the child support agenda had been set by a number of key research reports, were undoubtedly important influences. (This is not to diminish in any way the political will implied in making such a budgetary choice.) In this example, therefore, a Committee with a clear, short-term yet strategic focus came into being at an appropriate time. With the background support both of public and political opinion and of a group of key social policy experts, it played out a key role, albeit over a short period.

Report of the Expert Working Group on the Integration of Tax and Social Welfare, June 1996

The Context

The Group was established by the then Minister of State at the Department of Social Welfare, Joan Burton TD, in July 1993, arising from a commitment in the *Programme for Partnership Government*. The Group's membership came from a wide range of backgrounds and expertise under the chairmanship of Dónal Nevin. The government programme contained a commitment 'to study in consultation with the social partners the integration of the tax and social welfare codes'. At its inaugural meeting, the Minister of State indicated that 'the primary objective of integration is to address the problems of poverty traps and disincentives which can arise at present'. The issues the Group were asked to address had been a source of concern in the public domain for some time. Nonetheless, it was clear from the outset that integration could mean different things to different people.

The Group saw integration ranging from, at one extreme, total integration of the tax and welfare systems involving the merging of the tax system, social insurance system and social assistance system into a single unified tax/transfer system, to, at the other extreme, retention of the existing system, but with better coordination between them. This suggested that the approach should not be limited to a single definition of integration. So, in the Report the Group examined a range of options involving greater or lesser degrees of integration. The Group assessed options, from full structural integration of the systems, in the form of a Basic Income, to options which provide for better coordination of the existing systems. A broad range of specific options were evaluated against a number of policy criteria, including their impact on employment incentives (unemployment/poverty traps), income distribution, employment and equity. Within these criteria, the Group gave priority to the impact of reform on employment and the incentive to work.

Implicit in the Group's conclusions are a number of underlying policy principles which guided the Group's work. These were seen as a guide to future policy, which are important to note so that the impact of the Report can be seen over time, by reference to these criteria. The criteria are:

There must be a reward for working – people facing a job offer, or in lower paid employment, must be certain that they are identifiably better off by taking the available work than they would be if they stayed on unemployment payments;

The transition to work should be facilitated – the income tax and social welfare systems should not create difficulties for people moving between unemployment and employment;

Tax on the lower paid should be reduced – since many unemployed people, in particular the long-term unemployed, cannot command earnings at or about the average, every effort must be made over time to reduce or eliminate the tax wedge at lower income levels; where low earners pay no tax, subsidization through the benefit system provides an important and well targeted support to work;

The tax and social welfare systems should be simpler – complexity discourages movement between unemployment and employment;

Tax and social welfare reforms should be coordinated – many of the problems with the existing systems arise from the failure in the past to coordinate tax and welfare policies, particularly where they relate to unemployment/employment.

For the purposes of this article, it is not necessary to go into detail on the conclusions of the Report which span a very wide range of areas but its impact and significance should be viewed in the context of the degree to which progress is achieved in the light of the above underlying policy principles.

The Process

As stated earlier, the Group comprised a wide range of expertise. It met formally on 43 occasions. In addition, numerous sub-group meetings were held. The Group had meetings in Dublin with representatives of employers and with representatives of national anti-poverty networks. The Group also had meetings with unemployed people in Dublin and Cork. The Group did not advertise for submissions but views were received from the Conference of Religious of Ireland and from the Irish National Organisation of the Unemployed. The Group submitted an Interim Report to the Minister of State in December 1993. Research was commissioned from the Economic and Social Research Institute on the subject of Basic Income and published in September 1994 (Callan et al., 1994). A submission was made to the Minister for Social Welfare prior to the 1996 Budget.

The Impact

During its life, the Group provided interim advice to the Minister of State and the Minister for Social Welfare in the context of various Budgets. The Group made two specific budgetary recommendations in an Interim Report it submitted:

(*a*) An easing of the means test for Lone Parents Allowance in order to make it easier for lone parents to take up employment.

(*b*) Removal of the obligation on employers to pay the Health Contribution and Employment and Training Levy on behalf of medical card-holders.

Both of these issues were addressed in the 1994 Budget, and the necessary legislation was included in the 1994 Social Welfare Act.

The Group also submitted a number of Budget proposals for 1996, based on the conclusions they had reached at that stage. These recommendations were as follows:

(*a*) Medical Cards

Loss of the medical card on taking up employment, or on increasing earnings within employment, contributes to poverty and unemployment traps. The Group recommended that the long-term unemployed should be allowed to retain the medical card on taking up employment, subject to an earnings ceiling, and also subject to a two year time-limit. A variant of this was implemented in the Budget, without an earnings ceiling, and with a three-year time-limit.

(*b*) Child Dependant Allowances (CDAs)

The Group recommended allowing a long-term unemployed person to retain CDAs for up to 13 weeks on taking up employment, pending a decision on his/her FIS application. Again, this was implemented in the Budget.

(*c*) Means test for Unemployment Assistance (UA)

The Group recommended simplification of the means test for UA, to make it easier for people to take up part-time and/or casual employment. This was implemented in the Budget.

(*d*) Adult Dependant Allowance (ADA)

The Group noted that there was a poverty trap associated with the income cut-off for the ADA, and that the 1995 Social Welfare Act contained a provision allowing regulations to be made to allow for a more tapered withdrawal of the Adult Dependant Allowance. The

Group indicated support for the idea of a more tapered approach to ADAs and asked that the legislation be implemented as soon as possible. This has now happened.

Since both the publication of its Interim Report (December 1993) and its Final Report (June 1996), perusal of the literature would indicate that any public policy document dealing with the issues of work incentives or tax/social welfare coordination has drawn heavily on the Report's analysis and findings. While it may have been criticised to some degree for not coming forward with agreed recommendations in all of the areas it identified for action, its role in identifying the key options in areas of considerable complexity where agreement across the public domain is not simply achievable, in costing these options and in providing background analysis for the options and recommendations, it has clearly left an enduring legacy. Realistically, its overall impact will take a longer term framework, say ten years, to evaluate as it will take such a period to achieve long lasting change in areas of major resource distribution such as social welfare and taxation.

Sharing in Progress: The National Anti-Poverty Strategy, April 1997

The Context

At the UN World Summit for Social Development, held in Copenhagen in March 1995, the Irish Government, along with other Governments, endorsed a programme of action geared not only to eliminating absolute poverty in the developing world but to a substantial reduction of overall poverty and inequalities everywhere.

The following extract from the Copenhagen Declaration, Commitment 2, is relevant:

> (*a*) Formulate or strengthen, as a matter of urgency national policies and strategies geared to substantially reducing overall poverty in the shortest possible time, and reducing inequalities, and to eradicating absolute poverty by a target date to be specified by each country in its national context.
> (*b*) Focus our efforts and policies to address the root causes of poverty and to provide for the basic needs of all.
> (*c*) Seek to reduce inequalities, increase opportunities and access to resources and income, and remove any political, legal, economic and social factors and constraints that foster and sustain inequality.

Arising from this commitment the then government, following proposals brought by the Minister of Social Welfare, Proinsias de Rossa TD, approved the development of a National Anti-Poverty Strategy (NAPS). To this end, an Inter-Departmental Policy Committee, made up of representatives from government departments and national agencies with a contribution to make to addressing anti-poverty issues, was set up to prepare the Strategy.

The Strategy involved the following:

(*a*) the preparation of an overview statement setting out in broad terms the nature and extent of poverty, social exclusion and inequality in Ireland;

(*b*) the selection of key themes/policy areas to be addressed if poverty, social exclusion and inequality are to be tackled;

(*c*) the setting of specific targets within each theme against which progress can be addressed;

(*d*) the use of the Government's Strategic Management Initiative to reflect government commitment to an 'anti-poverty' strategy;

(*e*) recommending what type of institutional mechanisms should be put in place to ensure that the issue of reducing poverty, social exclusion and inequality is firmly on the agenda of all government departments and agencies, and that there is appropriate coordination across and between departments on policy in this area;

(*f*) specifically including the people directly affected by poverty in these processes of policy formulation and implementation through a wide-ranging consultative and participative exercise.

The Strategy statement published in April 1997 set out the strategic direction and overall objectives for the National Anti-Poverty Strategy which is now being put in place across all government departments.

The Process

The NAPS is a major cross-departmental policy initiative designed to place the needs of the poor and the socially excluded among the issues at the top of the national agenda in terms of Government policy development and action. The development of NAPS involved wide-ranging consultation and participation with the voluntary and community sector, the social partners, users of services and those with first hand experience of poverty. Nine regional public consultation seminars were held, attended by over 1000 people, while almost 300 written submissions from groups and individuals around the country were received and considered. These submissions were summarized in a separate document which was published in December 1995.

The NAPS sets out a framework within which poverty will be tackled over a ten-year period with an overall objective of reducing by half the numbers of people identified as consistently poor by 2007. Targets under five key headings have been identified: educational disadvantage, unemployment, income adequacy, disadvantaged urban areas and rural poverty.

The Impact

Firstly, at an institutional level, in recognition of the need to securely underpin the process, the following structures were approved by government in April 1997, and are now in place:

- the establishment of a Cabinet Committee to deal with issues of poverty and social exclusion to be chaired by the Taoiseach, and include all ministers whose brief includes policy areas relevant to tackling poverty. The role of the sub-committee has been extended to include issues relating to drugs and local development;

- the Minister for Social, Community and Family Affairs to have responsibility for the day to day political oversight of the strategy and to appear before the Social Affairs committee to update the Oireachtas on developments with NAPS. Individual ministers to have responsibility for development in areas under their remit;

- the NAPS Inter-Departmental Policy Committee to remain in place, chaired jointly by the Department of the Taoiseach and the Department of Social, Community and Family Affairs. The members of the Committee to comprise senior officers who will be designated as having responsibility for ensuring that the NAPS provisions relevant to their Departments are implemented;

- the establishment of an Strategic Management Initiative team in the Department of Social, Community and Family Affairs with core staffing (the NAPS Unit) to oversee the implementation of the Strategy;

- the National Economic and Social Forum to have responsibility for monitoring the progress of implementing the NAPS, in the context of its responsibility for monitoring the social inclusion element of Partnership 2000, and the Combat Poverty Agency to oversee an evaluation of the NAPS process;

- consultation with and the involvement of the voluntary and community sector to continue;

- drawing on the Department of the Environment report, *Better Local Government − A Programme for Change* (1996), and the work of the Devolution Commission, social inclusiveness and equality of opportunity to be fostered through a renewed system of local government.

A NAPS Unit is now located in the Department of Social, Community and Family Affairs (DSCFA). The role of the Unit is to:

- promote the concepts underlying the NAPS within the Department, across the public service, with community and voluntary groups, with business interests and with the general public;
- liaise with other departments in relation to their response to the NAPS and ensure that policies are audited to reflect a focus on poverty;
- monitor the activities and responses of departments to NAPS, in particular the extent to which they achieve their objectives;
- coordinate the activities of departments and organizations in relation to trans-departmental issues/projects (using the SMI approach to teams as a model);
- drive and coordinate the DSCFA response to NAPS in terms of both policy development and implementation of the strategy;
- liaise with agencies such as the Combat Poverty Agency, community and national anti-poverty networks etc.;
- develop a strategy for publicity, use of the media, etc., in order to keep the NAPS to the forefront of public policy.

Looking to the future, the objective is to embed the principles of the Strategy at political and departmental level and in the wider public service. Currently, ministers and the Cabinet sub-committee are kept informed of progress through reports and briefings. Departmental liaison officers are being asked to prioritize the commitments set out in the Strategy and devise a work-plan to deliver on those commitments, reporting annually to the Inter-Departmental Policy Committee on progress. It is planned that a process will be put in place to ensure that significant social inclusion issues are considered in any proposed government policy changes. A programme for public information and education for all sectors of the community is being developed. Various approaches, including public seminars, consultation meetings, publications and the Internet will be used for this purpose. Consideration is also being given to the role which the private sector and the broader community can play.

In summary, the NAPS has been a very ambitious cross-cutting initiative. Its success will clearly have to be judged over a ten-year period since changes as dramatic as encouraging further distribution of resources to the disadvantaged require considerable political will and widespread public support. Already however, the NAPS model has evoked considerable interest and is being drawn on by other governments. For instance, in a speech by the former British Secretary of State for Social Security, Harriet Harman, to Church Action on Poverty, she stated that in seeking solutions to problems of poverty in the UK, 'we have examined closely the Irish anti-poverty strategy'. There are of course people who feel that the Strategy is not sufficiently radical in vision and in the targets set but again, time and ongoing evaluation will be necessary to see if the Strategy's aims are both achievable, and indeed, ultimately achieved.

The National Pensions Policy Initiative

The Context

The issue of adequate and comprehensive pension cover has been under consideration in Ireland for over 20 years. During that time there has been a Green Paper on a *National Income Related Pension Scheme* in 1976 and the *Final Report of the National Pensions Board* in 1993. The Irish debate is set against an international background in which many countries are reforming or reviewing their pension systems. The most prominent reasons for this are the so-called demographic 'time-bomb' and the fact that many existing systems are facing severe financing difficulties. However, while similar problems could arise in Ireland, the timing is much different from that in other countries.

In 1995 the Economic and Social Research Institute (ESRI) was commissioned by the Department of Social Welfare and the Pensions Board to undertake a survey of occupational and personal pension coverage in Ireland (Hughes and Walsh, 1996). According to the survey, less that 50 per cent of the workforce have supplementary pension cover. This means that significant segments of the workforce and their dependants are at risk of experiencing a sharp drop in living standards when they become pensioners.

On 30 October 1996 the *National Pensions Policy Initiative* was launched. This was jointly sponsored by the Department of Social Welfare and the Pensions Board. The objective of the Initiative was to facilitate national debate on how to achieve a fully developed national pension system and to formulate a strategy and make recommendations for actions needed to achieve this system. The Report, which was published in May 1998 (National Pensions Board, 1998), set out a strategy for a fully developed national pension system. It stated the view that securing adequate provision for retirement income in the future would require both improvements to the basic Social Welfare old age pension (which itself should provide adequate minimum income guarantee for the avoidance of poverty) and development of the supplementary pension provision system to provide much more simplified access than exists at present. This should result in wider coverage, not only in terms of numbers covered but also in terms of the types of employment covered, with a particular objective of bringing into supplementary pension coverage groups hitherto not covered such as younger people, lower paid and atypical workers. The Report stated that these developments in the supplementary pension system would need to be supported by robust institutional arrangements to build confidence in supplementary schemes and an educational and information drive to convince people of the need to make sufficient retirement savings. If these did not prove sufficient, further steps, including mandatory contributions, should be considered in the context of a progress review to be undertaken as proposed in the Report.

In essence, the framework set out in the Report covers the following key elements:

- planning for future provision in a changing demographic context;

- addressing poverty concerns for the retired sector and in particular aiming to provide a minimum adequate pension in retirement;

- ensuring that funding arrangements take account of financial sustainability in the longer term;

- recommending a range of important innovations which will enable the potential of an established voluntary-funded Second Pillar system to be developed and extended considerably;

- setting specific targets both for the quality and extent of pension coverage in the future;

- providing a strong institutional framework for the above developments and ensuring a review mechanism to monitor progress achieved.

Interestingly, in developing its proposals for a minimum retirement income guarantee, the Board drew on the *National Anti-Poverty Strategy* (Ireland, 1997: 99), stating that 'adequate rates of payment under Social Welfare old age pensions should be a central instrument for the avoidance of poverty in retirement'. It went on to develop this argument in relation to what an 'adequate' level would be and how such a level would be funded.

The Process

The Initiative was progressed in two stages. The first stage involved the publication of a *Consultation Document* on 13 February 1997. The purpose of the *Consultation Document* was to provoke discussion by setting out background information, listing the main issues and possible ways forward. The Document was set out against an international background in which many countries are reforming or reviewing their system of providing for older people. 3,650 copies of this Document were distributed.

There was a very wide response to the Initiative from many different sources, showing a recognition of the importance of pensions and making use of the opportunity to influence future national pension policy. 143 submissions were received, ranging from detailed and research based documents to individual submissions. The range and scope of the submissions ensured that key issues of concern to organizations and individuals could be reflected, as far as possible, in what is, in effect, a national debate on the proposed way forward for securing future retirement provision. A National Pensions Conference was held on 2 July 1997 in Dublin Castle and all those who had made submissions came together to present and discuss them. This provided a further major contribution to the consultation process. In July 1997, the Pensions Board commenced work on the second stage of the Initiative. The second stage involved analysis of the responses to the Consultation Document, further investigation and discussion of specific ways forward leading to a report and recommendations from the Pensions Board to the Minister for Social, Community and Family Affairs. Many internal workshops were held over a nine-month period in which the Board discussed and debated issues raised in the consultation process, objectives, strategic approaches, practical alternatives to achieving these objectives and associated issues of implementation which would arise. These workshops were informed by the results of *the Actuarial Review of Social Welfare Pensions* published by the Department of Social, Community and Family Affairs in September 1997, and other economic forecasts, further analysis of data from the Economic and Social Research Institute, and inputs by expert practitioners on specific matter. Various meetings were also held with representative groups which proved very helpful.

The Impact

On publication of the Report in May 1998, the Minister for Social, Community and Family Affairs, Dermot Ahern TD, issued with the Report a detailed response on behalf of the government to the Report's findings in terms of the action to be taken on the key recommendations. The Minister stated:

> I am delighted to be able to set out the Government's response to the recommendations of the Pensions Board report and, for the first time in the history of the State, to set out a clear Government plan to secure the future of our older people. The recommendations of the Pensions Board involve the development of strong first pillar social welfare pensions,

based on social insurance, and major improvements in our second pillar (occupational and personal) pensions with the ultimate objective of ensuring that 70% of those at work over the age of 30 have second pillar cover. The Government, in its Action Programme, are already committed to a strong social welfare pension based on social insurance. We are committed to achieving a pension of £100 per week by the year 2002. The Government welcome the Board's target of achieving 70% second pillar pensions coverage and has, in principle, decided to introduce a new simplified Personal Retirement Savings Account (PRSA) which will make it easier for people to take out their own private pensions cover. I strongly believe that the implementation of this action plan will put our pension system on a sound basis as we move into the next Millennium (press release, 7 May 1998).

Many detailed responses have been made even in the month following the publication of the Report. In addition, seminars have been held on the Report's analysis and recommendations for a way forward on this strategic issue. Like the NAPS, it will take some years to gauge the impact of these recommendations in terms of increased coverage, level of provision for pensioners and financing of such provision. The Initiative was another key example of a large scale, cross-cutting initiative, where public opinion, industry, consumers, government and professional expertise was galvanized in a national effort on an important national issue.

The Commission on the Family

The Context

The Commission on the Family was established by the Minister for Social Welfare, Proinsias de Rossa, in October 1995:

> to examine the effects of legislation and policies on families and make recommendations to the Government on proposals which would strengthen the capacity of families to carry out their functions in a changing economic and social environment.

The terms of reference of the Commission were wide ranging. They included examining how government policies, programmes and services affect family life. The terms of reference were:

- to raise public awareness and improve understanding of issues affecting families;

- to examine the effects of legislation and policies on families and make recommendations to the government on proposals which would strengthen the capacity of families to carry out their functions in a

changing economic and social environment. The Commission would
also be expected to make proposals to the all–party Committee on the
Constitution on any changes which it believes might be necessary in
the constitutional provisions in relation to the family. Proposals
involving expenditure should be as far as practicable costed;

- to analyse recent economic and social change affecting the position
  of families, taking account of relevant research already carried out,
  including reports of commissions (e.g. Social Welfare, Taxation, Status
  of Women) and relevant working groups (e.g. Expert Working
  Group on the Integration of Taxation and Social Welfare, current
  anti–Poverty Strategy Policy Committee) and carry out limited
  research as necessary.

In carrying out its work, the Commission, while having due regard to
the provisions on the family in the Constitution intended to support the
family unit, was asked to reflect also in its deliberations on the definition
of the family outlined by the United Nations.

In its Final Report to the government, submitted in July 1998 (the
Commission also issued an Interim Report in November 1996), the
Commission concentrated on the welfare of children and vulnerable
families and how public policy can best strengthen and support families
in carrying out their important functions. It was the Commission's view
that a task such as theirs is the beginning. The report therefore aimed to
lay the foundations of future policy development to strengthen families
in our society. The overall thrust of the Commission's recommendations
centred on the need for public policy to focus on preventative and
supportive measures to strengthen families in carrying out their functions
and prevent difficulty.

The Commission's main findings and recommendations were presented
in terms of desirable outcomes for families. The pursuit of these desirable
outcomes were the core themes of this report. They relate to:

- Building strengths in families
- Supporting families in carrying out their functions – the caring and
  nurturing of children
- Promoting continuity and stability in family life
- Protecting and enhancing the position of children and vulnerable
  dependent family members.

The Commission set out its views on the policy approach in the various
areas which should be pursued in the years ahead. The Commission's
report also contained some original and significant research work which

the Commission had undertaken, including a national survey on the child-care arrangements which families make, sociological research on fathers and their role in family life and an overview of family policy in Ireland.

The Process

The Commission invited families, individuals and national and local voluntary organizations who work with families to assist with its work by making submissions setting out their views about the issues that affect family life and how policies, programmes and services can be improved to support families better. The Commission received 536 submissions from every part of the country. The majority of submissions were from individuals, families and small groups. The rest came from national organizations who work with families and voluntary and community groups. The submissions provide a broad picture of the concerns of families in Ireland today. The Commission also received contributions from the leading experts in the areas of family law, the Constitution, childcare and services for children, employment and workplace policies, poverty and healthcare who made valuable contributions to the Commission's work.

The Commission was also very active in pursuing its role of raising public awareness. During the period when it was seeking submissions, a freephone helpdesk was set up to advise callers about the work of the Commission and how they might contribute. There was a huge response from the public, with over 450 calls to the helpdesk. Nearly half of all callers went on to send in written submissions. On UN International Day of Families, 15 May 1996, the Commission hosted a Forum to hear what local community groups and families themselves see as the priority areas for action. The Forum was particularly aimed at local and community groups which have practical experience of working with families. UN International Day of Families 1997 was marked with a special exhibition in the National Gallery of Ireland, of the winning entries in the sculpture category of a national art competition for students in second-level Transition Year. The Commission hosted an expert workshop for the key providers of marriage and relationship counselling. A module of studies related to family issues was developed by the Commission with the Department of Education and Science, Transition Year Support Team, for teenage students in the 15 to 16 year age group who were taking the transition year at second level. 'Family Studies' is now available as an option to some 26,000 students throughout the country.

The Impact

In the forward to the Commission's final Report, the Minister for Social, Community and Family Affairs stated:

> The report 'Strengthening Families for Life' contains a comprehensive and in-depth analysis of the issues affecting families and wide-ranging recommendations across several different policy areas. . . . The Government is committed to adopting a families first approach by putting the family at the centre of all its policies. A new Family Affairs Unit has been established in the Department of Social, Community and Family Affairs to promote the coordination of family policy, pursue the findings in the Commission's final report following their consideration by the Government, to undertake research, and promote awareness about family issues. The Unit has responsibility for a number of family services including: support for the marriage and child counselling services, the Family Mediation Service, a pilot programme in relation to the local offices of the Department building on the one-stop-shop concept, with the aim of providing improved support at local level to families and an information programme on parenting issues . . . I am confident that the Commission's report will make a positive contribution to developing coherent, progressive and effective policies for families as promised in the Action Programme for the Millennium.

As with the other initiatives mentioned, the impact of the Commission's Report will best be judged over, say, a ten-year period. Part 10 of the Commission's Report discusses 'strengthening the institutional framework within which the State's response to families is developed and delivered and facilitating the development of a coherent policy approach to families across Government Departments and services'. In this context, the Commission recommends that 'family well-being' should be singled out as an area of critical importance for government in the years ahead. It will therefore be a challenge to ensure that both a supportive institutional framework *and* a range of supportive policies in this area are developed and maintained so that, over time, the required strategic changes take place.

CONCLUSION

The chosen examples described in this chapter are useful in drawing lessons in relation to some of the ingredients of successful, strategic cross-cutting initiatives which have or hopefully will have significant impact. The following points could be included in these ingredients:

• Clarity of objectives is important and the subject must be seen to be important and relevant to people's lives, and have long-term significance.

- Where submissions have been sought (e.g. the Commission on the Family, the National Anti-Poverty Strategy, the National Pensions Policy Initiative) it has been remarkable how willingly individuals and groups have become engaged in the topic and given enthusiastically of their time and views often in the form of lengthy submissions. The dynamism and creativity arising in such a process leaves an enduring legacy. The issues raised, some of which ultimately form the basis for recommendations, must of course be addressed in a coherent way in the implementation phase. (There must, indeed, be a few Masters or PhD theses waiting to be pursued in the analysis and perhaps follow-up of such exercises in tracking public opinion!)

- The analysis and research contained in these reports is often almost as important as the recommendations themselves. Important examples in this respect would include the analysis underlining the identification of options in the *Integration Report* and the research on fathers and on parents' use of child care possibilities (whether within or outside the home) in the Commission on the Family.

- The contribution of outside experts and civil servants, if the mix is right, can afford opportunities for cross-fertilization and creativity which can have far reaching results. In addition, the process can create a sense of ownership among the civil servants, which can be useful during the implementation phase. The role of the civil servants in these exercises can of course be a difficult one, depending on the circumstances. The constraints imposed by the legal and other require-ments under which they operate can at times be great. On the other hand, particularly in the context of greater openness now pertaining in the light of the SMI initiatives, the opportunity for dialogue with those 'outside' the system has probably never been greater. This requires a new mix of skills and approaches from the civil service, as the work involved in membership of such cross-cutting initiatives requires a different blend of skills to that required traditionally. Overall, this new situation creates both opportunities and threats which have to be managed.

RECOMMENDED READING

Readers are referred to the Reports of the Working Groups and Commissions referred to in this chapter, for full terms of reference, group membership and findings.

REFERENCES

Callan, T., C. O'Donoghue and C. O'Neill (1994) *Analysis of Basic Income Schemes for Ireland*, ESRI Policy Research Series, Paper No.21. Dublin: Economic and Social Research Institute.

Child Benefit Review Committee (1995) *Report to the Minister for Social Welfare*. Dublin: Stationery Office.

Commission on the Family (1996) *Interim Report*. Dublin: Stationery Office.

Commission on the Family (1998) *Strengthening Families for Life: Final Report of the Commission on the Family to the Minister for Social, Community and Family Affairs*. Dublin: Stationery Office.

Department of the Environment (1996) *Better Local Government: A Programme for Change*. Dublin: Stationery Office.

Department of Social Welfare (1976) *A National Income-Related Pension Scheme*. Dublin: Stationery Office.

Department of Social, Community and Family Affairs (1997) *Actuarial Review of Social Welfare Pensions*. Dublin: Stationery Office.

Expert Working Group on the Integration of Tax and Social Welfare (1996) *Report of the Expert Group on Integrating Tax and Social Welfare*. Dublin: Stationery Office.

Goodbody Economic Consultants (1997) *Progress in Achieving Equality for Women 1992–1997 and An Agenda for the Future: A Report for the National Women's Council of Ireland*. Dublin: National Women's Council of Ireland.

Hughes, G. and B. Walsh (1996) *Occupational and Personal Pension Coverage*. Dublin: Economic and Social Research Institute.

Ireland (1997) *Sharing in Progress: National Anti-Poverty Strategy*. Dublin: Stationery Office.

National Pensions Board (1993) *Developing the National Pension System. Final Report of the National Pensions Board*. Dublin: Stationery Office.

National Pensions Board (1998) *Securing Retirement Income. National Pensions Policy Initiative Report of the Pensions Board*. Dublin: Stationery Office.

Working Party on Women's Affairs and Family Law Reform (1985) *Irish Women: Agenda for Practical Action: Report of the Working Party on Women's Affairs and Family Law Reform*. Dublin: Stationery Office.

17
Social Policy Evaluation[1]

Nessa Winston

INTRODUCTION

On a daily basis, people make evaluations in relation to services, employees, films, sports teams, the weather and so on. Using our own criteria, we decide that *The Godfather* is a 'good' film, Mary is a 'First Class' student or that the 'best' racehorses are Irish.

Those responsible for implementing aspects of a social policy may wish to examine whether or not their programme or project is working and therefore they may decide to evaluate it. Alternatively, those who fund it may require an evaluation and this is increasingly the case, particularly for activities in receipt of European Social Funds. Not surprisingly, this has resulted in a growth in the 'evaluation industry' in Ireland. All kinds of organizations conduct evaluations, including the Combat Poverty Agency, the Economic and Social Research Institute, the European Social Fund Programme Evaluation Unit, EU Structural Funds Information and Evaluation Unit, the Social Science Research Centre, University College Dublin, the Work Research Centre and numerous independent consultants.

Based on the results of the evaluation, a number of decisions might be made, such as:

- The policy works well. Retain it.
- Parts of the policy are working; others have no positive impact. Improve or terminate those components that do not work.
- The policy is ineffective. Terminate it.
- The evaluation results are ignored.

It is obvious from the above that the implications of evaluation can be highly significant both for those implementing the policy and those on the receiving end of it. Consequently, it is important to ask the following questions:

- What is an evaluation and how should it be conducted?
- How do we find out if the policy is working or not?

In this chapter a specific method of evaluation, namely evaluation research will be examined. In addition, the focus is on evaluation research in relation to the social arena: policies, programmes, projects, and services such as drug treatment programmes or employment training schemes. For simplification purposes, this chapter will refer to programme evaluation rather than mentioning policies, projects and services each time. However, it should be noted that the comments made in relation to programmes apply to the evaluation of policies, projects and services unless otherwise stated.

EVALUATION AND EVALUATION RESEARCH DEFINED

The term evaluation implies some form of examination of a policy but also an assessment or judgement of it. Weiss defines evaluation thus:

> Evaluation is the systematic assessment of the operation and/or the outcomes of a programme or policy, compared to a set of explicit or implicit standards, as a means of contributing to the improvement of the programme or policy (Weiss, 1998: 4).

This definition contains a number of important points. First, she points out that evaluation involves a systematic assessment of a policy or programme. Second, Weiss notes that it can focus on the operation and/or the outcomes of the policy. This corresponds to a distinction often referred to in the literature on policy evaluation – that between formative and summative evaluations. When an evaluation is concerned only with the outcomes of a programme (investigating whether or not the programme works), it is a summative evaluation. Formative evaluations focus on the process of the programme ('what is the programme and how does it work?'). A comprehensive evaluation would include both summative and formative components. Another important aspect of the above definition is that evaluation involves assessing the programme in relation to its goals, both those that are explicit and also those implicit ones held by staff, management and client. For example, if a drug treatment programme was established to decrease drug use, an evaluation could assess whether or not it was meeting that explicit goal. Staff may also operate on the assumption that the programme increases the social skills and self-esteem of participants. These implicit goals would also need to be evaluated.

In order to make a reliable assessment of how a programme is functioning, evaluators use social science research methods to collect information about it and to make an appraisal. This process is known as evaluation research. Rossi and Freeman (1993: 5) define evaluation research as 'the systematic application of social research procedures for assessing the conceptualisation, design, implementation and utility of social intervention programmes'. Drawing on this and the significant dimensions of evaluation discussed above, evaluation research can be defined thus:

> Evaluation research refers to the systematic and reliable assessment of the operation and/or outcomes of a programme in relation to its goals, using research methods to improve that programme.

Evaluations can employ any research method or combination of methods to examine some aspect of or an entire policy (its conceptualization, operation and outcomes). Methods frequently used in evaluations are discussed in more detail below.

WHY UNDERTAKE EVALUATIONS?

When conducting an evaluation, it is important to understand why the evaluation is taking place, what purpose it serves. There are a variety of reasons for undertaking an evaluation.

1 *To assess the effectiveness of a programme.* Some evaluations focus on the question of whether or not the programme is working by examining (*a*) its outcomes and/or (*b*) the process involved in the programme. Outcome evaluations may concentrate on short and/or long-term effects. For example, in evaluating the effects of a drug treatment programme, the evaluator might be interested in the drug use of former participants one month, one year and/or five years after leaving the programme.

Alternatively, a process evaluation usually focuses on questions such as: what does the programme entail? Are all aspects of it being implemented and in the way stipulated by the programme developer? If not, why not? Are staff encountering problems with it and, if so, what are these problems? Are clients satisfied with it? These questions address what Mark (1996) calls the 'effort' involved in implementing a programme. Not all evaluations examine programme processes in detail. However, it is very difficult to understand programme outcomes without an in-depth understanding of its process. For example, if some clients of the drug treatment programme received different types of treatment or the same treatment from staff with different degrees of experience, this might affect whether or not their treatment was successful. Awareness of the details of a programme enhances the evaluator's understanding of the extent to which it is effective.

2 *To act as a tool for development of a programme* (Murray et al., 1994).
   Where this is the case, the evaluation is conducted to improve the
   effectiveness of a new programme while it is being implemented,
   recording changes as each component is put in place and examining
   the impact of these changes. In this way, the programme can be continually refined until the key stakeholders, those with a vested interest
   in it (funders, staff, administrators, clients) – are satisfied with it. These
   types of evaluations are required for small-scale, 'innovative' pilot
   schemes which have to be assessed before they can be introduced on
   a wider scale.

3 *To inform specific planning decisions.* If, for example, management is
   concerned about the future of one component of a programme, then
   the evaluation might focus on that component (Murray et al., 1994).

4 *For accountability purposes.* Increasingly, evaluations of publicly funded
   activities are required for accountability purposes. An external sponsor
   such as the government or the European Union usually imposes this
   type of evaluation. These evaluations address questions such as: was
   what was paid for actually undertaken? In the Irish context, the EU
   Structural Funds Information and Evaluation Unit, an independent
   unit within the Department of Finance, estimates that approximately
   £4 million of the current Community Support Framework (CSF
   1994–99) was spent on evaluating EU-funded activities by the end of
   1997 (EU Structural Funds Unit, 1998). Furthermore, the role of
   evaluation has greatly increased since the last CSF (1989–93) and this
   level of activity is expected to continue.

A special European Social Fund Programme Evaluation Unit was
established in 1992 in the Department of Enterprise and Employment
to assess the effectiveness of all human resource development interventions supported by the European Social Fund. The Unit operates in
partnership with the European Commission and has evaluated schemes
such as early school-leavers provisions, training for people with
disabilities, FÁS training programmes, and training for prisoners.

5 *To investigate the efficiency or cost-effectiveness of a programme.* Studies of
   this kind examine whether or not the benefits of the programme
   justify its costs (cost-benefit analysis) and whether there are alternative,
   less costly methods that might achieve the same results. Since the
   introduction of the Comptroller and Auditor General Amendment
   Act (1993), cost-effectiveness evaluations are conducted on a more
   regular basis. That Act gives legal power to the Comptroller and

Auditor General (CAG) to conduct 'Value for Money' examinations, investigating whether or not public bodies are employing cost-effective strategies. For example, the CAG reviewed the effectiveness of Regional Development Measures that formed part of the EU-aided Community Support Framework (CSF) for 1989–93. Government departments were required, as a condition of EU funding, to examine the effectiveness of these measures. On reviewing these evaluations, the CAG found that they were often extremely limited or that the projects were often of limited effectiveness and did not represent 'value for money' (e.g. some of the advanced technology pilot projects).

STAGES IN EVALUATION RESEARCH

Evaluation research is a process involving a number of interrelated steps. These steps provide a useful framework in which to describe the central issues that arise at different points.

The Evaluation Brief

Prior to conducting any evaluation, it is most important that it be planned in detail by the evaluator in conjunction with the various stakeholders. Murray et al. (1994: 49) refer to this plan as the 'evaluation brief' which 'specifies the scope, type and nature of the evaluation required'.

Consultation with key stakeholders (programme sponsors, managers, staff and recipients) is essential at this stage so that they help to inform the plans. Involving them from the outset means that their expectations of the evaluation are clear and realistic and it can also trigger an attachment on their part to the activity, a factor which can greatly facilitate the conduct of an evaluation and the way in which its results are received. Consulting key stakeholders also increases the likelihood that the evaluation results will be accepted and implemented (Patton, 1997: 41–3). While designing the evaluation brief is a time-consuming process, it is most valuable as it acts as a work programme for the evaluators and, when agreed on by the sponsors, as a form of contract between evaluator and sponsor.

Murray et al. (1994) contend that an evaluation brief should address the following questions.

What is to be Evaluated? It is most important that the evaluation brief outline what is to be evaluated as specifically as possible. Is it a policy, a programme, a project or a particular service within a project?

Why is an Evaluation Being Carried Out? As mentioned above, there are a variety of reasons for conducting an evaluation and in particular cases any combination of these reasons may apply. In drawing up the evaluation brief, it is essential to investigate and specify clearly the purpose of the evaluation. If the only reason for undertaking the evaluation is that sponsors require it, the evaluators should encourage management and staff to consider its possible benefits, such as increased effectiveness, rather than viewing it as an externally imposed and unwelcome procedure.

It is important to recognize that there may be both overt and covert reasons behind any evaluation. Politicians may call for an evaluation when they wish to postpone making a decision about a programme, but obviously they will not advertise this as one of the reasons for funding the research. Similarly, management may have a good idea what the results of an evaluation will be, but they sponsor it as a means of legitimizing a decision they wish to make, using the results as a lobbying tool, as a way of 'ducking responsibility', or as a form of public relations (Weiss, 1998: 22).

Who Wants the Evaluation? Prior to conducting the evaluation it is useful to know where the idea for evaluation originated. A key distinction here is whether or not the decision was an external or internal one. An internal decision implies that the programme management and/or staff wanted to assess their activities in some way. The implication of this for the evaluators is that staff tend to be more cooperative with the researchers than if the decision is made by an external organization such as the funding agency, a statutory body, senior management who are removed from the local operation of the programme, or consumers. When the decision is an external one, programme staff can view the evaluation as imposed and a threat to the services they provide and to their own jobs. They may feel, rightly or wrongly, that they themselves are being evaluated. In such cases, it is important for the evaluators to curtail such feelings of exclusion and 'impending doom' by involving the programme staff in evaluation decisions as much as possible and informing them about progress at regular intervals. Encouraging staff to view the evaluation as a useful planning tool can also help involve them in the process and enhance their willingness to cooperate with it.

Who is the Audience? The evaluation brief should also address the issue of who will be informed of the results of the study. The audience can include programme staff, funders, policy makers, decision takers, practitioners and the general public. Different types of presentation may be required for different audiences. For example, the funders might want a formal report while practitioners might prefer an oral and visual presentation of results.

What Resources are Available for the Evaluation? Evaluation research requires a variety of resources, all of which should be noted in the evaluation brief and agreed on by the sponsors. The necessary resources include financial resources, time, skills, availability of and access to information and key informants (Murray et al., 1994).

Understanding the Programme

Once the evaluation brief has been completed, the next step is to understand the programme to be evaluated, the context in which it operates and the politics of the situation. The best way to do this is to review documents and other relevant materials (videos, photos etc.) that describe the programme and talk about it with key stakeholders or their representatives. The aim here is to get a picture of how the programme is run and how it is linked to other programmes and organizations.

Understanding the goals of the programme is an essential aspect of this stage. In some cases, these objectives are outlined in the programme's literature. However, more often than not, identifying goals is a more difficult task than might be expected, for a number of reasons (Weiss, 1998). For example, the goals stated in the literature may be out of date or there may be no written goals. Another difficulty which may arise is that different stakeholders may have distinct objectives towards which each is working – employees can have one set of objectives, many of which, but not all, are shared by the programme management. Sometimes these can be conflicting goals, such as when management wish to provide a programme as cheaply as possible, while those administering it may feel it is best to provide as many different services as possible to those on the programme.

Defining Success

The next stage is to decide how programme success will be defined in the evaluation. This may involve defining successful outcomes, implementation and/or management. In evaluating a programme's outcomes, the evaluators must decide how much progress towards the desired outcome will be considered 'success'. For example, if half the people who attended a programme for young offenders were 'offence-free' three months after completing the programme, this might be considered a successful scheme. Alternatively, it might be better to examine ex-participants one year, or five years, later. This example demonstrates some of the decisions that must be made at this stage. One way to decide what constitutes success is to examine the results of similar programmes in other contexts and compare them with the expected results for their evaluation (Weiss, 1998). Whatever estimate of an acceptable success rate is chosen, it must be agreed with key stakeholders.

Figure 1. Measuring Programme Outcomes, Processes, Inputs and Environment

Evaluations can investigate a variety of concepts such as programme outcomes (intended and unintended), the processes involved in its operation, inputs to the programme and the environment in which it operates. The evaluators must decide which of these elements will be examined. For example, an evaluation of an AIDS Education Programme for physicians explored all four elements (Lewis, 1986). That is, Lewis investigated whether or not the physicians' level of knowledge about AIDS increased after the programme (programme outcome); types of education materials (programme process); resources allocated to the programme (inputs); and/or connections between the programme and other related sources of information (environment).

A comprehensive evaluation would measure programme outcomes, processes, inputs and environment. For simplification purposes, this chapter will focus on measuring outcomes of a programme. This is not to denigrate any other aspect of programme evaluation. Time and resources mean that all are rarely covered in most evaluations, but it must be emphasized that each dimension is important and that they are all interconnected. For example, programme processes are essential when you are concerned with how the programme functions, but they are also significant because they can lead to desired outcomes. In terms of the drug treatment example, we may be interested in how much treatment (intensity and duration of counselling) is offered to different categories of patients and the treatment characteristics of those who succeeded in remaining drug-free.

Programme Outcomes

When measuring outcomes, the evaluator starts by looking at the goals of the programme and translating these into measures. If examining its effects on the people who are served by the programme, the researchers might investigate changes in their behaviour and attitudes. Such changes can be explored by asking the participants themselves and/or by seeking expert judgments on their progress (judgments of those not working on the programme, but programme staff experts may also be included). An evaluation may also be concerned with the effect of a programme on public attitudes or values. For example, it may be a case of examining the impact of different types of health promotion campaigns on people's knowledge of health practices and health behaviour. The evaluation may want to know if individual contact with people works better than a media campaign in changing knowledge and behaviour (Weiss, 1998: 123).

In many cases, evaluators can employ existing measures, ones that have been tested by other researchers. An invaluable list of sources for evaluation measures is provided by Weiss (1998: 138–9). Using this list, an evaluator can find measures in the following areas: health, quality of life, self-confidence, crime and delinquency, child well-being, social gerontology, personality and social psychological attitudes, and organisational measures. When reliable measures of the concept do not exist, the evaluator has to create new measures. Any research methods textbook that deals with these issues can be examined to acquire the skills in this area (Cresswell, 1994; Hall and Hall, 1996; Hedrick, 1993; Judd et al., 1991; Mark, 1996). Regardless of whether or not the evaluator draws on existing measures or designs new ones, a key concern is that the measures be of high quality. Two main aspects of measurement quality are validity and reliability, and again these issues are dealt with in good methodology textbooks (Judd et al., 1991; Weiss, 1998). Weiss (1998: 148–50) discusses other measurement quality issues: direction, sensitivity to differences, currency, realistically connected, unbiased by the data collection method, accessibility, and system.

Great care needs to be taken when choosing and designing measures as one of the criteria used to judge the evaluation will be the measures it adopts. Indeed, the acceptance and implementation of the results of an evaluation can be controversial if there is disagreement in this area. Thus, consultation with key stakeholders on the choice of measures can greatly facilitate the acceptance of the findings.

Short-Term or Long-Term Measures?

One of the decisions the evaluator has to make is whether or not to include both short and long term measures of the outcomes. Policymakers tend to want results as soon as possible and certainly before the next election! But long-term measures can be extremely important and often the evaluator needs to convince the sponsors of their value. If evaluating the effects of pre-schooling on children, short-term measures might look at their scores on achievement tests before and after completing the course, while long-term measures might compare their Leaving Certificate results with a group of similar students who did not attend a pre-schooling programme. Key questions in this regard are whether or not an examination of long-term effects is necessary and will funding be available for that aspect of the evaluation? In a developmental evaluation, short-term measures are essential as they can be fed back to stakeholders to indicate which strategies are working. Those that are ineffective can then be improved or replaced by different ones.

Choosing Research Designs

When outlining the evaluation, researchers can choose any combination of designs from an array of different types used in social research. In this section, the focus will be on a number of strategies commonly employed in well-designed evaluations. (For a more detailed discussion of research designs in evaluation, including the advantages of each, see Weiss (1998).) It should be emphasized that each of these has limitations. Therefore, it is usual to choose a combination of approaches. A lot of space is devoted to this topic as it is often the weakest part of an evaluation, yet textbooks, with the exception of Weiss (1998), rarely cover the topic in a comprehensive and lucid manner.

Self-Evaluation

One way of assessing a programme is to ask the people involved in it (clients and staff) what they think about it. They can provide extremely useful information on the day-to-day running of the programme, its resources and their perceptions of its outcomes. However, there are limits to this type of data. For example, staff may be overly optimistic about the programme, especially if the evaluation results will be reported to programme sponsors, as they may have fears about cutbacks in their funding. Weiss (1998) points out that clients may also paint a rosy picture of the programme if it is the only resource of its type available to them and they are afraid of losing it. Thus, self-evaluation should be complemented by other forms of data. Note that external evaluators do not always carry out self-evaluations – they may be conducted by the programme staff themselves – a phenomenon which is frequently the case in community development projects.

External Expert Judgments

The evaluators might decide to invite a panel of experts from outside the programme to assess different aspects of it. The panel should consist of people with a variety of experiences so that it can provide a comprehensive assessment of the programme, contribute to its development plan and help it to maximize 'good practice'. Ideally, panel members should be people who have little or no stake in the programme. In reality, people like this can be difficult to find! However, a panel setting helps reduce this problem as no one expert's view holds too much weight.

In many cases, evaluations focus on one programme and one group of people, that is, there are no comparisons with people who are not involved in the project. Such designs can investigate the programme participants after the programme or they can examine them before and after the programme.

Single-Group 'After Only' Designs

This type of evaluation usually happens when the evaluator is called in after the programme has been running for some time and no data are available on participants before they began the programme. To supplement the 'after data', the evaluation should examine only records that might be available on participants when they started the programme to obtain as much information about them as possible. There may be some records on relevant variables (e.g. level of drug use just before the participant came on the programme) but this is often not the case. Another strategy which can be adopted is to ask those involved in the programme what the 'before' situation was like (clients and staff). However, if the duration of the programme was long, the reliability of this data can be questioned because it relies on accurate memories. If there are participants at different stages of the programme, the evaluator could examine newcomers to estimate what the participants may have been like before the programme, ensuring that there have been no changes in the criteria used to accept participants and that the numbers are large (Weiss, 1998).

Single-Group 'Before and After' Designs

Where possible, the evaluation should obtain relevant information on participants before they begin the programme and after they complete it. This provides some picture of whether or not the programme has had the desired impact on them. However, it is important to be aware of factors other than the programme that may have caused the changes in participants. For example, in evaluating an employment training scheme, some participants may also have taken evening classes on a related topic which could affect their success in getting a job at the end of the training programme. Thus, this approach needs to be supplemented with detailed information about the participants' lives during the programme and external events which might be responsible for the changes and not the programme itself (e.g. the overall unemployment rate and the economic climate).

One way of extending a single group design is to add a time series dimension to it. This is referred to as a time series design. Weiss describes this design thus:

> Time series involves a series of measurements on key outcome criteria at periodic intervals before the programme begins and continuing measurements after the programme ends. It thus becomes possible to learn a great deal about the condition that the programme aims to change – for example, unemployment or school-drop-out. Was the condition stable over the time period before the programme began, was it getting worse, or was it getting better even without the intervention of the programme? Then after the programme, did the condition improve immediately and remain fairly constant at the better level? Did it revert to its original problem status as effects of the programme faded out? Or did good results escalate over time, with success generating further success? (Weiss, 1998: 196–7).

An excellent example of the use of time series data is the evaluation of the Perry pre-school programme which explored whether or not a high-quality early childhood education programme would have short or long-term benefits for black children living in poverty (Schweinhart et al., 1993). The evaluators examined the abilities, attitudes and performance of the participants annually from age three to 11, at age 14–15, 19 and 27. They discovered that the pre-school programme had 'significant long-term benefits' for those who took part in it.

The major advantage of this type of design is that it adds additional evidence to 'before and after' changes, such as the extent to which the effects of a programme persist. This type of design is only possible when funds are made available for the long-term dimension of the evaluation and where data are available on the key variables prior to the establishment of a programme.

One of the limitations of this approach is that it does not indicate whether or not external factors, which have nothing to do with the programme, were responsible for the changes seen in programme participants. It may be that a decrease in unemployment accounts for the changes in the situation of unemployed participants on a training programme rather than the programme itself. Thus, there is a strong case for supplementing this type of data with other kinds of information.

Comparison Groups

Including a group(s) of people who do not participate in the programme is one way of extending single group designs. This group is generally referred to as the comparison group and it is used to investigate whether or not taking part in the programme evokes changes in the participants that do not occur in non-participants. Comparison groups increase the evaluators' ability to make causal inferences such as 'the programme changed the participants'.

Comparison groups' members should be as similar to those in the programme as possible with the only significant difference being that they do not take part in the programme. (See Weiss (1998) for different approaches to the use of comparison and control groups and the limitations of each approach.) The characteristics on which they are similar depend on the topic of the evaluation. For example, in evaluating training and employment programmes in Ireland, O'Connell and McGinnity (1997) compare post-programme labour market experiences of a sample of programme participants with those of a group similar to the participant group, except that they had not taken part in employment training schemes. Specifically, they were similar in terms of age and being unemployed at a certain point in time.

The Randomized Experiment (Control Groups)

When both the participant and comparison groups are chosen using random assignment procedures, the design is known as a randomized experiment and the comparison group is called a control group. This more scientific approach ensures that the two groups are similar to each other at the start of the programme and that whatever differences emerge are due to the programme.

The use of random assignment procedures provides the most rigorous test of the effects of a programme. It answers the question, has the programme evoked the desired changes in participants? With this approach, each member of the relevant population (e.g. the unemployed) has a known probability of ending up in the programme or control groups.[2]

For example, in the evaluation of a pilot-drug treatment programme in a United States prison, each participant was matched with a control, another person in the prison but not in the treatment unit, so that they were similar in terms of their history of heroin use, criminal convictions, duration of their prison sentence, age, education, and socio-economic background (Platt et al., 1977). At different stages during and after the programme, the evaluators were able to contrast changes in programme participants with those in the control group. Thus the evaluators were able to say that, six months after they left prison, those who had taken part in the programme were less likely to be using heroin than the control group, though the differences between the two groups were not significant. They could also reveal that programme participants were much less likely to have re-offended. Therefore, they concluded that the drug treatment programme was having some impact on its participants.

It is not always possible or desirable to use the randomized experiment. For example, evaluators cannot always control who gets onto a programme. Weiss (1998) lists a number of instances when it is feasible and desirable to use this approach. The first instance is when places on a programme are limited and the evaluator can advise programme staff on the assignment of people (or units of some kind) to the programme using random procedures. As Weiss (1998) points out, one of the chief objections that may be raised here relates to the fact that one group is being denied access to a social intervention because they are the control group. She counters that random assignment is an equitable way to allocate scarce resources and programme places, that is, it is more equitable than placing people on a programme on a first-come first-served basis (Weiss 1998: 217). There is also the argument that once the study has been completed and the programme shown to be effective, then the control group can be given places. (For additional arguments and counter-arguments on this approach, see Weiss, 1998: 217–22).

Another time when the randomized experiment may be used is when members of the control group can be assigned to an alternative programme, one that deals with a different need. Weiss gives an example of control group members for a new mathematics curriculum being assigned to a special arts class instead of the mathematics class.

Random assignment procedures can also be employed when a new programme is introduced in selected sites only. People attending those sites that do not have the new programme automatically become the control group. An experiment of this type can only be considered if there are enough sites, so that sites can be chosen using random procedures (See Weiss, 1998: 221 for a more detailed discussion of this approach). For example, random procedures could be used to decide which schools in Ireland were to receive a new mathematics curriculum.

Despite criticisms of this approach, it can be argued that when an outcome evaluation is required and random assignment procedures are possible, this design constitutes the best method of evaluating programme outcomes. 'Given its real attractions, the issue is how to realize its advantages without bogging down in its implementation problems and limitations' (Weiss, 1998: 233).

Data Collection

By this stage, it will be clear what type of information is required to evaluate the programme. The next step is to collect that information. Sometimes the evaluator can rely solely on existing data, such as records on clients and services. If so, then the researcher undertakes documentary research and/or secondary analysis of data (depending on the type of data available). See methodology texts for descriptions of these approaches (Cresswell, 1994; Hall and Hall, 1996; Judd et al., 1991; Mark, 1996). However, this is only the case when the information available is comprehensive or sufficient for the purpose of the evaluation. If not, new information must be collected. This may be done in a variety of ways, employing any combination of qualitative and/or quantitative methods.

Quantitative research methods involve focusing on things that can be counted and asks questions such as 'how many people remain drug-free after completing the programme'? or 'what proportion of people who completed employment training programmes obtain jobs?' This type of data is collected by means of standardized questionnaires using mostly closed-ended questions, standardized observation instruments and programme records (See methodology texts for descriptions of these approaches, e.g. Hall and Hall, 1996; Judd et al., 1991). Alternatively, qualitative methods are more concerned with detailed descriptions of outcomes or services and questions like 'what does the programme entail?' and 'how is it being implemented?' Such data may be collected by observation studies or in individual or group interviews (focus groups) using open-ended questions.

There is much debate about the value of each of these approaches with some people espousing quantitative methods to the exclusion of qualitative methods or vice versa. However, it is important to recognize the value and limitations of both approaches and that the method chosen should depend on the evaluation question, not the researcher's attachment to one form of research over another. Some methods are more suited to a particular evaluation question than others.

Data Analysis

Once the relevant information on the programme has been collected it is important to leave adequate time to analyse and interpret it. The analysis of data involves summarising the information that has been collected in such a way that it can answer the research questions e.g. does the programme work? In other words, this is the crux of the evaluation. There are a variety of strategies available for analysing data. The choice of technique depends on whether or not quantitative or qualitative data collection methods were employed in the study. If the evaluation involved conducting a large-scale survey, then a statistical analysis of the data can be performed using computer packages like the Statistical Package for the Social Sciences (SPSS). Evaluations involving qualitative data collection methods usually result in tapes of interviews, abstracts from documents, observation or field notes. Qualitative data is analysed as the information is being collected by exploring themes and differences that emerge in the data, by categorizing the data by event or by category of client etc. There are also statistical packages available to aid this process (e.g. Nudist, Qualpro).

After some preliminary analysis of the data, the evaluator should provide some feedback to the stakeholders and consult with them on the themes, patterns and issues that appear to be emerging.

Communicating Findings

The manner in which evaluation findings are communicated depends to some extent on whether or not the evaluation is summative or formative. When the formative approach is used, the findings are generally communicated to those involved in both formal (written reports) and informal ways (presentations) on an ongoing basis. If the evaluation is summative, findings may be communicated by means of report(s) (interim and final), seminars or presentations. The evaluation results should be presented in such a way that the audience can understand them. Some useful pointers here are

- avoid jargon
- think about presenting findings in report and/or seminar format.
- include an executive summary in all reports.

It is important to be aware of the fact that the evaluation may not produce the 'desired results' and some clients may be extremely dissatisfied with its findings. When clients are unhappy with the results of evaluation, they may keep coming back to the evaluators to request additional information until more acceptable results are uncovered or they may try to stop the results being made public. Alternatively, if they are made public and they do not like them, they may try to undermine the results by attacking the evaluation's methods and the intentions of the researchers. However, if evaluators follows the guidelines provided in this chapter, such attacks will be completely unjustified.

SUMMARY AND CONCLUSIONS

Social policy evaluation is a subject that has become extremely important for students of social policy. Not only is it good practice to evaluate pilot and ongoing programmes before mainstreaming or continuing them to ensure their relevance and effectiveness for clients but, increasingly, evaluations are required to account for the use of public funds and to demonstrate that a particular programme represents a value for money approach. Social policy analysts are ideally suited to evaluation as they have many of the research skills required to make a systematic and reliable assessment of policies.

A reliable evaluation of a particular social policy must be systematic. Designing an evaluation brief before conducting the research greatly facilitates a methodical approach as it clarifies the goals of the evaluation and identifies strategies to achieve these aims. In addition, a systematic evaluation follows these steps: understanding the programme; defining what is meant by success for the programme; measuring programme outcomes, inputs and environment; choosing a research design; data collection and analysis and communicating findings.

Consultation with key stakeholders is another important aspect of a systematic and reliable assessment of any social policy and it has been emphasized at different points in this chapter. By consulting staff, clients, management and other interested parties, the evaluator gains a more comprehensive understanding of the policy, helps to assuage any fears they may have about the evaluation and greatly increases the likelihood that the findings will be accepted.

NOTES

1 Thanks to Sarah Craig, Eithne Fitzgerald and Betty Hilliard for providing very helpful comments on this chapter.
2 Individuals, groups, staff, geographic areas can all be randomly assigned. A common method of random assignment is to make a list of all potential programme participants and give each a number. Then if a sample of 100 is required for each group (programme and control), choose 100 numbers from a

table of random numbers. Match them with those on the list of potential participants. The first 100 get placed in the programme and the next 100 go in the control group. Another method used is systematic sampling, in which the evaluator systematically chooses the first person (or unit) on a list and every nth person thereafter. For example, every tenth person on the list may be chosen. This approach requires that there be an adequate list to choose from in the first place. Finally, another random procedure that can be employed is to put all the names in a hat and pull out the number you need for each group.

RECOMMENDED READING

Murray, B., P. Faughnan and D. Redmond (1994) *Undertaking an Evaluation*. Maynooth: Sociology Association of Ireland. This book provides a very useful overview of the evaluation process. It is particularly interesting on the role of the evaluator and on the politics of this type of research.

Weiss, C. H. (1998) *Evaluation: Methods for Studying Programmes and Policies*. 2nd edition, New Jersey: Prentice Hall. This is an excellent textbook dealing with all of the key aspects of evaluation.

REFERENCES

Cresswell, J.W. (1994) *Research Design: Qualitative and Quantitative Approaches*. London: Sage.

Craig, S and K. McKeown (1994) *Progress through Partnership: Final Evaluation Report on the PESP Pilot Initiative on Long-term Unemployment*. Dublin: Combat Poverty Agency.

Hall, D. and I. Hall (1996) *Practical Social Research*. London: Macmillan.

Hedrick, T. (1993*) Applied Research Design: A Practical Guide*. London: Sage.

Judd, C. M., E. Smith and L. Kidder (1991) *Research Methods in Social Relations*. Texas: Harcourt Brace Jovanovich.

Lewis, C. (1986) 'The Impact of a Programme to Enhance the Competencies of Primary Care Physicians in Caring for Patients with AIDS', *Journal of General Internal Medicine*, 1: 287–94.

Mark, R. (1996) *Research Made Simple: A Handbook for Social Workers*. London: Sage.

Murray, B., P. Faughnan and D. Redmond (1994) *Undertaking an Evaluation*. Maynooth: Sociology Association of Ireland.

O'Connell, P. and F. McGinnity (1997) *Working Schemes? Active Labour Market Policies in Ireland*. Aldershot: Ashgate.

Patton, M. Q. (1997) *Utilization-focused Evaluation: The New Century Text*. 3rd edition, California: Sage.

Platt, J., C. Labate and R. Wicks (1977) *Evaluative Research in Correctional Drug Abuse Treatment*. Toronto: Lexington.

Rossi, P. and H. Freeman (1993) *Evaluation: A Systematic Approach*. 5th edition, London: Sage.

Schweinhart, L., H. Barnes and D. Weikart (1993) *Significant Benefits: The High/Scope Perry Preschool Study through Age 27*. Michigan: Hish/Scope Press.

Weiss, C. H. (1998) *Evaluation: Methods for Studying Programmes and Policies*. 2nd edition, Englewood, NJ: Prentice Hall.

Biographical Details of Authors

Helen Burke is Professor Emeritus in the Department of Social Policy and Social Work, University College Dublin. Her area of expertise is the historical development of social policy and her publications in this area include *The People and the Poor Law in Nineteenth-Century England* (1987) and *The Royal Hospital Donnybrook* (1993). With Olivia O'Leary she has written *Mary Robinson – The Authorised Biography*, the story of Ireland's first woman President who is now the United Nations High Commissioner for Human Rights.

Deirdre Carroll is Assistant Secretary in the Planning Unit of the Department of Social, Community and Family Affairs. She has worked in a number of government departments, including the Department of Finance and the Department of the Taoiseach. She is a graduate in Social Science of University College Dublin and has a Masters degree in Public Administration from University College Dublin. She represented the Minister on the Board of the Combat Poverty Agency and the Commission on the Family. She is currently the Minister's nominee on the Pensions Board.

Pauline Conroy is an expert with the European Commission on equality and is a guest lecturer in European Social Policy in the Department of Social Policy and Social Work, University College Dublin. She has held fellowships with the Council of Europe, Strasbourg, and the European University Institute, Florence, on the social protection of homeworkers and women's work in the underground economy. She is a graduate in Social Science of University College Dublin and of the London School of Economics.

Jennifer D'Arcy is the Research Teaching Fellow in the Department of Social Policy and Social Work. She is currently Research Officer with the Blanchardstown Local Area Drug Task Force. Her teaching interests include Social Gerontology and Substance Abuse. She is a Social Science graduate of University College Dublin.

Anne Doyle works in the Department of Justice, Equality and Law Reform. She had a leading role in the preparation of the Employment Equality Act, 1998 and has been involved with the development and implementation of equal opportunities policy and legislation at national and EU levels. She has also worked in a number of other government departments, primarily in the areas of industrial relations and employment law and practice. She is a graduate of University College Dublin and holds a Masters degree in Public Administration.

Catherine Earley is an independent social policy analyst and holds a Masters degree in Social Science from University College Dublin. She has worked for the National Economic and Social Council and the National Social Service Board. She has taught social policy at both undergraduate and postgraduate level in University College Dublin for a number of years. She has a particular interest in the process of policy making, and in the factors contributing to the creation of demand for policy change.

Bryan Fanning is a Lecturer in Social Policy in the Department of Social Policy and Social Work, University College Dublin. He has worked for a number of years for inner-city local authorities in London, during which time he undertook research on community activism and land-use planning in Haringey, a multi-ethnic borough. His current research interests include the implications of race and ethnicity for social policy in Ireland. He is a graduate of the University of Limerick and was awarded his PhD from the University of London.

Eithne Fitzgerald is a Lecturer in Social Policy in the Department of Social Policy and Social Work, University College Dublin. As Minister of State from 1993 to 1997, she drew up Ireland's National Development Plan, set up the National Economic and Social Forum, chaired the Task Force on Violence against Women, and enacted the Ethics in Public Office Act, the Freedom of Information Act and the Organisation of Working Time Act. She has written several social policy reports for the National Economic and Social Council and the Combat Poverty Agency. She was Research Officer with Threshold and is a former secretary of the National Campaign for the Homeless.

Rachel Iredale is a Senior Fellow at the Welsh Institute for Health and Social Care in the University of Glamorgan, Wales. Her current research is concerned with improving public participation in health policy planning. Her doctoral thesis was on the social policy implications of the new genetics in Ireland. She is a Social Science graduate of University College Dublin, undertook her Masters degree in St Patrick's College, Maynooth, and the universities of Bath and Tilburg, and her PhD studies in University College Dublin.

Helen Johnston is Head of Research at the Combat Poverty Agency and previously worked as a social policy researcher in the Northern Ireland civil service. She is an environmental science graduate from the University of Ulster and has a Masters degree in Town and Country Planning from Queen's University, Belfast. Her research interests are in analysing the impact of policies on people living in poverty. She has contributed to the development of the National Anti-Poverty Strategy and is involved in the evaluation of its implementation.

Patricia Kennedy is a Lecturer in Social Policy in the Department of Social Policy and Social Work, University College Dublin. She also lectures in the area of feminist social policy in the Women's Research and Resource Centre in University College Dublin. She has worked in the voluntary and community sector, as well as in the Department of Justice, Equality and Law Reform. A graduate of University College Cork, she completed her PhD in University College Dublin.

Gabriel Kiely holds the Jean Monnet Chair of Family Policies and European Integration in the Department of Social Policy and Social Work, University College Dublin. He is a graduate of University College Dublin, holds a Masters degree in Social Work from Florida State University and was awarded his PhD by the National University of Ireland. He is the Irish member of the European Observatory on National Family Policies.

Sylda Langford is an Assistant Secretary in the Department of Justice, Equality and Law Reform. She has worked in the Department of Social Welfare, the Office of the Ombudsman, the Eastern Health Board and the National Social Services Board. She studied at University College Cork and the London School of Economics. She is currently Chair of the National Social Work Qualifications Board.

Anne O'Donnell is a Research Officer at the Centre for Social Research, University of Malawi and was formerly Research/Teaching Fellow in the Department of Social Policy and Social work, University College Dublin. Her teaching areas include comparative social policy analysis and health policy. She has also worked as a nurse and midwife. She is a Social Science graduate of University College Dublin and of the London School of Economics.

Michael Rush is a Lecturer in Social Policy in the Department of Social Policy and Social Work, University College Dublin. He has worked with local development groups, cultural, educational and regenerative, in Ireland, England and Catalonia. He is a graduate of the Manchester Metropolitan University and of University College Dublin.

Nessa Winston is a Lecturer in Social Policy in the Department of Social Policy and Social Work, University College Dublin. Her particular area of teaching is research methodology. She has extensive experience as a researcher over the past decade, on topics concerned with European integration, education, rural development, ethnicity and single mothers. She is a graduate in Social Science of University College Dublin and was awarded her PhD by the University of Toronto, Canada.

Index